How Tomcat Works

A Guide to Developing Your Own Java Servlet Container

Budi Kurniawan and Paul Deck

How Tomcat Works: A Guide to Developing You Own Java Servlet Container

Copyright © 2004 by Budi Kurniawan and Paul Deck

First Edition: April 2004

International Standard Book Number: 0-9752128-0-X

Printed in the United States of America by Boyd Printing Company, Inc.

Book and Cover Designer: Yantoro

Indexer: Chris Mayle

Warning and Disclaimer

To all Tomcat developers,

Thank you for teaching us how to design and develop such an elegant solution.

Table of Contents

vi

Introduction

Welcome to *How Tomcat Works*. This book dissects Tomcat 4.1.12 and 5.0.18 and explains the internal workings of its free, open source, and most popular servlet container code-named Catalina. Tomcat is a complex system, consisting of many different components. Those who want to learn how Tomcat works often do know where to start. What this book does is provide the big picture and then build a simpler version of each component to make understanding that component easier. Only after that will the real component be explained.

You should start by reading this Introduction as it explains the structure of the book and gives you the brief outline of the applications built. The section "Preparing the Prerequisite Software" gives you instructions on what software you need to download, how to make a directory structure for your code, etc.

Who This Book Is for

This book is for anyone working with the Java technology.

- This book is for you if you are a servlet/JSP programmer or a Tomcat user and you are interested in knowing how a servlet container works.
- It is for you if you want to join the Tomcat development team because you need to first learn how the existing code works.
- If you have never been involved in web development but you have interest in software development in general, then you can learn from ths book how a large application such as Tomcat was designed and developed.
- If you need to configure and customize Tomcat, you should read this book.

To understand the discussion in this book, you need to understand object-oriented programming in Java as well as servlet programming. If you are not familiar with the latter, there are a plethora of books on servlets, including Budi's *Java for the Web with Servlets, JSP, and EJB*. To make the material easier to understand, each chapter starts with background information that will be required to understand the topic in discussion.

How A Servlet Container Works

A servlet container is a complex system. However, basically there are three things that a servlet container does to service a request for a servlet:

- Creating a request object and populate it with information that may be used by the invoked servlet, such as parameters, headers, cookies, query string, URI, etc. A request object is an instance of the `javax.servlet.ServletRequest` interface or the `javax.servlet.http.ServletRequest` interface.
- Creating a response object that the invoked servlet uses to send the response to the web client. A response object is an instance of the `javax.servlet.ServletResponse` interface or the `javax.servlet.http.ServletResponse` interface.
- Invoking the `service` method of the servlet, passing the request and response objects. Here the servlet reads the values from the request object and writes to the response object.

As you read the chapters, you will find detailed discussions of Catalina servlet container.

Catalina Block Diagram

Catalina is a very sophisticated piece of software, which was elegantly designed and developed. It is also modular too. Based on the tasks mentioned in the section "How A Servlet Container Works", you can view Catalina as consisting of two main modules: the connector and the container.

Figure I.1: Catalina's main modules

The block diagram in Figure I.1 is, of course, simplistic. Later in the following chapters you will unveil all smaller components one by one.

Now, back to Figure I.1, the connector is there to *connect* a request with the container. Its job is to construct a request object and a response object for each HTTP request it receives. It then passes processing to the container. The container receives the request and response objects from the connector and is responsible for invoking the servlet's `service` method.

Bear in mind though, that the description above is only the tip of the iceberg. There are a lot of things that a container does. For example, before it can invoke a servlet's `service` method, it must load the servlet, authenticate the user (if required), update the session for that user, etc. It's not surprising then that a container uses many different modules for processing. For example, the manager module is for processing user sessions, the loader is for loading servlet classess, etc.

Tomcat 4 and 5

This book covers both Tomcat 4 and 5. Here are some of the differences between the two:

- Tomcat 5 supports Servlet 2.4 and JSP 2.0 specifications, Tomcat 4 supports Servlet 2.3 and JSP 1.2.
- Tomcat 5 has a more efficient default connector than Tomcat 4.
- Tomcat 5 shares a thread for background processing whereas Tomcat 4's components all have their own threads for background processing. Therefore, Tomcat 5 uses less resources in this regard.
- Tomcat 5 does not need a mapper component to find a child component, therefore simplifying the code.

Overview of Each Chapter

There are 20 chapters in this book. The first two chapters serve as an introduction. Chapter 1 explains how an HTTP server works and Chapter 2 features a simple servlet container. The next two chapters focus on the connector and Chapters 5 to 20 cover each of the components in the container. The following is the summary of each of the chapters.

Note
For each chapter, there is an accompanying application similar to the component being explained.

Chapter 1 starts this book by presenting a simple HTTP server. To build a working HTTP server, you need to know the internal workings of two classes in the `java.net` package: `Socket` and `ServerSocket`. There is sufficient background information in this chapter about these two classes for you to understand how the accompanying application works.

Chapter 2 explains how simple servlet containers work. This chapter comes with two servlet container applications that can service requests for static resources as well as very simple servlets. In particular, you will learn how you can create request and response objects and pass them to the requested servlet's service method. There is also a servlet that can be run inside the servlet containers and that you can invoke from a web browser.

Chapter 3 presents a simplified version of Tomcat 4's default connector. The application built in this chapter serves as a learning tool to understand the connector discussed in Chapter 4.

Chapter 4 presents Tomcat 4's default connector. This connector has been deprecated in favor of a faster connector called Coyote. Nevertheless, the default connector is simpler and easier to understand.

Chapter 5 discusses the container module. A container is represented by the org.apache.catalina.Container interface and there are four types of containers: engine, host, context, and wrapper. This chapter offers two applications that work with contexts and wrappers.

Chapter 6 explains the Lifecycle interface. This interface defines the lifecycle of a Catalina component and provides an elegant way of notifying other components of events that occur in that component. In addition, the Lifecycle interface provides an elegant mechanism for starting and stopping all the components in Catalina by one single start/stop.

Chapter 7 covers loggers, which are components used for recording error messages and other messages.

Chapter 8 explains about loaders. A loader is an important Catalina module responsible for loading servlet and other classes that a web application uses. This chapter also shows how application reloading is achieved.

Chapter 9 discusses the manager, the component that manages sessions in session management. It explains the various types of managers and how a manager can persist session objects into a store. At the end of the chapter, you will learn how to build an application that uses a StandardManager instance to run a servlet that uses session objects to store values.

Chapter 10 covers web application security constraints for restricting access to certain contents. You will learn entities related to security such as principals, roles, login config, authenticators, etc. You will also write two applications that install an authenticator valve in the `StandardContext` object and uses basic authentication to authenticate users.

Chapter 11 explains in detail the `org.apache.catalina.core.StandardWrapper` class that represents a servlet in a web application. In particular, this chapter explains how filters and a servlet's `service` method are invoked. The application accompanying this chapter uses `StandardWrapper` instances to represents servlets.

Chapter 12 covers the `org.apache.catalina.core.StandardContext` class that represents a web application. In particular this chapter discusses how a `StandardContext` object is configured, what happens in it for each incoming HTTP request, how it supports automatic reloading, and how Tomcat 5 shares a thread that executes periodic tasks in its associated components.

Chapter 13 presents the two other containers: host and engine. You can also find the standard implementation of these two containers: `org.apache.catalina.core.StandardHost` and `org.apache.catalina.core.StandardEngine`.

Chapter 14 offers the server and service components. A server provides an elegant start and stop mechanism for the whole servlet container, a service serves as a holder for a container and one or more connectors. The application accompanying this chapter shows how to use a server and a service.

Chapters 15 explains the configuration of a web application through Digester, an exciting open source project from the Apache Software Foundation. For those not initiated, this chapter presents a section that gently introduces the digester library and how to use it to convert the nodes in an XML document to Java objects. It then explains the `ContextConfig` object that configures a StandardContext instance.

Chapter 16 explains the shutdown hook that Tomcat uses to always get a chance to do clean-up regardless how the user stops it (i.e. either appropriately by sending a shutdown command or inappropriately by simply closing the console.)

Chapter 17 discusses the starting and stopping of Tomcat through the use of batch files and shell scripts.

Chapter 18 presents the deployer, the component responsible for deploying and installing web applications.

Chapter 19 discusses a special interface, `ContainerServlet`, to give a servlet access to the Catalina internal objects. In particular, it discusses the Manager application that you can use to manage deployed applications.

Chapter 20 discusses JMX and how Tomcat make its internal objects manageable by creating MBeans for those objects.

The Application for Each Chapter

Each chapter comes with one or more applications that focus on a specific component in Catalina. Normally you'll find the simplified version of the component being explained or code that explains how to use a Catalina component. All classes and interfaces in the chapters' applications reside in the `ex[chapter number].pyrmont` package or its subpackages. For example, the classes in the application in Chapter 1 are part of the `ex01.pyrmont` package.

Preparing the Prerequisite Software

The applications accompanying this book run with J2SE version **1.4**. The zipped source files can be downloaded from the authors' web site www.brainysoftware.com. It contains the source code for Tomcat 4.1.12 and the applications used in this book. Assuming you have installed J2SE 1.4 and your `path` environment variable includes the location of the JDK, follow these steps:

1. Extract the zip files. All extracted files will reside in a new directory called **HowTomcatWorks**. HowTomcatWorks is your working directory. There will be several subdirectories under HowTomcatWorks, including **lib** (containing all needed libraries), **src** (containing the source files), **webroot** (containing an HTML file and three sample servlets), and **webapps** (containing sample applications).
2. Change directory to the working directory and compile the java files. If you are using Windows, run the **win-compile.bat** file. If your computer is a Linux machine, type the following: (don't forget to chmod the file if necessary)

```
./linux-compile.sh
```

Note
More information can be found in the Readme.txt file included in the ZIP file.

Chapter 1
A Simple Web Server

This chapter explains how Java web servers work. A web server is also called a Hypertext Transfer Protocol (HTTP) server because it uses HTTP to communicate with its clients, which are usually web browsers. A Java-based web server uses two important classes: `java.net.Socket` and `java.net.ServerSocket`, and communications are done through HTTP messages. It is therefore natural to start this chapter with a discussion of HTTP and the two classes. Afterwards, it goes on to explain the simple web server application that accompanies this chapter.

The Hypertext Transfer Protocol (HTTP)

HTTP is the protocol that allows web servers and browsers to send and receive data over the Internet. It is a request and response protocol. The client requests a file and the server responds to the request. HTTP uses reliable TCP connections—by default on TCP port 80. The first version of HTTP was HTTP/0.9, which was then overridden by HTTP/1.0. Replacing HTTP/1.0 is the current version of HTTP/1.1, which is defined in Request for Comments (RFC) 2616 and downloadable from http://www.w3.org/Protocols/HTTP/1.1/rfc2616.pdf.

> **Note**
> This section covers HTTP 1.1 only briefly and is intended to help you understand the messages sent by web server applications. If you are interested in more details, read RFC 2616.

In HTTP, it is always the client who initiates a transaction by establishing a connection and sending an HTTP request. The web server is in no position to contact a client or make a callback connection to the client. Either the client or the server can prematurely terminate a connection. For example, when using a web browser you can click the Stop button on your browser to stop the download process of a file, effectively closing the HTTP connection with the web server.

HTTP Requests

An HTTP request consists of three components:

- Method—Uniform Resource Identifier (URI)—Protocol/Version
- Request headers
- Entity body

An example of an HTTP request is the following:

```
POST /examples/default.jsp HTTP/1.1
Accept: text/plain; text/html
Accept-Language: en-gb
Connection: Keep-Alive
Host: localhost
User-Agent: Mozilla/4.0 (compatible; MSIE 4.01; Windows 98)
Content-Length: 33
Content-Type: application/x-www-form-urlencoded
Accept-Encoding: gzip, deflate

lastName=Franks&firstName=Michael
```

The method—URI—protocol version appears as the first line of the request.

```
POST /examples/default.jsp HTTP/1.1
```

where POST is the request method, /examples/default.jsp represents the URI and HTTP/1.1 the Protocol/Version section.

Each HTTP request can use one of the many request methods as specified in the HTTP standards. The HTTP 1.1 supports seven types of request: GET, POST, HEAD, OPTIONS, PUT, DELETE, and TRACE. GET and POST are the most commonly used in Internet applications.

The URI specifies an Internet resource completely. A URI is usually interpreted as being relative to the server's root directory. Thus, it should always begin with a forward slash /. A Uniform Resource Locator (URL) is actually a type of URI (see http://www.ietf.org/rfc/rfc2396.txt). The protocol version represents the version of the HTTP protocol being used.

The request header contains useful information about the client environment and the entity body of the request. For example, it could contain the language the browser is set for, the length of the entity body, and so on. Each header is separated by a carriage return/linefeed (CRLF) sequence.

Between the headers and the entity body, there is a blank line (CRLF) that is important to the HTTP request format. The CRLF tells the HTTP server where the entity body begins. In some Internet programming books, this CRLF is considered the fourth component of an HTTP request.

In the previous HTTP request, the entity body is simply the following line:

```
lastName=Franks&firstName=Michael
```

The entity body can easily become much longer in a typical HTTP request.

HTTP Responses

Similar to an HTTP request, an HTTP response also consists of three parts:

- Protocol—Status code—Description
- Response headers
- Entity body

The following is an example of an HTTP response:

```
HTTP/1.1 200 OK
Server: Microsoft-IIS/4.0
Date: Mon, 5 Jan 2004 13:13:33 GMT
Content-Type: text/html
Last-Modified: Mon, 5 Jan 2004 13:13:12 GMT
Content-Length: 112

<html>
<head>
<title>HTTP Response Example</title>
</head>
<body>
Welcome to Brainy Software
</body>
</html>
```

The first line of the response header is similar to the first line of the request header. The first line tells you that the protocol used is HTTP version 1.1, the request succeeded (200 = success), and that everything went okay.

The response headers contain useful information similar to the headers in the request. The entity body of the response is the HTML content of the response itself. The headers and the entity body are separated by a sequence of CRLFs.

The Socket Class

A socket is an endpoint of a network connection. A socket enables an application to read from and write to the network. Two software applications residing on two different computers can communicate with each other by sending and receiving byte streams over a connection. To send a message from your application to another application, you need to know the IP address as well as the port number of the socket of the other application. In Java, a socket is represented by the `java.net.Socket` class.

To create a socket, you can use one of the many constructors of the `Socket` class. One of these constructors accepts the host name and the port number:

```
public Socket (java.lang.String host, int port)
```

where *host* is the remote machine name or IP address and *port* is the port number of the remote application. For example, to connect to yahoo.com at port 80, you would construct the following `Socket` object:

```
new Socket ("yahoo.com", 80);
```

Once you create an instance of the `Socket` class successfully, you can use it to send and receive streams of bytes. To send byte streams, you must first call the `Socket` class's `getOutputStream` method to obtain a `java.io.OutputStream` object. To send text to a remote application, you often want to construct a `java.io.PrintWriter` object from the `OutputStream` object returned. To receive byte streams from the other end of the connection, you call the `Socket` class's `getInputStream` method that returns a `java.io.InputStream`.

The following code snippet creates a socket that can communicate with a local HTTP server (127.0.0.1 denotes a local host), sends an HTTP request, and receives the response from the server. It creates a `StringBuffer` object to hold the response and prints it on the console.

```
Socket socket = new Socket("127.0.0.1", "8080");
OutputStream os = socket.getOutputStream();
boolean autoflush = true;
PrintWriter out = new PrintWriter(
  socket.getOutputStream(), autoflush);
BufferedReader in = new BufferedReader(
  new InputStreamReader( socket.getInputStream() ));

// send an HTTP request to the web server
out.println("GET /index.jsp HTTP/1.1");
out.println("Host: localhost:8080");
```

```
out.println("Connection: Close");
out.println();

// read the response
boolean loop = true;
StringBuffer sb = new StringBuffer(8096);
while (loop) {
  if ( in.ready() ) {
    int i=0;
    while (i!=-1) {
      i = in.read();
      sb.append((char) i);
    }
    loop = false;
  }
  Thread.currentThread().sleep(50);
}

// display the response to the out console
System.out.println(sb.toString());
socket.close();
```

Note that to get a proper response from the web server, you need to send an HTTP request that complies with the HTTP protocol. If you have read the previous section, The Hypertext Transfer Protocol (HTTP), you should be able to understand the HTTP request in the code above.

> **Note**
> You can use the `com.brainysoftware.pyrmont.util.HttpSniffer` class included with this book to send an HTTP request and display the response. To use this Java program, you must be connected to the Internet. Be warned, though, that it may not work if you are behind a firewall.

The ServerSocket Class

The `Socket` class represents a "client" socket, i.e. a socket that you construct whenever you want to connect to a remote server application. Now, if you want to implement a server application, such as an HTTP server or an FTP server, you need a different approach. This is because your server must stand by all the time as it does not know when a client application will try to connect to it. In order for your application to be able to stand by all the time, you need to use the `java.net.ServerSocket` class. This is an implementation of a server socket.

`ServerSocket` is different from `Socket`. The role of a server socket is to wait for connection requests from clients. Once the server socket gets a connection request, it creates a `Socket` instance to handle the communication with the client.

To create a server socket, you need to use one of the four constructors the `ServerSocket` class provides. You need to specify the IP address and port number the server socket will be listening on. Typically, the IP address will be 127.0.0.1, meaning that the server socket will be listening on the local machine. The IP address the server socket is listening on is referred to as the binding address. Another important property of a server socket is its backlog, which is the maximum queue length of incoming connection requests before the server socket starts to refuse the incoming requests.

One of the constructors of the `ServerSocket` class has the following signature:

```
public ServerSocket(int port, int backLog, InetAddress bindingAddress);
```

Notice that for this constructor, the binding address must be an instance of `java.net.InetAddress`. An easy way to construct an `InetAddress` object is by calling its static method `getByName`, passing a `String` containing the host name, such as in the following code.

```
InetAddress.getByName("127.0.0.1");
```

The following line of code constructs a `ServerSocket` that listens on port 8080 of the local machine. The `ServerSocket` has a backlog of 1.

```
new ServerSocket(8080, 1, InetAddress.getByName("127.0.0.1"));
```

Once you have a `ServerSocket` instance, you can tell it to wait for an incoming connection request to the binding address at the port the server socket is listening on. You do this by calling the `ServerSocket` class's `accept` method. This method will only return when there is a connection request and its return value is an instance of the `Socket` class. This `Socket` object can then be used to send and receive byte streams from the client application, as explained in the previous section, "The Socket Class". Practically, the `accept` method is the only method used in the application accompanying this chapter.

The Application

Our web server application is part of the `ex01.pyrmont` package and consists of three classes:

- `HttpServer`
- `Request`
- `Response`

The entry point of this application (the static `main` method) can be found in the `HttpServer` class. The `main` method creates an instance of `HttpServer` and calls its `await` method. The `await` method, as the name implies, waits for HTTP requests on a designated port, processes them, and sends responses back to the clients. It keeps waiting until a shutdown command is received.

The application cannot do more than sending static resources, such as HTML files and image files, residing in a certain directory. It also displays the incoming HTTP request byte streams on the console. However, it does not send any header, such as dates or cookies, to the browser.

We will now take a look at the three classes in the following subsections.

The HttpServer Class

The `HttpServer` class represents a web server and is presented in Listing 1.1. Note that the `await` method is given in Listing 1.2 and is not repeated in Listing 1.1 to save space.

Listing 1.1: The **HttpServer** class

```
package ex01.pyrmont;

import java.net.Socket;
import java.net.ServerSocket;
import java.net.InetAddress;
import java.io.InputStream;
import java.io.OutputStream;
import java.io.IOException;
import java.io.File;

public class HttpServer {

  /** WEB_ROOT is the directory where our HTML and other files reside.
   *  For this package, WEB_ROOT is the "webroot" directory under the
   *  working directory.
   *  The working directory is the location in the file system
   *  from where the java command was invoked.
   */
  public static final String WEB_ROOT =
    System.getProperty("user.dir") + File.separator  + "webroot";

  // shutdown command
  private static final String SHUTDOWN_COMMAND = "/SHUTDOWN";

  // the shutdown command received
  private boolean shutdown = false;

  public static void main(String[] args) {
    HttpServer server = new HttpServer();
```

```
    server.await();
  }

  public void await() {
    ...
  }
}
```

This web server can serve static resources found in the directory indicated by the public static final `WEB_ROOT` and all subdirectories under it. `WEB_ROOT` is initialized as follows:

```
public static final String WEB_ROOT =
  System.getProperty("user.dir") + File.separator + "webroot";
```

The code listings include a directory called webroot that contains some static resources that you can use for testing this application. You can also find several servlets in the same directory for testing applications in the next chapters.

To request for a static resource, you type the following URL in your browser's Address or URL box:

```
http://machineName:port/staticResource
```

If you are sending a request from a different machine from the one running your application, *machineName* is the name or IP address of the computer running this application. If your browser is on the same machine, you can use `localhost` for the *machineName*. *port* is 8080 and *staticResource* is the name of the file requested and must reside in `WEB_ROOT`.

For instance, if you are using the same computer to test the application and you want to ask the `HttpServer` object to send the index.html file, you use the following URL:

```
http://localhost:8080/index.html
```

To stop the server, you send a shutdown command from a web browser by typing the pre-defined string in the browser's Address or URL box, after the *host:port* section of the URL. The shutdown command is defined by the `SHUTDOWN` static final variable in the `HttpServer` class:

```
private static final String SHUTDOWN_COMMAND = "/SHUTDOWN";
```

Therefore, to stop the server, you use the following URL:

```
http://localhost:8080/SHUTDOWN
```

Now, let's look at the `await` method printed in Listing 1.2.

Listing 1.2: The `HttpServer` class's `await` method

```java
public void await() {
  ServerSocket serverSocket = null;
  int port = 8080;
  try {
    serverSocket =  new ServerSocket(port, 1,
      InetAddress.getByName("127.0.0.1"));
  }
  catch (IOException e) {
    e.printStackTrace();
    System.exit(1);
  }
  // Loop waiting for a request
  while (!shutdown) {
    Socket socket = null;
    InputStream input = null;
    OutputStream output = null;

    try {
      socket = serverSocket.accept();
      input = socket.getInputStream();
      output = socket.getOutputStream();
      // create Request object and parse
      Request request = new Request(input);
      request.parse();

      // create Response object
      Response response = new Response(output);
      response.setRequest(request);
      response.sendStaticResource();

      // Close the socket
      socket.close();

      //check if the previous URI is a shutdown command
      shutdown = request.getUri().equals(SHUTDOWN_COMMAND);
    }
    catch (Exception e) {
      e.printStackTrace();
      continue;
    }
  }
}
```

The method name `await` is used instead of wait because `wait` is an important
method in the `java.lang.Object` class for working with threads.

The `await` method starts by creating an instance of `ServerSocket` and
then going into a `while` loop.

```java
    serverSocket =  new ServerSocket(port, 1,
      InetAddress.getByName("127.0.0.1"));
    ...
    // Loop waiting for a request
```

```
while (!shutdown) {
  ...
}
```

The code inside the `while` loop stops at the `accept` method of `ServerSocket`, which returns only when an HTTP request is received on port 8080:

```
socket = serverSocket.accept();
```

Upon receiving a request, the `await` method obtains `java.io.InputStream` and `java.io.OutputStream` objects from the `Socket` instance returned by the `accept` method.

```
input = socket.getInputStream();
output = socket.getOutputStream();
```

The `await` method then creates an `ex01.pyrmont.Request` object and calls its `parse` method to parse the HTTP request raw data.

```
// create Request object and parse
Request request = new Request(input);
request.parse();
```

Afterwards, the `await` method creates a `Response` object, sets the `Request` object to it, and calls its `sendStaticResource` method.

```
// create Response object
Response response = new Response(output);
response.setRequest(request);
response.sendStaticResource();
```

Finally, the `await` method closes the `Socket` and calls the `getUri` method of `Request` to check if the URI of the HTTP request is a shutdown command. If it is, the `shutdown` variable is set to `true` and the program exits the `while` loop.

```
// Close the socket
socket.close();

//check if the previous URI is a shutdown command
shutdown = request.getUri().equals(SHUTDOWN_COMMAND);
```

The Request Class

The `ex01.pyrmont.Request` class represents an HTTP request. An instance of this class is constructed by passing the `InputStream` object obtained from a `Socket` that handles the communication with the client. You call one of the read methods of the `InputStream` object to obtain the HTTP request raw data.

The Request class is offered in Listing 1.3. The `Request` class has two public methods, `parse` and `getUri`, which are given in Listings 1.4 and 1.5, respectively.

Listing 1.3: The **Request** class

```
package ex01.pyrmont;

import java.io.InputStream;
import java.io.IOException;

public class Request {
  private InputStream input;
  private String uri;

  public Request(InputStream input) {
    this.input = input;
  }

  public void parse() {
    ...
  }

  private String parseUri(String requestString) {
    ...
  }

  public String getUri() {
    return uri;
  }
}
```

The `parse` method parses the raw data in the HTTP request. Not much is done by this method. The only information it makes available is the URI of the HTTP request that it obtains by calling the private method `parseUri`. The `parseUri` method stores the URI in the `uri` variable. The public `getUri` method is invoked to return the URI of the HTTP request.

> **Note**
> More processing of the HTTP request raw data will be done in the applications accompanying Chapter 3 and the subsequent chapters.

To understand how the `parse` and `parseUri` methods work, you need to know the structure of an HTTP request, discussed in the previous section, "The Hypertext Transfer Protocol (HTTP)". In this chapter, we are only interested in the first part of the HTTP request, the request line. A request line begins with a method token, followed by the request URI and the protocol version, and ends with carriage-return linefeed (CRLF) characters. Elements in a request line are separated by a space character. For instance, the request line for a request for the index.html file using the GET method is as follows.

```
GET /index.html HTTP/1.1
```

The parse method reads the whole byte stream from the socket's InputStream that is passed to the Request object and stores the byte array in a buffer. It then populates a StringBuffer object called request using the bytes in the buffer byte array, and passes the String representation of the StringBuffer to the parseUri method.

The parse method is given in Listing 1.4.

Listing 1.4: The **Request** class's **parse** method

```java
public void parse() {
  // Read a set of characters from the socket
  StringBuffer request = new StringBuffer(2048);
  int i;
  byte[] buffer = new byte[2048];
  try {
    i = input.read(buffer);
  }
  catch (IOException e) {
    e.printStackTrace();
    i = -1;
  }
  for (int j=0; j<i; j++) {
    request.append((char) buffer[j]);
  }
  System.out.print(request.toString());
  uri = parseUri(request.toString());
}
```

The parseUri method then obtains the URI from the request line. Listing 1.5 presents the parseUri method. The parseUri method searches for the first and the second spaces in the request and obtains the URI from it.

Listing 1.5: the **Request** class's **parseUri** method

```java
private String parseUri(String requestString) {
  int index1, index2;
  index1 = requestString.indexOf(' ');
  if (index1 != -1) {
    index2 = requestString.indexOf(' ', index1 + 1);
    if (index2 > index1)
      return requestString.substring(index1 + 1, index2);
  }
  return null;
}
```

The Response Class

The ex01.pyrmont.Response class represents an HTTP response and is given in Listing 1.6.

Listing 1.6: The Response class

```
package ex01.pyrmont;

import java.io.OutputStream;
import java.io.IOException;
import java.io.FileInputStream;
import java.io.File;

/*
  HTTP Response = Status-Line
    *(( general-header | response-header | entity-header ) CRLF)
    CRLF
    [ message-body ]
    Status-Line = HTTP-Version SP Status-Code SP Reason-Phrase CRLF
*/

public class Response {

  private static final int BUFFER_SIZE = 1024;
  Request request;
  OutputStream output;

  public Response(OutputStream output) {
    this.output = output;
  }

  public void setRequest(Request request) {
    this.request = request;
  }

  public void sendStaticResource() throws IOException {
    byte[] bytes = new byte[BUFFER_SIZE];
    FileInputStream fis = null;
    try {
      File file = new File(HttpServer.WEB_ROOT, request.getUri());
      if (file.exists()) {
        fis = new FileInputStream(file);
        int ch = fis.read(bytes, 0, BUFFER_SIZE);
        while (ch!=-1) {
          output.write(bytes, 0, ch);
          ch = fis.read(bytes, 0, BUFFER_SIZE);
        }
      }
      else {
        // file not found
        String errorMessage = "HTTP/1.1 404 File Not Found\r\n" +
          "Content-Type: text/html\r\n" +
          "Content-Length: 23\r\n" +
          "\r\n" +
```

```
        "<h1>File Not Found</h1>";
      output.write(errorMessage.getBytes());
    }
  }
  catch (Exception e) {
    // thrown if cannot instantiate a File object
    System.out.println(e.toString() );
  }
  finally {
    if (fis!=null)
      fis.close();
  }
  }
}
```

First note that its constructor accepts a `java.io.OutputStream` object, such as the following.

```
public Response(OutputStream output) {
  this.output = output;
}
```

A `Response` object is constructed by the `HttpServer` class's `await` method by passing the `OutputStream` object obtained from the socket.

The `Response` class has two public methods: `setRequest` and `sendStaticResource` method. The `setRequest` method is used to pass a `Request` object to the `Response` object.

The `sendStaticResource` method is used to send a static resource, such as an HTML file. It first instantiates the `java.io.File` class by passing the parent path and child path to the `File` class's constructor.

```
File file = new File(HttpServer.WEB_ROOT, request.getUri());
```

It then checks if the file exists. If it does, `sendStaticResource` constructs a `java.io.FileInputStream` object by passing the `File` object. Then, it invokes the `read` method of the `FileInputStream` and writes the byte array to the `OutputStream` output. Note that in this case the content of the static resource is sent to the browser as raw data.

```
      if (file.exists()) {
        fis = new FileInputStream(file);
        int ch = fis.read(bytes, 0, BUFFER_SIZE);
        while (ch!=-1) {
          output.write(bytes, 0, ch);
          ch = fis.read(bytes, 0, BUFFER_SIZE);
        }
      }
```

If the file does not exist, the `sendStaticResource` method sends an error message to the browser.

```
String errorMessage = "HTTP/1.1 404 File Not Found\r\n" +
  "Content-Type: text/html\r\n" +
  "Content-Length: 23\r\n" +
  "\r\n" +
  "<h1>File Not Found</h1>";
output.write(errorMessage.getBytes());
```

Running the Application

To run the application, from the working directory, type the following:

```
java ex01.pyrmont.HttpServer
```

To test the application, open your browser and type the following in the URL or Address box:

```
http://localhost:8080/index.html
```

You will see the index.html page displayed in your browser, as in Figure 1.1.

On the console, you can see the HTTP request similar to the following:

```
GET /index.html HTTP/1.1
Accept: image/gif, image/x-xbitmap, image/jpeg, image/pjpeg,
application/vnd.ms-excel, application/msword, application/vnd.ms-
powerpoint, application/x-shockwave-flash, application/pdf, */*
Accept-Language: en-us
Accept-Encoding: gzip, deflate
User-Agent: Mozilla/4.0 (compatible; MSIE 6.0; Windows NT 5.1; .NET CLR
1.1.4322)
Host: localhost:8080
Connection: Keep-Alive

GET /images/logo.gif HTTP/1.1
Accept: */*
Referer: http://localhost:8080/index.html
Accept-Language: en-us
Accept-Encoding: gzip, deflate
User-Agent: Mozilla/4.0 (compatible; MSIE 6.0; Windows NT 5.1; .NET CLR
1.1.4322)
Host: localhost:8080
Connection: Keep-Alive
```

22

Figure 1.1: The output from the web server

Summary

In this chapter you have seen how a simple web server works. The application accompanying this chapter consists of only three classes and is not fully functional. Nevertheless, it serves as a good learning tool. The next chapter will discuss the processing of dynamic contents.

Chapter 2
A Simple Servlet Container

This chapter explains how you can develop your own servlet container by presenting two applications. The first application has been designed to be as simple as possible to make it easy for you to understand how a servlet container works. It then evolves into the second servlet container, which is slightly more complex.

> **Note**
> Every servlet container application in each chapter gradually evolves from the application in the previous chapter, until a fully-functional Tomcat servlet container is built in Chapter 17.

Both servlet containers can process simple servlets as well as static resources. You can use `PrimitiveServlet` to test this container. `PrimitiveServlet` is given in Listing 2.1 and its class file can be found in the webroot directory. More complex servlets are beyond the capabilities of these containers, but you will learn how to build more sophisticated servlet containers in the next chapters.

The classes for both applications are part of the `ex02.pyrmont` package. To understand how the applications work, you need to be familiar with the `javax.servlet.Servlet` interface. To refresh your memory, this interface is discussed in the first section of this chapter. After that, you will learn what a servlet container has to do to serve HTTP requests for a servlet.

The javax.servlet.Servlet Interface

Servlet programming is made possible through the classes and interfaces in two packages: `javax.servlet` and `javax.servlet.http`. Of those classes and interfaces, the `javax.servlet.Servlet` interface is of the utmost importance. All servlets must implement this interface or extend a class that does.

The `Servlet` interface has five methods whose signatures are as follows.

```
public void init(ServletConfig config) throws ServletException
public void service(ServletRequest request, ServletResponse response)
  throws ServletException, java.io.IOException
public void destroy()
public ServletConfig getServletConfig()
public java.lang.String getServletInfo()
```

Of the five methods in `Servlet`, the `init`, `service`, and `destroy` methods are the servlet's life cycle methods. The `init` method is called by the servlet container after the servlet class has been instantiated. The servlet container calls this method exactly once to indicate to the servlet that the servlet is being placed into service. The `init` method must complete successfully before the servlet can receive any requests. A servlet programmer can override this method to write initialization code that needs to run only once, such as loading a database driver, initializing values, and so on. In other cases, this method is normally left blank.

The servlet container calls the `service` method of a servlet whenever there is a request for the servlet. The servlet container passes a `javax.servlet.ServletRequest` object and a `javax.servlet.ServletResponse` object. The `ServletRequest` object contains the client's HTTP request information and the `ServletResponse` object encapsulates the servlet's response. The service method is `invoked` many times during the life of the servlet.

The servlet container calls the `destroy` method before removing a servlet instance from service. This normally happens when the servlet container is shut down or the servlet container needs some free memory. This method is called only after all threads within the servlet's `service` method have exited or after a timeout period has passed. After the servlet container has called the `destroy` method, it will not call the `service` method again on the same servlet. The `destroy` method gives the servlet an opportunity to clean up any resources that are being held, such as memory, file handles, and threads, and make sure that any persistent state is synchronized with the servlet's current state in memory.

Listing 2.1 presents the code for a servlet named `PrimitiveServlet`, which is a very simple servlet that you can use to test the servlet container applications in this chapter. The `PrimitiveServlet` class implements `javax.servlet.Servlet` (as all servlets must) and provides implementations for all the five methods of `Servlet`. What `PrimitiveServlet` does is very simple. Each time any of the `init`, `service`, or `destroy` methods is called, the servlet writes the method's name to the standard console. In addition, the `service` method obtains the `java.io.PrintWriter` object from the `ServletResponse` object and sends strings to the browser.

Listing 2.1 PrimitiveServlet.java

```java
import javax.servlet.*;
import java.io.IOException;
import java.io.PrintWriter;

public class PrimitiveServlet implements Servlet {

  public void init(ServletConfig config) throws ServletException {
    System.out.println("init");
  }

  public void service(ServletRequest request, ServletResponse response)
    throws ServletException, IOException {
    System.out.println("from service");
    PrintWriter out = response.getWriter();
    out.println("Hello. Roses are red.");
    out.print("Violets are blue.");
  }

  public void destroy() {
    System.out.println("destroy");
  }

  public String getServletInfo() {
    return null;
  }
  public ServletConfig getServletConfig() {
    return null;
  }
}
```

Application 1

Now, let's examine servlet programming from a servlet container's perspective. In a nutshell, a fully-functional servlet container does the following for each HTTP request for a servlet:

- When the servlet is called for the first time, load the servlet class and call the servlet's `init` method (once only)
- For each request, construct an instance of `javax.servlet.ServletRequest` and an instance of `javax.servlet.ServletResponse`.
- Invoke the servlet's `service` method, passing the ServletRequest and ServletResponse objects.

- When the servlet class is shut down, call the servlet's destroy method and unload the servlet class.

The first servlet container for this chapter is not fully functional. Therefore, it cannot run other than very simple servlets and does not call the servlets' init and destroy methods. Instead, it does the following:

- Wait for HTTP requests.
- Construct a ServletRequest object and a ServletResponse object.
- If the request is for a static resource, invoke the process method of the StaticResourceProcessor instance, passing the ServletRequest and ServletResponse objects.
- If the request is for a servlet, load the servlet class and invoke the service method of the servlet, passing the ServletRequest and ServletResponse objects.

Note
In this servlet container, the servlet class is loaded every time the servlet is requested.

The first application consists of six classes:

- HttpServer1
- Request
- Response
- StaticResourceProcessor
- ServletProcessor1
- Constants

Figure 2.1 displays the UML diagram of the first servlet container.

The entry point of this application (the static main method) is in the HttpServer1 class. The main method creates an instance of HttpServer1 and calls its await method. The await method waits for HTTP requests, creates a Request object and a Response object for every request, and dispatch them either to a StaticResourceProcessor instance or a ServletProcessor instance, depending on whether the request is for a static resource or a servlet.

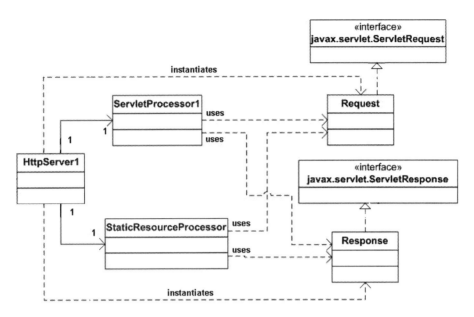

Figure 2.1: The UML diagram of the first servlet container

The `Constants` class contains the static final `WEB_ROOT` that is referenced from other classes. `WEB_ROOT` indicates the location of `PrimitiveServlet` and the static resource that can be served by this container.

The `HttpServer1` instance keeps waiting for HTTP requests until a shutdown command is received. You issue a shutdown command the same way as you did it in Chapter 1.

Each of the classes in the application is discussed in the following sections.

The HttpServer1 Class

The `HttpServer1` class in this application is similar to the `HttpServer` class in the simple web server application in Chapter 1. However, in this application the `HttpServer1` class can serve both static resources and servlets. To request a static resource, you type a URL in the following format in your browser's Address or URL box:

```
http://machineName:port/staticResource
```

This is exactly how you requested a static resource in the web server application in Chapter 1.

To request a servlet, you use the following URL:

```
http://machineName:port/servlet/servletClass
```

Therefore, if you are using a browser locally to request a servlet called PrimitiveServlet, you enter the following URL in the browser's Address or URL box:

```
http://localhost:8080/servlet/PrimitiveServlet
```

This servlet container can serve PrimitiveServlet. However, if you invoke the other servlet, ModernServlet, the servlet container will throw an exception. At the later chapters, you will build applications that can process both.

The HttpServer1 class is presented in Listing 2.2.

Listing 2.2: The HttpServer1 Class's await method

```java
package ex02.pyrmont;

import java.net.Socket;
import java.net.ServerSocket;
import java.net.InetAddress;
import java.io.InputStream;
import java.io.OutputStream;
import java.io.IOException;

public class HttpServer1 {

  /** WEB_ROOT is the directory where our HTML and other files reside.
   *  For this package, WEB_ROOT is the "webroot" directory under the
   *  working directory.
   *  The working directory is the location in the file system
   *  from where the java command was invoked.
   */
  // shutdown command
  private static final String SHUTDOWN_COMMAND = "/SHUTDOWN";

  // the shutdown command received
  private boolean shutdown = false;

  public static void main(String[] args) {
    HttpServer1 server = new HttpServer1();
    server.await();
  }

  public void await() {
    ServerSocket serverSocket = null;
    int port = 8080;
    try {
      serverSocket =  new ServerSocket(port, 1,
        InetAddress.getByName("127.0.0.1"));
    }
```

```
  catch (IOException e) {
    e.printStackTrace();
    System.exit(1);
  }

  // Loop waiting for a request
  while (!shutdown) {
    Socket socket = null;
    InputStream input = null;
    OutputStream output = null;
    try {
      socket = serverSocket.accept();
      input = socket.getInputStream();
      output = socket.getOutputStream();

      // create Request object and parse
      Request request = new Request(input);
      request.parse();

      // create Response object
      Response response = new Response(output);
      response.setRequest(request);

      // check if this is a request for a servlet or
      // a static resource
      // a request for a servlet begins with "/servlet/"
      if (request.getUri().startsWith("/servlet/")) {
        ServletProcessor1 processor = new ServletProcessor1();
        processor.process(request, response);
      }
      else {
        StaticResourceProcessor processor =
          new StaticResourceProcessor();
        processor.process(request, response);
      }

      // Close the socket
      socket.close();
      //check if the previous URI is a shutdown command
      shutdown = request.getUri().equals(SHUTDOWN_COMMAND);
    }
    catch (Exception e) {
      e.printStackTrace();
      System.exit(1);
    }
  }
}
}
```

The class's await method waits for HTTP requests until a shutdown command
is issued, and reminds you of the await method in Chapter 1. The difference
between the await method in Listing 2.2 and the one in Chapter 1 is that in
Listing 2.2 the request can be dispatched to either a
StaticResourceProcessor or a ServletProcessor. The request is

forwarded to the latter if the URI contains the string /servlet/. Otherwise, the request is passed to the StaticResourceProcessor instance. Notice that that part is greyed in Listing 2.2.

The Request Class

A servlet's service method receives a javax.servlet.ServletRequest instance and a javax.servlet.ServletResponse instance from the servlet container. This is to say that for every HTTP request, a servlet container must construct a ServletRequest object and a ServletResponse object and pass them to the service method of the servlet it is serving.

The ex02.pyrmont.Request class represents a request object to be passed to the servlet's service method. As such, it must implement the javax.servlet.ServletRequest interface. This class has to provide implementations for all methods in the interface. However, we would like to make it very simple and provide the implementations of some of the methods only.we leave the full method implementations for the chapters to come. In order to compile the Request class, you need to provide "blank" implementations for those methods. If you look at the Request class in Listing 2.3, you will see that all methods whose signatures return an object instance return a null.

Listing 2.3: The Request class

```
package ex02.pyrmont;

import java.io.InputStream;
import java.io.IOException;
import java.io.BufferedReader;
import java.io.UnsupportedEncodingException;
import java.util.Enumeration;
import java.util.Locale;
import java.util.Map;
import javax.servlet.RequestDispatcher;
import javax.servlet.ServletInputStream;
import javax.servlet.ServletRequest;


public class Request implements ServletRequest {

  private InputStream input;
  private String uri;

  public Request(InputStream input) {
    this.input = input;
  }
```

```
public String getUri() {
  return uri;
}

private String parseUri(String requestString) {
  int index1, index2;
  index1 = requestString.indexOf(' ');
  if (index1 != -1) {
    index2 = requestString.indexOf(' ', index1 + 1);
    if (index2 > index1)
      return requestString.substring(index1 + 1, index2);
  }
  return null;
}

public void parse() {
  // Read a set of characters from the socket
  StringBuffer request = new StringBuffer(2048);
  int i;
  byte[] buffer = new byte[2048];
  try {
    i = input.read(buffer);
  }
  catch (IOException e) {
    e.printStackTrace();
    i = -1;
  }
  for (int j=0; j<i; j++) {
    request.append((char) buffer[j]);
  }
  System.out.print(request.toString());
  uri = parseUri(request.toString());
}
```

```
/* implementation of ServletRequest */
public Object getAttribute(String attribute) {
  return null;
}
public Enumeration getAttributeNames() {
  return null;
}
public String getRealPath(String path) {
  return null;
}
public RequestDispatcher getRequestDispatcher(String path) {
  return null;
}
public boolean isSecure() {
  return false;
}
public String getCharacterEncoding() {
  return null;
}
public int getContentLength() {
  return 0;
}
```

```
public String getContentType() {
  return null;
}
public ServletInputStream getInputStream() throws IOException {
  return null;
}
public Locale getLocale() {
  return null;
}
public Enumeration getLocales() {
  return null;
}
public String getParameter(String name) {
  return null;
}
public Map getParameterMap() {
  return null;
}
public Enumeration getParameterNames() {
  return null;
}
public String[] getParameterValues(String parameter) {
  return null;
}
public String getProtocol() {
  return null;
}
public BufferedReader getReader() throws IOException {
  return null;
}
public String getRemoteAddr() {
  return null;
}
public String getRemoteHost() {
  return null;
}
public String getScheme() {
  return null;
}
public String getServerName() {
  return null;
}
public int getServerPort() {
  return 0;
}
public void removeAttribute(String attribute) {  }
public void setAttribute(String key, Object value) {  }
public void setCharacterEncoding(String encoding)
  throws UnsupportedEncodingException {  }
}
```

In addition, the Request class still has the parse and the getUri methods which were discussed in Chapter 1.

The Response Class

The ex02.pyrmont.Response class, given in Listing 2.4, implements javax.servlet.ServletResponse. As such, the class must provide implementations for all the methods in the interface. Similar to the Request class, we leave the implementations of all methods "blank", except for the getWriter method.

Listing 2.4: The Response class

```
package ex02.pyrmont;

import java.io.OutputStream;
import java.io.IOException;
import java.io.FileInputStream;
import java.io.FileNotFoundException;
import java.io.File;
import java.io.PrintWriter;
import java.util.Locale;
import javax.servlet.ServletResponse;
import javax.servlet.ServletOutputStream;

public class Response implements ServletResponse {

  private static final int BUFFER_SIZE = 1024;
  Request request;
  OutputStream output;
  PrintWriter writer;

  public Response(OutputStream output) {
    this.output = output;
  }

  public void setRequest(Request request) {
    this.request = request;
  }

  /* This method is used to serve static pages */
  public void sendStaticResource() throws IOException {
    byte[] bytes = new byte[BUFFER_SIZE];
    FileInputStream fis = null;
    try {
      /* request.getUri has been replaced by request.getRequestURI */
      File file = new File(Constants.WEB_ROOT, request.getUri());
      fis = new FileInputStream(file);
      /*
      HTTP Response = Status-Line
        *(( general-header | response-header | entity-header ) CRLF)
        CRLF
        [ message-body ]
        Status-Line = HTTP-Version SP Status-Code SP Reason-Phrase CRLF
      */
      int ch = fis.read(bytes, 0, BUFFER_SIZE);
      while (ch!=-1) {
```

```
        output.write(bytes, 0, ch);
        ch = fis.read(bytes, 0, BUFFER_SIZE);
      }
    }
    catch (FileNotFoundException e) {
      String errorMessage = "HTTP/1.1 404 File Not Found\r\n" +
        "Content-Type: text/html\r\n" +
        "Content-Length: 23\r\n" +
        "\r\n" +
        "<h1>File Not Found</h1>";
      output.write(errorMessage.getBytes());
    }
    finally {
      if (fis!=null)
        fis.close();
    }
  }


  /** implementation of ServletResponse  */
  public void flushBuffer() throws IOException {  }
  public int getBufferSize() {
    return 0;
  }
  public String getCharacterEncoding() {
    return null;
  }
  public Locale getLocale() {
    return null;
  }
  public ServletOutputStream getOutputStream() throws IOException {
    return null;
  }
  public PrintWriter getWriter() throws IOException {
    // autoflush is true, println() will flush,
    // but print() will not.
    writer = new PrintWriter(output, true);
    return writer;
  }
  public boolean isCommitted() {
    return false;
  }
  public void reset() {   }
  public void resetBuffer() {  }
  public void setBufferSize(int size) {  }
  public void setContentLength(int length) {  }
  public void setContentType(String type) {  }
  public void setLocale(Locale locale) {  }
}
```

In the getWriter method, the second argument to the PrintWriter class's constructor is a boolean indicating whether or not autoflush is enabled. Passing true as the second argument will make any call to a println method flush the output. However, a print method does not flush the output.

Therefore, if a call to a `print` method happens to be the last line in a servlet's `service` method, *the output will not be sent to the browser.* This imperfection will be fixed in the later applications.

The `Response` class still has the `sendStaticResource` method discussed in Chapter 1.

The StaticResourceProcessor Class

The `ex02.pyrmont.StaticResourceProcessor` class is used to serve requests for static resources. The only method it has is the process method. Listing 2.5 offers the StaticResourceProcessor class.

Listing 2.5: The StaticResourceProcessor class

```
package ex02.pyrmont;

import java.io.IOException;

public class StaticResourceProcessor {

  public void process(Request request, Response response) {
    try {
      response.sendStaticResource();
    }
    catch (IOException e) {
      e.printStackTrace();
    }
  }
}
```

The `process` method receives two arguments: an `ex02.pyrmont.Request` instance and an `ex02.pyrmont.Response` instance. This method simply calls the `sendStaticResource` method on the `Response` object.

The ServletProcessor1 Class

The `ex02.pyrmont.ServletProcessor1` class in Listing 2.6 is there to process HTTP requests for servlets.

Listing 2.6: The ServletProcessor1 class

```
package ex02.pyrmont;

import java.net.URL;
import java.net.URLClassLoader;
import java.net.URLStreamHandler;
import java.io.File;
```

```java
import java.io.IOException;
import javax.servlet.Servlet;
import javax.servlet.ServletRequest;
import javax.servlet.ServletResponse;

public class ServletProcessor1 {

  public void process(Request request, Response response) {
    String uri = request.getUri();
    String servletName = uri.substring(uri.lastIndexOf("/") + 1);
    URLClassLoader loader = null;
    try {
      // create a URLClassLoader
      URL[] urls = new URL[1];
      URLStreamHandler streamHandler = null;
      File classPath = new File(Constants.WEB_ROOT);
      // the forming of repository is taken from the
      // createClassLoader method in
      // org.apache.catalina.startup.ClassLoaderFactory
      String repository =
       (new URL("file", null, classPath.getCanonicalPath() +
       File.separator)).toString() ;
      // the code for forming the URL is taken from
      // the addRepository method in
      // org.apache.catalina.loader.StandardClassLoader.
      urls[0] = new URL(null, repository, streamHandler);
      loader = new URLClassLoader(urls);
    }
    catch (IOException e) {
      System.out.println(e.toString() );
    }
    Class myClass = null;
    try {
      myClass = loader.loadClass(servletName);
    }
    catch (ClassNotFoundException e) {
      System.out.println(e.toString());
    }

    Servlet servlet = null;

    try {
      servlet = (Servlet) myClass.newInstance();
      servlet.service((ServletRequest) request,
        (ServletResponse) response);
    }
    catch (Exception e) {
      System.out.println(e.toString());
    }
    catch (Throwable e) {
      System.out.println(e.toString());
    }

  }
}
```

The `ServletProcessor1` class is surprisingly simple, consisting only of one method: `process`. This method accepts two arguments: an instance of `javax.servlet.ServletRequest` and an instance of `javax.servlet.ServletResponse`. From the `ServletRequest`, the method obtains the URI by calling the `getRequestUri` method:

```
String uri = request.getUri();
```

Remember that the URI is in the following format:

```
/servlet/servletName
```

where *servletName* is the name of the servlet class.

To load the servlet class, we need to know the servlet name from the URI. We can get the servlet name using the next line of the `process` method:

```
String servletName = uri.substring(uri.lastIndexOf("/") + 1);
```

Next, the `process` method loads the servlet. To do this, you need to create a class loader and tell this class loader the location to look for the class to be loaded. For this servlet container, the class loader is directed to look in the directory pointed by `Constants.WEB_ROOT`, which points to the webroot directory under the working directory.

> **Note**
> Class loaders are discussed in detail in Chapter 8.

To load a servlet, you use the `java.net.URLClassLoader` class, which is an indirect child class of the `java.lang.ClassLoader` class. Once you have an instance of `URLClassLoader`, you use its `loadClass` method to load a servlet class. Instantiating the `URLClassLoader` class is straightforward. This class has three constructors, the simplest of which being:

```
public URLClassLoader(URL[] urls);
```

where *urls* is an array of `java.net.URL` objects pointing to the locations on which searches will be conducted when loading a class. Any URL that ends with a / is assumed to refer to a directory. Otherwise, the URL is assumed to refer to a JAR file, which will be downloaded and opened as needed.

> **Note**
> In a servlet container, the location where a class loader can find servlet classes is called a repository.

In our application, there is only one location that the class loader must look, i.e. the `webroot` directory under the working directory. Therefore, we start by creating an array of a single URL. The URL class provides a number of constructors, so there are many ways of constructing a URL object. For this application, we used the same constructor used in another class in Tomcat. The constructor has the following signature.

```
public URL(URL context, java.lang.String spec, URLStreamHandler hander)
  throws MalformedURLException
```

You can use this constructor by passing a specification for the second argument and null for both the first and the third arguments. However, there is another constructor that accepts three arguments:

```
public URL(java.lang.String protocol, java.lang.String host,
  java.lang.String file) throws MalformedURLException
```

Therefore, the compiler will not know which constructor you mean if you simply write the following code:

```
new URL(null, aString, null);
```

You can get around this by telling the compiler the type of the third argument, like this.

```
URLStreamHandler streamHandler = null;
new URL(null, aString, streamHandler);
```

For the second argument, you pass a String containing the repository (the directory where servlet classes can be found), which you form by using the following code:

```
String repository = (new URL("file", null,
  classPath.getCanonicalPath() + File.separator)).toString() ;
```

Combining all the pieces together, here is the part of the process method that constructs the appropriate URLClassLoader instance:

```
// create a URLClassLoader
URL[] urls = new URL[1];
URLStreamHandler streamHandler = null;
File classPath = new File(Constants.WEB_ROOT);
String repository = (new URL("file", null,
  classPath.getCanonicalPath() + File.separator)).toString() ;
urls[0] = new URL(null, repository, streamHandler);
loader = new URLClassLoader(urls);
```

Note
The code that forms the repository is taken from the createClassLoader method in org.apache.catalina.startup.ClassLoaderFactory and the code for forming the URL is taken from the addRepository method in org.apache.catalina.loader.StandardClassLoader. However, you don't have to worry about these classes until the later chapters.

Having a class loader, you can load a servlet class using the `loadClass` method:

```
Class myClass = null;
try {
  myClass = loader.loadClass(servletName);
}
catch (ClassNotFoundException e) {
  System.out.println(e.toString());
}
```

Next, the `process` method creates an instance of the servlet class loaded, downcasts it to `javax.servlet.Servlet`, and invokes the servlet's `service` method:

```
Servlet servlet = null;
try {
  servlet = (Servlet) myClass.newInstance();
  servlet.service((ServletRequest) request,
    (ServletResponse) response);
}
catch (Exception e) {
  System.out.println(e.toString());
}
catch (Throwable e) {
  System.out.println(e.toString());
}
```

Running the application

To run the application on Windows, type the following command from the working directory:

```
java -classpath ./lib/servlet.jar;./ ex02.pyrmont.HttpServer1
```

In Linux, you use a colon to separate two libraries:

```
java -classpath ./lib/servlet.jar:./ ex02.pyrmont.HttpServer1
```

To test the application, type the following in your URL or Address box of your browser:

```
http://localhost:8080/index.html
```

or

```
http://localhost:8080/servlet/PrimitiveServlet
```

When invoking `PrimitiveServlet`, you will see the following text in your browser:

```
Hello. Roses are red.
```

Note that you cannot see the second string Violets are blue, because only the first string is flushed to the browser. We will fix this problem in Chapter 3, though.

Application 2

There is a serious problem in the first application. In the ServletProcessor1 class's process method, you upcast the instance of ex02.pyrmont.Request to javax.servlet.ServletRequest and pass it as the first argument to the servlet's service method. You also upcast the instance of ex02.pyrmont.Response to javax.servlet.ServletResponse and pass it as the second argument to the servlet's service method.

```
try {
  servlet = (Servlet) myClass.newInstance();
  servlet.service((ServletRequest) request,
    (ServletResponse) response);
}
```

This compromises security. Servlet programmers who know the internal workings of this servlet container can downcast the ServletRequest and ServletResponse instances back to ex02.pyrmont.Request and ex02.pyrmont.Response respectively and call their public methods. Having a Request instance, they can call its parse method. Having a Response instance, they can call its sendStaticResource method.

You cannot make the parse and sendStaticResource methods private because they will be called from other classes. However, these two methods are not supposed to be available from inside a servlet. One solution is to make both Request and Response classes have default access modifier, so that they cannot be used from outside the ex02.pyrmont package. However, there is a more elegant solution: by using façade classes. See the UML diagram in Figure 2.2.

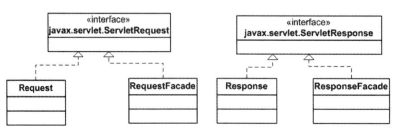

Figure 2.2: Façade classes

In this second application, we add two façade classes: `RequestFacade` and `ResponseFacade`. `RequestFacade` implements the `ServletRequest` interface and is instantiated by passing a `Request` instance that it assigns to a `ServletRequest` object reference in its constructor. Implementation of each method in the `ServletRequest` interface invokes the corresponding method of the `Request` object. However, the `ServletRequest` object itself is private and cannot be accessed from outside the class. Instead of upcasting the `Request` object to `ServletRequest` and passing it to the `service` method, we construct a `RequestFacade` object and pass it to the `service` method. Servlet programmers can still downcast the `ServletRequest` instance back to `RequestFacade`, however they can only access the methods available in the `ServletRequest` interface. Now, the `parseUri` method is safe.

Listing 2.7 shows an incomplete `RequestFacade` class.

Listing 2.7: The RequestFacade class

```
package ex02.pyrmont;
public class RequestFacade implements ServletRequest {
  private ServletRequest request = null;

  public RequestFacade(Request request) {
    this.request = request;
  }

  /* implementation of the ServletRequest*/
  public Object getAttribute(String attribute) {
    return request.getAttribute(attribute);
  }

  public Enumeration getAttributeNames() {
    return request.getAttributeNames();
  }

  . . .
}
```

Notice the constructor of `RequestFacade`. It accepts a `Request` object but immediately assigns it to the private `servletRequest` object reference. Notice also each method in the `RequestFacade` class invokes the corresponding method in the `ServletRequest` object.

The same applies to the `ResponseFacade` class.

Here are the classes used in Application 2:

- `HttpServer2`
- `Request`
- `Response`

- StaticResourceProcessor
- ServletProcessor2
- Constants

The HttpServer2 class is similar to HttpServer1, except that it uses ServletProcessor2 in its await method, instead of ServletProcessor1:

```
if (request.getUri().startsWith("/servlet/")) {
    ServletProcessor2 processor = new ServletProcessor2();
    processor.process(request, response);
}
else {
    ...
}
```

The ServletProcessor2 class is similar to ServletProcessor1, except in the following part of its process method:

```
Servlet servlet = null;
RequestFacade requestFacade = new RequestFacade(request);
ResponseFacade responseFacade = new ResponseFacade(response);
try {
  servlet = (Servlet) myClass.newInstance();
  servlet.service((ServletRequest) requestFacade,
    (ServletResponse) responseFacade);
}
```

Running the application

To run the application on Windows, type this from the working directory:

```
java -classpath ./lib/servlet.jar;./ ex02.pyrmont.HttpServer2
```

In Linux, you use a colon to separate two libraries.

```
java -classpath ./lib/servlet.jar:./ ex02.pyrmont.HttpServer2
```

You can use the same URLs as in Application1 and you will get the same result.

Summary

This chapter discussed two simple servlet containers that can be used to serve static resources as well as process servlets as simple as PrimitiveServlet. Background information on the javax.servlet.Servlet interface and related types was also given.

Chapter 3
Connector

As mentioned in Introduction, there are two main modules in Catalina: the connector and the container. In this chapter you will enhance the applications in Chapter 2 by writing a connector that creates better request and response objects. A connector compliant with Servlet 2.3 and 2.4 specifications must create instances of `javax.servlet.http.HttpServletRequest` and `javax.servlet.http.HttpServletResponse` to be passed to the invoked servlet's `service` method. In Chapter 2 the servlet containers could only run servlets that implement `javax.servlet.Servlet` and passed instances of `javax.servlet.ServletRequest` and `javax.servlet.ServletResponse` to the `service` method. Because the connector does not know the type of the servlet (i.e. whether it implements `javax.servlet.Servlet`, extends `javax.servlet.GenericServlet`, or extends `javax.servlet.http.HttpServlet`), the connector must always provide instances of `HttpServletRequest` and `HttpServletResponse`.

In this chapter's application, the connector parses HTTP request headers and enables a servlet to obtain headers, cookies, parameter names/values, etc. You will also perfect the `getWriter` method in the `Response` class in Chapter 2 so that it will behave correctly. Thanks to these enhancements, you will get a complete response from `PrimitiveServlet` and be able to run the more complex `ModernServlet`.

The connector you build in this chapter is a simplified version of the default connector that comes with Tomcat 4, which is discussed in detail in Chapter 4. Tomcat's default connector is deprecated as of version 4 of Tomcat, however it still serves as a great learning tool. For the rest of the chapter, "connector" refers to the module built in our application.

Note
Unlike the applications in the previous chapters, in this chapter's application the connector is separate from the container.

The application for this chapter can be found in the `ex03.pyrmont` package and its sub-packages. The classes that make up the connector are part of the `ex03.pyrmont.connector` and `ex03.pyrmont.connector.http` packages. Starting from this chapter, every accompanying application has a bootstrap class used to start the application. However, at this stage, there is not yet a mechanism to stop the application. Once run, you must stop the application abruptly by closing the console (in Windows) or by killing the process (in UNIX/Linux).

Before we explain the application, let me start with the `StringManager` class in the `org.apache.catalina.util` package. This class handles the internationalization of error messages in different modules in this application and in Catalina itself. The discussion of the accompanying application is presented afterwards.

The StringManager Class

A large application such as Tomcat needs to handle error messages carefully. In Tomcat error messages are useful for both system administrators and servlet programmers. For example, Tomcat logs error messages in order for system administrator to easily pinpoint any abnormality that happened. For servlet programmers, Tomcat sends a particular error message inside every `javax.servlet.ServletException` thrown so that the programmer knows what has gone wrong with his/her servlet.

The approach used in Tomcat is to store error messages in a properties file, so that editing them is easy. However, there are hundreds of classes in Tomcat. Storing all error messages used by all classes in one big properties file will easily create a maintenance nightmare. To avoid this, Tomcat allocates a properties file for each package. For example, the properties file in the `org.apache.catalina.connector` package contains all error messages that can be thrown from any class in that package. Each properties file is handled by an instance of the `org.apache.catalina.util.StringManager` class. When Tomcat is run, there will be many instances of `StringManager`, each of which reads a properties file specific to a package. Also, due to Tomcat's popularity, it makes sense to provide error messages in multi languages. Currently, three languages are supported. The properties file for English error messages is named `LocalStrings.properties`. The other two are for the Spanish and Japanese languages, in the LocalStrings_es.properties and LocalStrings_ja.properties files respectively.

When a class in a package needs to look up an error message in that package's properties file, it will first obtain an instance of StringManager. However, many classes in the same package may need a StringManager and it is a waste of resources to create a StringManager instance for every object that needs error messages. The StringManager class therefore has been designed so that an instance of StringManager is shared by all objects inside a package. If you are familiar with design patterns, you'll guess correctly that StringManager is a singleton class. The only constructor it has is private so that you cannot use the new keyword to instantiate it from outside the class. You get an instance by calling its public static method getManager, passing a package name. Each instance is stored in a Hashtable with package names as its keys.

```
private static Hashtable managers = new Hashtable();
public synchronized static StringManager
  getManager(String packageName) {
  StringManager mgr = (StringManager)managers.get(packageName);
  if (mgr == null) {
    mgr = new StringManager(packageName);
    managers.put(packageName, mgr);
  }
  return mgr;
}
```

Note
An article on the Singleton pattern entitled "The Singleton Pattern" can be found in the accompanying ZIP file.

For example, to use StringManager from a class in the ex03.pyrmont.connector.http package, pass the package name to the StringManager class's getManager method:

```
StringManager sm =
  StringManager.getManager("ex03.pyrmont.connector.http");
```

In the ex03.pyrmont.connector.http package, you can find three properties files: LocalStrings.properties, LocalStrings_es.properties and LocalStrings_ja.properties. Which of these files will be used by the StringManager instance depends on the locale of the server running the application. If you open the LocalStrings.properties file, the first non-comment line reads:

```
httpConnector.alreadyInitialized=HTTP connector has already been
initialized
```

To get an error message, use the StringManager class's getString, passing an error code. Here is the signature of one of its overloads:

```
public String getString(String key)
```

Calling getString by passing httpConnector.alreadyInitialized as the argument returns HTTP connector has already been initialized.

The Application

Starting from this chapter, the accompanying application for each chapter is divided into modules. This chapter's application consists of three modules: connector, startup, and core.

The startup module consists only of one class, Bootstrap, which starts the application. The connector module has classes that can be grouped into five categories:

- The connector and its supporting class (HttpConnector and HttpProcessor).
- The class representing HTTP requests (HttpRequest) and its supporting classes.
- The class representing HTTP responses (HttpResponse) and its supporting classes.
- Façade classes (HttpRequestFacade and HttpResponseFacade).
- The Constant class.

The core module consists of two classes: ServletProcessor and StaticResourceProcessor.

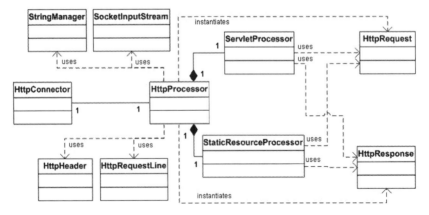

Figure 3.1 The UML diagram of the application

Figure 3.1 shows the UML diagram of the classes in this application. To make the diagram more readable, the classes related to `HttpRequest` and `HttpResponse` have been omitted. You can find UML diagrams for both when we discuss `Request` and `Response` objects respectively.

Compare the diagram with the one in Figure 2.1. The `HttpServer` class in Chapter 2 has been broken into two classes: `HttpConnector` and `HttpProcessor`, `Request` has been replaced by `HttpRequest`, and `Response` by `HttpResponse`. Also, more classes are used in this chapter's application.

The `HttpServer` class in Chapter 2 is responsible for waiting for HTTP requests and creating request and response objects. In this chapter's application, the task of waiting for HTTP requests is given to the `HttpConnector` instance, and the task of creating request and response objects is assigned to the `HttpProcessor` instance.

In this chapter, HTTP request objects are represented by the `HttpRequest` class, which implements `javax.servlet.http.HttpServletRequest`. An `HttpRequest` object will be cast to a `HttpServletRequest` instance and passed to the invoked servlet's `service` method. Therefore, every `HttpRequest` instance must have its fields properly populated so that the servlet can use them. Values that need to be assigned to the `HttpRequest` object include the URI, query string, parameters, cookies and other headers, etc. Because the connector does not know which values will be needed by the invoked servlet, the connector must parse all values that can be obtained from the HTTP request. However, parsing an HTTP request involves expensive string and other operations, and the connector can save lots of CPU cycles if it parses only values that will be needed by the servlet. For example, if the servlet does not need any request parameter (i.e. it does not call the `getParameter`, `getParameterMap`, `getParameterNames`, or `getParameterValues` methods of `javax.servlet.http.HttpServletRequest`), the connector does not need to parse these parameters from the query string and or from the HTTP request body. Tomcat's default connector (and the connector in this chapter's application) tries to be more efficient by leaving the parameter parsing until it is really needed by the servlet.

Tomcat's default connector and our connector use the `SocketInputStream` class for reading byte streams from the socket's `InputStream`. An instance of `SocketInputStream` wraps the `java.io.InputStream` instance returned by the socket's `getInputStream` method. The `SocketInputStream` class provides two important methods:

readRequestLine and readHeader. readRequestLine returns the first line in an HTTP request, i.e. the line containing the URI, method and HTTP version. Because processing byte stream from the socket's input stream means reading from the first byte to the last (and never moves backwards), readRequestLine must be called only once and must be called before readHeader is called. readHeader is called to obtain a header name/value pair each time it is called and should be called repeatedly until all headers are read. The return value of readRequestLine is an instance of HttpRequestLine and the return value of readHeader is an HttpHeader object. We will discuss the HttpRequestLine and HttpHeader classes in the sections to come.

The HttpProcessor object creates instances of HttpRequest and therefore must populate fields in them. The HttpProcessor class, using its parse method, parses both the request line and headers in an HTTP request. The values resulting from the parsing are then assigned to the fields in the HttpProcessor objects. However, the parse method does not parse the parameters in the request body or query string. This task is left to the HttpRequest objects themselves. Only if the servlet needs a parameter will the query string or request body be parsed.

Another enhancement over the previous applications is the presence of the bootstrap class ex03.pyrmont.startup.Bootstrap to start the application.

We will explain the application in detail in these sub-sections:

- Starting the Application
- The Connector
- Creating an HttpRequest Object
- Creating an HttpResponse Object
- Static resource processor and servlet processor
- Running the Application

Starting the Application

You start the application from the ex03.pyrmont.startup.Bootstrap class. This class is given in Listing 3.1.

Listing 3.1: The Bootstrap class

```
package ex03.pyrmont.startup;
import ex03.pyrmont.connector.http.HttpConnector;
```

```
public final class Bootstrap {
  public static void main(String[] args) {
    HttpConnector connector = new HttpConnector();
    connector.start();
  }
}
```

The `main` method in the `Bootstrap class` instantiates the `HttpConnector` class and calls its `start` method. The `HttpConnector` class is given in Listing 3.2.

The Connector

The `ex03.pyrmont.connector.http.HttpConnector` class represents a connector responsible for creating a server socket that waits for incoming HTTP requests. This class is presented in Listing 3.2.

Listing 3.2: The HttpConnector class's start method

```
package ex03.pyrmont.connector.http;

import java.io.IOException;
import java.net.InetAddress;
import java.net.ServerSocket;
import java.net.Socket;

public class HttpConnector implements Runnable {
  boolean stopped;
  private String scheme = "http";

  public String getScheme() {
    return scheme;
  }

  public void run() {
    ServerSocket serverSocket = null;
    int port = 8080;
    try {
      serverSocket =  new
        ServerSocket(port, 1, InetAddress.getByName("127.0.0.1"));
    }
    catch (IOException e) {
      e.printStackTrace();
      System.exit(1);
    }
    while (!stopped) {
      // Accept the next incoming connection from the server socket
      Socket socket = null;
      try {
        socket = serverSocket.accept();
      }
```

```
    catch (Exception e) {
      continue;
    }
    // Hand this socket off to an HttpProcessor
    HttpProcessor processor = new HttpProcessor(this);
    processor.process(socket);
  }
}

public void start() {
  Thread thread = new Thread(this);
  thread.start();
}
}
```

The `HttpConnector` class implements `java.lang.Runnable` so that it can be dedicated a thread of its own. When you start the application, an instance of `HttpConnector` is created and its `run` method executed.

Note
You can read the article "Working with Threads" to refresh your memory about how to create Java threads.

The `run` method contains a `while` loop that does the following:

- Waits for HTTP requests
- Creates an instance of `HttpProcessor` for each request.
- Calls the `process` method of the `HttpProcessor`.

Note
The `run` method is similar to the `await` method of the `HttpServer1` class in Chapter 2.

You can see right away that the `HttpConnector` class is very similar to the `ex02.pyrmont.HttpServer1` class, except that after a socket is obtained from the `accept` method of `java.net.ServerSocket`, an `HttpProcessor` instance is created and its `process` method is called, passing the socket.

Note
The `HttpConnector` class has another method calls `getScheme`, which returns the scheme (HTTP).

The `HttpProcessor` class's `process` method receives the socket from an incoming HTTP request. For each incoming HTTP request, it does the following:

1. Create an `HttpRequest` object.
2. Create an `HttpResponse` object.

3. Parse the HTTP request's first line and headers and populate the HttpRequest object.
4. Pass the HttpRequest and HttpResponse objects to either a ServletProcessor or a StaticResourceProcessor. Like in Chapter 2, the ServletProcessor invokes the service method of the requested servlet and the StaticResourceProcessor sends the content of a static resource.

The process method is given in Listing 3.3.

Listing 3.3: The HttpProcessor class's process method.

```
public void process(Socket socket) {
  SocketInputStream input = null;
  OutputStream output = null;
  try {
    input = new SocketInputStream(socket.getInputStream(), 2048);
    output = socket.getOutputStream();

    // create HttpRequest object and parse
    request = new HttpRequest(input);

    // create HttpResponse object
    response = new HttpResponse(output);
    response.setRequest(request);

    response.setHeader("Server", "Pyrmont Servlet Container");

    parseRequest(input, output);
    parseHeaders(input);

    //check if this is a request for a servlet or a static resource
    //a request for a servlet begins with "/servlet/"
    if (request.getRequestURI().startsWith("/servlet/")) {
      ServletProcessor processor = new ServletProcessor();
      processor.process(request, response);
    }
    else {
      StaticResourceProcessor processor = new
        StaticResourceProcessor();
      processor.process(request, response);
    }

    // Close the socket
    socket.close();
    // no shutdown for this application
  }
  catch (Exception e) {
    e.printStackTrace();
  }
}
```

The process method starts by obtaining the input stream and output stream of the socket. Note, however, in this method we use the SocketInputStream class that extends java.io.InputStream.

```
SocketInputStream input = null;
OutputStream output = null;
try {
  input = new SocketInputStream(socket.getInputStream(), 2048);
  output = socket.getOutputStream();
```

Then, it creates an HttpRequest instance and an HttpResponse instance and assigns the HttpRequest to the HttpResponse.

```
// create HttpRequest object and parse
request = new HttpRequest(input);

// create HttpResponse object
response = new HttpResponse(output);
response.setRequest(request);
```

The HttpResponse class in this chapter's application is more sophisticated than the Response class in Chapter 2. For one, you can send headers to the client by calling its setHeader method.

```
response.setHeader("Server", "Pyrmont Servlet Container");
```

Next, the process method calls two private methods in the HttpProcessor class for parsing the request.

```
parseRequest(input, output);
parseHeaders(input);
```

Then, it hands off the HttpRequest and HttpResponse objects for processing to either a ServletProcessor or a StaticResourceProcessor, depending the URI pattern of the request.

```
if (request.getRequestURI().startsWith("/servlet/")) {
  ServletProcessor processor = new ServletProcessor();
  processor.process(request, response);
}
else {
  StaticResourceProcessor processor =
    new StaticResourceProcessor();
  processor.process(request, response);
}
```

Finally, it closes the socket.

```
socket.close();
```

Note also that the `HttpProcessor` class uses the `org.apache.catalina.util.StringManager` class for sending error messages:

```
protected StringManager sm =
  StringManager.getManager("ex03.pyrmont.connector.http");
```

The private methods in the `HttpProcessor` class--`parseRequest`, `parseHeaders`, and `normalize`--are called to help populate the `HttpRequest`. These methods will be discussed in the next section, "Creating an `HttpRequest` Object".

Creating an HttpRequest Object

The `HttpRequest` class implements `javax.servlet.http.HttpServletRequest`. Accompanying it is a façade class called `HttpRequestFacade`. Figure 3.2 shows the UML diagram of the `HttpRequest` class and its related classes.

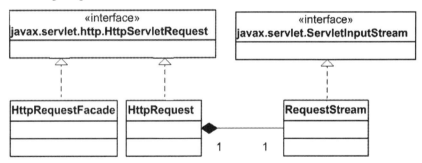

Figure 3.2: The HttpRequest class and related classes

Many of the methods in the `HttpRequest` class are left blank (you have to wait until Chapter 4 for a full implementation), but servlet programmers can already retrieve the headers, cookies and parameters of the incoming HTTP request. These three types of values are stored in the following reference variables:

```
protected HashMap headers = new HashMap();
protected ArrayList cookies = new ArrayList();
protected ParameterMap parameters = null;
```

Note

`ParameterMap` class will be explained in the section "Obtaining Parameters".

Therefore, a servlet programmer can get the correct return values from the following methods in `javax.servlet.http.HttpServletRequest`: `getCookies`, `getDateHeader`, `getHeader`, `getHeaderNames`, `getHeaders`, `getParameter`, `getPrameterMap`, `getParameterNames`, and `getParameterValues`. Once you get headers, cookies, and parameters populated with the correct values, the implementation of the related methods are easy, as you can see in the `HttpRequest` class.

Needless to say, the main challenge here is to parse the HTTP request and populate the `HttpRequest` object. For headers and cookies, the `HttpRequest` class provides the `addHeader` and `addCookie` methods that are called from the `parseHeaders` method of `HttpProcessor`. Parameters are parsed when they are needed, using the `HttpRequest` class's `parseParameters` method. All methods are discussed in this section.

Since HTTP request parsing is a rather complex task, this section is divided into the following subsections:

- Reading the socket's input stream
- Parsing the request line
- Parsing headers
- Parsing cookies
- Obtaining parameters

Reading the socket's input stream

In Chapters 1 and 2 you did a bit of request parsing in the `ex01.pyrmont.HttpRequest` and `ex02.pyrmont.HttpRequest` classes. You obtained the request line containing the method, the URI, and the HTTP version by invoking the `read` method of the `java.io.InputStream` class:

```
byte[] buffer = new byte[2048];
try {
  // input is the InputStream from the socket.
  i = input.read(buffer);
}
```

You did not attempt to parse the request further for the two applications. In the application for this chapter, however, you have the `ex03.pyrmont.connector.http.SocketInputStream` class, a copy of `org.apache.catalina.connector.http.SocketInputStream`. This class provides methods for obtaining not only the request line, but also the request headers.

You construct a `SocketInputStream` instance by passing an `InputStream` and an integer indicating the buffer size used in the instance. In this application, you create a `SocketInputStream` object in the `process` method of `ex03.pyrmont.connector.http.HttpProcessor`, as in the following code fragment:

```
SocketInputStream input = null;
OutputStream output = null;
try {
  input = new SocketInputStream(socket.getInputStream(), 2048);
  ...
```

As mentioned previously, the reason for having a `SocketInputStream` is for its two important methods: `readRequestLine` and `readHeader`. Read on.

Parsing the Request Line

The `process` method of `HttpProcessor` calls the private `parseRequest` method to parse the request line, i.e. the first line of an HTTP request. Here is an example of a request line:

```
GET /myApp/ModernServlet?userName=tarzan&password=pwd HTTP/1.1
```

The second part of the request line is the URI plus an optional query string. In the example above, here is the URI:

```
/myApp/ModernServlet
```

And, anything after the question mark is the query string. Therefore the query string is the following:

```
userName=tarzan&password=pwd
```

The query string can contain zero or more parameters. In the example above, there are two parameter name/value pairs: `userName`/`tarzan` and `password`/`pwd`. In servlet/JSP programming, the parameter name `jsessionid` is used to carry a session identifier. Session identifiers are usually embedded as cookies, but the programmer can opt to embed the session identifiers in query strings, for example if the browser's support for cookies is being turned off.

When the `parseRequest` method is called from the `HttpProcessor` class's `process` method, the `request` variable points to an instance of `HttpRequest`. The `parseRequest` method parses the request line to obtain several values and assigns these values to the `HttpRequest` object. Now, let's take a close look at the `parseRequest` method in Listing 3.4.

Listing 3.4: The parseRequest method in the HttpProcessor class

```
private void parseRequest(SocketInputStream input, OutputStream output)
  throws IOException, ServletException {

  // Parse the incoming request line
  input.readRequestLine(requestLine);
  String method =
    new String(requestLine.method, 0, requestLine.methodEnd);
  String uri = null;
  String protocol = new String(requestLine.protocol, 0,
    requestLine.protocolEnd);

  // Validate the incoming request line
  if (method.length() < 1) {
    throw new ServletException("Missing HTTP request method");
  }
  else if (requestLine.uriEnd < 1) {
    throw new ServletException("Missing HTTP request URI");
  }
  // Parse any query parameters out of the request URI
  int question = requestLine.indexOf("?");
  if (question >= 0) {
    request.setQueryString(new String(requestLine.uri, question + 1,
      requestLine.uriEnd - question - 1));
    uri = new String(requestLine.uri, 0, question);
  }
  else {
    request.setQueryString(null);
    uri = new String(requestLine.uri, 0, requestLine.uriEnd);
  }

  // Checking for an absolute URI (with the HTTP protocol)
  if (!uri.startsWith("/")) {
    int pos = uri.indexOf("://");
    // Parsing out protocol and host name
    if (pos != -1) {
      pos = uri.indexOf('/', pos + 3);
      if (pos == -1) {
        uri = "";
      }
      else {
        uri = uri.substring(pos);
      }
    }
  }

  // Parse any requested session ID out of the request URI
  String match = ";jsessionid=";
  int semicolon = uri.indexOf(match);
  if (semicolon >= 0) {
    String rest = uri.substring(semicolon + match.length());
    int semicolon2 = rest.indexOf(';');
    if (semicolon2 >= 0) {
      request.setRequestedSessionId(rest.substring(0, semicolon2));
      rest = rest.substring(semicolon2);
```

```
    }
    else {
      request.setRequestedSessionId(rest);
      rest = "";
    }
    request.setRequestedSessionURL(true);
    uri = uri.substring(0, semicolon) + rest;
  }
  else {
    request.setRequestedSessionId(null);
    request.setRequestedSessionURL(false);
  }

  // Normalize URI (using String operations at the moment)
  String normalizedUri = normalize(uri);
  // Set the corresponding request properties
  ((HttpRequest) request).setMethod(method);
  request.setProtocol(protocol);
  if (normalizedUri != null) {
    ((HttpRequest) request).setRequestURI(normalizedUri);
  }
  else {
    ((HttpRequest) request).setRequestURI(uri);
  }
  if (normalizedUri == null) {
    throw new ServletException("Invalid URI: " + uri + "'");
  }
}
```

The `parseRequest` method starts by calling the `SocketInputStream` class's `readRequestLine` method:

```
    input.readRequestLine(requestLine);
```

where *requestLine* is an instance of HttpRequestLine inside HttpProcessor:

```
private HttpRequestLine requestLine = new HttpRequestLine();
```

Invoking its `readRequestLine` method tells the `SocketInputStream` to populate the `HttpRequestLine` instance.

Next, the `parseRequest` method obtains the method, URI, and protocol of the request line:

```
    String method =
      new String(requestLine.method, 0, requestLine.methodEnd);
    String uri = null;
    String protocol = new String(requestLine.protocol, 0,
      requestLine.protocolEnd);
```

However, there may be a query string after the URI. If present, the query string is separated by a question mark. Therefore, the `parseRequest` method attempts to first obtain the query string and populates the `HttpRequest` object by calling its `setQueryString` method:

```
// Parse any query parameters out of the request URI
int question = requestLine.indexOf("?");
if (question >= 0) { // there is a query string.
  request.setQueryString(new String(requestLine.uri, question + 1,
    requestLine.uriEnd - question - 1));
  uri = new String(requestLine.uri, 0, question);
}
else {
  request.setQueryString(null);
  uri = new String(requestLine.uri, 0, requestLine.uriEnd);
}
```

However, while most often a URI points to a relative resource, a URI can also be an absolute value, such as the following:

```
http://www.brainysoftware.com/index.html?name=Tarzan
```

The `parseRequest` method also checks this:

```
// Checking for an absolute URI (with the HTTP protocol)
if (!uri.startsWith("/")) {
  // not starting with /, this is an absolute URI
  int pos = uri.indexOf("://");
  // Parsing out protocol and host name
  if (pos != -1) {
    pos = uri.indexOf('/', pos + 3);
    if (pos == -1) {
      uri = "";
    }
    else {
      uri = uri.substring(pos);
    }
  }
}
```

Then, the query string may also contain a session identifier, indicated by the `jsessionid` parameter name. Therefore, the `parseRequest` method checks for a session identifier too. If `jsessionid` is found in the query string, the method obtains the session identifier and assigns the value to the `HttpRequest` instance by calling its `setRequestedSessionId` method:

```
// Parse any requested session ID out of the request URI
String match = ";jsessionid=";
int semicolon = uri.indexOf(match);
if (semicolon >= 0) {
  String rest = uri.substring(semicolon + match.length());
  int semicolon2 = rest.indexOf(';');
  if (semicolon2 >= 0) {
    request.setRequestedSessionId(rest.substring(0, semicolon2));
    rest = rest.substring(semicolon2);
  }
```

```
    else {
      request.setRequestedSessionId(rest);
      rest = "";
    }
    request.setRequestedSessionURL(true);
    uri = uri.substring(0, semicolon) + rest;
  }
  else {
    request.setRequestedSessionId(null);
    request.setRequestedSessionURL(false);
  }
```

If `jsessionid` is found, this also means that the session identifier is carried in the query string, and not in a cookie. Therefore, pass `true` to the request's `setRequestSessionURL` method. Otherwise, pass `false` to the `setRequestSessionURL` method and `null` to the `setRequestedSessionURL` method.

At this point, the value of `uri` has been stripped off the `jsessionid`.

Then, the `parseRequest` method passes `uri` to the `normalize` method to correct an "abnormal" URI. For example, any occurrence of \ will be replaced by /. If `uri` is in good format or if the abnormality can be corrected, `normalize` returns the same URI or the corrected one. If the URI cannot be corrected, it will be considered invalid and `normalize` returns null. On such an occasion (`normalize` returning null), the `parseRequest` method will throw an exception at the end of the method.

Finally, the `parseRequest` method sets some properties of the `HttpRequest` object:

```
((HttpRequest) request).setMethod(method);
request.setProtocol(protocol);
if (normalizedUri != null) {
  ((HttpRequest) request).setRequestURI(normalizedUri);
}
else {
  ((HttpRequest) request).setRequestURI(uri);
}
```

And, if the return value from the `normalize` method is null, the method throws an exception:

```
if (normalizedUri == null) {
  throw new ServletException("Invalid URI: " + uri + "'");
}
```

Parsing Headers

An HTTP header is represented by the HttpHeader class. This class will be explained in detail in Chapter 4, for now it is sufficient to know the following:

- You can construct an HttpHeader instance by using its class's no-argument constructor.
- Once you have an HttpHeader instance, you can pass it to the readHeader method of SocketInputStream. If there is a header to read, the readHeader method will populate the HttpHeader object accordingly. If there is no more header to read, both nameEnd and valueEnd fields of the HttpHeader instance will be zero.
- To obtain the header name and value, use the following:

```
String name = new String(header.name, 0, header.nameEnd);
String value = new String(header.value, 0, header.valueEnd);
```

The parseHeaders method contains a while loop that keeps reading headers from the SocketInputStream until there is no more header. The loop starts by constructing an HttpHeader instance and passing it to the SocketInputStream class's readHeader:

```
HttpHeader header = new HttpHeader();
// Read the next header
input.readHeader(header);
```

Then, you can test whether or not there is a next header to be read from the input stream by testing the nameEnd and valueEnd fields of the HttpHeader instance:

```
if (header.nameEnd == 0) {
  if (header.valueEnd == 0) {
    return;
  }
  else {
    throw new ServletException
      (sm.getString("httpProcessor.parseHeaders.colon"));
  }
}
```

If there is a next header, the header name and value can then be retrieved:

```
String name = new String(header.name, 0, header.nameEnd);
String value = new String(header.value, 0, header.valueEnd);
```

Once you get the header name and value, you add it to the headers HashMap in the HttpRequest object by calling its addHeader method:

```
request.addHeader(name, value);
```

Some headers also require the setting of some properties. For instance, the value of the content-length header is to be returned when the servlet calls the `getContentLength` method of `javax.servlet.ServletRequest`, and the cookie header contains cookies to be added to the cookie collection. Thus, here is some processing:

```
if (name.equals("cookie")) {
  ... // process cookies here
}
else if (name.equals("content-length")) {
  int n = -1;
  try {
    n = Integer.parseInt(value);
  }
  catch (Exception e) {
    throw new ServletException(sm.getString(
      "httpProcessor.parseHeaders.contentLength"));
  }
  request.setContentLength(n);
}
else if (name.equals("content-type")) {
  request.setContentType(value);
}
```

Cookie parsing is discussed in the next section, Parsing Cookies.

Parsing Cookies

Cookies are sent by a browser as an HTTP request header. Such a header has the name "cookie" and the value is the cookie name/value pair(s). Here is an example of a cookie header containing two cookies: `userName` and `password`.

```
Cookie: userName=budi; password=pwd;
```

Cookie parsing is done using the `parseCookieHeader` method of the `org.apache.catalina.util.RequestUtil` class. This method accepts the cookie header and returns an array of `javax.servlet.http.Cookie`. The number of elements in the array is the same as the number of cookie name/value pairs in the header. The `parseCookieHeader` method is given in Listing 3.5.

Listing 3.5: The org.apache.catalina.util.RequestUtil class's parseCookieHeader method

```
public static Cookie[] parseCookieHeader(String header) {
  if ((header == null) || (header.length() < 1))
    return (new Cookie[0]);

  ArrayList cookies = new ArrayList();
  while (header.length() > 0) {
```

```
int semicolon = header.indexOf(';');
if (semicolon < 0)
  semicolon = header.length();
  if (semicolon == 0)
    break;
  String token = header.substring(0, semicolon);
  if (semicolon < header.length())
    header = header.substring(semicolon + 1);
  else
    header = "";
  try {
    int equals = token.indexOf('=');
    if (equals > 0) {
      String name = token.substring(0, equals).trim();
      String value = token.substring(equals+1).trim();
      cookies.add(new Cookie(name, value));
    }
  }
  catch (Throwable e) {
    ;
  }
}
return ((Cookie[]) cookies.toArray(new Cookie[cookies.size()]));
}
```

And, here is the part of the `HttpProcessor` class's `parseHeader` method that processes the cookies:

```
else if (header.equals(DefaultHeaders.COOKIE_NAME)) {
  Cookie cookies[] = RequestUtil.parseCookieHeader(value);
  for (int i = 0; i < cookies.length; i++) {
    if (cookies[i].getName().equals("jsessionid")) {
      // Override anything requested in the URL
      if (!request.isRequestedSessionIdFromCookie()) {
        // Accept only the first session id cookie
        request.setRequestedSessionId(cookies[i].getValue());
        request.setRequestedSessionCookie(true);
        request.setRequestedSessionURL(false);
      }
    }
    request.addCookie(cookies[i]);
  }
}
```

Obtaining Parameters

You don't parse the query string or HTTP request body to get parameters until the servlet needs to read one or all of them by calling the `getParameter`, `getParameterMap`, `getParameterNames`, or `getParameterValues` methods of `javax.servlet.http.HttpServletRequest`. Therefore, the implementations of these four methods in `HttpRequest` always start with a call to the `parseParameter` method.

The parameters only needs to be parsed once and may only be parsed once because if the parameters are to be found in the request body, parameter parsing causes the `SocketInputStream` to reach the end of its byte stream. The `HttpRequest` class employs a `boolean` called `parsed` to indicate whether or not parsing has been done.

Parameters can be found in the query string or in the request body. If the user requested the servlet using the GET method, all parameters are on the query string. If the POST method is used, you may find some in the request body too. All the name/value pairs are stored in a `HashMap`. Servlet programmers can obtain the parameters as a `Map` (by calling `getParameterMap` of `HttpServletRequest`) and the parameter name/value. There is a catch, though. Servlet programmers are not allowed to change parameter values. Therefore, a special `HashMap` is used: `org.apache.catalina.util.ParameterMap`.

The `ParameterMap` class extends `java.util.HashMap` and employs a `boolean` called `locked`. The name/value pairs can only be added, updated or removed if `locked` is `false`. Otherwise, an `IllegalStateException` is thrown. Reading the values, however, can be done any time. The `ParameterMap` class is given in Listing 3.6. It overrides the methods for adding, updating and removing values. Those methods can only be called when `locked` is `false`.

Listing 3.6: The org.apache.Catalina.util.ParameterMap class.

```
package org.apache.catalina.util;
import java.util.HashMap;
import java.util.Map;

public final class ParameterMap extends HashMap {
  public ParameterMap() {
    super();
  }
  public ParameterMap(int initialCapacity) {
    super(initialCapacity);
  }
  public ParameterMap(int initialCapacity, float loadFactor) {
    super(initialCapacity, loadFactor);
  }
  public ParameterMap(Map map) {
    super(map);
  }
  private boolean locked = false;
  public boolean isLocked() {
    return (this.locked);
```

```
  }
  public void setLocked(boolean locked) {
    this.locked = locked;
  }
  private static final StringManager sm =
    StringManager.getManager("org.apache.catalina.util");
  public void clear() {
    if (locked)
      throw new IllegalStateException
        (sm.getString("parameterMap.locked"));
    super.clear();
  }
  public Object put(Object key, Object value) {
    if (locked)
      throw new IllegalStateException
        (sm.getString("parameterMap.locked"));
    return (super.put(key, value));
  }
  public void putAll(Map map) {
    if (locked)
      throw new IllegalStateException
        (sm.getString("parameterMap.locked"));
    super.putAll(map);
  }

  public Object remove(Object key) {
    if (locked)
      throw new IllegalStateException
        (sm.getString("parameterMap.locked"));
    return (super.remove(key));
  }
}
```

Now, let's see how the parseParameters method works.

Because parameters can exist in the query string and or the HTTP request body, the parseParameters method checks both the query string and the request body. Once parsed, parameters can be found in the object variable parameters, so the method starts by checking the parsed boolean, which is true if parsing has been done before.

```
if (parsed)
  return;
```

Then, the parseParameters method creates a ParameterMap called results and points it to parameters. It creates a new ParameterMap if parameters is null.

```
ParameterMap results = parameters;
if (results == null)
  results = new ParameterMap();
```

Then, the `parseParameters` method opens the `parameterMap`'s lock to enable writing to it.

```
results.setLocked(false);
```

Next, the `parseParameters` method checks the encoding and assigns a default encoding if the encoding is `null`.

```
String encoding = getCharacterEncoding();
if (encoding == null)
  encoding = "ISO-8859-1";
```

Then, the `parseParameters` method tries the query string. Parsing parameters is done using the `parseParameters` method of `org.apache.Catalina.util.RequestUtil`.

```
// Parse any parameters specified in the query string
String queryString = getQueryString();
try {
  RequestUtil.parseParameters(results, queryString, encoding);
}
catch (UnsupportedEncodingException e) {
  ;
}
```

Next, the method tries to see if the HTTP request body contains parameters. This happens if the user sends the request using the POST method, the content length is greater than zero, and the content type is `application/x-www-form-urlencoded`. So, here is the code that parses the request body.

```
// Parse any parameters specified in the input stream
String contentType = getContentType();
if (contentType == null)
  contentType = "";
int semicolon = contentType.indexOf(';');
if (semicolon >= 0) {
  contentType = contentType.substring(0, semicolon).trim();
}
else {
  contentType = contentType.trim();
}
if ("POST".equals(getMethod()) && (getContentLength() > 0)
  && "application/x-www-form-urlencoded".equals(contentType)) {
  try {
    int max = getContentLength();
    int len = 0;
    byte buf[] = new byte[getContentLength()];
    ServletInputStream is = getInputStream();
    while (len < max) {
      int next = is.read(buf, len, max - len);
      if (next < 0 ) {
        break;
      }
```

```
    len += next;
  }
  is.close();
  if (len < max) {
    throw new RuntimeException("Content length mismatch");
  }
  RequestUtil.parseParameters(results, buf, encoding);
}
catch (UnsupportedEncodingException ue) {
  ;
}
catch (IOException e) {
  throw new RuntimeException("Content read fail");
}
}
```

Finally, the parseParameters method locks the ParameterMap back, sets parsed to true and assigns results to parameters.

```
// Store the final results
results.setLocked(true);
parsed = true;
parameters = results;
```

Creating a HttpResponse Object

The HttpResponse class implements javax.servlet.http.HttpServletResponse. Accompanying it is a façade class named HttpResponseFacade. Figure 3.3 shows the UML diagram of HttpResponse and its related classes.

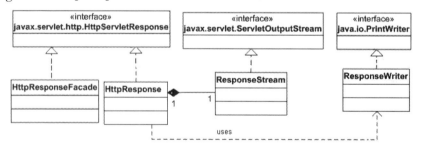

Figure 3.3: The HttpResponse class and related classes

In Chapter 2, you worked with an HttpResponse class that was only partially functional. For example, its getWriter method returned a java.io.PrintWriter object that does not flush automatically when one of its `print` methods is called. The application in this chapter fixes this problem. To understand how it is fixed, you need to know what a `Writer` is.

From inside a servlet, you use a `PrintWriter` to write characters. You may use any encoding you desire, however the characters will be sent to the browser as byte streams. Therefore, it's not surprising that in Chapter 2, the `ex02.pyrmont.HttpResponse` class has the following `getWriter` method:

```
public PrintWriter getWriter() {
  // if autoflush is true, println() will flush,
  // but print() will not.
  // the output argument is an OutputStream
  writer = new PrintWriter(output, true);
  return writer;
}
```

See, how we construct a `PrintWriter` object? By passing an instance of `java.io.OutputStream`. Anything you pass to the `print` or `println` methods of `PrintWriter` will be translated into byte streams that will be sent through the underlying `OutputStream`.

In this chapter you use an instance of the `ex03.pyrmont.connector.ResponseStream` class as the `OutputStream` for the `PrintWriter`. Note that the `ResponseStream` class is indirectly derived from the `java.io.OutputStream` class.

You also have the `ex03.pyrmont.connector.ResponseWriter` class that extends the `PrintWriter` class. The `ResponseWriter` class overrides all the `print` and `println` methods and makes any call to these methods automatically flush the output to the underlying `OutputStream`. Therefore, we use a `ResponseWriter` instance with an underlying `ResponseStream` object.

We could instantiate the `ResponseWriter` class by passing an instance of `ResponseStream` object. However, we use a `java.io.OutputStreamWriter` object to serve as a bridge between the `ResponseWriter` object and the `ResponseStream` object.

With an `OutputStreamWriter`, characters written to it are encoded into bytes using a specified charset. The charset that it uses may be specified by name or may be given explicitly, or the platform's default charset may be accepted. Each invocation of a write method causes the encoding converter to be invoked on the given character(s). The resulting bytes are accumulated in a buffer before being written to the underlying output stream. The size of this buffer may be specified, but by default it is large enough for most purposes. Note that the characters passed to the write methods are not buffered.

Therefore, here is the getWriter method:

```
public PrintWriter getWriter() throws IOException {
  ResponseStream newStream = new ResponseStream(this);
  newStream.setCommit(false);
  OutputStreamWriter osr =
    new OutputStreamWriter(newStream, getCharacterEncoding());
  writer = new ResponseWriter(osr);
  return writer;
}
```

Static resource processor and servlet processor

The ServletProcessor class is similar to the
ex02.pyrmont.ServletProcessor class in Chapter 2. They both have only
one method: process. However, the process method in
ex03.pyrmont.connector.ServletProcessor accepts an
HttpRequest and an HttpResponse, instead of instances of Request and
Response. Here is the signature of the process method in this chapter's
application:

```
public void process(HttpRequest request, HttpResponse response) {
```

In addition, the process method uses HttpRequestFacade and
HttpResponseFacade as façade classes for the request and the response.
Also, it calls the HttpResponse class's finishResponse method after
calling the servlet's service method.

```
servlet = (Servlet) myClass.newInstance();
HttpRequestFacade requestFacade = new HttpRequestFacade(request);
HttpResponseFacade responseFacade = new
  HttpResponseFacade(response);
servlet.service(requestFacade, responseFacade);
((HttpResponse) response).finishResponse();
```

The StaticResourceProcessor class is almost identical to the
ex02.pyrmont.StaticResourceProcessor class.

Running the Application

To run the application in Windows, from the working directory, type the
following:

```
java -classpath ./lib/servlet.jar;./ ex03.pyrmont.startup.Bootstrap
```

In Linux, you use a colon to separate two libraries.

```
java -classpath ./lib/servlet.jar:./ ex03.pyrmont.startup.Bootstrap
```

To display index.html, use the following URL:

```
http://localhost:8080/index.html
```

To invoke PrimitiveServlet, direct your browser to the following URL:

```
http://localhost:8080/servlet/PrimitiveServlet
```

You'll see the following on your browser:

```
Hello. Roses are red.
Violets are blue.
```

> **Note**
> Running `PrimitiveServlet` in Chapter 2 did not give you the second line.

You can also call `ModernServet`, which would not run in the servlet containers in Chapter 2. Here is the URL:

```
http://localhost:8080/servlet/ModernServlet
```

> **Note**
> The source code for ModernServlet can be found in the webroot directory under the working directory.

You can append a query string to the URL to test the servlet. Figure 3.4 shows the result if you run ModernServlet with the following URL.

```
http://localhost:8080/servlet/ModernServlet?userName=tarzan&password=pw
d
```

Summary

In this chapter you have learned how connectors work. The connector built is a simplified version of the default connector in Tomcat 4. As you know, the default connector has been deprecated because it is not efficient. For example, all HTTP request headers are parsed, even though they might not be used in the servlet. As a result, the default connector is slow and has been replaced by Coyote, a faster connector, whose source code can be downloaded from the Apache Software Foundation's web site. The default connector, nevertheless, serves as a good learning tool and will be discussed in detail in Chapter 4.

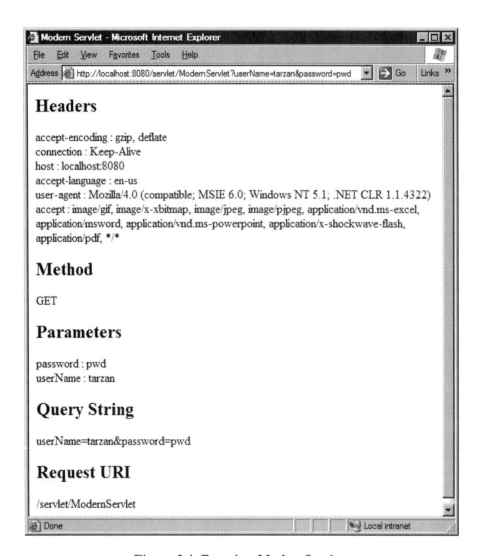

Figure 3.4: Running ModernServlet

Chapter 4
Tomcat Default Connector

The connector in Chapter 3 worked fine and could have been perfected to achieve much more. However, it was designed as an educational tool, an introduction to Tomcat 4's default connector. Understanding the connector in Chapter 3 is key to understanding the default connector that comes with Tomcat 4. Chapter 4 will now discuss what it takes to build a real Tomcat connector by dissecting the code of Tomcat 4's default connector.

> **Note**
> The "default connector" in this chapter refers to Tomcat 4's default connector. Even though the default connector has now been deprecated, replaced by a faster connector code-named Coyote, it is still a great learning tool.

A Tomcat connector is an independent module that can be plugged into a servlet container. There are already many connectors in existence. Examples include Coyote, mod_jk, mod_jk2, and mod_webapp. A Tomcat connector must meet the following requirements:

1. It must implement the `org.apache.catalina.Connector` interface.
2. It must create request objects whose class implements the `org.apache.catalina.Request` interface.
3. It must create response objects whose class implements the `org.apache.catalina.Response` interface.

Tomcat 4's default connector works similarly to the simple connector in Chapter 3. It waits for incoming HTTP requests, creates request and response objects, then passes the request and response objects to the container. A connector passes the request and response objects to the container by calling the `org.apache.catalina.Container` interface's `invoke` method, which has the following signature.

```
public void invoke(
  org.apache.catalina.Request request,
  org.apache.catalina.Response response);
```

Inside the invoke method, the container loads the servlet class, call its service method, manage sessions, log error messages, etc.

The default connector also employs a few optimizations not used in Chapter 3's connector. The first is to provide a pool of various objects to avoid the expensive object creation. Secondly, in many places it uses char arrays instead of strings.

The application in this chapter is a simple container that will be associated with the default connector. However, the focus of this chapter is not this simple container but the default connector. Containers will be discussed in Chapter 5. Nevertheless, the simple container will be discussed in the section "The Simple Container Application" towards the end of this chapter, to show how to use the default connector.

Another point that needs attention is that the default connector implements all features new to HTTP 1.1 as well as able to serve HTTP 0.9 and HTTP 1.0 clients. To understand the new features in HTTP 1.1, you first need to understand these features, which we will explain in the first section of this chapter. Thereafter, we discuss the org.apache.catalina.Connector interface and how to create the request and response objects. If you understand how the connector in Chapter 3 works, you should not find any problem understanding the default connector.

This chapter starts with three new features in HTTP 1.1. Understanding them is crucial to understanding the internal working of the default connector. Afterwards, it introduces org.apache.catalina.Connector, the interface that all connectors must implement. You then will find classes you have encountered in Chapter 3, such as HttpConnector, HttpProcessor, etc. This time, however, they are more advanced than the similar classes in Chapter 3.

HTTP 1.1 New Features

This section explains three new features of HTTP 1.1. Understanding them is crucial to understanding how the default connector processes HTTP requests.

Persistent Connections

Prior to HTTP 1.1, whenever a browser connected to a web server, the connection was closed by the server right after the requested resource was sent.

However, an Internet page can contain other resources, such as image files, applets, etc. Therefore, when a page is requested, the browser also needs to download the resources referenced by the page. If the page and all resources it references are downloaded using different connections, the process will be very slow. That's why HTTP 1.1 introduced persistent connections. With a persistent connection, when a page is downloaded, the server does not close the connection straight away. Instead, it waits for the web client to request all resources referenced by the page. This way, the page and referenced resources can be downloaded using the same connection. This saves a lot of work and time for the web server, client, and the network, considering that establishing and tearing down HTTP connections are expensive operations.

The persistent connection is the default connection of HTTP 1.1. Also, to make it explicit, a browser can send the request header `connection` with the value `keep-alive`:

```
connection: keep-alive
```

Chunked Encoding

The consequence of establishing a persistent connection is that the server can send byte streams from multiple resources, and the client can send multiple requests using the same connection. As a result, the sender must send the content length header of each request or response so that the recipient would know how to interpret the bytes. However, often the case is that the sender does not know how many bytes it will send. For example, a servlet container can start sending the response when the first few bytes become available and not wait until all of them ready. This means, there must be a way to tell the recipient how to interpret the byte stream in the case that the content-length header cannot be known earlier.

Even without having to send multiple requests or many responses, a server or a client does not necessarily know how much data it will send. In HTTP 1.0, a server could just leave out the `content-length` header and keep writing to the connection. When it was finished, it would simply close the connection. In this case, the client would keep reading until it got a -1 as an indication that the end of file had been reached.

HTTP 1.1 employs a special header called `transfer-encoding` to indicate that the byte stream will be sent in chunks. For every chunk, the length (in hexadecimal) followed by CR/LF is sent prior to the data. A transaction is marked with a zero length chunk. Suppose you want to send the following 38 bytes in 2 chunks, the first with the length of 29 and the second 9.

```
I'm as helpless as a kitten up a tree.
```

You would send the following:

```
1D\r\n
I'm as helpless as a kitten u
9\r\n
p a tree.
0\r\n
```

1D, the hexadecimal of 29, indicates that the first chunk consists of 29 bytes. 0\r\n indicates the end of the transaction.

Use of the 100 (Continue) Status

HTTP 1.1 clients may send the `Expect: 100-continue` header to the server before sending the request body and wait for acknowledgement from the server. This normally happens if the client is going to send a long request body but is not sure that the server is willing to accept it. It would be a waste if the client sent the long body just to find out the server turned it down.

Upon receipt of the `Expect: 100-continue` header, the server responds with the following `100-continue` header if it is willing to or can process the request, followed by two pairs of CRLF characters.

```
HTTP/1.1 100 Continue
```

The server should then continue reading the input stream.

The Connector interface

A Tomcat connector must implement the `org.apache.catalina.Connector` interface. Of many methods in this interface, the most important are `getContainer`, `setContainer`, `createRequest`, and `createResponse`.

`setContainer` is used to associate the connector with a container. `getContainer` returns the associated container. `createRequest` constructs a request object for the incoming HTTP request and `createResponse` creates a response object.

The `org.apache.catalina.connector.http.HttpConnector` class is an implementation of the `Connector` interface and is discussed in the next section, "The HttpConnector Class". Now, take a close look at Figure 4.1

for the UML class diagram of the default connector. Note that the implementation of the `Request` and `Response` interfaces have been omitted to keep the diagram simple. The `org.apache.catalina` prefix has also been omitted from the type names, except for the `SimpleContainer` class. Therefore, `Connector` should be read `org.apache.catalina.Connector`, `util.StringManager` `org.apache.catalina.util.StringManager`, etc.

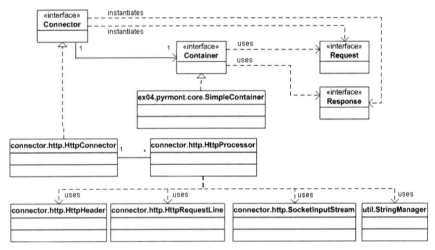

Figure 4.1: The default connector class diagram

A `Connector` has one-to-one relationship with a `Container`. The navigability of the arrow representing the relationship reveals that the `Connector` knows about the `Container` but not the other way around. Also note that, unlike in Chapter 3, the relationship between `HttpConnector` and `HttpProcessor` is one-to-many.

The HttpConnector Class

You already know how this class works because the simplified version of `org.apache.catalina.connector.http.HttpConnector` was explained in Chapter 3. It implements `org.apache.catalina.Connector` (to make it eligible to work with Catalina), `java.lang.Runnable` (so that its instance can work in its own thread), and `org.apache.catalina.Lifecycle`. The `Lifecycle` interface is used to maintain the life cycle of every Catalina component that implements it.

`Lifecycle` is explained in Chapter 6 and for now you don't have to worry about it except to know this: by implementing `Lifecycle`, after you have created an instance of `HttpConnector`, you should call its `initialize` and `start` methods. Both methods must only called once during the life time of the component. We will now look at those aspects that are different from the `HttpConnector` class in Chapter 3: how `HttpConnector` creates a server socket, how it maintains a pool of `HttpProcessor`, and how it serves HTTP requests.

Creating a Server Socket

The `initialize` method of `HttpConnector` calls the `open` private method that returns an instance of `java.net.ServerSocket` and assigns it to `serverSocket`. However, instead of calling the `java.net.ServerSocket` constructor, the `open` method obtains an instance of `ServerSocket` from a server socket factory. If you want to know the details of this factory, read the `ServerSocketFactory` interface and the `DefaultServerSocketFactory` class in the org.apache.catalina.net package. They are easy to understand.

Maintaining HttpProcessor Instances

In Chapter 3, the `HttpConnector` instance had only one instance of `HttpProcessor` at a time, so it can only process one HTTP request at a time. In the default connector, the `HttpConnector` has a pool of `HttpProcessor` objects and each instance of `HttpProcessor` has a thread of its own. Therefore, the `HttpConnector` can serve multiple HTTP requests simultaneously.

The `HttpConnector` maintains a pool of `HttpProcessor` instances to avoid creating `HttpProcessor` objects all the time. The `HttpProcessor` instances are stored in a `java.io.Stack` called `processors`:

```
private Stack processors = new Stack();
```

In `HttpConnector`, the number of `HttpProcessor` instances created is determined by two variables: `minProcessors` and `maxProcessors`. By default, `minProcessors` is set to 5 and `maxProcessors` 20, but you can change their values through the `setMinProcessors` and `setMaxProcessors` methods.

```
protected int minProcessors = 5;
```

```
private int maxProcessors = 20;
```

Initially, the `HttpConnector` object creates `minProcessors` instances of `HttpProcessor`. If there are more requests than the `HttpProcessor` instances can serve at a time, the `HttpConnector` creates more `HttpProcessor` instances until the number of instances reaches `maxProcessors`. After this point is reached and there are still not enough `HttpProcessor` instances, the incoming HTTP requests will be ignored. If you want the `HttpConnector` to keep creating `HttpProcessor` instances, set `maxProcessors` to a negative number. In addition, the `curProcessors` variable keeps the current number of `HttpProcessor` instances.

Here is the code that creates an initial number of `HttpProcessor` instances in the `HttpConnector` class's `start` method:

```
while (curProcessors < minProcessors) {
  if ((maxProcessors > 0) && (curProcessors >= maxProcessors))
    break;
  HttpProcessor processor = newProcessor();
  recycle(processor);
}
```

The `newProcessor` method constructs a new `HttpProcessor` object and increments `curProcessors`. The `recycle` method pushes the `HttpProcessor` back to the stack.

Each `HttpProcessor` instance is responsible for parsing the HTTP request line and headers and populates a request object. Therefore, each instance is associated with a request object and a response object. The `HttpProcessor` class's constructor contains calls to the `HttpConnector` class's `createRequest` and `createResponse` methods.

Serving HTTP Requests

The `HttpConnector` class has its main logic in its `run` method, just like in Chapter 3. The `run` method contains a `while` loop where the server socket waits for an HTTP request until the HttpConnector is stopped.

```
while (!stopped) {
  Socket socket = null;
  try {
    socket = serverSocket.accept();
  ...
```

For each incoming HTTP request, it obtains an `HttpProcessor` instance by calling the `createProcessor` private method.

```
HttpProcessor processor = createProcessor();
```

However, most of the time the `createProcessor` method does not create a
new `HttpProcessor` object. Instead, it gets one from the pool. If there is still
an `HttpProcessor` instance in the stack, `createProcessor` pops one. If
the stack is empty and the maximum number of `HttpProcessor` instances has
not been exceeded, `createProcessor` creates one. However, if the maximum
number has been reached, `createProcessor` returns null. If this happens, the
socket is simply closed and the incoming HTTP request is not processed.

```
if (processor == null) {
  try {
    log(sm.getString("httpConnector.noProcessor"));
    socket.close();
  }
  ...
  continue;
```

If `createProcessor` does not return `null`, the client socket is passed to the
`HttpProcessor` class's `assign` method:

```
processor.assign(socket);
```

It's now the `HttpProcessor` instance's job to read the socket's input stream
and parse the HTTP request. An important note is this. The `assign` method
must return straight away and not wait until the `HttpProcessor` finishes the
parsing, so the next incoming HTTP request can be served. Since each
`HttpProcessor` instance has a thread of its own for the parsing, this is not
very hard to achieve. You will see how this is done in the next section, "The
HttpProcessor Class".

The HttpProcessor Class

The `HttpProcessor` class in the default connector is the full version of the
similarly named class in Chapter 3. You've learned how it worked and in this
chapter we're most interested in knowing how the `HttpProcessor` class makes
its `assign` method asynchronous so that the `HttpConnector` instance can
serve many HTTP requests at the same time.

Note
Another important method of the `HttpProcessor` class is the private
`process` method which parses the HTTP request and invoke the container's
`invoke` method. We'll have a look at it in the section, "Processing Requests"
later in this chapter.

In Chapter 3, the `HttpConnector` runs in its own thread. However, it has to wait for the currently processed HTTP request to finish before it can process the next request. Here is part of the `HttpConnector` class's `run` method in Chapter 3:

```
public void run() {
  ...
  while (!stopped) {
    Socket socket = null;
    try {
      socket = serverSocket.accept();
    }
    catch (Exception e) {
      continue;
    }
    // Hand this socket off to an HttpProcessor
    HttpProcessor processor = new HttpProcessor(this);
    processor.process(socket);
  }
}
```

The `process` method of the `HttpProcessor` class in Chapter 3 is synchronous. Therefore, its `run` method waits until the `process` method finishes before accepting another request.

In the default connector, however, the `HttpProcessor` class implements `java.lang.Runnable` and each instance of `HttpProcessor` runs in its own thread, which we call the "processor thread". For each `HttpProcessor` instance the `HttpConnector` creates, its `start` method is called, effectively starting the "processor thread" of the `HttpProcessor` instance. Listing 4.1 presents the `run` method in the `HttpProcessor` class in the default connector:

Listing 4.1: The `HttpProcessor` class's `run` method.

```
public void run() {
  // Process requests until we receive a shutdown signal
  while (!stopped) {
    // Wait for the next socket to be assigned
    Socket socket = await();
    if (socket == null)
      continue;
    // Process the request from this socket
    try {
      process(socket);
    }
    catch (Throwable t) {
      log("process.invoke", t);
    }
    // Finish up this request
    connector.recycle(this);
  }
  // Tell threadStop() we have shut ourselves down successfully
```

```
  synchronized (threadSync) {
    threadSync.notifyAll();
  }
}
```

The `while` loop in the `run` method keeps going in this order: gets a socket, process it, calls the connector's `recycle` method to push the current `HttpProcessor` instance back to the stack. Here is the HttpConenctor class's `recycle` method:

```
void recycle(HttpProcessor processor) {
   processors.push(processor);
}
```

Notice that the `while` loop in the run method stops at the `await` method. The `await` method holds the control flow of the "processor thread" until it gets a new socket from the `HttpConnector`. In other words, until the `HttpConnector` calls the `HttpProcessor` instance's `assign` method. However, the `await` method runs on a different thread than the assign method. The `assign` method is called from the `run` method of the `HttpConnector`. We name the thread that the `HttpConnector` instance's `run` method runs on the "connector thread". How does the `assign` method tell the `await` method that it has been called? By using a `boolean` called `available`, and by using the `wait` and `notifyAll` methods of `java.lang.Object`.

Note
The `wait` method causes the current thread to wait until another thread invokes the `notify` or the `notifyAll` method for this object.

Here is the `HttpProcessor` class's `assign` and `await` methods:

```
synchronized void assign(Socket socket) {
  // Wait for the Processor to get the previous Socket
  while (available) {
    try {
      wait();
    }
    catch (InterruptedException e) {
    }
  }
  // Store the newly available Socket and notify our thread
  this.socket = socket;
  available = true;
  notifyAll();
  ...
}

private synchronized Socket await() {
  // Wait for the Connector to provide a new Socket
```

```
  while (!available) {
    try {
      wait();
    }
    catch (InterruptedException e) {
    }
  }

  // Notify the Connector that we have received this Socket
  Socket socket = this.socket;
  available = false;
  notifyAll();
  if ((debug >= 1) && (socket != null))
    log("  The incoming request has been awaited");
  return (socket);
}
```

The program flows of both methods are summarized in Table 4.1.

The processor thread (the `await` method)	The connector thread (the `assign` method)

`while (!available) {`
`  wait();`
`}`
`Socket socket = this.socket;`
`available = false;`
`notifyAll();`
`return socket; // to the run`
`                // method`
	`while (available) {`
	`  wait();`
	`}`
	`this.socket = socket;`
	`available = true;`
	`notifyAll();`
	`...`

Table 4.1: Summary of the `await` and `assign` method

Initially, when the "processor thread" has just been started, `available` is `false`, so the thread waits inside the `while` loop (see Column 1 of Table 4.1). It will wait until another thread calls `notify` or `notifyAll`. This is to say that calling the `wait` method causes the "processor thread" to pause until the "connector thread" invokes the `notifyAll` method for the `HttpProcessor` instance.

Now, look at Column 2. When a new socket is assigned, the "connector thread" calls the `HttpProcessor`'s `assign` method. The value of `available` is `false`, so the `while` loop is skipped and the socket is assigned to the `HttpProcessor` instance's `socket` variable:

```
this.socket = socket;
```

The "connector thread" then sets `available` to `true` and calls `notifyAll`. This wakes up the processor thread and now the value of `available` is `true` so the program controls goes out of the `while` loop: assigning the instance's socket to a local variable, sets `available` to false, calls `notifyAll`, and returns the socket, which eventually causes the socket to be processed.

Why does the `await` method need to use a local variable (`socket`) and not return the instance's `socket` variable? So that the instance's `socket` variable can be assigned to the next incoming socket before the current socket gets processed completely.

Why does the `await` method need to call `notifyAll`? Just in case another socket arrives when the value of `available` is `true`. In this case, the "connector thread" will stop inside the `assign` method's `while` loop until the `nofifyAll` call from the "processor thread" is received.

Request Objects

The HTTP Request object in the default connector is represented by the `org.apache.catalina.Request` interface. This interface is directly implemented by the `RequestBase` class, which is the parent of `HttpRequest`. The ultimate implementation is `HttpRequestImpl`, which extends `HttpRequest`. Like in Chapter 3, there are façade classes: `RequestFacade` and `HttpRequestFacade`. The UML diagram for the `Request` interface and its implementation classes is given in Figure 4.2. Note that except for the types belonging to the `javax.servlet` and `javax.servlet.http` packages, the prefix `org.apache.catalina` has been omitted.

If you understand about the request object in Chapter 3, you should not have problems understanding the diagram.

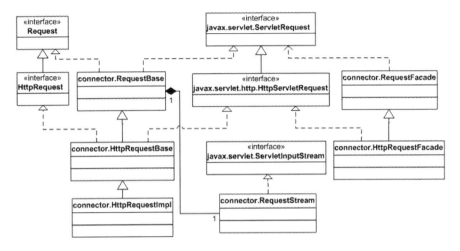

Figure 4.2: The Request interface and related types

Response Objects

The UML diagram of the Response interface and its implementation classes is given in Figure 4.3.

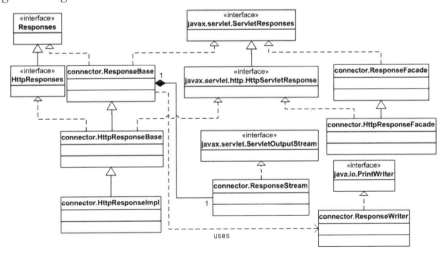

Figure 4.3: The Response interface and its implementation classes

Processing Requests

At this point, you already understand about the request and response objects and how the HttpConnector object creates them. Now is the last bit of the process. In this section we focus on the process method of the HttpProcessor class, which is called by the HttpProcessor class's run method after a socket is assigned to it. The process method does the following:

- parse the connection
- parse the request
- parse headers

Each operation is discussed in the sub-sections of this section after the process method is explained.

The process method uses the boolean ok to indicate that there is no error during the process and the boolean finishResponse to indicate that the finishResponse method of the Response interface should be called.

```
boolean ok = true;
boolean finishResponse = true;
```

In addition, the process method also uses the instance boolean variables keepAlive, stopped, and http11. keepAlive indicates that the connection is persistent, stopped indicates that the HttpProcessor instance has been stopped by the connector so that the process method should also stop, and http11 indicates that the HTTP request is coming from a web client that supports HTTP 1.1.

Like in Chapter 3, a SocketInputStream instance is used to wrap the socket's input stream. Note that, the constructor of SocketInputStream is also passed the buffer size from the connector, not from a local variable in the HttpProcessor class. This is because HttpProcessor is not accessible by the user of the default connector. By putting the buffer size in the Connector interface, this allows anyone using the connector to set the buffer size.

```
SocketInputStream input = null;
OutputStream output = null;
// Construct and initialize the objects we will need
try {
  input = new SocketInputStream(socket.getInputStream(),
    connector.getBufferSize());
}
catch (Exception e) {
  ok = false;
}
```

Then, there is a `while` loop which keeps reading the input stream until the `HttpProcessor` is stopped, an exception is thrown, or the connection is closed.

```
keepAlive = true;
while (!stopped && ok && keepAlive) {
  ...
}
```

Inside the `while` loop, the `process` method starts by setting `finishResponse` to `true` and obtaining the output stream and performing some initialization to the request and response objects.

```
finishResponse = true;
try {
  request.setStream(input);
  request.setResponse(response);
  output = socket.getOutputStream();
  response.setStream(output);
  response.setRequest(request);
  ((HttpServletResponse) response.getResponse()).setHeader
    ("Server", SERVER_INFO);
}
catch (Exception e) {
  log("process.create", e);  //logging is discussed in Chapter 7
  ok = false;
}
```

Afterwards, the `process` method start parsing the incoming HTTP request by calling the `parseConnection`, `parseRequest`, and `parseHeaders` methods, all of which are discussed in the sub-sections in this section.

```
try {
  if (ok) {
    parseConnection(socket);
    parseRequest(input, output);
    if (!request.getRequest().getProtocol()
      .startsWith("HTTP/0"))
      parseHeaders(input);
```

The `parseConnection` method obtains the value of the protocol, which can be HTTP 0.9, HTTP 1.0 or HTTP 1.1. If the protocol is HTTP 1.0, the `keepAlive` boolean is set to `false` because HTTP 1.0 does not support persistent connections. The `parseHeaders` method will set the `sendAck` boolean to `true` if an `Expect: 100-continue` header is found in the HTTP request.

If the protocol is HTTP 1.1, it will respond to the `Expect: 100-continue` header, if the web client sent this header, by calling the `ackRequest` method. It will also check if chunking is allowed.

```
if (http11) {
  // Sending a request acknowledge back to the client if
  // requested.
  ackRequest(output);
  // If the protocol is HTTP/1.1, chunking is allowed.
  if (connector.isChunkingAllowed())
    response.setAllowChunking(true);
}
```

The ackRequest method checks the value of sendAck and sends the following string if sendAck is true:

```
HTTP/1.1 100 Continue\r\n\r\n
```

During the parsing of the HTTP request, one of the many exceptions might be thrown. Any exception will set ok or finishResponse to false. After the parsing, the process method passes the request and response objects to the container's invoke method.

```
try {
  ((HttpServletResponse) response).setHeader
    ("Date", FastHttpDateFormat.getCurrentDate());
  if (ok) {
    connector.getContainer().invoke(request, response);
  }
}
```

Afterwards, if finishResponse is still true, the response object's finishResponse method and the request's object finishRequest methods are called, and the output is flushed.

```
if (finishResponse) {
  ...
  response.finishResponse();
  ...
  request.finishRequest();
  ...
  output.flush();
```

The last part of the while loop checks if the response's Connection header has been set to close from inside the servlet or if the protocol is HTTP 1.0. If this is the case, keepAlive is set to false. Also, the request and response objects are then recycled.

```
if ( "close".equals(response.getHeader("Connection")) ) {
  keepAlive = false;
}
// End of request processing
status = Constants.PROCESSOR_IDLE;
// Recycling the request and the response objects
request.recycle();
response.recycle();
}
```

At this stage, the `while` loop will start from the beginning if `keepAlive` is `true`, there is no error during the previous parsing and from the container's `invoke` method, or the `HttpProcessor` instance has not been stopped. Otherwise, the `shutdownInput` method is called and the socket is closed.

```
try {
  shutdownInput(input);
  socket.close();
}
...
```

The `shutdownInput` method checks if there are any unread bytes. If there are, it skips those bytes.

Parsing the Connection

The `parseConnection` method obtains the Internet address from the socket and assigns it to the `HttpRequestImpl` object. It also checks if a proxy is used and assigns the socket to the request object. The `parseConnection` method is given in Listing 4.2.

Listing 4.2: The `parseConnection` method

```
private void parseConnection(Socket socket)
  throws IOException, ServletException {
  if (debug >= 2)
    log(" parseConnection: address=" + socket.getInetAddress() +
      ", port=" + connector.getPort());
  ((HttpRequestImpl) request).setInet(socket.getInetAddress());
  if (proxyPort != 0)
    request.setServerPort(proxyPort);
  else
    request.setServerPort(serverPort);
  request.setSocket(socket);
}
```

Parsing the Request

The parseRequest method is the full version of the similar method in Chapter 3. If you understand Chapter 3 well, you should be able to understand how this method works by reading the method.

88

Parsing Headers

The parseHeaders method in the default connector uses the HttpHeader and DefaultHeaders classes in the org.apache.catalina.connector.http package. The HttpHeader class represents an HTTP request header. Instead of working with strings like in Chapter 3, the HttpHeader class uses character arrays to avoid expensive string operations. The DefaultHeaders class is a final class containing the standard HTTP request headers in character arrays:

```
static final char[] AUTHORIZATION_NAME =
  "authorization".toCharArray();
static final char[] ACCEPT_LANGUAGE_NAME =
  "accept-language".toCharArray();
static final char[] COOKIE_NAME = "cookie".toCharArray();
...
```

The parseHeaders method contains a while loop that keeps reading the HTTP request until there is no more header to read. The while loop starts by calling the allocateHeader method of the request object to obtain an instance of empty HttpHeader. The instance is passed to the readHeader method of SocketInputStream.

```
HttpHeader header = request.allocateHeader();

// Read the next header
input.readHeader(header);
```

If all headers have been read, the readHeader method will assign no name to the HttpHeader instance, and this is time for the parseHeaders method to return.

```
if (header.nameEnd == 0) {
  if (header.valueEnd == 0) {
    return;
  }
  else {
    throw new ServletException
      (sm.getString("httpProcessor.parseHeaders.colon"));
  }
}
```

If there is a header name, there must also be a header value:

```
String value = new String(header.value, 0, header.valueEnd);
```

Next, like in Chapter 3, the parseHeaders method compares the header name with the standard names in DefaultHeaders. Note that comparison is performed between two character arrays, not between two strings.

```
if (header.equals(DefaultHeaders.AUTHORIZATION_NAME)) {
  request.setAuthorization(value);
}
else if (header.equals(DefaultHeaders.ACCEPT_LANGUAGE_NAME)) {
  parseAcceptLanguage(value);
}
else if (header.equals(DefaultHeaders.COOKIE_NAME)) {
  // parse cookie
}
else if (header.equals(DefaultHeaders.CONTENT_LENGTH_NAME)) {
  // get content length
}
else if (header.equals(DefaultHeaders.CONTENT_TYPE_NAME)) {
    request.setContentType(value);
}
else if (header.equals(DefaultHeaders.HOST_NAME)) {
  // get host name
}
else if (header.equals(DefaultHeaders.CONNECTION_NAME)) {
  if (header.valueEquals(DefaultHeaders.CONNECTION_CLOSE_VALUE)) {
    keepAlive = false;
    response.setHeader("Connection", "close");
  }
}
else if (header.equals(DefaultHeaders.EXPECT_NAME)) {
  if (header.valueEquals(DefaultHeaders.EXPECT_100_VALUE))
    sendAck = true;
  else
    throw new ServletException(sm.getString
      ("httpProcessor.parseHeaders.unknownExpectation"));
}
else if (header.equals(DefaultHeaders.TRANSFER_ENCODING_NAME)) {
  //request.setTransferEncoding(header);
}

request.nextHeader();
```

The Simple Container Application

The main purpose of the application in this chapter is to show how to use the default connector. It consists of two classes: ex04.pyrmont.core.SimpleContainer and ex04.pyrmont.startup.Bootstrap. The SimpleContainer class implements org.apache.catalina.container so that it can be associated with the connector. The Bootstrap class is used to start the application. we have removed the connector module and the ServletProcessor and

`StaticResourceProcessor` classes in the application accompanying Chapter 3, so you cannot request a static page.

The SimpleContainer class is presented in Listing 4.3.

Listing 4.3: The `SimpleContainer` class

```
package ex04.pyrmont.core;

import java.beans.PropertyChangeListener;
import java.net.URL;
import java.net.URLClassLoader;
import java.net.URLStreamHandler;
import java.io.File;
import java.io.IOException;
import javax.naming.directory.DirContext;
import javax.servlet.Servlet;
import javax.servlet.ServletException;
import javax.servlet.http.HttpServletRequest;
import javax.servlet.http.HttpServletResponse;
import org.apache.catalina.Cluster;
import org.apache.catalina.Container;
import org.apache.catalina.ContainerListener;
import org.apache.catalina.Loader;
import org.apache.catalina.Logger;
import org.apache.catalina.Manager;
import org.apache.catalina.Mapper;
import org.apache.catalina.Realm;
import org.apache.catalina.Request;
import org.apache.catalina.Response;

public class SimpleContainer implements Container {

  public static final String WEB_ROOT =
    System.getProperty("user.dir") + File.separator  + "webroot";

  public SimpleContainer() {   }
  public String getInfo() {
    return null;
  }
  public Loader getLoader() {
    return null;
  }
  public void setLoader(Loader loader) {   }
  public Logger getLogger() {
    return null;
  }
  public void setLogger(Logger logger) {   }
  public Manager getManager() {
    return null;
  }
  public void setManager(Manager manager) {   }
  public Cluster getCluster() {
    return null;
  }
  public void setCluster(Cluster cluster) {   }
```

```
  public String getName() {
    return null;
  }
  public void setName(String name) {  }
  public Container getParent() {
    return null;
  }
  public void setParent(Container container) {  }
  public ClassLoader getParentClassLoader() {
    return null;
  }
  public void setParentClassLoader(ClassLoader parent) {  }
  public Realm getRealm() {
    return null;
  }
  public void setRealm(Realm realm) {  }
  public DirContext getResources() {
    return null;
  }
  public void setResources(DirContext resources) {  }
  public void addChild(Container child) {  }
  public void addContainerListener(ContainerListener listener) {  }
  public void addMapper(Mapper mapper) {  }
  public void addPropertyChangeListener(
    PropertyChangeListener listener) {  }
  public Container findChild(String name) {
    return null;
  }
  public Container[] findChildren() {
    return null;
  }
  public ContainerListener[] findContainerListeners() {
    return null;
  }
  public Mapper findMapper(String protocol) {
    return null;
  }
  public Mapper[] findMappers() {
    return null;
  }
  public void invoke(Request request, Response response)
    throws IOException, ServletException {

    String servletName = ( (HttpServletRequest)
request).getRequestURI();
    servletName = servletName.substring(servletName.lastIndexOf("/") +
1);
    URLClassLoader loader = null;
    try {
      URL[] urls = new URL[1];
      URLStreamHandler streamHandler = null;
      File classPath = new File(WEB_ROOT);
      String repository = (new URL("file", null,
classPath.getCanonicalPath() + File.separator)).toString() ;
      urls[0] = new URL(null, repository, streamHandler);
      loader = new URLClassLoader(urls);
```

92

```
    }
    catch (IOException e) {
      System.out.println(e.toString() );
    }
    Class myClass = null;
    try {
      myClass = loader.loadClass(servletName);
    }
    catch (ClassNotFoundException e) {
      System.out.println(e.toString());
    }

    Servlet servlet = null;

    try {
      servlet = (Servlet) myClass.newInstance();
      servlet.service((HttpServletRequest) request,
(HttpServletResponse) response);
    }
    catch (Exception e) {
      System.out.println(e.toString());
    }
    catch (Throwable e) {
      System.out.println(e.toString());
    }
  }

  public Container map(Request request, boolean update) {
    return null;
  }
  public void removeChild(Container child) {  }
  public void removeContainerListener(ContainerListener listener) {  }
  public void removeMapper(Mapper mapper) {  }
  public void removePropertyChangeListener(
    PropertyChangeListener listener) {
  }
}
```

I only provide the implementation of the `invoke` method in the
`SimpleContainer` class because the default connector will call this method.
The `invoke` method creates a class loader, loads the servlet class, and calls its
`service` method. This method is very similar to the `process` method in the
ServletProcessor class in Chapter 3.

The `Bootstrap` class is given in Listing 4.4.

Listing 4.4: The ex04.pyrmont.startup.Bootstrap class

```
package ex04.pyrmont.startup;
import ex04.pyrmont.core.SimpleContainer;
import org.apache.catalina.connector.http.HttpConnector;

public final class Bootstrap {
  public static void main(String[] args) {
```

```
    HttpConnector connector = new HttpConnector();
    SimpleContainer container = new SimpleContainer();
    connector.setContainer(container);
    try {
      connector.initialize();
      connector.start();

      // make the application wait until we press any key.
      System.in.read();
    }
    catch (Exception e) {
      e.printStackTrace();
    }
  }
}
```

The main method of the Bootstrap class constructs an instance of
org.apache.catalina.connector.http.HttpConnector and a
SimpleContainer instance. It then associates the connector with the
container by calling the connector's setContainer method, passing the
container. Next, it calls the connector's initialize and start methods. This
will make the connector ready for processing any HTTP request on port 8080.

You can terminate the application by pressing a key on the console.

Running the Application

To run the application in Windows, from the working directory, type the
following:

```
java -classpath ./lib/servlet.jar;./ ex04.pyrmont.startup.Bootstrap
```

In Linux, you use a colon to separate two libraries.

```
java -classpath ./lib/servlet.jar:./ ex04.pyrmont.startup.Bootstrap
```

You can invoke PrimitiveServlet and ModernServlet the way you did
in Chapter 3. Note that you cannot request the index.html file because there
is no processor for static resources.

Summary

This chapter showed what it takes to build a Tomcat connector that can work
with Catalina. It dissected the code of Tomcat 4's default connector and built a
small application that used the connector. All applications in the upcoming
chapters use the default connector.

94

Chapter 5
Container

A container is a module that processes the requests for a servlet and populates the response objects for web clients. A container is represented by the `org.apache.catalina.Container` interface and there are four types of containers: `Engine`, `Host`, `Context`, and `Wrapper`. This chapter covers Context and Wrapper and leaves Engine and Host to Chapter 13. This chapter starts with the discussion of the `Container` interface, followed by the pipelining mechanism in a container. It then looks at the `Wrapper` and `Context` interfaces. Two applications conclude this chapter by presenting a simple wrapper and a simple context respectively.

The Container Interface

A container must implement `org.apache.catalina.Container`. As you have seen in Chapter 4, you pass an instance of `Container` to the `setContainer` method of the connector, so that the `connector` can call the container's `invoke` method. Recall the following code from the `Bootstrap` class in the application in Chapter 4.

```
HttpConnector connector = new HttpConnector();
SimpleContainer container = new SimpleContainer();
connector.setContainer(container);
```

The first thing to note about containers in Catalina is that there are four types of containers at different conceptual levels:

- Engine. Represents the entire Catalina servlet engine.
- Host. Represents a virtual host with a number of contexts.
- Context. Represents a web application. A context contains one or more wrappers.
- Wrapper. Represents an individual servlet.

Each conceptual level above is represented by an interface in the `org.apache.catalina` package. These interfaces are `Engine`, `Host`,

`Context`, and `Wrapper`. All the four extends the `Container` interface. Standard implementations of the four containers are `StandardEngine`, `StandardHost`, `StandardContext`, and `StandardWrapper`, respectively, all of which are part of the `org.apache.catalina.core` package.

Figure 5.1 shows the class diagram of the `Container` interface and its sub-interfaces and implementations. Note that all interfaces are part of the org.apache.catalina package and all classes are part of the `org.apache.catalina.core` package.

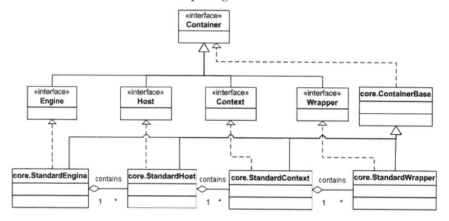

Figure 5.1: The class diagram of Container and its related types

Note
All implementation classes derive from the abstract class `ContainerBase`.

A functional Catalina deployment does not need all the four types of containers. For example, the container module in this chapter's first application consists of only a wrapper. The second application is a container module with a context and a wrapper. Neither host nor engine is needed in the applications accompanying this chapter.

A container can have zero or more child containers of the lower level. For instance, a context normally has one or more wrappers and a host can have zero or more contexts. However, a wrapper, being the lowest in the 'hierarchy', cannot contain a child container. To add a child container to a container, you use the `Container` interface's `addChild` method whose signature is as follows.

```
public void addChild(Container child);
```

To remove a child container from a container, call the `Container` interface's `removeChild` method. The `remove` method's signature is as follows.

```
public void removeChild(Container child);
```

In addition, the `Container` interface supports the finding of a child container or a collection of all child containers through the `findChild` and `findChildren` methods. The signatures of both methods are the following.

```
public Container findChild(String name);
public Container[] findChildren();
```

A container can also contain a number of support components such as Loader, Logger, Manager, Realm, and Resources. We will discuss these components in later chapters. One thing worth noting here is that the `Container` interface provides the get and set methods for associating itself with those components. These methods include `getLoader` and `setLoader`, `getLogger` and `setLogger`, `getManager` and `setManager`, `getRealm` and `setRealm`, and `getResources` and `setResources`.

More interestingly, the `Container` interface has been designed in such a way that at the time of deployment a Tomcat administrator can determine what a container performs by editing the configuration file (server.xml). This is achieved by introducing a pipeline and a set of valves in a container, which we will discuss in the next section, "Pipelining Tasks".

Note
The `Container` interface in Tomcat 4 is slightly different from that in Tomcat 5. For example, in Tomcat 4 this interface has a map method, which no longer exists in the `Container` interface in Tomcat 5.

Pipelining Tasks

This section explains what happens when a container's `invoke` method is called by the connector. This section then discusses in the sub-sections the four related interfaces in the `org.apache.catalina` package: `Pipeline`, `Valve`, `ValveContext`, and `Contained`.

A pipeline contains tasks that the container will invoke. A valve represents a specific task. There is one basic valve in a container's pipeline, but you can add as many valves as you want. The number of valves is defined to be the number of additional valves, i.e. not including the basic valve. Interestingly, valves can be added dynamically by editing Tomcat's configuration file (server.xml). Figure 5.2 shows a pipeline and its valves.

98

| Valve-1 | Valve-2 | . . . | Valve-n |

Figure 5.2: Pipeline and valves

If you understand servlet filters, it is not hard to imagine how a pipeline and its valve work. A pipeline is like a filter chain and each valve is a filter. Like a filter, a valve can manipulate the request and response objects passed to it. After a valve finishes processing, it calls the next valve in the pipeline. The basic valve is always called the last.

A container can have one pipeline. When a container's invoke method is called, the container passes processing to its pipeline and the pipeline invokes the first valve in it, which will then invoke the next valve, and so on, until there is no more valve in the pipeline. You might imagine that you could have the following pseudo code inside the pipeline's invoke method:

```
// invoke each valve added to the pipeline
for (int n=0; n<valves.length; n++) {
  valve[n].invoke( ... );
}
// then, invoke the basic valve
basicValve.invoke( ... );
```

However, the Tomcat designer chose a different approach by introducing the org.apache.catalina.ValveContext interface. Here is how it works.

A container does not hard code what it is supposed to do when its invoke method is called by the connector. Instead, the container calls its pipeline's invoke method. The Pipeline interface's invoke method has the following signature, which is exactly the same as the invoke method of the Container interface.

```
public void invoke(Request request, Response response)
  throws IOException, ServletException;
```

Here is the implementation of the Container interface's invoke method in the org.apache.catalina.core.ContainerBase class.

```
public void invoke(Request request, Response response)
  throws IOException, ServletException {
  pipeline.invoke(request, response);
}
```

where pipeline is an instance of the Pipeline interface inside the container.

Now, the pipeline has to make sure that all the valves added to it as well as its basic valve must be invoked once. The pipeline does this by creating an instance of the `ValveContext` interface. The `ValveContext` is implemented as an inner class of the pipeline so that the `ValveContext` has access to all members of the pipeline. The most important method of the `ValveContext` interface is `invokeNext`:

```
public void invokeNext(Request request, Response response)
  throws IOException, ServletException
```

After creating an instance of `ValveContext`, the pipeline calls the `invokeNext` method of the `ValveContext`. The `ValveContext` will first invoke the first valve in the pipeline and the first valve will invoke the next valve before the first valve does its task. The `ValveContext` passes itself to each valve so that the valve can call the `invokeNext` method of the `ValveContext`. Here is the signature of the `invoke` method of the `Valve` interface.

```
public void invoke(Request request, Response response,
  ValveContext valveContext) throws IOException, ServletException
```

An implementation of a valve's `invoke` method will be something like the following.

```
public void invoke(Request request, Response response,
  ValveContext valveContext) throws IOException, ServletException {
  // Pass the request and response on to the next valve in our pipeline
  valveContext.invokeNext(request, response);
  // now perform what this valve is supposed to do
    ...
}
```

The `org.apache.catalina.core.StandardPipeline` class is the implementation of `Pipeline` in all containers. In Tomcat 4, this class has an inner class called `StandardPipelineValveContext` that implements the `ValveContext` interface. Listing 5.1 presents the StandardPipelineValveContext class.

Listing 5.1: The `StandardPipelineValveContext` class in Tomcat 4

```
protected class StandardPipelineValveContext implements ValveContext {
  protected int stage = 0;
  public String getInfo() {
    return info;
  }
  public void invokeNext(Request request, Response response)
    throws IOException, ServletException {

    int subscript = stage;
    stage = stage + 1;
```

```
    // Invoke the requested Valve for the current request thread
    if (subscript < valves.length) {
      valves[subscript].invoke(request, response, this);
    }
    else if ((subscript == valves.length) && (basic != null)) {
      basic.invoke(request, response, this);
    }
    else {
      throw new ServletException
        (sm.getString("standardPipeline.noValve"));
    }
  }
}
}
```

The invokeNext method uses subscript and stage to remember which valve is being invoked. When first invoked from the pipeline's invoke method, the value of subscript is 0 and the value of stage is 1. Therefore, the first valve (array index 0) is invoked. The first valve in the pipeline receives the ValveContext instance and invokes its invokeNext method. This time, the value of subscript is 1 so that the second valve is invoked, and so on.

When the invokeNext method is called from the last valve, the value of subscript is equal to the number of valves. As a result, the basic valve is invoked.

Tomcat 5 removes the StandardPipelineValveContext class from StandardPipeline and instead relies on the org.apache.catalina.core.StandardValveContext class, which is presented in Listing 5.2.

Listing 5.2: The StandardValveContext class in Tomcat 5

```
package org.apache.catalina.core;

import java.io.IOException;
import javax.servlet.ServletException;
import org.apache.catalina.Request;
import org.apache.catalina.Response;
import org.apache.catalina.Valve;
import org.apache.catalina.ValveContext;
import org.apache.catalina.util.StringManager;

public final class StandardValveContext implements ValveContext {
  protected static StringManager sm =
    StringManager.getManager(Constants.Package);
  protected String info =
    "org.apache.catalina.core.StandardValveContext/1.0";
  protected int stage = 0;
  protected Valve basic = null;
  protected Valve valves[] = null;
  public String getInfo() {
    return info;
```

```
    }

  public final void invokeNext(Request request, Response response)
    throws IOException, ServletException {
    int subscript = stage;
    stage = stage + 1;
    // Invoke the requested Valve for the current request thread
    if (subscript < valves.length) {
      valves[subscript].invoke(request, response, this);
    }
    else if ((subscript == valves.length) && (basic != null)) {
      basic.invoke(request, response, this);
    }
    else {
      throw new ServletException
        (sm.getString("standardPipeline.noValve"));
    }
  }

  void set(Valve basic, Valve valves[]) {
    stage = 0;
    this.basic = basic;
    this.valves = valves;
  }
}
```

Can you see the similarities between the StandardPipelineValveContext class in Tomcat 4 and the StandardValveContext class in Tomcat 5?

We will now explain the `Pipeline`, `Valve`, and `ValveContext` interfaces in more detail. Also discussed is the `org.apache.catalina.Contained` interface that a valve class normally implements.

The Pipeline Interface

The first method of the `Pipeline` interface that we mentioned was the `invoke` method, which a container calls to start invoking the valves in the pipeline and the basic valve. The `Pipeline` interface allows you to add a new valve through its `addValve` method and remove a valve by calling its `removeValve` method. Finally, you use its `setBasic` method to assign a basic valve to a pipeline and its `getBasic` method to obtain the basic valve. The basic valve, which is invoked last, is responsible for processing the request and the corresponding response. The `Pipeline` interface is given in Listing 5.3.

Listing 5.3: The **Pipeline** interface

```
package org.apache.catalina;
import java.io.IOException;
```

```
import javax.servlet.ServletException;

public interface Pipeline {
  public Valve getBasic();
  public void setBasic(Valve valve);
  public void addValve(Valve valve);
  public Valve[] getValves();
  public void invoke(Request request, Response response)
    throws IOException, ServletException;
  public void removeValve(Valve valve);
}
```

The Valve Interface

The Valve interface represents a valve, the component responsible for processing a request. This interface has two methods: invoke and getInfo. The invoke method has been discussed above. The getInfo method returns information about the valve implementation. The Valve interface is given in Listing 5.4.

Listing 5.4: The Valve interface

```
package org.apache.catalina;
import java.io.IOException;
import javax.servlet.ServletException;

public interface Valve {
  public String getInfo();
  public void invoke(Request request, Response response,
    ValveContext context) throws IOException, ServletException;
}
```

The ValveContext Interface

This interface has two methods: the invokeNext method, which has been discussed above, and the getInfo method, which returns information about the ValveContext implementation. The ValveContext interface is given in Listing 5.5.

Listing 5.5: The ValveContext interface

```
package org.apache.catalina;
import java.io.IOException;
import javax.servlet.ServletException;

public interface ValveContext {
  public String getInfo();
  public void invokeNext(Request request, Response response)
    throws IOException, ServletException;
```

}

The Contained Interface

A valve class can optionally implement the
`org.apache.catalina.Contained` interface. This interface specifies that
the implementing class is associated with at most one container instance. The
`Contained` interface is given in Listing 5.6.

Listing 5.6: The Contained interface

```
package org.apache.catalina;
public interface Contained {
  public Container getContainer();
  public void setContainer(Container container);
}
```

The Wrapper Interface

The `org.apache.catalina.Wrapper` interface represents a wrapper. A
wrapper is a container representing an individual servlet definition. The
`Wrapper` interface extends `Container` and adds a number of methods.
Implementations of `Wrapper` are responsible for managing the servlet life cycle
for their underlying servlet class, i.e. calling the `init`, `service`, and `destroy`
methods of the servlet. Since a wrapper is the lowest level of container, you must
not add a child to it. A wrapper throws an `IllegalArgumantException` if
its `addChild` method is called.

Important methods in the `Wrapper` interface include `allocate` and `load`.
The `allocate` method allocates an initialized instance of the servlet the
wrapper represents. The `allocate` method must also take into account
whether or not the servlet implements the
`javax.servlet.SingleThreadModel` interface, but we will discuss this
later in Chapter 11. The load method loads and initializes an instance of the
servlet the wrapper represents. The signatures of the allocate and load methods
are as follows.

```
public javax.servlet.Servlet allocate() throws
javax.servlet.ServletException;
public void load() throws javax.servlet.ServletException;
```

The other methods will be covered in Chapter 11 when we discuss the
`org.apache.catalina.core.StandardWrapper` class.

The Context Interface

A context is a container that represents a web application. A context usually has one or more wrappers as its child containers.

Important methods include `addWrapper`, `createWrapper`, etc. This interface will be covered in more detail in Chapter 12.

The Wrapper Application

This application demonstrates how to write a minimal container module. The core class of this application is `ex05.pyrmont.core.SimpleWrapper`, an implementation of the `Wrapper` interface. The `SimpleWrapper` class contains a `Pipeline` (implemented by the `ex05.pyrmont.core.SimplePipeline` class) and uses a `Loader` (implemented by the `ex05.pyrmont.core.SimpeLoader`) to load the servlet. The `Pipeline` contains a basic valve (`ex05.pyrmont.core.SimpleWrapperValve`) and two additional valves (`ex05.pyrmont.core.ClientIPLoggerValve` and `ex05.pyrmont.core.HeaderLoggerValve`). The class diagram of the application is given in Figure 5.3.

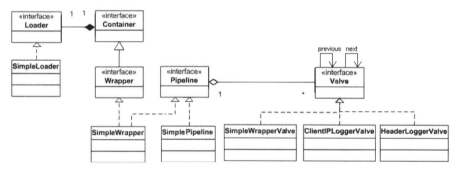

Figure 5.3: The Class Diagram of the Wrapper Application

Note
The container uses Tomcat 4's default connector.

The wrapper wraps the `ModernServlet` that you have used in the previous chapters. This application proves that you can have a servlet container consisting only of one wrapper. All classes are not fully developed, implementing only methods that must be present in the class. Let's now look at the classes in detail.

ex05.pyrmont.core.SimpleLoader

The task of loading servlet classes in a container is assigned to a `Loader` implementation. In this application, the `SimpleLoader` class is that implementation. It knows the location of the servlet class and its `getClassLoader` method returns a `java.lang.ClassLoader` instance that searches the servlet class location. The `SimpleLoader` class declares three variables. The first is `WEB_ROOT`, which points to the directory where the servlet class is to be found.

```
public static final String WEB_ROOT =
  System.getProperty("user.dir") + File.separator  + "webroot";
```

The other two variables are object references of type `ClassLoader` and `Container`:

```
ClassLoader classLoader = null;
Container container = null;
```

The `SimpleLoader` class's constructor initializes the class loader so that it is ready to be returned to the `SimpleWrapper` instance.

```
  public SimpleLoader() {
    try {
      URL[] urls = new URL[1];
      URLStreamHandler streamHandler = null;
      File classPath = new File(WEB_ROOT);
      String repository = (new URL("file", null,
        classPath.getCanonicalPath() + File.separator)).toString() ;
      urls[0] = new URL(null, repository, streamHandler);
      classLoader = new URLClassLoader(urls);
    }
    catch (IOException e) {
      System.out.println(e.toString() );
    }
  }
```

The code in the constructor has been used to initialize class loaders in the applications in previous chapters and won't be explained again.

The `container` variable represents the container associated with this loader.

Note
Loaders will be discussed in detail in Chapter 8.

ex05.pyrmont.core.SimplePipeline

The `SimplePipeline` class implements the `org.apache.catalina.Pipeline` interface. The most important method in this class is the `invoke` method, which contains an inner class called `SimplePipelineValveContext`. The `SimplePipelineValveContext` implements the `org.apache.catalina.ValveContext` interface and has been explained in the section "Pipelining Tasks" above.

ex05.pyrmont.core.SimpleWrapper

This class implements the `org.apache.catalina.Wrapper` interface and provides implementation for the `allocate` and `load` methods. Among others, this class declares the following variables:

```
private Loader loader;
protected Container parent = null;
```

The `loader` variable is a `Loader` that is used to load the servlet class. The `parent` variable represents a parent container for this wrapper. This means that this wrapper can be a child container of another container, such as a `Context`.

Pay special attention to its `getLoader` method, which is given in Listing 5.7.

Listing 5.7: The SimpleWrapper class's getLoader method

```
public Loader getLoader() {
  if (loader != null)
    return (loader);
  if (parent != null)
    return (parent.getLoader());
  return (null);
}
```

The `getLoader` method returns a `Loader` that is used to load a servlet class. If the wrapper is associated with a `Loader`, this `Loader` will be returned. If not, it will return the `Loader` of the parent container. If no parent is available, the `getLoader` method returns null.

The `SimpleWrapper` class has a pipeline and sets a basic valve for the pipeline. You do this in the `SimpleWrapper` class's constructor, given in Listing 5.8.

Listing 5.8: The SimpleWrapper class's constructor

```
public SimpleWrapper() {
```

```
    pipeline.setBasic(new SimpleWrapperValve());
  }
```

Here, `pipeline` is an instance of `SimplePipeline` as declared in the class:

```
private SimplePipeline pipeline = new SimplePipeline(this);
```

ex05.pyrmont.core.SimpleWrapperValve

The `SimpleWrapperValve` class is the basic valve that is dedicated to processing the request for the `SimpleWrapper` class. It implements the `org.apache.catalina.Valve` interface and the `org.apache.catalina.Contained` interface. The most important method in the `SimpleWrapperValve` is the `invoke` method, given in Listing 5.9.

Listing 5.9: The `SimpleWrapperValve` class's `invoke` method

```
public void invoke(Request request, Response response,
  ValveContext valveContext)
  throws IOException, ServletException {

  SimpleWrapper wrapper = (SimpleWrapper) getContainer();
  ServletRequest sreq = request.getRequest();
  ServletResponse sres = response.getResponse();
  Servlet servlet = null;
  HttpServletRequest hreq = null;
  if (sreq instanceof HttpServletRequest)
    hreq = (HttpServletRequest) sreq;
  HttpServletResponse hres = null;
  if (sres instanceof HttpServletResponse)
    hres = (HttpServletResponse) sres;
  // Allocate a servlet instance to process this request
  try {
    servlet = wrapper.allocate();
    if (hres!=null && hreq!=null) {
      servlet.service(hreq, hres);
    }
    else {
      servlet.service(sreq, sres);
    }
  }
  catch (ServletException e) {
  }
}
```

Because `SimpleWrapperValve` is used as a basic valve, its `invoke` method does not need to call the `invokeNext` method of the `ValveContext` passed to it. The `invoke` method calls the `allocate` method of the `SimpleWrapper` class to obtain an instance of the servlet the wrapper represents. It then calls the servlet's `service` method. Notice that the basic

valve of the wrapper's pipeline invokes the servlet's `service` method, not the
wrapper itself.

ex05.pyrmont.valves.ClientIPLoggerValve

The `ClientIPLoggerValve` class is a valve that prints the client's IP address
to the console. This class is given in Listing 5.10.

Listing 5.10: The `ClientIPLoggerValve` class

```
package ex05.pyrmont.valves;

import java.io.IOException;
import javax.servlet.ServletRequest;
import javax.servlet.ServletException;
import org.apache.catalina.Request;
import org.apache.catalina.Response;
import org.apache.catalina.Valve;
import org.apache.catalina.ValveContext;
import org.apache.catalina.Contained;
import org.apache.catalina.Container;

public class ClientIPLoggerValve implements Valve, Contained {
  protected Container container;
  public void invoke(Request request, Response response,
    ValveContext valveContext) throws IOException, ServletException {

    // Pass this request on to the next valve in our pipeline
    valveContext.invokeNext(request, response);
    System.out.println("Client IP Logger Valve");
    ServletRequest sreq = request.getRequest();
    System.out.println(sreq.getRemoteAddr());
    System.out.println("----------------------------------");
  }

  public String getInfo() {
    return null;
  }
  public Container getContainer() {
    return container;
  }
  public void setContainer(Container container) {
    this.container = container;
  }
}
```

Pay attention to the `invoke` method. The first thing the invoke method does is
call the `invokeNext` method of the valve context to invoke the next valve in
the pipeline, if any. It then prints a few lines of string including the output of the
`getRemoteAddr` method of the request object.

ex05.pyrmont.valves.HeaderLoggerValve

This class is very similar to the ClientIPLoggerValve class. The HeaderLoggerValve class is a valve that prints the request header to the console. This class is given in Listing 5.11.

Listing 5.11: The `HeaderLoggerValve` class

```
package ex05.pyrmont.valves;

import java.io.IOException;
import java.util.Enumeration;
import javax.servlet.ServletRequest;
import javax.servlet.ServletException;
import javax.servlet.http.HttpServletRequest;
import org.apache.catalina.Request;
import org.apache.catalina.Response;
import org.apache.catalina.Valve;
import org.apache.catalina.ValveContext;
import org.apache.catalina.Contained;
import org.apache.catalina.Container;

public class HeaderLoggerValve implements Valve, Contained {
  protected Container container;

  public void invoke(Request request, Response response,
    ValveContext valveContext) throws IOException, ServletException {

    // Pass this request on to the next valve in our pipeline
    valveContext.invokeNext(request, response);
    System.out.println("Header Logger Valve");
    ServletRequest sreq = request.getRequest();
    if (sreq instanceof HttpServletRequest) {
      HttpServletRequest hreq = (HttpServletRequest) sreq;
      Enumeration headerNames = hreq.getHeaderNames();
      while (headerNames.hasMoreElements()) {
        String headerName = headerNames.nextElement().toString();
        String headerValue = hreq.getHeader(headerName);
        System.out.println(headerName + ":" + headerValue);
      }

    }
    else
      System.out.println("Not an HTTP Request");

    System.out.println("------------------------------------");
  }

  public String getInfo() {
    return null;
  }
  public Container getContainer() {
    return container;
  }
  public void setContainer(Container container) {
```

```
    this.container = container;
  }
}
```

Again, pay special attention to the `invoke` method. The first thing the `invoke` method does is call the invokeNext method of the valve context to invoke the next valve in the pipeline, if any. It then prints the values of some headers.

ex05.pyrmont.startup.Bootstrap1

The `Bootstrap1` class is used to start the application. It is given in Listing 5.12.

Listing 5.12: The Bootstrap1 class

```
package ex05.pyrmont.startup;
import ex05.pyrmont.core.SimpleLoader;
import ex05.pyrmont.core.SimpleWrapper;
import ex05.pyrmont.valves.ClientIPLoggerValve;
import ex05.pyrmont.valves.HeaderLoggerValve;
import org.apache.catalina.Loader;
import org.apache.catalina.Pipeline;
import org.apache.catalina.Valve;
import org.apache.catalina.Wrapper;
import org.apache.catalina.connector.http.HttpConnector;

public final class Bootstrap1 {
  public static void main(String[] args) {
    HttpConnector connector = new HttpConnector();
    Wrapper wrapper = new SimpleWrapper();
    wrapper.setServletClass("ModernServlet");
    Loader loader = new SimpleLoader();
    Valve valve1 = new HeaderLoggerValve();
    Valve valve2 = new ClientIPLoggerValve();

    wrapper.setLoader(loader);
    ((Pipeline) wrapper).addValve(valve1);
    ((Pipeline) wrapper).addValve(valve2);

    connector.setContainer(wrapper);

    try {
      connector.initialize();
      connector.start();

      // make the application wait until we press a key.
      System.in.read();
    }
    catch (Exception e) {
      e.printStackTrace();
    }
  }
}
```

After creating an instance of `HttpConnector` and `SimpleWrapper`, the `main` method of the `Bootstrap` class assigns `ModernServlet` to the `setServletClass` method of `SimpleWrapper`, telling the wrapper the name of the class to be loaded.

```
wrapper.setServletClass("ModernServlet");
```

It then creates a loader and two valves and sets the loader to the wrapper:

```
Loader loader = new SimpleLoader();
Valve valve1 = new HeaderLoggerValve();
Valve valve2 = new ClientIPLoggerValve();
wrapper.setLoader(loader);
```

The two valves are then added to the wrapper's pipeline.

```
((Pipeline) wrapper).addValve(valve1);
((Pipeline) wrapper).addValve(valve2);
```

Finally, the wrapper is set as the container of the connector and the connector is initialized and started.

```
connector.setContainer(wrapper);

try {
  connector.initialize();
  connector.start();
```

The next line allows the user to stop the application by typing Enter in the console.

```
// make the application wait until we press Enter.
System.in.read();
```

Running the Application

To run the application in Windows, from the working directory, type the following:

```
java –classpath ./lib/servlet.jar;./ ex05.pyrmont.startup.Bootstrap1
```

In Linux, you use a colon to separate two libraries.

```
java –classpath ./lib/servlet.jar:./ ex05.pyrmont.startup.Bootstrap1
```

You can invoke the servlet using the following URL:

```
http://localhost:8080
```

The browser will display the response from the `ModernServlet`. Note also that something similar to the following is printed on the console.

```
ModernServlet -- init
Client IP Logger Valve
127.0.0.1
------------------------------------
Header Logger Valve
accept:image/gif, image/x-xbitmap, image/jpeg, image/pjpeg,
application/vnd.ms-excel, application/msword, application/vnd.ms-
powerpoint, */*
accept-language:en-us
accept-encoding:gzip, deflate
user-agent:Mozilla/4.0 (compatible; MSIE 6.0; Windows NT 5.0; .NET CLR
1.1.4322)
host:localhost:8080
connection:Keep-Alive
------------------------------------
```

The Context Application

In the first application in this chapter, you learned how to deploy a simple web application consisting of only one wrapper. This application only had one servlet. While it is possible that some applications might only need one single servlet, most web applications require more. In such applications, you need a different type of container than a wrapper. You need a context.

This second application demonstrates how to use a context with two wrappers that wrap two servlet classes. Having more than one wrapper, you need a mapper, a component that helps a container--in this case a context--select a child container that will process a particular request.

> **Note**
> A mapper can only be found in Tomcat 4. Tomcat 5 uses another approach to finding a child container.

In this application your mapper is an instance of the `ex05.pyrmont.core.SimpleContextMapper` class, which implements the `org.apache.catalina.Mapper` interface in Tomcat 4. A container can also use multiple mappers to support multiple protocols. In this case, one mapper supports one request protocol. For example, a container may have a mapper for the HTTP protocol and another mapper for the HTTPS protocol. Listing 5.13 offers the `Mapper` interface in Tomcat 4.

Listing 5.13: The **Mapper** interface

```
package org.apache.catalina;
public interface Mapper {
```

```
    public Container getContainer();
    public void setContainer(Container container);
    public String getProtocol();
    public void setProtocol(String protocol);
    public Container map(Request request, boolean update);
}
```

The getContainer method returns the container this mapper is associated with and the setContainer method is used to associate a container with this mapper. The getProtocol method returns the protocol this mapper is responsible for and the setProtocol method is used to assign the name of the protocol this mapper is responsible for. The map method returns a child container that will process a particular request.

Figure 5.4 presents the class diagram of this application.

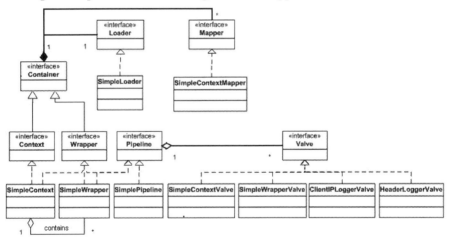

Figure 5.4: The Context application class diagram.

The SimpleContext class represents a context. It uses the SimpleContextMapper as its mapper and SimpleContextValve as its basic valve. Two valves, ClientIPLoggerValve and HeaderLoggerValve, are added to the context. Two wrappers, each represented by SimpleWrapper, are added as child containers of the context. The wrappers use SimpleWrapperValve as their basic valve but do not have additional valves.

The Context application uses the same loader and the two valves. However, the loader and valves are associated with the context, not a wrapper. This way, the loader can be used by both wrappers. The context is assigned as the container for the connector. Therefore, the connector will call the invoke method of the context every time it receives an HTTP request. The rest is not hard to figure out if you recall our discussion above:

1. A container has a pipeline. The container's invoke method calls the pipeline's invoke method.
2. The pipeline's invoke method invokes all the valves added to its container and then calls its basic valve's invoke method.
3. In a wrapper, the basic valve is responsible to load the associated servlet class and respond to the request.
4. In a context with child containers, the basic valve uses a mapper to find a child container that is responsible for processing the request. If a child container is found, it calls the invoke method of the child container. It then goes back to Step 1.

Now let's see the order of processing in the implementation.

The SimpleContext class's invoke method calls the pipeline's invoke method.

```
public void invoke(Request request, Response response)
  throws IOException, ServletException {
  pipeline.invoke(request, response);
}
```

The pipeline is represented by the SimplePipeline class. Its invoke method is as follows.

```
public void invoke(Request request, Response response)
  throws IOException, ServletException {
  // Invoke the first Valve in this pipeline for this request
  (new SimplePipelineValveContext()).invokeNext(request, response);
}
```

As explained in the "Pipelining Tasks" section above, the code invokes all the valves added to it and then calls the basic valve's invoke method. In SimpleContext, the SimpleContextValve class represents the basic valve. In its invoke method, SimpleContextValve uses the context's mapper to find a wrapper:

```
// Select the Wrapper to be used for this Request
Wrapper wrapper = null;
try {
  wrapper = (Wrapper) context.map(request, true);
}
```

If a wrapper is found, its invoke method is called.

```
wrapper.invoke(request, response);
```

A wrapper in this application is represented by the `SimpleWrapper` class. Here is the `invoke` method of `SimpleWrapper`, which is exactly the same as the `SimpleContext` class's `invoke` method.

```
public void invoke(Request request, Response response)
  throws IOException, ServletException {
  pipeline.invoke(request, response);
}
```

The pipeline is an instance of `SimplePipeline` whose `invoke` method has been listed above. The wrappers in this application do not have valves except the basic valve, which is an instance of `SimpleWrapperValve`. The wrapper's pipeline calls the `SimpleWrapperValve` class's `invoke` method that allocates a servlet and calls its `service` method, as explained in the section "The Wrapper Application" above.

Note that the wrapper is not associated with a loader, but the context is. Therefore, the `getLoader` method of the `SimpleWrapper` class returns the parent's loader.

The four classes--`SimpleContext`, `SimpleContextValve`, `SimpleContextMapper`, and `Bootstrap2`—have not been explained in the previous section and will be discussed below.

ex05.pyrmont.core.SimpleContextValve

This class represents the basic valve for `SimpleContext`. Its most important method is the invoke method, given in Listing 5.14.

Listing 5.14: The SimpleContextValve class's invoke method

```
public void invoke(Request request, Response response,
  ValveContext valveContext)
  throws IOException, ServletException {
  // Validate the request and response object types
  if (!(request.getRequest() instanceof HttpServletRequest) ||
    !(response.getResponse() instanceof HttpServletResponse)) {
    return;
  }

  // Disallow any direct access to resources under WEB-INF or META-INF
  HttpServletRequest hreq = (HttpServletRequest) request.getRequest();
  String contextPath = hreq.getContextPath();
  String requestURI = ((HttpRequest) request).getDecodedRequestURI();
  String relativeURI =
    requestURI.substring(contextPath.length()).toUpperCase();

  Context context = (Context) getContainer();
  // Select the Wrapper to be used for this Request
```

```
  Wrapper wrapper = null;
  try {
    wrapper = (Wrapper) context.map(request, true);
  }
  catch (IllegalArgumentException e) {
    badRequest(requestURI, (HttpServletResponse)
      response.getResponse());
    return;
  }
  if (wrapper == null) {
    notFound(requestURI, (HttpServletResponse) response.getResponse());
    return;
  }
  // Ask this Wrapper to process this Request
  response.setContext(context);
  wrapper.invoke(request, response);
}
```

ex05.pyrmont.core.SimpleContextMapper

The SimpleContextMapper class, given in Listing 5.15, implements the org.apache.catalina.Mapper interface in Tomcat 4 and is designed to be associated with an instance of SimpleContext.

Listing 5.15: The SimpleContext class

```
package ex05.pyrmont.core;

import javax.servlet.http.HttpServletRequest;
import org.apache.catalina.Container;
import org.apache.catalina.HttpRequest;
import org.apache.catalina.Mapper;
import org.apache.catalina.Request;
import org.apache.catalina.Wrapper;

public class SimpleContextMapper implements Mapper {

  private SimpleContext context = null;
  public Container getContainer() {
    return (context);
  }
  public void setContainer(Container container) {
    if (!(container instanceof SimpleContext))
      throw new IllegalArgumentException
        ("Illegal type of container");
    context = (SimpleContext) container;
  }

  public String getProtocol() {
    return null;
  }
  public void setProtocol(String protocol) {  }
```

```
public Container map(Request request, boolean update) {
    // Identify the context-relative URI to be mapped
    String contextPath =
      ((HttpServletRequest) request.getRequest()).getContextPath();
    String requestURI = ((HttpRequest) request).getDecodedRequestURI();
    String relativeURI = requestURI.substring(contextPath.length());
    // Apply the standard request URI mapping rules from
    // the specification
    Wrapper wrapper = null;
    String servletPath = relativeURI;
    String pathInfo = null;
    String name = context.findServletMapping(relativeURI);
    if (name != null)
      wrapper = (Wrapper) context.findChild(name);
    return (wrapper);
  }
}
```

The setContainer method throws an IllegalArgumentException if
you pass a container that is not an instance of SimpleContext. The map
method returns a child container (a wrapper) that is responsible for processing
the request. The map method is passed two arguments, a request object and a
boolean. This implementation ignores the second argument. What the method
does is retrieve the context path from the request object and uses the context's
findServletMapping method to obtain a name associated with the path. If a
name is found, it uses the context's findChild method to get an instance of
Wrapper.

ex05.pyrmont.core.SimpleContext

The SimpleContext class is the context implementation for this application. It
is the main container that is assigned to the connector. However, processing of
each individual servlet is performed by a wrapper. This application has two
servlets, PrimitiveServlet and ModernServlet, and thus two wrappers.
Each wrapper has a name. The name of the wrapper for PrimitiveServlet
is Primitive, and the wrapper for ModernServlet is Modern. For
SimpleContext to determine which wrapper to invoke for every request, you
must map request URL patterns with wrappers' names. In this application, we
have two URL patterns that can be used to invoke the two wrappers. The first
pattern is /Primitive, which is mapped to the wrapper Primitive. The
second pattern is /Modern, which is mapped to the wrapper Modern. Of
course, you can use more than one pattern for a given servlet. You just need to
add those patterns.

There are a number of methods from the `Container` and `Context` interfaces that `SimpleContext` must implement. Most methods are blank methods, however those methods related to mapping are given real code. These methods are as follows.

- `addServletMapping`. Adds a URL pattern/wrapper name pair. You add every pattern that can be used to invoke the wrapper with the given name.
- `findServletMapping`. Obtains a wrapper name given a URL pattern. This method is used to find which wrapper should be invoked for a particular URL pattern. If the given pattern has not yet been registered using the `addServletMapping`, the method returns `null`.
- `addMapper`. Adds a mapper to the context. The `SimpleContext` class declares the `mapper` and `mappers` variables. `mapper` is for the default mapper and `mappers` contains all mappers for the `SimpleContext` instance. The first mapper added to this context becomes the default mapper.
- `findMapper`. Finds the correct mapper. In `SimpleContext`, this returns the default mapper.
- `map`. Returns the wrapper that is responsible for processing this request.

In addition, `SimpleContext` also provides the implementation of the `addChild`, `findChild`, and `findChildren` methods. The `addChild` method is used to add a wrapper to the context, the `findChild` method is used to find a wrapper given a name, and `findChildren` returns all wrappers in the `SimpleContext` instance.

ex05.pyrmont.startup.Bootstrap2

The `Bootstrap2` class is used to start the application. This class is similar to `BootStrap1` and is given in Listing 5.16.

Listing 5.16: The Bootstrap2 class

```
package ex05.pyrmont.startup;
import ex05.pyrmont.core.SimpleContext;
import ex05.pyrmont.core.SimpleContextMapper;
import ex05.pyrmont.core.SimpleLoader;
import ex05.pyrmont.core.SimpleWrapper;
import ex05.pyrmont.valves.ClientIPLoggerValve;
import ex05.pyrmont.valves.HeaderLoggerValve;
import org.apache.catalina.Connector;
import org.apache.catalina.Context;
import org.apache.catalina.Loader;
import org.apache.catalina.Mapper;
```

```
import org.apache.catalina.Pipeline;
import org.apache.catalina.Valve;
import org.apache.catalina.Wrapper;
import org.apache.catalina.connector.http.HttpConnector;

public final class Bootstrap2 {
  public static void main(String[] args) {
    HttpConnector connector = new HttpConnector();
    Wrapper wrapper1 = new SimpleWrapper();
    wrapper1.setName("Primitive");
    wrapper1.setServletClass("PrimitiveServlet");
    Wrapper wrapper2 = new SimpleWrapper();
    wrapper2.setName("Modern");
    wrapper2.setServletClass("ModernServlet");

    Context context = new SimpleContext();
    context.addChild(wrapper1);
    context.addChild(wrapper2);

    Valve valve1 = new HeaderLoggerValve();
    Valve valve2 = new ClientIPLoggerValve();

    ((Pipeline) context).addValve(valve1);
    ((Pipeline) context).addValve(valve2);

    Mapper mapper = new SimpleContextMapper();
    mapper.setProtocol("http");
    context.addMapper(mapper);
    Loader loader = new SimpleLoader();
    context.setLoader(loader);
    // context.addServletMapping(pattern, name);
    context.addServletMapping("/Primitive", "Primitive");
    context.addServletMapping("/Modern", "Modern");
    connector.setContainer(context);
    try {
      connector.initialize();
      connector.start();

      // make the application wait until we press a key.
      System.in.read();
    }
    catch (Exception e) {
      e.printStackTrace();
    }
  }
}
```

The `main` method starts by instantiating the Tomcat default connector and two
wrappers, `wrapper1` and `wrapper2`. These wrappers are given names
`Primitive` and `Modern`. The servlet classes for `Primitive` and `Modern` are
`PrimitiveServlet` and `ModernServlet`, respectively.

```
HttpConnector connector = new HttpConnector();
Wrapper wrapper1 = new SimpleWrapper();
wrapper1.setName("Primitive");
```

```
wrapper1.setServletClass("PrimitiveServlet");
Wrapper wrapper2 = new SimpleWrapper();
wrapper2.setName("Modern");
wrapper2.setServletClass("ModernServlet");
```

Then, the `main` method creates an instance of `SimpleContext` and adds `wrapper1` and `wrapper2` as child containers of `SimpleContext`. It also instantiates the two valves, `ClientIPLoggerValve` and `HeaderLoggerValve`, and adds them to `SimpleContext`.

```
Context context = new SimpleContext();
context.addChild(wrapper1);
context.addChild(wrapper2);

Valve valve1 = new HeaderLoggerValve();
Valve valve2 = new ClientIPLoggerValve();

((Pipeline) context).addValve(valve1);
((Pipeline) context).addValve(valve2);
```

Next, it constructs a mapper object from the `SimpleMapper` class and adds it to `SimpleContext`. This mapper is responsible for finding child containers in the context that will process HTTP requests.

```
Mapper mapper = new SimpleContextMapper();
mapper.setProtocol("http");
context.addMapper(mapper);
```

To load a servlet class, you need a loader. Here you use the `SimpleLoader` class, just like in the first application. However, instead of adding it to both wrappers, the loader is added to the context. The wrappers will find the loader using its `getLoader` method because the context is their parent.

```
Loader loader = new SimpleLoader();
context.setLoader(loader);
```

Now, it's time to add servlet mappings. You add two patterns for the two wrappers.

```
// context.addServletMapping(pattern, name);
context.addServletMapping("/Primitive", "Primitive");
context.addServletMapping("/Modern", "Modern");
```

Finally, assign the context as the container for the connector and initialize and start the connector.

```
connector.setContainer(context);
try {
  connector.initialize();
  connector.start();
```

Running the Application

To run the application in Windows, from the working directory, type the following:

```
java -classpath ./lib/servlet.jar;./ ex05.pyrmont.startup.Bootstrap2
```

In Linux, you use a colon to separate between libraries.

```
java -classpath ./lib/servlet.jar:./ ex05.pyrmont.startup.Bootstrap2
```

To invoke `PrimitiveServlet`, you use the following URL in your browser.

```
http://localhost:8080/Primitive
```

To invoke `ModernServlet`, you use the following URL.

```
http://localhost:8080/Modern
```

Summary

The container is the second main module after the connector. The container uses many other modules, such as Loader, Logger, Manager, etc. There are four types of containers: Engine, Host, Context, and Wrapper. A Catalina deployment does not need all four containers to be present. The two applications in this chapter show that a deployment can have one single wrapper or a context with a few wrappers.

122

Chapter 6
Lifecycle

Catalina consists of many components. When Catalina is started, these components need to be started as well. When Catalina is stopped, these components must also be given a chance to do a clean-up. For example, when the container is stopped, it must invoke the `destroy` method of all loaded servlets and the session manager must save the session objects to secondary storage. A consistent mechanism for starting and stopping components is achieved by implementing the `org.apache.catalina.Lifecycle` interface.

A component implementing the `Lifecycle` interface can also trigger one or many of the following events: `BEFORE_START_EVENT`, `START_EVENT`, `AFTER_START_EVENT`, `BEFORE_STOP_EVENT`, `STOP_EVENT`, and `AFTER_STOP_EVENT`. The first three events are normally fired when the component is started and the last three when the component is stopped. An event is represented by the org.apache.catalina.LifecycleEvent class. And, of course, if a Catalina component can trigger events, there must be event listeners that you can write to respond to those events. A listener is represented by the `org.apache.catalina.LifecycleListener` interface.

This chapter will discuss these three types `Lifecycle`, `LifecycleEvent`, and `LifecycleListener`. In addition, it will also explain a utility class called `LifecycleSupport` that provides an easy way for a component to fire lifecycle events and deal with lifecycle listeners. In this chapter, you will build a project with classes that implement the `Lifecycle` interface. The application is based on the application in Chapter 5.

The Lifecycle Interface

The design of Catalina allows a component to contain other components. For example, a container can contain components such as a loader, a manager, etc. A parent component is responsible for starting and stopping its child components.

The design of Catalina is such that all components but one are put "in custody" of a parent component so that a bootstrap class needs only start one single component. This single start/stop mechanism is made possible through the Lifecycle interface. Take a look at the Lifecycle interface in Listing 6.1.

Listing 6.1: The Lifecycle interface

```
package org.apache.catalina;
public interface Lifecycle {
  public static final String START_EVENT = "start";
  public static final String BEFORE_START_EVENT = "before_start";
  public static final String AFTER_START_EVENT = "after_start";
  public static final String STOP_EVENT = "stop";
  public static final String BEFORE_STOP_EVENT = "before_stop";
  public static final String AFTER_STOP_EVENT = "after_stop";

  public void addLifecycleListener(LifecycleListener listener);
  public LifecycleListener[] findLifecycleListeners();
  public void removeLifecycleListener(LifecycleListener listener);
  public void start() throws LifecycleException;
  public void stop() throws LifecycleException;
}
```

The most important methods in Lifecycle are start and stop. A component provides implementations of these methods so that its parent component can start and stop it. The other three methods—addLifecycleListener, findLifecycleListeners, and removeLifecycleListener—are related to listeners. A component can have listeners that are interested in an event that occurs in that component. When an event occurs, the listener interested in that event will be notified. The names of the six events that can be triggered by a Lifecycle instance are defined in public static final Strings of the interface.

The LifecycleEvent Class

The org.apache.catalina.LifecycleEvent class represents a lifecycle event and is presented in Listing 6.2.

Listing 6.2: The org.apache.catalinaLifecycleEvent interface

```
package org.apache.catalina;
import java.util.EventObject;

public final class LifecycleEvent extends EventObject {
  public LifecycleEvent(Lifecycle lifecycle, String type) {
    this(lifecycle, type, null);
  }
  public LifecycleEvent(Lifecycle lifecycle, String type,
    Object data) {
```

```
    super(lifecycle);
    this.lifecycle = lifecycle;
    this.type = type;
    this.data = data;
  }
  private Object data = null;
  private Lifecycle lifecycle = null;
  private String type = null;

  public Object getData() {
    return (this.data);
  }
  public Lifecycle getLifecycle() {
    return (this.lifecycle);
  }
  public String getType() {
    return (this.type);
  }
}
```

The LifecycleListener Interface

The org.apache.catalina.LifecycleListener interface represents a lifecycle listener and is given in Listing 6.3.

Listing 6.3: The org.apache.catalina.LifecycleListener interface

```
package org.apache.catalina;
import java.util.EventObject;
public interface LifecycleListener {
  public void lifecycleEvent(LifecycleEvent event);
}
```

There is only one method in this interface, lifecycleEvent. This method is invoked when an event the listener is interested in fires.

The LifecycleSupport Class

A component implementing Lifecycle and allowing a listener to register its interest in its events must provide code for the three listener-related methods in the Lifecycle interface (addLifecycleListener, findLifecycleListeners, and removeLifecycleListener). That component then has to store all listeners added to it in an array or ArrayList or a similar object. Catalina provides a utility class for making it easy for a component to deal with listeners and fire lifecycle events:

`org.apache.catalina.util.LifecycleSupport`. The
LifecycleSupport class is given in Listing 6.4.

Listing 6.4: The LifecycleSupport class

```
package org.apache.catalina.util;
import org.apache.catalina.Lifecycle;
import org.apache.catalina.LifecycleEvent;
import org.apache.catalina.LifecycleListener;

public final class LifecycleSupport {
  public LifecycleSupport(Lifecycle lifecycle) {
    super();
    this.lifecycle = lifecycle;
  }

  private Lifecycle lifecycle = null;
  private LifecycleListener listeners[] = new LifecycleListener[0];
  public void addLifecycleListener(LifecycleListener listener) {
    synchronized (listeners) {
      LifecycleListener results[] =
        new LifecycleListener[listeners.length + 1];
      for (int i = 0; i < listeners.length; i++)
        results[i] = listeners[i];
      results[listeners.length] = listener;
      listeners = results;
    }
  }

  public LifecycleListener[] findLifecycleListeners() {
    return listeners;
  }

  public void fireLifecycleEvent(String type, Object data) {
    LifecycleEvent event = new LifecycleEvent(lifecycle, type, data);
    LifecycleListener interested[] = null;
    synchronized (listeners) {
      interested = (LifecycleListener[]) listeners.clone();
    }
    for (int i = 0; i < interested.length; i++)
      interested[i].lifecycleEvent(event);
  }

  public void removeLifecycleListener(LifecycleListener listener) {
    synchronized (listeners) {
      int n = -1;
      for (int i = 0; i < listeners.length; i++) {
        if (listeners[i] == listener) {
          n = i;
          break;
        }
      }
      if (n < 0)
        return;
      LifecycleListener results[] =
        new LifecycleListener[listeners.length - 1];
```

```
    int j = 0;
    for (int i = 0; i < listeners.length; i++) {
      if (i != n)
      results[j++] = listeners[i];
    }
    listeners = results;
  }
 }
}
```

As you can see in Listing 6.4, the `LifecycleSupport` class stores all lifecycle listeners in an array called `listeners` that initially has no member.

```
private LifecycleListener listeners[] = new LifecycleListener[0];
```

When a listener is added in the `addLifecycleListener` method, a new array is created with the size of the number of elements in the old array plus one. Then, all elements from the old array are copied to the new array and the new listener is added. When a listener is removed in the `removeLifecycleListener` method, a new array is also created with the size of the number of elements in the old array minus one. Then, all elements except the one removed are copied to the new array.

The `fireLifecycleEvent` method fires a lifecycle event. First, it clones the `listeners` array. Then, it calls the `lifecycleEvent` method of each member, passing the triggered event.

A component implementing `Lifecycle` can use the `LifecycleSupport` class. For example, the `SimpleContext` class in the application accompanying this chapter declares the following variable:

```
protected LifecycleSupport lifecycle = new LifecycleSupport(this);
```

To add a lifecycle listener, the `SimpleContext` class calls the `addLifecycleListener` method of the `LifecycleSupport` class:

```
public void addLifecycleListener(LifecycleListener listener) {
  lifecycle.addLifecycleListener(listener);
}
```

To remove a lifecycle listener, the `SimpleContext` class calls the `removeLifecycleListener` method of the `LifecycleSupport` class.

```
public void removeLifecycleListener(LifecycleListener listener) {
  lifecycle.removeLifecycleListener(listener);
}
```

To fire an event, the `SimpleContext` class calls the `fireLifecycleEvent` method of the `LifecycleSupport` class, such as in the following line of code:

```
lifecycle.fireLifecycleEvent(START_EVENT, null);
```

The Application

The application accompanying this chapter builds upon the application in Chapter 5 and illustrates the use of the `Lifecycle` interface and lifecycle-related types. It contains one context and two wrappers as well as a loader and a mapper. The components in this application implement the `Lifecycle` interface and a listener is used for the context. The two valves in Chapter 5 are not used here to make the application simpler. The class diagram of the application is shown in Figure 6.1. Note that a number of interfaces (`Container`, `Wrapper`, `Context`, `Loader`, `Mapper`) and classes (`SimpleContextValve`, `SimpleContextMapper`, and `SimpleWrapperValve`) are not included in the diagram.

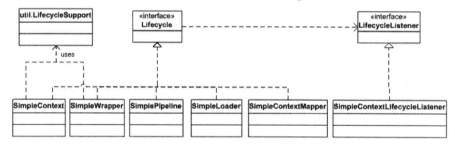

Figure 6.1 The class diagram of the accompanying application

Note that the `SimpleContextLifecycleListener` class represents a listener class for the `SimpleContext` class. The `SimpleContextValve`, `SimpleContextMapper`, and `SimpleWrapperValve` classes are the same as the ones in Chapter 5 and will not be discussed again here.

ex06.pyrmont.core.SimpleContext

The `SimpleContext` class in this application is similar to the one in Chapter 5, except that it now implements the `Lifecycle` interface. The `SimpleContext` class uses the following variable to reference a `LifecycleSupport` instance.

```
protected LifecycleSupport lifecycle = new LifecycleSupport(this);
```

It also uses a boolean named `started` to indicate if the `SimpleContext` instance has been started. The `SimpleContext` class provides implementation of the methods from the `Lifecycle` interface. Listing 6.5 presents these methods.

Listing 6.5: Methods from the Lifecycle interface.

```
public void addLifecycleListener(LifecycleListener listener) {
  lifecycle.addLifecycleListener(listener);
}
public LifecycleListener[] findLifecycleListeners() {
  return null;
}
public void removeLifecycleListener(LifecycleListener listener) {
  lifecycle.removeLifecycleListener(listener);
}
public synchronized void start() throws LifecycleException {
  if (started)
    throw new LifecycleException("SimpleContext has already started");
  // Notify our interested LifecycleListeners
  lifecycle.fireLifecycleEvent(BEFORE_START_EVENT, null);
  started = true;
  try {
    // Start our subordinate components, if any
    if ((loader != null) && (loader instanceof Lifecycle))
      ((Lifecycle) loader).start();

    // Start our child containers, if any
    Container children[] = findChildren();
    for (int i = 0; i < children.length; i++) {
      if (children[i] instanceof Lifecycle)
        ((Lifecycle) children[i]).start();
    }

    // Start the Valves in our pipeline (including the basic),
    // if any
    if (pipeline instanceof Lifecycle)
      ((Lifecycle) pipeline).start();
    // Notify our interested LifecycleListeners
    lifecycle.fireLifecycleEvent(START_EVENT, null);
  }
  catch (Exception e) {
    e.printStackTrace();
  }
  // Notify our interested LifecycleListeners
  lifecycle.fireLifecycleEvent(AFTER_START_EVENT, null);
}

public void stop() throws LifecycleException {
  if (!started)
    throw new LifecycleException("SimpleContext has not been started");
  // Notify our interested LifecycleListeners
  lifecycle.fireLifecycleEvent(BEFORE_STOP_EVENT, null);
  lifecycle.fireLifecycleEvent(STOP_EVENT, null);
  started = false;
  try {
    // Stop the Valves in our pipeline (including the basic), if any
    if (pipeline instanceof Lifecycle) {
```

```
      ((Lifecycle) pipeline).stop();
   }

   // Stop our child containers, if any
   Container children[] = findChildren();
   for (int i = 0; i < children.length; i++) {
     if (children[i] instanceof Lifecycle)
       ((Lifecycle) children[i]).stop();
   }
   if ((loader != null) && (loader instanceof Lifecycle)) {
     ((Lifecycle) loader).stop();
   }
 }
 catch (Exception e) {
   e.printStackTrace();
 }
 // Notify our interested LifecycleListeners
 lifecycle.fireLifecycleEvent(AFTER_STOP_EVENT, null);
}
```

Notice how the start method starts all child containers and associated components such as the Loader, Pipeline, and Mapper, and how the stop method stops them? Using this mechanism, to start all the components in the container module, you just need to start the highest component in the hierarchy (in this case the SimpleContext instance). To stop them, you only have to stop the same single component.

The start method in SimpleContext begins by checking if the component has been started previously. If it has, it throws a LifecycleException.

```
if (started)
  throw new LifecycleException(
    "SimpleContext has already started");
```

It then raises the BEFORE_START_EVENT event.

```
// Notify our interested LifecycleListeners
lifecycle.fireLifecycleEvent(BEFORE_START_EVENT, null);
```

As a result, every listener that has registered its interest in the SimpleContext instance's events will be notified. In this application, one listener of type SimpleContextLifecycleListener registers its interest. We will see what happens with this listener when we discuss the SimpleContextLifecycleListener class.

Next, the start method sets the started boolean to true to indicate that the component has been started.

```
started = true;
```

The `start` method then starts all the components and its child container. Currently there are two components that implement the `Lifecycle` interface, `SimpleLoader` and `SimplePipeline`. The `SimpleContext` has two wrappers as its children. These wrappers are of type `SimpleWrapper` that also implements the `Lifecycle` interface.

```
try {
  // Start our subordinate components, if any
  if ((loader != null) && (loader instanceof Lifecycle))
    ((Lifecycle) loader).start();

  // Start our child containers, if any
  Container children[] = findChildren();
  for (int i = 0; i < children.length; i++) {
    if (children[i] instanceof Lifecycle)
      ((Lifecycle) children[i]).start();
  }

  // Start the Valves in our pipeline (including the basic),
  // if any
  if (pipeline instanceof Lifecycle)
    ((Lifecycle) pipeline).start();
```

After the components and children are started, the start method raises two events: START_EVENT and AFTER_START_EVENT.

```
// Notify our interested LifecycleListeners
lifecycle.fireLifecycleEvent(START_EVENT, null);
.
.
.
// Notify our interested LifecycleListeners
lifecycle.fireLifecycleEvent(AFTER_START_EVENT, null);
```

The `stop` method first checks if the instance has been started. If not, it throws a `LifecycleException`.

```
if (!started)
  throw new LifecycleException(
    "SimpleContext has not been started");
```

It then generates the BEFORE_STOP_EVENT and STOP_EVENT events, and reset the `started` boolean.

```
// Notify our interested LifecycleListeners
lifecycle.fireLifecycleEvent(BEFORE_STOP_EVENT, null);
lifecycle.fireLifecycleEvent(STOP_EVENT, null);
started = false;
```

Next, the `stop` method stops all components associated with it and the `SimpleContext` instance's child containers.

```
try {
```

```
// Stop the Valves in our pipeline (including the basic), if any
if (pipeline instanceof Lifecycle) {
  ((Lifecycle) pipeline).stop();
}

// Stop our child containers, if any
Container children[] = findChildren();
for (int i = 0; i < children.length; i++) {
  if (children[i] instanceof Lifecycle)
    ((Lifecycle) children[i]).stop();
}
if ((loader != null) && (loader instanceof Lifecycle)) {
  ((Lifecycle) loader).stop();
}
}
```

Finally, it raises the AFTER_STOP_EVENT event.

```
// Notify our interested LifecycleListeners
lifecycle.fireLifecycleEvent(AFTER_STOP_EVENT, null);
```

ex06.pyrmont.core.SimpleContextLifecycleListener

The SimpleContextLifecycleListener class represents a listener for a SimpleContext instance. It is given in Listing 6.6.

Listing 6.6: The SimpleContextLifecycleListener class

```
package ex06.pyrmont.core;
import org.apache.catalina.Context;
import org.apache.catalina.Lifecycle;
import org.apache.catalina.LifecycleEvent;
import org.apache.catalina.LifecycleListener;

public class SimpleContextLifecycleListener implements
LifecycleListener {

  public void lifecycleEvent(LifecycleEvent event) {
    Lifecycle lifecycle = event.getLifecycle();
    System.out.println("SimpleContextLifecycleListener's event " +
      event.getType().toString());
    if (Lifecycle.START_EVENT.equals(event.getType())) {
      System.out.println("Starting context.");
    }
    else if (Lifecycle.STOP_EVENT.equals(event.getType())) {
      System.out.println("Stopping context.");
    }
  }
}
```

The implementation of the lifecycleEvent method in the SimpleContextLifecycleListener class is simple. It simply prints the type of the event raised. If it is a START_EVENT, the lifecycleEvent method prints Starting context. If the event is a STOP_EVENT, then it prints Stopping context.

ex06.pyrmont.core.SimpleLoader

The SimpleLoader class is similar to the one in Chapter 5, except that in this application the class implements the Lifecycle interface. The method implementation for the Lifecycle interface for this class does not do anything other than printing a string to the console. More importantly, however, by implementing the Lifecycle interface, a SimpleLoader instance can be started by its associated container.

The methods from the Lifecycle interface in SimpleLoader are given in Listing 6.7.

Listing 6.7: The methods from Lifecycle in the SimpleLoader class

```
public void addLifecycleListener(LifecycleListener listener) { }
public LifecycleListener[] findLifecycleListeners() {
  return null;
}
public void removeLifecycleListener(LifecycleListener listener) { }
public synchronized void start() throws LifecycleException {
  System.out.println("Starting SimpleLoader");
}
public void stop() throws LifecycleException { }
```

ex06.pyrmont.core.SimplePipeline

In addition to the Pipeline interface, the SimplePipeline class implements the Lifecycle interface. The methods from the Lifecycle interface are left blank but now an instance of this class can be started from its associated container. The rest of the class is similar to the SimplePipeline class in Chapter 5.

ex06.pyrmont.core.SimpleWrapper

This class is similar to the ex05.pyrmont.core.SimpleWrapper class. In this application, it implements the Lifecycle interface so that it can be started from its parent container. In this application most of the methods from the

Lifecycle interface are left blank except the start and stop methods. Listing 6.8 presents the method implementation from the Lifecycle interface.

Listing 6.8: The methods from the Lifecycle interface

```
public void addLifecycleListener(LifecycleListener listener) {   }
public LifecycleListener[] findLifecycleListeners() {
  return null;
}
public void removeLifecycleListener(LifecycleListener listener) { }
public synchronized void start() throws LifecycleException {
  System.out.println("Starting Wrapper " + name);
  if (started)
    throw new LifecycleException("Wrapper already started");
  // Notify our interested LifecycleListeners
  lifecycle.fireLifecycleEvent(BEFORE_START_EVENT, null);
  started = true;

  // Start our subordinate components, if any
  if ((loader != null) && (loader instanceof Lifecycle))
    ((Lifecycle) loader).start();
  // Start the Valves in our pipeline (including the basic), if any
  if (pipeline instanceof Lifecycle)
    ((Lifecycle) pipeline).start();
  // Notify our interested LifecycleListeners
  lifecycle.fireLifecycleEvent(START_EVENT, null);
  // Notify our interested LifecycleListeners
  lifecycle.fireLifecycleEvent(AFTER_START_EVENT, null);
}

public void stop() throws LifecycleException {
  System.out.println("Stopping wrapper " + name);
  // Shut down our servlet instance (if it has been initialized)
  try {
    instance.destroy();
  }
  catch (Throwable t) {
  }
  instance = null;
  if (!started)
    throw new LifecycleException("Wrapper " + name + " not started");
  // Notify our interested LifecycleListeners
  lifecycle.fireLifecycleEvent(BEFORE_STOP_EVENT, null);
  // Notify our interested LifecycleListeners
  lifecycle.fireLifecycleEvent(STOP_EVENT, null);
  started = false;

  // Stop the Valves in our pipeline (including the basic), if any
  if (pipeline instanceof Lifecycle) {
    ((Lifecycle) pipeline).stop();
  }
  // Stop our subordinate components, if any
  if ((loader != null) && (loader instanceof Lifecycle)) {
    ((Lifecycle) loader).stop();
  }
  // Notify our interested LifecycleListeners
```

```
  lifecycle.fireLifecycleEvent(AFTER_STOP_EVENT, null);
}
```

The `start` method in `SimpleWrapper` is similar to the `start` method in the `SimpleContext` class. It starts any components added to it (currently, there is none) and triggers the BEFORE_START_EVENT, START_EVENT, and AFTER_START_EVENT events.

The `stop` method in `SimpleWrapper` is even more interesting. After printing a simple string, it invokes the `destroy` method of the servlet instance.

```
System.out.println("Stopping wrapper " + name);
// Shut down our servlet instance (if it has been initialized)
try {
  instance.destroy();
}
catch (Throwable t) {
}
instance = null;
```

Then, it checks if the wrapper has been started. If not, it throws a `LifecycleException`.

```
if (!started)
  throw new LifecycleException("Wrapper " + name + " not started");
```

Next, it triggers the BEFORE_STOP_EVENT and STOP_EVENT events and reset the `started` boolean.

```
// Notify our interested LifecycleListeners
lifecycle.fireLifecycleEvent(BEFORE_STOP_EVENT, null);
// Notify our interested LifecycleListeners
lifecycle.fireLifecycleEvent(STOP_EVENT, null);
started = false;
```

Next, it stops the loader and pipeline components associated with it. In this application, the `SimpleWrapper` instances do not have a loader.

```
// Stop the Valves in our pipeline (including the basic), if any
if (pipeline instanceof Lifecycle) {
  ((Lifecycle) pipeline).stop();
}
// Stop our subordinate components, if any
if ((loader != null) && (loader instanceof Lifecycle)) {
  ((Lifecycle) loader).stop();
}
```

Finally, it triggers the AFTER_STOP_EVENT event.

```
// Notify our interested LifecycleListeners
lifecycle.fireLifecycleEvent(AFTER_STOP_EVENT, null);
```

Running the Application

To run the application in Windows, from the working directory, type the following:

```
java -classpath ./lib/servlet.jar;./ ex06.pyrmont.startup.Bootstrap
```

In Linux, you use a colon to separate two libraries.

```
java -classpath ./lib/servlet.jar:./ ex06.pyrmont.startup.Bootstrap
```

You will see the following message on the console. Notice how the various events are fired?

```
HttpConnector Opening server socket on all host IP addresses
HttpConnector[8080] Starting background thread
SimpleContextLifecycleListener's event before_start
Starting SimpleLoader
Starting Wrapper Modern
Starting Wrapper Primitive
SimpleContextLifecycleListener's event start
Starting context.
SimpleContextLifecycleListener's event after_start
```

To invoke PrimitiveServlet, you use the following URL in your browser.

```
http://localhost:8080/Primitive
```

To invoke ModernServlet, you use the following URL.

```
http://localhost:8080/Modern
```

Summary

In this chapter you have learned how to work with the Lifecycle interface. This interface defines the lifecycle for a component and provides an elegant way to send events to other components. In addition, the Lifecycle interface also makes it possible to start and stop all the components in Catalina by one single start/stop.

Chapter 7
Logger

A logger is a component for recording messages. In Catalina a logger is associated with a container and is relatively simpler than other components. Tomcat provides various loggers in the `org.apache.catalina.logger` package. The application that accompanies this chapter can be found in the `ex07.pyrmont` package. Two classes, `SimpleContext` and `Bootstrap`, have changed from the application in Chapter 6.

There are three sections in this chapter. The first section covers the `org.apache.catalina.Logger` interface, the interface that all loggers must implement. The second section explains the loggers in Tomcat and the third details the application for this chapter that uses Tomcat's loggers.

The Logger Interface

A logger must implement the `org.apache.catalina.Logger` interface, which is given in Listing 7.1.

Listing 7.1: The Logger interface

```
package org.apache.catalina;
import java.beans.PropertyChangeListener;

public interface Logger {
  public static final int FATAL = Integer.MIN_VALUE;
  public static final int ERROR = 1;
  public static final int WARNING = 2;
  public static final int INFORMATION = 3;
  public static final int DEBUG = 4;

  public Container getContainer();
  public void setContainer(Container container);
  public String getInfo();
  public int getVerbosity();
  public void setVerbosity(int verbosity);
  public void addPropertyChangeListener(PropertyChangeListener
    listener);
  public void log(String message);
```

```
    public void log(Exception exception, String msg);
    public void log(String message, Throwable throwable);
    public void log(String message, int verbosity);
    public void log(String message, Throwable throwable, int verbosity);
    public void removePropertyChangeListener(PropertyChangeListener
      listener);
}
```

The Logger interface provides a number of log methods that the implementing class can choose to invoke. The simplest of these methods is the one that accepts a String as the message to be recorded.

The last two log methods accept a verbosity level. If the number passed is lower than the verbosity level set for the class's instance, the message is logged. Otherwise, the message is ignored. Five verbosity levels are defined as public static variables: FATAL, ERROR, WARNING, INFORMATION, and DEBUG. The getVerbosity and setVerbosity methods are used to obtain and set this value.

In addition, the Logger interface has the getContainer and setContainer methods to associate a Logger instance with a container. It also provides the addPropertyChangeListener and removePropertyChangeListener methods to add and remove a PropertyChangeListener.

These methods will be clearer when you see their implementations in the Tomcat logger classes.

Tomcat's Loggers

Tomcat provides three loggers whose classes are FileLogger, SystemErrLogger, and SystemOutLogger. These classes can be found in the org.apache.catalina.logger package and they all extend the org.apache.catalina.logger.LoggerBase class. In Tomcat 4 the LoggerBase class implements the org.apache.catalina.Logger interface. In Tomcat 5, it also implements Lifecycle (discussed in Chapter 6) and MBeanRegistration (explained in Chapter 20).

The UML diagram of these classes is shown in Figure 7.1.

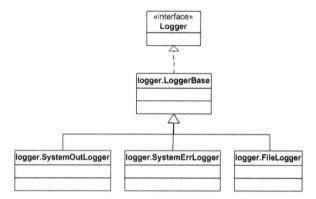

Figure 7.1: Tomcat's Loggers

The LoggerBase Class

In Tomcat 5 the `LoggerBase` class is quite complex because it incorporates code for creating MBeans, which will only be discussed in Chapter 20. We therefore look at the `LoggerBase` class in Tomcat 4. You will be able to understand the `LoggerBase` class in Tomcat 5 if you understand the discussion in Chapter 20.

In Tomcat 4, the `LoggerBase` class is an abstract class that provides the implementation of all methods in the `Logger` interface except the `log(String msg)` method.

```
public abstract void log(String msg);
```

This method overload is the one that does the logging in the child classes. All the other `log` method overloads call this overload. Because each child class logs messages to a different destination, this method overload is left blank in the `LoggerBase` class.

Now let's look at the verbosity level of this class. It is defined by a protected variable named verbosity, with ERROR as its default value:

```
protected int verbosity = ERROR;
```

The verbosity level can be changed by calling the `setVerbosity` method, passing one of the following strings: FATAL, ERROR, WARNING, INFORMATION, or DEBUG. Listing 7.2 presents the `setVerbosity` method in the `LoggerBase` class.

Listing 7.2: The setVerbosity method

```
public void setVerbosityLevel(String verbosity) {
  if ("FATAL".equalsIgnoreCase(verbosity))
    this.verbosity = FATAL;
  else if ("ERROR".equalsIgnoreCase(verbosity))
    this.verbosity = ERROR;
  else if ("WARNING".equalsIgnoreCase(verbosity))
    this.verbosity = WARNING;
  else if ("INFORMATION".equalsIgnoreCase(verbosity))
    this.verbosity = INFORMATION;
  else if ("DEBUG".equalsIgnoreCase(verbosity))
    this.verbosity = DEBUG;
}
```

Two `log` methods accept an integer as the verbosity level. In these method overloads, the `log(String message)` overload is only called if the verbosity level passed is lower than the instance's verbosity levels. Listing 7.3 provides these method overloads.

Listing 7.3: The log method overloads that accept verbosity

```
public void log(String message, int verbosity) {
  if (this.verbosity >= verbosity)
    log(message);
}
public void log(String message, Throwable throwable, int verbosity) {
  if (this.verbosity >= verbosity)
    log(message, throwable);
}
```

In the three child classes of `LoggerBase` discussed in the following sections, you will see the implementation of the `log(String message)` method overload.

The SystemOutLogger Class

This child class of `LoggerBase` provides the implementation of the `log(String message)` method overload. Every message received is passed to the `System.out.println` method. The `SystemOutLogger` class is given in Listing 7.4.

Listing 7.4: The SystemOutLogger Class

```
package org.apache.catalina.logger;
public class SystemOutLogger extends LoggerBase {

  protected static final String info =
    "org.apache.catalina.logger.SystemOutLogger/1.0";
```

```
  public void log(String msg) {
    System.out.println(msg);
  }
}
```

The SystemErrLogger Class

This class is very similar to the SystemOutLogger class, except that the message argument to the log(String message) method overload calls the System.err.println() method. The SystemErrLogger class is given in Listing 7.5.

Listing 7.5: The SystemErrLogger class

```
package org.apache.catalina.logger;
public class SystemErrLogger extends LoggerBase {

  protected static final String info =
    "org.apache.catalina.logger.SystemErrLogger/1.0";
  public void log(String msg) {
    System.err.println(msg);
  }
}
```

The FileLogger Class

The FileLogger class is the most sophisticated child class of LoggerBase. It writes the messages it receives from its associated container to a file and each message can be optionally time-stamped. When first instantiated, an instance of this class creates a file whose name contains the date information of today's date. If the date changes, it will create a new file for the new date and writes everything there. The class instance allows you to add a prefix and suffix to the name of its log file.

In Tomcat 4, the FileLogger class implements the Lifecycle interface so that it can be started and stopped just like any other components that implement org.apache.catalina.Lifecycle. In Tomcat 5, it is the LoggerBase class (the parent of FileLogger) that implements Lifecycle.

The start and stop methods in the LoggerBase class in Tomcat 4 (inherited from the Lifecycle interface) do not do much more than trigger lifecycle events of the listeners interested in the starting and stopping of the file logger. The two methods are given in Listing 7.6. Note that the stop method also calls the private close method that closes the log file. The close method will be discussed later in this section.

Listing 7.6: The start and stop methods

```
public void start() throws LifecycleException {
  // Validate and update our current component state
  if (started)
    throw new LifecycleException
      (sm.getString("fileLogger.alreadyStarted"));
  lifecycle.fireLifecycleEvent(START_EVENT, null);
  started = true;
}

public void stop() throws LifecycleException {
  // Validate and update our current component state
  if (!started)
    throw new LifecycleException
      (sm.getString("fileLogger.notStarted"));
  lifecycle.fireLifecycleEvent(STOP_EVENT, null);
  started = false;
  close();
}
```

The most important method of the FileLogger class is the log method, given in Listing 7.7.

Listing 7.7: The log method

```
public void log(String msg) {
  // Construct the timestamp we will use, if requested
  Timestamp ts = new Timestamp(System.currentTimeMillis());
  String tsString = ts.toString().substring(0, 19);
  String tsDate = tsString.substring(0, 10);

  // If the date has changed, switch log files
  if (!date.equals(tsDate)) {
    synchronized (this) {
      if (!date.equals(tsDate)) {
        close();
        date = tsDate;
        open();
      }
    }
  }

  // Log this message, timestamped if necessary
  if (writer != null) {
    if (timestamp) {
      writer.println(tsString + " " + msg);
    }
    else {
      writer.println(msg);
    }
  }
}
```

The `log` method receives a message and writes to a log file. During the lifetime of a `FileLogger` instance, the `log` method may open and close multiple log files. Typically, the log method rotates the log files by closing the current file and opening a new one if the date changes. Let's have a look at how the `open`, `close`, and `log` methods work.

The open method

The `open` method, given in Listing 7.8, creates a new log file in the designated directory.

Listing 7.8: The open method

```
private void open() {
  // Create the directory if necessary
  File dir = new File(directory);
  if (!dir.isAbsolute())
    dir = new File(System.getProperty("catalina.base"), directory);
  dir.mkdirs();

  // Open the current log file
  try {
    String pathname = dir.getAbsolutePath() + File.separator +
      prefix + date + suffix;
    writer = new PrintWriter(new FileWriter(pathname, true), true);
  }
  catch (IOException e) {
    writer = null;
  }
}
```

The `open` method first checks if the directory in which it is supposed to create a log file exists. If the directory does not exist, the method also creates the directory. The directory is stored in the class variable `directory`.

```
File dir = new File(directory);
if (!dir.isAbsolute())
  dir = new File(System.getProperty("catalina.base"), directory);
dir.mkdirs();
```

It then composes the pathname of the file to open based on the directory path, the prefix, current date, and the suffix.

```
try {
  String pathname = dir.getAbsolutePath() + File.separator +
    prefix + date + suffix;
```

Next, it constructs an instance of `java.io.PrintWriter` whose writer is a `java.io.FileWriter` object that writes `pathname`. The `PrintWriter` instance is then assigned to the class variable writer. The log method uses writer to log the message.

```
writer = new PrintWriter(new FileWriter(pathname, true), true);
```

The close method

The close method flushes the PrintWriter writer, flushes its content, closes the PrintWriter, sets the PrintWriter to null, and sets the date to an empty string. The close method is given in Listing 7.9.

Listing 7.9: The close method

```
private void close() {
  if (writer == null)
    return;
  writer.flush();
  writer.close();
  writer = null;
  date = "";
}
```

The log method

The log method starts by creating an instance of java.sql.Timestamp class, which is a thin wrapper of the java.util.Date class. The purpose of instantiating the Timestamp class in the log method is to easily obtain the current date. The log method constructs a Timestamp instance by passing the current time in long to the Timestamp class's constructor.

```
Timestamp ts = new Timestamp(System.currentTimeMillis());
```

Using the Timestamp class's toString method, you can get the string representation of the current date. The toString method's output has the following format.

```
yyyy-mm-dd hh:mm:ss.fffffffff
```

where fffffffff indicates the number of nanoseconds that has elapsed from 00:00:00. To get the date and hour only, the log method calls the substring method of the String class:

```
String tsString = ts.toString().substring(0, 19);
```

Then, from tsString, to obtain the date part, the log method uses the following line:

```
String tsDate = tsString.substring(0, 10);
```

The `log` method then compares `tsDate` with the value of the String variable `date`, which initially contains an empty string. If the values of `tsDate` and `date` are not the same, it closes the current log file, assigns the value of `tsDate` to `date`, and opens a new log file.

```
// If the date has changed, switch log files
if (!date.equals(tsDate)) {
  synchronized (this) {
    if (!date.equals(tsDate)) {
      close();
      date = tsDate;
      open();
    }
  }
}
```

Finally, the `log` method writes to the `PrintWriter` instance whose output stream is the log file. If the value of the boolean `timestamp` is `true`, it prefixes the message with the `timestamp (tsString)`. Otherwise, it logs the message without a prefix.

```
// Log this message, timestamped if necessary
if (writer != null) {
  if (timestamp) {
    writer.println(tsString + " " + msg);
  }
  else {
    writer.println(msg);
  }
}
```

The Application

The application is very similar to the application in Chapter 6, except that you have a `FileLogger` that is associated with a `SimpleContext` object. The change to the application in Chapter 6 can be found in the `ex07.pyrmont.startup.Bootstrap` class's `main` method, given in Listing 7.10. In particular, take a close look at the highlighted code.

Listing 7.10: The Bootstrap class

```
package ex07.pyrmont.startup;

import ex07.pyrmont.core.SimpleContext;
import ex07.pyrmont.core.SimpleContextLifecycleListener;
import ex07.pyrmont.core.SimpleContextMapper;
import ex07.pyrmont.core.SimpleLoader;
import ex07.pyrmont.core.SimpleWrapper;
import org.apache.catalina.Connector;
import org.apache.catalina.Context;
```

```java
import org.apache.catalina.Lifecycle;
import org.apache.catalina.LifecycleListener;
import org.apache.catalina.Loader;
import org.apache.catalina.logger.FileLogger;
import org.apache.catalina.Mapper;
import org.apache.catalina.Wrapper;
import org.apache.catalina.connector.http.HttpConnector;

public final class Bootstrap {
  public static void main(String[] args) {
    Connector connector = new HttpConnector();
    Wrapper wrapper1 = new SimpleWrapper();
    wrapper1.setName("Primitive");
    wrapper1.setServletClass("PrimitiveServlet");
    Wrapper wrapper2 = new SimpleWrapper();
    wrapper2.setName("Modern");
    wrapper2.setServletClass("ModernServlet");
    Loader loader = new SimpleLoader();

    Context context = new SimpleContext();
    context.addChild(wrapper1);
    context.addChild(wrapper2);

    Mapper mapper = new SimpleContextMapper();
    mapper.setProtocol("http");
    LifecycleListener listener = new SimpleContextLifecycleListener();
    ((Lifecycle) context).addLifecycleListener(listener);
    context.addMapper(mapper);
    context.setLoader(loader);
    // context.addServletMapping(pattern, name);
    context.addServletMapping("/Primitive", "Primitive");
    context.addServletMapping("/Modern", "Modern");

    // ------ add logger --------
    System.setProperty("catalina.base",
System.getProperty("user.dir"));
    FileLogger logger = new FileLogger();
    logger.setPrefix("FileLog_");
    logger.setSuffix(".txt");
    logger.setTimestamp(true);
    logger.setDirectory("webroot");
    context.setLogger(logger);

    //----------------------------

    connector.setContainer(context);
    try {
      connector.initialize();
      ((Lifecycle) connector).start();
      ((Lifecycle) context).start();

      // make the application wait until we press a key.
      System.in.read();
      ((Lifecycle) context).stop();
    }
    catch (Exception e) {
```

```
        e.printStackTrace();
      }
    }
}
```

Summary

In this chapter you have learned about the logger components, reviewed the `org.apache.catalina.Logger` interface, and taken a close look of the three Tomcat implementations of the `Logger` interface. In addition, the application that accompanies this chapter uses the `FileLogger` class, the most advanced logger available in Tomcat.

Chapter 8
Loader

You have seen a simple loader implementation in the previous chapters, which was used for loading servlet classes. This chapter explains the standard web application loader, or loader for short, in Catalina. A servlet container needs a customized loader and cannot simply use the system's class loader because it should not trust the servlets it is running. If it were to load all servlets and other classes needed by the servlets using the system's class loader, as we did in the previous chapters, then a servlet would be able to access any class and library included in the CLASSPATH environment variable of the running Java Virtual Machine (JVM). This would be a breach of security. A servlet is only allowed to load classes in the WEB-INF/classes directory and its subdirectories and from the libraries deployed into the WEB-INF/lib directory. That's why a servlet container requires a loader of its own. Each web application (context) in a servlet container has its own loader. A loader employs a class loader that applies certain rules to loading classes. In Catalina, a loader is represented by the org.apache.catalina.Loader interface.

Another reason why Tomcat needs its own loader is to support automatic reloading whenever a class in the WEB-INF/classes or WEB-INF/lib directories has been modified. The class loader in the Tomcat loader implementation uses a separate thread that keeps checking the time stamps of the servlet and supporting class files. To support automatic reloading, a class loader must implement the org.apache.catalina.loader.Reloader interface.

The first section of this chapter briefly reviews the class loading mechanism in Java. Next, it covers the Loader interface, which all loaders must implement, followed by the Reloader interface. After a look at the implementation of the loader and class loader, the chapter presents an application that demonstrates how to use a Tomcat's loader.

Two terms are used extensively in this chapter: repository and resources. A repository is a place that will be searched by the class loader. The term resources refers to a `DirContext` object in a class loader whose document base points to the context's document base.

Java Class Loader

Every time you create an instance of a Java class, the class must first be loaded into memory. The JVM uses a class loader to load classes. The class loader normally searches some core Java libraries and all directories included in the `CLASSPATH` environment variable. If it does not find the required class, it throws a `java.lang.ClassNotFoundException`.

Starting from J2SE 1.2, the JVM employs three class loaders: bootstrap class loader, extension class loader, and system class loader. Each of the three class loaders has a parent-child relationship with each other, in which the bootstrap class loader sits at the top of the hierarchy and the system class loader at the bottom.

The bootstrap class loader is used to bootstrap the JVM. It starts working whenever you call the java.exe program. As such, it must be implemented using the native code because it is used to load the classes required for the JVM to function. Also, it is responsible for loading all the core Java classes, such as those in `java.lang` and `java.io` packages. The bootstrap class loader searches the core libraries such as rt.jar, i18n.jar, etc. Which libraries are searched depends on the version of the JVM and the operating system.

The extension class loader is responsible for loading classes in a standard extension directory. This is to make the programmer's life easier because they can just copy JAR files into this extension directory and the jar files will be searched automatically. The extension library differs from one vendor to another. Sun's JVM's standard extension directory is /jdk/jre/lib/ext.

The system class loader is the default class loader and searches the directories and JAR files specified in the `CLASSPATH` environment variable.

So, which class loader does the JVM use? The answer lies in the **delegation model**, which is there for security reasons. Every time a class needs to be loaded, the system class loader is first called. However, it does not load the class right away. Instead, it delegates the task to its parent, the extension class loader. The extension class loader also delegates it to its parent, the bootstrap class loader. Therefore, the bootstrap class loader is always given the first chance to load a class. If the bootstrap class loader can't find the class needed, the extension class loader will try to load the class. If the extension class loader also fails, the system class loader will perform the task. If the system class loader can't find the class, a `java.lang.ClassNotFoundException` is thrown. Why the round trip?

The delegation model is very important for security. As you know, you can use the security manager to restrict access to a certain directory. Now, someone with malicious intents can write a class called `java.lang.Object` that can be used to access any directory in the hard disk. Because the JVM trusts the `java.lang.Object` class, it will not watch its activity in this regard. As a result, if the custom `java.lang.Object` was allowed to be loaded, the security manager would be easily paralyzed. Fortunately, this will not happen because of the delegation model. Here is how it works.

When the custom `java.lang.Object` class is called somewhere in the program, the system class loader delegates the request to the extension class loader, which delegates to the bootstrap class loader. The bootstrap class loader searches its core libraries, and finds the standard `java.lang.Object` and instantiates it. As a result, the custom `java.lang.Object` will never be loaded.

The great thing about the class loading mechanism in Java is that you can write your own class loader by extending the abstract `java.lang.ClassLoader` class. The reasons why Tomcat needs a custom class loader include the following:

- To specify certain rules in loading classes.
- To cache the previously loaded classes.
- To pre-load classes so they are ready to use.

The Loader Interface

There are rules in loading servlet and other classes in a web application. For example, a servlet in an application can use classes deployed to the WEB-INF/classes directory and any sub-directory under it. However, servlets do not have access to other classes, even though those classes are included in the CLASSPATH of the JVM running Tomcat. Also, a servlet can only access libraries deployed under the WEB-INF/lib directory and not other directories.

A Tomcat loader represents a web application loader rather than a class loader. A loader must implement the `org.apache.catalina.Loader` interface. The loader implementation uses a custom class loader represented by the `org.apache.catalina.loader.WebappClassLoader` class. You can obtain the `ClassLoader` inside a web loader using the `Loader` interface's `getClassLoader` method.

Among others, the Loader interface defines methods to work with a collection of repositories. The WEB-INF/classes and WEB-INF/lib of a web application are directories to be added as repositories. The Loader interface's addRepository method is used to add a repository and its findRepositories method returns an array of all repositories.

A Tomcat loader implementation is usually associated with a context, and the getContainer and setContainer methods of the Loader interface are used for building this association. A loader can also supports reloading, if one or more classes in a context have been modified. This way, a servlet programmer can recompile a servlet or a supporting class and the new class will be reloaded without restarting Tomcat. For the reloading purpose, the Loader interface has the modified method. In a loader implementation, the modified method must return true if one or more classes in its repositories have been modified, and therefore reloading is required. A loader does not do the reloading itself, however. Instead, it calls the Context interface's reload method. Two other methods, setReloadable and getReloadable, are used to determine if reloading is enabled in the Loader. By default, in the standard implementation of Context (the org.apache.catalina.core.StandardContext class, which is discussed in Chapter 12), reloading is not enabled. Therefore, to enable reloading of a context, you need to add a Context element for that context in your server.xml file, such as the following:

```
<Context path="/myApp" docBase="myApp" debug="0" reloadable="true"/>
```

Also, a Loader implementation can be told whether or not to delegate to a parent class loader. For this purpose, the Loader interface provides the getDelegate and setDelegate methods.

The Loader interface is given in Listing 8.1.

Listing 8.1: The Loader interface

```
package org.apache.catalina;
import java.beans.PropertyChangeListener;

public interface Loader {
  public ClassLoader getClassLoader();
  public Container getContainer();
  public void setContainer(Container container);
  public DefaultContext getDefaultContext();
  public void setDefaultContext(DefaultContext defaultContext);
  public boolean getDelegate();
  public void setDelegate(boolean delegate);
  public String getInfo();
  public boolean getReloadable();
  public void setReloadable(boolean reloadable);
  public void addPropertyChangeListener(PropertyChangeListener
```

```
    listener);
  public void addRepository(String repository);
  public String[] findRepositories();
  public boolean modified();
  public void removePropertyChangeListener(PropertyChangeListener
    listener);
}
```

Catalina provides the `org.apache.catalina.loader.WebappLoader` as an implementation of the `Loader` interface. For its class loader, the `WebappLoader` object contains an instance of the `org.apache.catalina.loader.WebappClassLoader` class, which extends the `java.net.URLClassLoader` class.

> **Note**
> Whenever the container associated with a loader needs a servlet class, i.e. when its `invoke` method is called, the container first calls the loader's `getClassLoader` method to obtain the class loader. The container then calls the `loadClass` method of the class loader to load the servlet class. More details on this can be found in Chapter 11, "StandardWrapper".

The class diagram for the `Loader` interface and its implementation is given in Figure 8.1.

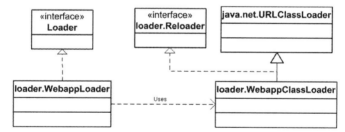

Figure 8.1: The Loader interface and its implementation

The Reloader Interface

To support automatic reloading, a class loader implementation must implement the `org.apache.catalina.loader.Reloader` interface in Listing 8.2.

Listing 8.2: The Reloader interface

```
package org.apache.catalina.loader;
public interface Reloader {
  public void addRepository(String repository);
  public String[] findRepositories();
```

```
  public boolean modified();
}
```

The most important method of the Reloader interface is modified, which returns true if one of the servlet or supporting classes in a web application has been modified. The addRepository method is used to add a repository and the findRepositories method returns a String array of all repositories in the class loader implementing Reloader.

The WebappLoader Class

The org.apache.catalina.loader.WebappLoader class is the implementation of the Loader interface and represents a web application loader responsible for loading classes for a web application. WebappLoader creates an instance of the org.apache.catalina.loader.WebappClassLoader class as its class loader. Like other Catalina components, WebappLoader implements org.apache.catalina.Lifecycle and it is started and stopped by the associated container. The WebappLoader class also implements the java.lang.Runnable interface so that it can dedicate a thread for repeatedly calling the modified method of its class loader. If the modified method returns true, the WebappLoader instance notifies its associated container (in this case a context). The class reloading itself is performed by the Context, not by the WebappLoader. How the Context does this is discussed in Chapter 12, "StandardContext".

Important tasks are performed when the WebappLoader class's start method is called:

- Creating a class loader
- Setting repositories
- Setting the class path
- Setting permissions
- Starting a new thread for auto-reload.

Each of these tasks is discussed in the following sub-sections.

Creating A Class Loader

For loading classes, a WebappLoader instance employs an internal class loader. You may recall from the discussion of the Loader interface that this interface provides the getClassLoader method but there is no setClassLoader.

Therefore, you cannot instantiate a class loader and pass it to the WebappLoader. Does it mean that the WebappLoader does not have the flexibility to work with a non-default class loader?

The answer is no. The WebappLoader provides the getLoaderClass and setLoaderClass methods to obtain and change the value of its private variable loaderClass. This variable is a String representing the name of the class of the class loader. By default, the value of loaderClass is org.apache.catalina.loader.WebappClassLoader. If you wish, you can create your own class loader that extends WebappClassLoader and call the setLoaderClass to force your WebappLoader to use your custom class loader. Otherwise, when it is started, the WebappLoader will create an instance of WebappClassLoader by calling its private createClassLoader method. This method is given in Listing 8.3.

Listing 8.3: The createClassLoader method

```
private WebappClassLoader createClassLoader() throws Exception {
  Class clazz = Class.forName(loaderClass);
  WebappClassLoader classLoader = null;
  if (parentClassLoader == null) {
    // Will cause a ClassCast if the class does not extend
    // WebappClassLoader, but this is on purpose (the exception will be
    // caught and rethrown)
    classLoader = (WebappClassLoader) clazz.newInstance();
    // in Tomcat 5, this if block is replaced by the following:
    // if (parentClassLoader == null) {
    //   parentClassLoader =
    //     Thread.currentThread().getContextClassLoader();
    // }

  }
  else {
    Class[] argTypes = { ClassLoader.class };
    Object[] args = { parentClassLoader };
    Constructor constr = clazz.getConstructor(argTypes);
    classLoader = (WebappClassLoader) constr.newInstance(args);
  }
  return classLoader;
}
```

It is possible to use a different class loader other than an instance of WebappClassLoader. Note, however, that the createClassLoader method returns a WebappClassLoader. Therefore, if your custom class loader does not extend WebappClassLoader, this method will throw an exception.

Setting Repositories

The `WebappLoader` class's `start` method calls the `setRepositories` method to add repositories to its class loader. The WEB-INF/classes directory is passed to the class loader's `addRepository` method and the WEB-INF/lib directory is passed to the class loader's `setJarPath` method. This way, the class loader will be able to load classes in the WEB-INF/classes directory and from any library deployed to the WEB-INF/lib directory.

Setting the Class Path

This task is performed by the `start` method by calling the `setClassPath` method. The `setClassPath` method assigns to an attribute in the servlet context a string containing the class path information for the Jasper JSP compiler. It will not be discussed here.

Setting Permissions

If the security manager is used when running Tomcat, the `setPermissions` method adds the permissions to the class loader to access necessary directories, such as WEB-INF/classes and WEB-INF/lib. If no security manager is used, this method returns right away.

Starting a New Thread for Auto-Reload

`WebappLoader` supports auto-reload. If a class in the WEB-INF/classes or WEB-INF/lib directories is re-compiled, the class must be reloaded automatically without restarting Tomcat. For this purpose, `WebappLoader` has a thread that continuously checks the date stamp of each resource every x seconds. The x here is defined by the value of the `checkInterval` variable. By default its value is 15, meaning that a check for auto-reload is performed every 15 seconds. The `getCheckInterval` and `setCheckInterval` methods are used to access this variable.

In Tomcat 4 `WebappLoader` implements the `java.lang.Runnable` interface to support auto-reload. The implementation of the `run` method in `WebappLoader` is given in Listing 8.3.

Listing 8.3: The run method

```
public void run() {
  if (debug >= 1)
    log("BACKGROUND THREAD Starting");

  // Loop until the termination semaphore is set
  while (!threadDone) {
    // Wait for our check interval
    threadSleep();
    if (!started)
      break;
    try {
      // Perform our modification check
      if (!classLoader.modified())
        continue;
    }
    catch (Exception e) {
      log(sm.getString("webappLoader.failModifiedCheck"), e);
      continue;
    }
    // Handle a need for reloading
    notifyContext();
    break;
  }

  if (debug >= 1)
    log("BACKGROUND THREAD Stopping");
}
```

Note

In Tomcat 5 the task of checking for modified classes is performed by the `backgroundProcess` method of the `org.apache.catalina.core.StandardContext` object. This method is called periodically by a dedicated thread in the `org.apache.catalina.core.ContainerBase` class, the parent class of `StandardContext`. Check the `ContainerBase` class's `ContainerBackgroundProcessor` inner class that implements `Runnable`.

At its core, the `run` method in Listing 8.3 contains a `while` loop that will run until the `started` variable (used to indicate that the `WebappLoader` has been started) is set to `false`. The `while` loop does the following:

- Sleep for the period specified by the `checkInterval` variable.
- Check if any class it loaded has been modified by calling the modified method of the `WebappLoader` instance's class loader. If not, continue.
- If a class has been modified, call the `notifyContext` private method to ask the `Context` associated with this `WebappLoader` to reload.

The `notifyContext` method is given in Listing 8.4.

Listing 8.4: The notifyContext method

```
private void notifyContext() {
  WebappContextNotifier notifier = new WebappContextNotifier();
  (new Thread(notifier)).start();
}
```

The notifyContext method does not call the Context interface's reload method directly. Instead, it instantiates the inner class WebappContextNotifier and passes the thread object and calls its start method. This way, the execution of reload will be performed by a different thread. The WebappContextNotifier class is given in Listing 8.5.

Listing 8.5: The WebappContextNotifier inner class

```
protected class WebappContextNotifier implements Runnable {
  public void run() {
    ((Context) container).reload();
  }
}
```

When an instance of WebappContextNotifier is passed to a Thread and the Thread object's start method is invoked, the run method of the WebappContextNotifier instance will be executed. In turn, the run method calls the reload method of the Context interface. You can see how the reload method is implemented in the org.apache.catalina.core.StandardContext class in Chapter 12.

The WebappClassLoader Class

The org.apache.catalina.loader.WebappClassLoader class represents the class loader responsible for loading the classes used in a web application. WebappClassLoader extends the java.net.URLClassLoader class, the class we used for loading Java classes in the applications in the previous chapters.

WebappClassLoader was designed for optimization and security in mind. For example, it caches the previously loaded classes to enhance performance. It also caches the names of classes it has failed to find, so that the next time the same classes are requested to be loaded, the class loader can throw the ClassNotFoundException without first trying to find them. WebappClassLoader searches for classes in the list of repositories as well as the specified JAR files.

With regard to security, the WebappClassLoader will not allow certain classes to be loaded. These classes are stored in a String array triggers and currently has one member:

```
private static final String[] triggers = {
  "javax.servlet.Servlet"                    // Servlet API
};
```

Also, you are not allowed to load classes belonging to these packages and subpackages under them, without first delegating to the system class loader:

```
private static final String[] packageTriggers = {
  "javax",                                    // Java extensions
  "org.xml.sax",                              // SAX 1 & 2
  "org.w3c.dom",                              // DOM 1 & 2
  "org.apache.xerces",                        // Xerces 1 & 2
  "org.apache.xalan"                          // Xalan
};
```

Let's now look at how this class performs caching and class loading in the following sub-sections.

Caching

For better performance, classes that are loaded are cached so that the next time a class is required, it can be taken from the cache. Caching can be done locally, meaning that the cache is managed by the WebappClassLoader instance. In addition, the java.lang.ClassLoader maintains a Vector of previously loaded classes to prevent those classes from being garbage-collected. In this case, caching is managed by the super class.

Each class (either deployed as a class file under WEB-INF/classes or from a JAR file) that may be loaded by WebappClassLoader is referred to as a resource. A resource is represented by the org.apache.catalina.loader.ResourceEntry class. A ResourceEntry instance holds the byte array representation of the class, the last modified date, the Manifest (if the resource is from a JAR file), etc.

The ResourceEntry class is given in Listing 8.6.

Listing 8.6: The ResourceEntry class.

```
package org.apache.catalina.loader;
import java.net.URL;
import java.security.cert.Certificate;
import java.util.jar.Manifest;

public class ResourceEntry {
```

```
    public long lastModified = -1;
    // Binary content of the resource.
    public byte[] binaryContent = null;
    public Class loadedClass = null;
    // URL source from where the object was loaded.
    public URL source = null;
    // URL of the codebase from where the object was loaded.
    public URL codeBase = null;
    public Manifest manifest = null;
    public Certificate[] certificates = null;
}
```

All cached resources are stored in a `HashMap` called `resourceEntries`. The keys are the resource names. All resources that were not found are stored in another `HashMap` called `notFoundResources`.

Loading Classes

When loading a class, the `WebappClassLoader` class applies these rules:

- All previously loaded classes are cached, so first check the local cache.
- If not found in the local cache, check in the cache, i.e. by calling the `findLoadedClass` of the `java.lang.ClassLoader` class.
- If not found in both caches, use the system's class loader to prevent the web application from overriding J2EE class.
- If `SecurityManager` is used, check if the class is allowed to be loaded. If the class is not allowed, throw a `ClassNotFoundException`.
- If the delegate flag is on or if the class to be loaded belongs to the package name in the package trigger, use the parent class loader to load the class. If the parent class loader is `null`, use the system class loader.
- Load the class from the current repositories.
- If the class is not found in the current repositories, and if the `delegate` flag is not on, use the parent class loader. If the parent class loader is `null`, use the system class loader.
- If the class is still not found, throw a `ClassNotFoundException`.

The Application

The application accompanying this chapter demonstrates how to use a `WebappLoader` instance associated with a context. The standard implementation of `Context` is the `org.apache.catalina.core.StandardContext` class, therefore this application instantiates the `StandardContext` class. However, the discussion of StandardContext itself will be deferred until Chapter 12. You do not need to understand the details of this class at this stage. All you need to know about StandardContext is that it works with a listener that listens to events it fires, such as the START_EVENT and STOP_EVENT. The listener must implement the org.apache.catalina.lifecycle.LifecycleListener interface and call the StandardContext class's setConfigured method. For this application, the listener is represented by the ex08.pyrmont.core.SimpleContextConfig class, which is given in Listing 8.6.

Listing 8.6: The SimpleContextConfig class

```
package ex08.pyrmont.core;
import org.apache.catalina.Context;
import org.apache.catalina.Lifecycle;
import org.apache.catalina.LifecycleEvent;
import org.apache.catalina.LifecycleListener;

public class SimpleContextConfig implements LifecycleListener {
  public void lifecycleEvent(LifecycleEvent event) {
    if (Lifecycle.START_EVENT.equals(event.getType())) {
      Context context = (Context) event.getLifecycle();
      context.setConfigured(true);
    }
  }
}
```

All you need to do is instantiate both StandardContext and SimpleContextConfig and then register the latter with StandardContext by calling the addLifecycleListener method of the org.apache.catalina.Lifecycle interface. This interface was discussed in detail in Chapter 6, "Lifecycles".

In addition, the application retains the following classes from the previous chapter: SimplePipeline, SimpleWrapper, and SimpleWrapperValve.

The application can be tested using both PrimitiveServlet and ModernServlet, but this time the use of StandardContext dictates the servlets be stored under the WEB-INF/classes of an application directory. The application directory is called myApp and should have been created when you deployed the downloadable ZIP file the first time. To tell the StandardContext instance where to find the application directory, you set a system property called catalina.base with the value of the user.dir property, as follows.

```
System.setProperty("catalina.base", System.getProperty("user.dir"));
```

In fact, that is the first line in the main method of the Bootstrap class. Afterwards, the main method instantiates the default connector.

```
Connector connector = new HttpConnector();
```

It then creates two wrappers for the two servlets and initialize them, just like the application in the previous chapter.

```
Wrapper wrapper1 = new SimpleWrapper();
wrapper1.setName("Primitive");
wrapper1.setServletClass("PrimitiveServlet");
Wrapper wrapper2 = new SimpleWrapper();
wrapper2.setName("Modern");
wrapper2.setServletClass("ModernServlet");
```

It then creates an instance of StandardContext and set the path as well as the document base of the context.

```
Context context = new StandardContext();
// StandardContext's start method adds a default mapper
context.setPath("/myApp");
context.setDocBase("myApp");
```

This is equivalent to having the following element in the server.xml file.

```
<Context path="/myApp" docBase="myApp"/>
```

Then, the two wrappers are added to the context, and it adds the mapping for both so that the context can locate the wrappers.

```
context.addChild(wrapper1);
context.addChild(wrapper2);
context.addServletMapping("/Primitive", "Primitive");
context.addServletMapping("/Modern", "Modern");
```

The next step is to instantiate a listener and register it with the context.

```
LifecycleListener listener = new SimpleContextConfig();
((Lifecycle) context).addLifecycleListener(listener);
```

Next, it instantiates the WebappLoader and associates it with the context.

```
Loader loader = new WebappLoader();
context.setLoader(loader);
```

Afterwards, the context is associated with the default connector, and the connector's initialize and start methods are called, followed by the context's start method. This puts the servlet container into service.

```
connector.setContainer(context);
try {
  connector.initialize();
  ((Lifecycle) connector).start();
```

```
((Lifecycle) context).start();
```

The next lines simply display the value of the resources' `docBase` and all the repositories in the class loader.

```
// now we want to know some details about WebappLoader
WebappClassLoader classLoader = (WebappClassLoader)
  loader.getClassLoader();
System.out.println("Resources' docBase: " +
  ((ProxyDirContext)classLoader.getResources()).getDocBase());
String[] repositories = classLoader.findRepositories();
for (int i=0; i<repositories.length; i++) {
  System.out.println("  repository: " + repositories[i]);
}
```

These lines will make `docBase` and the list of repositories displayed when you run the application.

```
Resources' docBase: C:\HowTomcatWorks\myApp
  repository: /WEB-INF/classes/
```

The value of docBase may be different on your machine, depending where you install the application.

Finally, the application waits until the user presses Enter on the console to stop the application.

```
// make the application wait until we press a key.
System.in.read();
((Lifecycle) context).stop();
```

Running the Application

To run the application in Windows, from the working directory, type the following:

```
java -classpath ./lib/servlet.jar;./lib/commons-collections.jar;./
ex08.pyrmont.startup.Bootstrap
```

In Linux, you use a colon to separate two libraries.

```
java -classpath ./lib/servlet.jar:./lib/commons-collections.jar:./
ex08.pyrmont.startup.Bootstrap
```

To invoke `PrimitiveServlet` servlet, you use the following URL in your browser.

```
http://localhost:8080/Primitive
```

To invoke `ModernServlet`, you use the following URL.

```
http://localhost:8080/Modern
```

Summary

The web application loader, or simply a loader, is a most important component in Catalina. A loader is responsible for loading classes and therefore employs an internal class loader. This internal class loader is a customized class that is used by Tomcat to apply certain rules to the class loading within an application context. Also, the customized class loader supports caching and can check whether or not one or more classes have been modified.

Chapter 9
Session Management

Catalina supports session management through a component called manager, which is represented by the `org.apache.catalina.Manager` interface. A manager is always associated with a context. Among others, a manager is responsible for creating, updating, and destroying (invalidating) session objects as well as returning a valid session object to any requesting component.

A servlet can obtain a session object by calling the `getSession` method of the `javax.servlet.http.HttpServletRequest` interface, which is implemented by the `org.apache.catalina.connector.HttpRequestBase` class in the default connector. Here are some related methods in the `HttpRequestBase` class.

```
public HttpSession getSession() {
  return (getSession(true));
}
public HttpSession getSession(boolean create) {
  ...
  return doGetSession(create);
}
private HttpSession doGetSession(boolean create) {
  // There cannot be a session if no context has been assigned yet
  if (context == null)
    return (null);
  // Return the current session if it exists and is valid
  if ((session != null) && !session.isValid())
    session = null;
  if (session != null)
    return (session.getSession());

  // Return the requested session if it exists and is valid
  Manager manager = null;
  if (context != null)
    manager = context.getManager();
  if (manager == null)
    return (null);        // Sessions are not supported
  if (requestedSessionId != null) {
    try {
      session = manager.findSession(requestedSessionId);
    }
```

```
   catch (IOException e) {
     session = null;
   }
   if ((session != null) && !session.isValid())
     session = null;
   if (session != null) {
     return (session.getSession());
   }
 }

 // Create a new session if requested and the response is not
 // committed
 if (!create)
   return (null);
 ...
 session = manager.createSession();
 if (session != null)
   return (session.getSession());
 else
   return (null);
}
```

By default, a manager stores its session objects in memory. However, Tomcat also allows a manager to persist its session objects into a file store or a database (through JDBC). Catalina provides the `org.apache.catalina.session` package that contains types related to session objects and session management.

This chapter explains the session management in Catalina in three sections, "Sessions", "Managers", and "Stores". The last section explains the application that uses a context with an associated Manager.

Sessions

In servlet programming, a session object is represented by the `javax.servlet.http.HttpSession` interface. The implementation of this interface is the `StandardSession` class in the `org.apache.catalina.session` package. However, for security reasons, a manager does not pass a `StandardSession` instance to a servlet. Instead, it uses a façade class `StandardSessionFacade` in the `org.apache.catalina.session` package. Internally, a manager works with another façade: the `org.apache.catalina.Session` interface. The UML diagram for the session-related types are given in Figure 9.1. Note that for brevity, the `org.apache.catalina` prefix on `Session`, `StandardSession`, and `StandardSessionFacade` has been omitted.

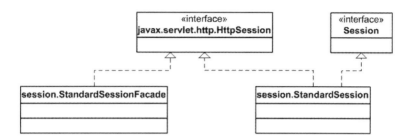

Figure 9.1: Session-related types

The Session interface

The Session interface acts as a Catalina-internal façade. The standard implementation of the Session interface, StandardSession, also implements the javax.servlet.http.HttpSession interface. The Session interface is given in Listing 9.1.

Listing 9.1: The Session interface

```java
package org.apache.catalina;
import java.io.IOException;
import java.security.Principal;
import java.util.Iterator;
import javax.servlet.ServletException;
import javax.servlet.http.HttpSession;

public interface Session {
  public static final String SESSION_CREATED_EVENT = "createSession";
  public static final String SESSION_DESTROYED_EVENT =
    "destroySession";
  public String getAuthType();
  public void setAuthType(String authType);
  public long getCreationTime();
  public void setCreationTime(long time);
  public String getId();
  public void setId(String id);
  public String getInfo();
  public long getLastAccessedTime();
  public Manager getManager();
  public void setManager(Manager manager);
  public int getMaxInactiveInterval();
  public void setMaxInactiveInterval(int interval);
  public void setNew(boolean isNew);
  public Principal getPrincipal();
  public void setPrincipal(Principal principal);
  public HttpSession getSession();
  public void setValid(boolean isValid);
  public boolean isValid();
```

```
    public void access();
    public void addSessionListener(SessionListener listener);
    public void expire();
    public Object getNote(String name);
    public Iterator getNoteNames();
    public void recycle();
    public void removeNote(String name);
    public void removeSessionListener(SessionListener listener);
    public void setNote(String name, Object value);
}
```

A Session object is always contained in a manager, and the setManager and getManager methods are used for associating a Session instance with a manager. A Session instance also has a unique identifier throughout the context associated with its manager. Session identifiers are accessed through the setId and getId methods. The getLastAccessedTime method is invoked by the manager to determine a Session object's validity. The manager calls the setValid method to set or reset a session's validity. Every time a Session instance is accessed, its access method is called to update its last accessed time. Finally, the manager can expire a session by calling its expire method and the getSession method returns an HttpSession object wrapped by this façade.

The StandardSession Class

The StandardSession class is the standard implementation of the Session interface. In addition to implementing javax.servlet.http.HttpSession and org.apache.catalina.Session, StandardSession implements java.lang.Serializable to make Session objects serializable.

The constructor of this class accepts a Manager instance, forcing a Session object to always have a Manager.

```
public StandardSession(Manager manager);
```

The following are some important private variables for maintaining states. Note that the transient keyword makes a variable non-serializable.

```
// session attributes
private HashMap attributes = new HashMap();
// the authentication type used to authenticate our cached Principal,
if any
private transient String authType = null;
private long creationTime = 0L;
private transient boolean expiring = false;
private transient StandardSessionFacade facade = null;
private String id = null;
private long lastAccessedTime = creationTime;
// The session event listeners for this Session.
```

```
private transient ArrayList listeners = new ArrayList();
private Manager manager = null;
private int maxInactiveInterval = -1;
// Flag indicating whether this session is new or not.
private boolean isNew = false;
private boolean isValid = false;
private long thisAccessedTime = creationTime;
```

Note

In Tomcat 5 the above variables are protected, in Tomcat 4 they are private. Each of these variables has an accessor and a mutator (the get/set methods).

The getSession method creates a StandardSessionFacade object by passing this instance:

```
public HttpSession getSession() {
  if (facade == null)
    facade = new StandardSessionFacade(this);
  return (facade);
}
```

A Session object that has not been accessed for a period of time exceeding the value of the maxInactiveInterval variable in the Manager will be made expired. Expiring a Session object is achieved by calling the expire method of the Session interface. The implementation of this method in StandardSession in Tomcat 4 is given in Listing 9.2.

Listing 9.2: The expire method

```
public void expire(boolean notify) {
  // Mark this session as "being expired" if needed
  if (expiring)
    return;
  expiring = true;
  setValid(false);

  // Remove this session from our manager's active sessions
  if (manager != null)
    manager.remove(this);
  // Unbind any objects associated with this session
  String keys[] = keys();
  for (int i = 0; i < keys.length; i++)
    removeAttribute(keys[i], notify);
  // Notify interested session event listeners
  if (notify) {
    fireSessionEvent(Session.SESSION_DESTROYED_EVENT, null);
  }

  // Notify interested application event listeners
  // FIXME - Assumes we call listeners in reverse order
  Context context = (Context) manager.getContainer();
  Object listeners[] = context.getApplicationListeners();
  if (notify && (listeners != null)) {
    HttpSessionEvent event = new HttpSessionEvent(getSession());
```

```
    for (int i = 0; i < listeners.length; i++) {
      int j = (listeners.length - 1) - i;
      if (!(listeners[j] instanceof HttpSessionListener))
        continue;
      HttpSessionListener listener =
       (HttpSessionListener) listeners[j];
      try {
        fireContainerEvent(context, "beforeSessionDestroyed",
          listener);
        listener.sessionDestroyed(event);
        fireContainerEvent(context, "afterSessionDestroyed", listener);
      }
      catch (Throwable t) {
        try {
          fireContainerEvent(context, "afterSessionDestroyed",
            listener);
        }
        catch (Exception e) {
          ;
        }
        // FIXME - should we do anything besides log these?
        log(sm.getString("standardSession.sessionEvent"), t);
      }
    }
  }

  // We have completed expire of this session
  expiring = false;
  if ((manager != null) && (manager instanceof ManagerBase)) {
    recycle();
  }
}
```

The expiring process as shown in Listing 9.2 includes the setting of an internal variable called `expiring`, removing the `Session` instance from `Manager`, and firing of a few events.

The StandardSessionFacade Class

To pass a `Session` object to a servlet, Catalina could instantiate the `StandardSession` class, populate it, and then pass it to the servlet. However, instead, it passes it to an instance of `StandardSessionFacade` that provides only implementation of the methods in `javax.servlet.http.HttpSession`. This way, the servlet programmers cannot downcast the `HttpSession` object back to `StandardSessionFacade` and access its public methods that are not supposed to be available to the programmer.

Manager

A manager manages session objects. For example, it creates session objects and invalidates them. A manager is represented by the `org.apache.catalina.Manager` interface. In Catalina, the `org.apache.catalina.session` package contains the `ManagerBase` class that provides implementation of common functionality. `ManagerBase` has two direct subclasses: `StandardManager` and `PersistentManagerBase`.

When running, `StandardManager` stores session objects in memory. However, when stopped, it saves all the session objects currently in memory to a file. When it is started again, it loads back these session objects.

`PersistentManagerBase` is a base class for manager components that store session objects in secondary storage. It has two sub-classes: `PersistentManager` and `DistributedManager` (`DistributedManager` is only available in Tomcat 4). The UML diagram of the `Manager` interface and its implementation classes is given in Figure 9.2.

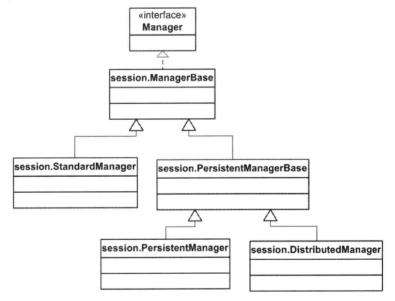

Figure 9.2: The Manager interface and its implementations

The Manager Interface

The Manager interface represents a Manager component. It is given in Listing 9.3.

Listing 9.3: The Manager interface

```
package org.apache.catalina;
import java.beans.PropertyChangeListener;
import java.io.IOException;

public interface Manager {
  public Container getContainer();
  public void setContainer(Container container);
  public DefaultContext getDefaultContext();
  public void setDefaultContext(DefaultContext defaultContext);
  public boolean getDistributable();
  public void setDistributable(boolean distributable);
  public String getInfo();
  public int getMaxInactiveInterval();
  public void setMaxInactiveInterval(int interval);
  public void add(Session session);
  public void addPropertyChangeListener(PropertyChangeListener
    listener);
  public Session createSession();
  public Session findSession(String id) throws IOException;
  public Session[] findSessions();
  public void load() throws ClassNotFoundException, IOException;
  public void remove(Session session);
  public void removePropertyChangeListener(PropertyChangeListener
    listener);
  public void unload() throws IOException;
}
```

First of all, the Manager interface has the getContainer and setContainer methods to associate a Manager implementation with a context. The createSession method creates a Session object. The add method adds a Session instance to the session pool and the remove method removes the Session object from the pool. The getMaxInactiveInterval and the setMaxInactiveInterval methods return and specifies the number of seconds the Manager will wait for the user associated with a session to come back before destroying the session.

Finally, the load and unload methods are there to support persisting sessions to a secondary storage in a Manager implementation that supports a kind of persistence mechanism. The unload method saves currently active sessions to a store specified by the Manager implementation, and the load method brings back the sessions persisted to the memory.

The ManagerBase Class

The `ManagerBase` class is an abstract class from which all `Manager` classes derive. This class provides common functionality for its child classes. Among others, `ManagerBase` has the `createSession` method for creating a `Session` object. Each session has a unique identifier, and the `ManagerBase` class's protected method `generateSessionId` returns a unique identifier.

> **Note**
> An active session is a session object that is still valid (has not expired)

The instance of `Manager` for a given context manages all active sessions in the context. These active sessions are stored in a `HashMap` called `sessions`:

```
protected HashMap sessions = new HashMap();
```

The `add` method adds a `Session` object to the `sessions` HashMap. This method is given below.

```
public void add(Session session) {
  synchronized (sessions) {
    sessions.put(session.getId(), session);
  }
}
```

The `remove` method removes a `Session` from the `sessions` HashMap. Here is the `remove` method.

```
public void remove(Session session) {
  synchronized (sessions) {
    sessions.remove(session.getId());
  }
}
```

The no-argument `findSession` method returns all active sessions from the `sessions` HashMap as an array of `Session` instances. The `findSession` method that accepts a session identifier as an argument returns the `Session` instance with that identifier. These method overloads are given below.

```
public Session[] findSessions() {
  Session results[] = null;
  synchronized (sessions) {
    results = new Session[sessions.size()];
    results = (Session[]) sessions.values().toArray(results);
  }
  return (results);
}
public Session findSession(String id) throws IOException {
  if (id == null)
    return (null);
  synchronized (sessions) {
```

```
    Session session = (Session) sessions.get(id);
    return (session);
  }
}
```

StandardManager

The StandardManager class is the standard implementation of Manager and stores session objects in memory. It implements the Lifecycle interface (See Chapter 6, "Lifecycles") so that it can be started and stopped. The implementation of the stop method calls the unload method that serializes valid Session instances to a file called SESSIONS.ser for each context. The SESSIONS.ser file can be found under the work directory under CATALINA_HOME. For example, in Tomcat 4 and 5, if you have run the examples application, you can find a SESSIONS.ser file under CATALINA_HOME/work/Standalone/localhost/examples. When StandardManager is started again, these Session objects are read back to memory by calling the load method.

A manager is also responsible for destroying session objects that are no longer valid. In StandardManager in Tomcat 4, this is achieved by employing a dedicated thread. For this reason, StandardManager implements java.lang.Runnable. Listing 9.4 presents the run method of the StandardManager class in Tomcat 4.

Listing 9.4: The run method of StandardManager in Tomcat 4

```
public void run() {
  // Loop until the termination semaphore is set
  while (!threadDone) {
    threadSleep();
    processExpires();
  }
}
```

The threadSleep method puts the thread to sleep for the number of seconds specified by the checkInterval variable, which by default has a value of 60. You can change this value by calling the setCheckInterval method.

The processExpire method loops through all Session objects managed by StandardManager and compares each Session instance's lastAccessedTime with the current time. If the difference between the two exceeds maxInactiveInterval, the method calls the Session interface's expire method to expire the Session instance. The value of maxInactiveInternal can be changed by calling the `setMaxInactiveInterval` method. The default value of `maxInactiveInterval` variable in `StandardManager` is 60. Don't be fooled into thinking that this is the value used in a Tomcat deployment, though. The `setContainer` method, which is called by the `setManager` method in the `org.apache.catalina.core.ContainerBase` class (you always call `setManager` to associate a manager with a context), overwrites this value. Here is the piece of code in the `setContainer` method:

```
setMaxInactiveInterval( ((Context)
this.container).getSessionTimeout()*60 );
```

> **Note**
> The default value of the `sessionTimeOut` variable in the
> org.apache.catalina.core.StandardContext class is 30.

In Tomcat 5, the `StandardManager` class does not implement `java.lang.Runnable`. The `processExpires` method in a `StandardManager` object in Tomcat 5 is directly called by the `backgroundProcess` method, which is not available in Tomcat 4.

```
public void backgroundProcess() {
  processExpires();
}
```

The `backgroundProcess` method in `StandardManager` is invoked by the `backgroundProcess` method of the `org.apache.catalina.core.StandardContext` instance, the container associated with this manager. `StandardContext` invokes its `backgroundProcess` method periodically and will be discussed in Chapter 12.

PersistentManagerBase

The `PersistentManagerBase` class is the parent class of all persistent managers. The main difference between a `StandardManager` and a persistent manager is the presence of a store in the latter. A store represents a secondary storage for the managed session objects. The `PersistentManagerBase` class uses a private object reference called `store`.

```
private Store store = null;
```

In a persistent manager, session objects can be backed up as well as swapped out. When a session object is backed up, the session object is copied into a store and the original stays in memory. Therefore, if the server crashes, the active session objects can be retrieved from the store. When a session object is swapped out, it is *moved* to the store because the number of active session objects exceeds a specified number or the session object has been idle for too long. The purpose of swapping out is to save memory.

In Tomcat 4 `PersistentManagerBase` implements `java.lang.Runnable` to employ a separate thread that routinely backs up and swaps out active sessions. Here is its run method implementation:

```
public void run() {
  // Loop until the termination semaphore is set
  while (!threadDone) {
    threadSleep();
    processExpires();
    processPersistenceChecks();
  }
}
```

The `processExpired` method, just like in `StandardManager`, checks for expiring session objects. The `processPersistenceChecks` method calls three other methods:

```
public void processPersistenceChecks() {
  processMaxIdleSwaps();
  processMaxActiveSwaps();
  processMaxIdleBackups();
}
```

In Tomcat 5 `PersistentManagerBase` does not implement `java.lang.Runnable`. Backing up and swapping out is done by its `backgroundProcess` manager, which is periodically invoked by the associated `StandardContext` instance.

Swap out and back up are discussed in the following sub-sections.

Swap Out

The `PersistentManagerBase` class applies a number of rules in swapping out session objects. A session object is swapped out either because the number of active sessions has exceeded the value of `maxActiveSessions` variable or because the session has been idle for too long.

In the case where there are too many session objects, a `PersistentManagerBase` instance simply swaps out any session objects until the number of active session objects is equal to `maxActiveSessions`. (See the `processMaxActiveSwaps` method)

In the case where a session object has been idle for too long, the `PersistentManagerBase` class uses two variables to determine whether or not a session object should be swapped out: `minIdleSwap` and

maxIdleSwap. A session object will be swapped out if its
lastAccessedTime is exceeds both minIdleSwap and maxIdleSwap. To
prevent any swapping out, you can set the maxIdleSwap to a negative number.
(See the processMaxIdleSwaps method)

Because an active session can be swapped out, it can either reside in memory
or in a store. Therefore, the findSession(String id) method first looks
for the Session instance in the memory and, if none is found, in the store.
Here is the method implementation in the PersistentManagerBase class.

```
public Session findSession(String id) throws IOException {
  Session session = super.findSession(id);
  if (session != null)
    return (session);
  // not found in memory, see if the Session is in the Store
  session = swapIn(id); // swapIn returns an active session in the
                        // Store
  return (session);
}
```

Back-up

Not all active session objects are backed up. A PersistentManagerBase
instance only backs up session objects that have been idle longer than the value
of maxIdleBackup. The processMaxIdleBackups method performs the
session object back-up.

PersistentManager

The PersistentManager class extends PersistentManagerBase. There
is not much addition here, except two properties. The PersistentManager
class is given in Listing 9.5.

Listing 9.5: The PersistentManager class

```
package org.apache.catalina.session;
public final class PersistentManager extends PersistentManagerBase {
  // The descriptive information about this implementation.
  private static final String info = "PersistentManager/1.0";
  // The descriptive name of this Manager implementation (for logging).
  protected static String name = "PersistentManager";
  public String getInfo() {
    return (this.info);
  }
  public String getName() {
    return (name);
  }
}
```

DistributedManager

Tomcat 4 provides the `DistrubutedManager` class. A subclass of `PersistentManagerBase`, `DistributedManager` is used in a clustered environment with two or more nodes. A node represents a Tomcat deployment. Nodes in a cluster can exist in different machines or the same machine. In a clustered environment, each node must use an instance of `DistributedManager` as its `Manager` to support session replication, which is the main responsibility of `DistributedManager`.

For the replication purpose, `DistributedManager` sends notification to other nodes whenever a session object is created or destroyed. In addition, a node must be able to receive notification from other nodes as well. This way, an HTTP request can be served by any node in the cluster.

For sending and receiving notification to and from other instances of `DistributedManager` in other nodes, Catalina provides classes in the `org.apache.catalina.cluster` package. Among others, the `ClusterSender` class is used for sending notifications to other nodes and the `ClusterReceiver` class for receiving notifications from other nodes.

The `createSession` method of `DistrbutedManager` must create a session object to be stored in the current instance *and* use a `ClusterSender` instance to send notification to other nodes. Listing 9.6 presents the `createSession` method.

Listing 9.6: The createSession method

```
public Session createSession() {
  Session session = super.createSession();
  ObjectOutputStream oos = null;
  ByteArrayOutputStream bos = null;
  ByteArrayInputStream bis = null;

  try {
    bos = new ByteArrayOutputStream();
    oos = new ObjectOutputStream(new BufferedOutputStream(bos));

    ((StandardSession)session).writeObjectData(oos);
    oos.close();
    byte[] obs = bos.toByteArray();
    clusterSender.send(obs);
    if(debug > 0)
      log("Replicating Session: "+session.getId());
  }
  catch (IOException e) {
    log("An error occurred when replicating Session: " +
      session.getId());
  }
```

```
  return (session);
}
```

First, the `createSession` method calls the super class's `createSession` method to create a session object for itself. Then, it sends the session object as an array of bytes using the `ClusterSender`.

The `DistributedManager` class also implements `java.lang.Runnable` to have a separate thread for expiring session objects and receive notification from other nodes. The `run` method is as follows.

```
public void run() {
  // Loop until the termination semaphore is set
  while (!threadDone) {
    threadSleep();
    processClusterReceiver();
    processExpires();
    processPersistenceChecks();
  }
}
```

What's worth noting in this method is the call to the `processClusterReceiver` method that processes session create notification from other nodes.

Stores

A store, represented by the `org.apache.catalina.Store` interface, is a component that provides a permanent storage for sessions managed by a manager. The `Store` interface is given in Listing 9.7.

Listing 9.7: The Store interface

```
package org.apache.catalina;
import java.beans.PropertyChangeListener;
import java.io.IOException;

public interface Store {
  public String getInfo();
  public Manager getManager();
  public void setManager(Manager manager);
  public int getSize() throws IOException;
  public void addPropertyChangeListener(PropertyChangeListener
    listener);
  public String[] keys() throws IOException;
  public Session load(String id)
    throws ClassNotFoundException, IOException;
  public void remove(String id) throws IOException;
  public void clear() throws IOException;
  public void removePropertyChangeListener(PropertyChangeListener
```

```
    listener);
  public void save(Session session) throws IOException;
}
```

The two most important methods in the `Store` interface are `save` and `load`. The `save` method saves the specified session object to a permanent storage. The `load` method loads the session object with a given session identifier from the storage. Also, the `keys` method returns a `String` array containing all session identifiers.

The UML diagram for the `Store` interface and its implementation classes is given in Figure 9.3. Note that the `org.apache.catalina` prefix has been omitted from all type names.

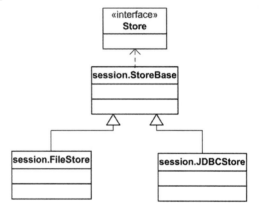

Figure 9.3: The Store interface and its implementations

The following sub-sections discuss the `StoreBase`, `FileStore`, and `JDBCStore` classes.

StoreBase

The `StoreBase` class is an abstract class that provides common functionality for the two child classes: `FileStore` and `JDBCStore`. The `StoreBase` class does not implement the `Store` interface's `save` and `load` methods because the implementations of these methods depend on the type of storage to persist sessions to.

The `StoreBase` class in Tomcat 4 employs a separate thread to regularly check for expired session and remove expired sessions from the collection of active sessions. Here is the `run` method in `StoreBase` in Tomcat 4.

```
public void run() {
  // Loop until the termination semaphore is set
  while (!threadDone) {
    threadSleep();
    processExpires();
  }
}
```

The `processExpires` method retrieves all active sessions and checks the `lastAccessedTime` value of each session, and removes the session objects that have been inactive for too long. The `processExpires` method is given in Listing 9.7.

Listing 9.7: the processExpires method

```
protected void processExpires() {
  long timeNow = System.currentTimeMillis();
  String[] keys = null;
  if (!started)
    return;
  try {
    keys = keys();
  }
  catch (IOException e) {
    log (e.toString());
    e.printStackTrace();
    return;
  }

  for (int i = 0; i < keys.length; i++) {
    try {
      StandardSession session = (StandardSession) load(keys[i]);
      if (!session.isValid())
        continue;
      int maxInactiveInterval = session.getMaxInactiveInterval();
      if (maxInactiveInterval < 0)
        continue;
      int timeIdle = // Truncate, do not round up
        (int) ((timeNow - session.getLastAccessedTime()) / 1000L);
      if (timeIdle >= maxInactiveInterval) {
        if ( ( (PersistentManagerBase) manager).isLoaded( keys[i] )) {
          // recycle old backup session
          session.recycle();
        }
        else {
          // expire swapped out session
          session.expire();
        }
        remove(session.getId());
      }
    }
    catch (IOException e) {
      log (e.toString());
      e.printStackTrace();
```

```
    }
    catch (ClassNotFoundException e) {
      log (e.toString());
      e.printStackTrace();
    }
  }
}
```

In Tomcat 5 there is no special thread for calling the `processExpires` method. Instead, this method is periodically called by the `backgroundProcess` method of the associated `PersistentManagerBase` instance.

FileStore

The `FileStore` class stores session objects in a file. The file is named the same as the identifier of the session object plus the extension .session. This file resides in the temporary work directory. You can change the temporary directory by calling the `FileStore` class's `setDirectory`.

The `java.io.ObjectOutputStream` class is used in the `save` method to serialize the session objects. Therefore, all objects stored in a `Session` instance must implement `java.lang.Serializable`. To deserialize a session object in the `load` method, the `java.io.ObjectInputStream` class is used.

JDBCStore

The `JDBCStore` class stores session objects in a database and transfers are done through JDBC. As such, to use `JDBCStore` you need to set the driver name and the connection URL by calling the `setDriverName` and `setConnectionURL` respectively.

The Application

The application accompanying this article is similar to the one in Chapter 8. It uses the default connector and has a context as its main container with one wrapper. One difference, however, is that the context in this application has a `StandardManager` instance to manage session objects. To test this application, you use the third example servlet `SessionServlet`. This servlet is represented by a wrapper named `wrapper1`.

Note
You can find the `SessionServlet` class under the myApp/WEB-INF/classes directory.

The application has two packages, `ex09.pyrmont.core` and `ex09.pyrmont.startup`, and uses various classes in Catalina. There are four classes in the `ex09.pyrmont.core` package: `SimpleContextConfig`, `SimplePipeline`, `SimpleWrapper`, and `SimpleWrapperValve`. The first three classes are simply copies of the same classes in Chapter 8. There are, however, two additional lines of code in the `SimpleWrapperValve` class. The `ex09.pyrmont.startup` package has one class: `Bootstrap`.

The `Bootstrap` class is explained in the first sub-section of this section and the `SimpleWrapperValve` class in the second sub-section. The last sub-section discusses how to run the application.

The Bootstrap Class

The `Bootstrap` class starts the application and it is very similar to the `Bootstrap` class in Chapter 8. However, the `Bootstrap` class in this chapter creates an instance of the `org.apache.catalina.session.StandardManager` class and associate it with the `Context`.

The `main` method starts by setting the `catalina.base` system property and instantiating the default connector.

```
System.setProperty("catalina.base",
  System.getProperty("user.dir"));
Connector connector = new HttpConnector();
```

For the `SessionServlet`, it creates a wrapper called `wrapper1`.

```
Wrapper wrapper1 = new SimpleWrapper();
wrapper1.setName("Session");
wrapper1.setServletClass("SessionServlet");
```

Then, it creates a `StandardContext` object, sets its `path` and `docBase` properties, and adds the wrapper to the context.

```
Context context = new StandardContext();
context.setPath("/myApp");
context.setDocBase("myApp");
context.addChild(wrapper1);
```

Next, the `start` method continues by adding a servlet mapping. The mapping is different from the ones in the application in Chapter 8. Instead of `/Session`, we use `/myApp/Session` as the pattern. This is required because we set the path name of the context to `/myApp`. The path name will be used to send the session cookie, and the browser will only send the cookie back to the server if the path is also `/myApp`.

```
context.addServletMapping("/myApp/Session", "Session");
```

The URL used to request SessionServlet is as follows.

```
http://localhost:8080/myApp/Session.
```

Just like in Chapter 8, we need a listener and a loader for the context.

```
LifecycleListener listener = new SimpleContextConfig();
((Lifecycle) context).addLifecycleListener(listener);

// here is our loader
Loader loader = new WebappLoader();
// associate the loader with the Context
context.setLoader(loader);
connector.setContainer(context);
```

Now, new to this application is a manager. We use an instance of `StandardManager` and pass it to the context.

```
Manager manager = new StandardManager();
context.setManager(manager);
```

Finally, we initialize and start the connector and start the context.

```
connector.initialize();
((Lifecycle) connector).start();
((Lifecycle) context).start();
```

The SimpleWrapperValve Class

Recall that at the beginning of this chapter, we mentioned that the servlet can get a session object by calling the `getSession` method of the `javax.servlet.http.HttpServletRequest` interface. When the `getSession` method is invoked, the request object must somehow call the manager associated with the context. The manager either creates a new session object or returns the existing one. For the request object to be able to access the manager, it must have access to the context. To achieve this, in the `invoke` method of the `SimpleWrapperValve` class, you call the `setContext` method of the `org.apache.catalina.Request` interface, passing the `Context`. Remember that the `SimpleWrapperValve` class's `invoke` method calls the requested servlet's `service` method. Therefore, you must set the `Context` before the servlet's `service` method is called. The `invoke` method of the `SimpleWrapperValve` class is given in Listing 9.8. The highlighted lines are the addition to this class.

Listing 9.8: The invoke method of the SimpleWrapperValve class

```
public void invoke(Request request, Response response,
  ValveContext valveContext) throws IOException, ServletException {

  SimpleWrapper wrapper = (SimpleWrapper) getContainer();
  ServletRequest sreq = request.getRequest();
  ServletResponse sres = response.getResponse();
  Servlet servlet = null;
  HttpServletRequest hreq = null;
  if (sreq instanceof HttpServletRequest)
    hreq = (HttpServletRequest) sreq;
  HttpServletResponse hres = null;
  if (sres instanceof HttpServletResponse)
    hres = (HttpServletResponse) sres;

  // pass the Context to the Request object so that
  // the Request object can call the Manager
  Context context = (Context) wrapper.getParent();
  request.setContext(context);

  // Allocate a servlet instance to process this request
  try {
    servlet = wrapper.allocate();
    if (hres!=null && hreq!=null) {
      servlet.service(hreq, hres);
    }
    else {
      servlet.service(sreq, sres);
    }
  }
  catch (ServletException e) {
  }
}
```

You have access to the wrapper, therefore you can obtain the context by calling the `getParent` method of the `Container` interface. Note that the wrapper was added to a context. Once you have the context, you can then call the `setContext` method of the `Request` interface.

As explained at the beginning of the chapter, the private `doGetSession` method in the `org.apache.catalina.connector.HttpRequestBase` class can then call the `getManager` method of the `Context` interface to obtain the manager.

```
  // Return the requested session if it exists and is valid
  Manager manager = null;
  if (context != null)
```

```
manager = context.getManager();
```

Once you have the manager, obtaining a session object or creating a new one is straightforward.

Running the Application

To run the application in Windows, from the working directory, type the following:

```
java -classpath ./lib/servlet.jar;./lib/commons-collections.jar;./
ex09.pyrmont.startup.Bootstrap
```

In Linux, you use a colon to separate between libraries.

```
java -classpath ./lib/servlet.jar:./lib/commons-collections.jar:./
ex09.pyrmont.startup.Bootstrap
```

To invoke the `SessionServlet` servlet, you use the following URL in your browser.

```
http://localhost:8080/myApp/Session
```

`SessionServlet` uses a session object to store a value. This servlet displays the previous value and the current value in the Session object. It also displays a form that the user can use to enter a new value. Figure 9.4 displays the output from `SessionServlet` when it is first invoked.

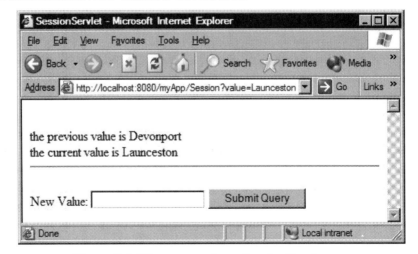

Figure 9.4: The output from SessionServlet

Summary

This chapter discussed the manager, the component that manages sessions in the session management. It explained the types of managers and how a manager can persist session objects into a store. At the end of the chapter, you have learned how to build an application that uses a `StandardManager` instance to run a servlet that uses session objects to store values.

188

Chapter 10
Security

Some contents of a web application are restricted, and only authorized users are allowed to view them, after they supplied the correct user name and password. The servlet technology supports applying security constraint to those contents via the configuration of the deployment descriptor (web.xml file). Now, in this chapter, we will look at how a web container supports the security constraint feature.

A servlet container supports security constraint through a valve called authenticator. The authenticator valve is added to a context's pipeline when the servlet container is started. Read Chapter 6 again if you have forgotten about how a pipeline works.

The authenticator valve is called before the wrapper valve. The authenticator valve authenticates the user. If the user enters the correct user name and password, the authenticator valve calls the next valve, which displays the requested servlet. If the authentication fails, the authenticator valve returns without invoking the next valve. As a result of a failed authentication, the user does not see the requested servlet.

The authenticator valve calls the `authenticate` method of the context's realm to authenticate the user, passing the user name and password. A realm has access to the collection of valid user names and passwords.

This chapter starts with the classes that represent the objects related to the security feature in servlet programming (realms, principals, roles, etc). It then presents an application that demonstrates how you can apply basic authentication to your servlets.

Note
It is assumed that you are familiar with the security constraint concept in servlet programming, including principals, roles, realms, login configuration, etc. If you do not understand them, read my own *Java for the Web with Servlets, JSP, and EJB* or any other decent servlet programming book.

Realm

A realm is a component used for authenticating a user. It can tell you whether or not a pair of user name and password is valid. A realm is normally attached to a context, and a container can only have one realm. You attach a realm to a container by passing the realm to the setRealm method of the container.

How does a realm know how to authenticate a user? Well, it contains all user names and passwords of valid users or it has access to the store that holds them. Where this information is stored depends on the realm implementation. In Tomcat, by default valid users are stored in the tomcat-users.xml file. However, you can use other realm implementation that authenticates against other sources, such as a relational database.

In Catalina, a realm is represented by the org.apache.catalina.Realm interface. The most important methods are its four authenticate method overloads:

```
public Principal authenticate(String username, String credentials);
public Principal authenticate(String username, byte[] credentials);
public Principal authenticate(String username, String digest,
   String nonce, String nc, String cnonce, String qop, String realm,
   String md5a2);
public Principal authenticate(X509Certificate certs[]);
```

The first overload is normally used. The Realm interface also has the hasRole method whose signature is as follows:

```
public boolean hasRole(Principal principal, String role);
```

Also, the getContainer and setContainer methods are used to associate a realm with a container.

A base implementation for the Realm interface is provided in the form of the abstract class org.apache.catalina.realm.RealmBase. The org.apache.catalina.realm package also provides a number of implementation classes that extend RealmBase: JDBCRealm, JNDIRealm, MemoryRealm, and UserDatabaseRealm. By default, MemoryRealm is used. When the MemoryRealm is first started, it reads the tomcat-users.xml document. In the application accompanying this chapter, however, you will build a simple realm that stores user information in the object itself.

Note
In Catalina, the authenticator valve calls the authenticate method of the attached realm to authenticate a user.

GenericPrincipal

A principal is represented by the `java.security.Principal` interface. Its implementation in Catalina is the `org.apache.catalina.realm.GenericPrincipal` class. A `GenericPrincipal` must always be associated with a realm, as shown by the two constructors of `GenericPrincipal`:

```
public GenericPrincipal(Realm realm, String name, String password) {
  this(realm, name, password, null);
}
public GenericPrincipal(Realm realm, String name, String password,
  List roles) {
  super();
  this.realm = realm;
  this.name = name;
  this.password = password;
  if (roles != null) {
    this.roles = new String[roles.size()];
    this.roles = (String[]) roles.toArray(this.roles);
    if (this.roles.length > 0)
      Arrays.sort(this.roles);
  }
}
```

A `GenericPrincipal` must also have a name and a password. Optionally, you can pass a list of roles to it. You can then check if this principal has a specified role by calling its `hasRole` method, passing the string representation of the role. Here is the `hasRole` method in Tomcat 4.

```
public boolean hasRole(String role) {
  if (role == null)
    return (false);
  return (Arrays.binarySearch(roles, role) >= 0);
}
```

Tomcat 5 supports Servlet 2.4 and therefore must recognize that the special character * represents any role.

```
public boolean hasRole(String role) {
  if ("*".equals(role)) // Special 2.4 role meaning everyone
    return true;
  if (role == null)
    return (false);
  return (Arrays.binarySearch(roles, role) >= 0);
}
```

LoginConfig

A login configuration contains a realm name and is represented by the
`org.apache.catalina.deploy.LoginConfig` final class. The
`LoginConfig` instance encapsulates the realm name and the authentication
method used. You obtain the realm name by calling the `LoginConfig`
instance's `getRealmName` method and the authentication method by invoking
its `getAuthName` method. The value of the authentication name must be one
of the following: `BASIC`, `DIGEST`, `FORM`, or `CLIENT-CERT`. If form-based
authentication is used, the `LoginConfig` object also contains the string
representations of the URLs to the login and error pages in its `loginPage` and
`errorPage` properties, respectively.

In a deployment, Tomcat reads the web.xml file at start-up. If the web.xml
file contains a `login-config` element, Tomcat creates a `LoginConfig` object
and sets its properties accordingly. The authenticator valve calls the
`getRealmName` method of the `LoginConfig` and sends the realm name to
the browser to be displayed in the Login dialog. If the `getRealmName` method
returns `null`, the server name and port is sent to the browser instead. Figure
10.1 shows a basic authentication login dialog in Internet Explorer 6 on
Windows XP.

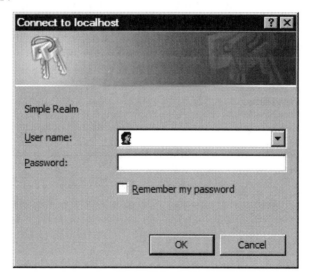

Figure 10.1: The basic authentication dialog

Authenticator

The org.apache.catalina.Authenticator interface represents an authenticator. It does not have a method and acts as a marker so that other components can detect whether or not a component is an authenticator by using an instanceof test.

Catalina provides a base implementation of the Authenticator interface: the org.apache.catalina.authenticator.AuthenticatorBase class. In addition to implementing the Authenticator interface, AuthenticatorBase extends the org.apache.catalina.valves.ValveBase class. That means, AuthenticatorBase is also a valve. A number of implementation classes can be found in the org.apache.catalina.authenticator package, including the BasicAuthenticator class that can be used for basic authentication, the FormAuthenticator class for form-based authentication, DigestAuthentication for digest authentication, and SSLAuthenticator for SSL authentication. In addition, the NonLoginAuthenticator class is used if the user of Tomcat does not specify a value for the auth-method element. The NonLoginAuthenticator class represents an authenticator that only checks security constraints but does not involve user authentication.

The UML class diagram of the members of the org.apache.catalina.authenticator package is given in Figure 10.2.

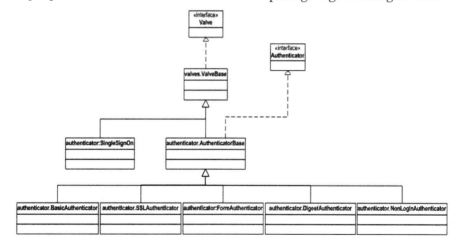

Figure 10.2: Authenticator-related classes

The main job of an authenticator is to authenticate users. Therefore, it's not surprising that the invoke method of AuthenticatorBase calls the abstract method authenticate whose implementation depends on the child class. In BasicAuthenticator, for example, the authenticate method uses basic authentication to authenticate the user.

Installing the Authenticator Valve

The login-config element can only appear once in the deployment descriptor, and the login-config element contains the auth-method element that specifies the authentication method. This is to say a context can only have one instance of LoginConfig object and employs one authentication class implementation.

Which child class of AuthenticatorBase will be used as the authenticator valve in a context depends on the value of the auth-method element in the deployment descriptor. Table 10.1 presents the class name of the authenticator that will be used for a given auth-method element value.

Value of the auth-method element	Authenticator class
BASIC	BasicAuthenticator
FORM	FormAuthenticator
DIGEST	DigestAuthenticator
CLIENT-CERT	SSLAuthenticator

Table 10.1: The authenticator implementation class

If the auth-method element is not present, the value of the auth-method property of the LoginConfig object is assumed to be NONE, and the NonLoginAuthenticator class will be used.

Because the authenticator class is only known at runtime, the class is dynamically loaded. The StandardContext class uses the org.apache.catalina.startup.ContextConfig class to configure many settings of the StandardContext instance. This configuration includes the instantiation of an authenticator class and associating the instance with the context. The application that accompanies this chapter employs a simple context config of type ex10.pyrmont.core.SimpleContextConfig. As you can see later, the instance of this class is responsible for dynamically loading the

`BasicAuthenticator` class, instantiating it, and installing it as a valve in the `StandardContext` instance.

Note
The `org.apache.catalina.startup.ContextConfig` class will be discussed in Chapter 15.

The Applications

The applications accompanying this chapter use several Catalina classes that are related to security constraint. Both also employ the `SimplePipeline`, `SimpleWrapper`, and `SimpleWrapperValve` classes that are similar to the application in Chapter 9. In addition, the `SimpleContextConfig` class is similar to the `SimpleContextConfig` class in Chapter 9, except that it has the `authenticatorConfig` method that adds a `BasicAuthenticator` instance to the `StandardContext`. Both applications also use two servlets: `PrimitiveServlet` and `ModernServlet`. These classes are used in both accompanying applications.

There are two classes in the first application, `ex10.pyrmont.startup.Bootstrap1` and `ex10.pyrmont.realm.SimpleRealm`. The second application uses `ex10.pyrmont.startup.Bootstrap2` and `ex10.pyrmont.realm.SimpleUserDatabaseRealm`. Each of these classes will be explained in the sections below.

The ex10.pyrmont.core.SimpleContextConfig Class

The `SimpleContextConfig` class in Listing 10.1 is similar to `SimpleContextConfig` in Chapter 9. It is required by the `org.apache.catalina.core.StandardContext` instance to set its `configured` property to `true`. However, the `SimpleContextConfig` class in the application in this chapter adds the `authenticatorConfig` method that is called from the `lifeCycleEvent` method. The `authenticatorConfig` method instantiates the `BasicAuthenticator` class and adds it as a valve to the `StandardContext` instance's pipeline.

Listing 10.1: The SimpleContextConfig class

```
package ex10.pyrmont.core;

import org.apache.catalina.Authenticator;
```

```java
import org.apache.catalina.Context;
import org.apache.catalina.Lifecycle;
import org.apache.catalina.LifecycleEvent;
import org.apache.catalina.LifecycleListener;
import org.apache.catalina.Pipeline;
import org.apache.catalina.Valve;
import org.apache.catalina.core.StandardContext;
import org.apache.catalina.deploy.SecurityConstraint;
import org.apache.catalina.deploy.LoginConfig;

public class SimpleContextConfig implements LifecycleListener {
  private Context context;
  public void lifecycleEvent(LifecycleEvent event) {
    if (Lifecycle.START_EVENT.equals(event.getType())) {
      context = (Context) event.getLifecycle();
      authenticatorConfig();
      context.setConfigured(true);
    }
  }

  private synchronized void authenticatorConfig() {
    // Does this Context require an Authenticator?
    SecurityConstraint constraints[] = context.findConstraints();
    if ((constraints == null) || (constraints.length == 0))
      return;
    LoginConfig loginConfig = context.getLoginConfig();
    if (loginConfig == null) {
      loginConfig = new LoginConfig("NONE", null, null, null);
      context.setLoginConfig(loginConfig);
    }

    // Has an authenticator been configured already?
    Pipeline pipeline = ((StandardContext) context).getPipeline();
    if (pipeline != null) {
      Valve basic = pipeline.getBasic();
      if ((basic != null) && (basic instanceof Authenticator))
        return;
      Valve valves[] = pipeline.getValves();
      for (int i = 0; i < valves.length; i++) {
        if (valves[i] instanceof Authenticator)
        return;
      }
    }
    else { // no Pipeline, cannot install authenticator valve
      return;
    }
    // Has a Realm been configured for us to authenticate against?
    if (context.getRealm() == null) {
      return;
    }
    // Identify the class name of the Valve we should configure
    String authenticatorName =
      "org.apache.catalina.authenticator.BasicAuthenticator";
    // Instantiate and install an Authenticator of the requested class
    Valve authenticator = null;
    try {
```

```
      Class authenticatorClass = Class.forName(authenticatorName);
      authenticator = (Valve) authenticatorClass.newInstance();
      ((StandardContext) context).addValve(authenticator);
      System.out.println("Added authenticator valve to Context");
    }
    catch (Throwable t) {
    }
  }
}
```

The `authenticatorConfig` method starts by checking if there is a security constraint in the associated context. If there is none, the method returns without installing an authenticator.

```
// Does this Context require an Authenticator?
SecurityConstraint constraints[] = context.findConstraints();
if ((constraints == null) || (constraints.length == 0))
  return;
```

If one or more security constraint is found, the `authenticatorConfig` method checks if the context has a `LoginConfig` object. If it does not have a `LoginConfig`, an instance is created.

```
LoginConfig loginConfig = context.getLoginConfig();
if (loginConfig == null) {
  loginConfig = new LoginConfig("NONE", null, null, null);
  context.setLoginConfig(loginConfig);
}
```

The `authenticatorConfig` method then checks if the basic valve or another additional valve in the `StandardContext` object's pipeline is an authenticator. Since a context can only have one authenticator, the `authenticatorConfig` method will return if one of the valves is an authenticator.

```
// Has an authenticator been configured already?
Pipeline pipeline = ((StandardContext) context).getPipeline();
if (pipeline != null) {
  Valve basic = pipeline.getBasic();
  if ((basic != null) && (basic instanceof Authenticator))
    return;
  Valve valves[] = pipeline.getValves();
  for (int i = 0; i < valves.length; i++) {
    if (valves[i] instanceof Authenticator)
    return;
  }
}
else { // no Pipeline, cannot install authenticator valve
  return;
}
```

It then checks if a realm has been associated with the context. If no realm is found, there is no need to install an authenticator because the user cannot be authenticated against.

```
// Has a Realm been configured for us to authenticate against?
if (context.getRealm() == null) {
  return;
}
```

At this point, the authenticatorConfig method will load the BasicAuthenticator class dynamically, creates an instance of the class, and adds it as a valve to the StandardContext instance.

```
// Identify the class name of the Valve we should configure
String authenticatorName =
  "org.apache.catalina.authenticator.BasicAuthenticator";
// Instantiate and install an Authenticator of the requested class
Valve authenticator = null;
try {
  Class authenticatorClass = Class.forName(authenticatorName);
  authenticator = (Valve) authenticatorClass.newInstance();
  ((StandardContext) context).addValve(authenticator);
  System.out.println("Added authenticator valve to Context");
}
catch (Throwable t) {    }
}
```

The ex10.pyrmont.realm.SimpleRealm Class

The SimpleRealm class in Listing 10.2 demonstrates how a realm works. This class is used in the first application in this chapter and contains two hard-coded user names and password.

Listing 10.2: The SimpleRealm Class

```
package ex10.pyrmont.realm;

import java.beans.PropertyChangeListener;
import java.security.Principal;
import java.security.cert.X509Certificate;
import java.util.ArrayList;
import java.util.Iterator;
import org.apache.catalina.Container;
import org.apache.catalina.Realm;
import org.apache.catalina.realm.GenericPrincipal;


public class SimpleRealm implements Realm {
  public SimpleRealm() {
    createUserDatabase();
  }
  private Container container;
```

```java
  private ArrayList users = new ArrayList();
  public Container getContainer() {
    return container;
  }
  public void setContainer(Container container) {
    this.container = container;
  }
  public String getInfo() {
    return "A simple Realm implementation";
  }
  public void addPropertyChangeListener(PropertyChangeListener
    listener) {  }
  public Principal authenticate(String username, String credentials) {
    System.out.println("SimpleRealm.authenticate()");
    if (username==null || credentials==null)
      return null;
    User user = getUser(username, credentials);
    if (user==null)
      return null;
    return new GenericPrincipal(this, user.username,
      user.password, user.getRoles());
  }

  public Principal authenticate(String username, byte[] credentials) {
    return null;
  }
  public Principal authenticate(String username, String digest,
    String nonce, String nc, String cnonce, String qop, String realm,
    String md5a2) {
    return null;
  }
  public Principal authenticate(X509Certificate certs[]) {
    return null;
  }
  public boolean hasRole(Principal principal, String role) {
    if ((principal == null) || (role == null) ||
      !(principal instanceof GenericPrincipal))
      return (false);
    GenericPrincipal gp = (GenericPrincipal) principal;
    if (!(gp.getRealm() == this))
      return (false);
    boolean result = gp.hasRole(role);
    return result;
  }
  public void removePropertyChangeListener(PropertyChangeListener
    listener) {  }
  private User getUser(String username, String password) {
    Iterator iterator = users.iterator();
    while (iterator.hasNext()) {
      User user = (User) iterator.next();
      if (user.username.equals(username) &&
        user.password.equals(password))
        return user;
    }
    return null;
  }
```

```
private void createUserDatabase() {
  User user1 = new User("ken", "blackcomb");
  user1.addRole("manager");
  user1.addRole("programmer");
  User user2 = new User("cindy", "bamboo");
  user2.addRole("programmer");

  users.add(user1);
  users.add(user2);
}

class User {
  public User(String username, String password) {
    this.username = username;
    this.password = password;
  }
  public String username;
  public ArrayList roles = new ArrayList();
  public String password;
  public void addRole(String role) {
    roles.add(role);
  }
  public ArrayList getRoles() {
    return roles;
  }
}
}
```

The SimpleRealm class implements the Realm interface. From the constructor, it calls the createUserDatabase method that creates two users. Internally, a user is represented by the inner class User. The first user has the user name ken and password blackcomb. This user has two roles, manager and programmer. The second user's user name and password are cindy and bamboo, respectively. This user has the programmer role. Then, the two users are added to the users ArrayList. The code that creates the two users are as follows:

```
User user1 = new User("ken", "blackcomb");
user1.addRole("manager");
user1.addRole("programmer");
User user2 = new User("cindy", "bamboo");
user2.addRole("programmer");
users.add(user1);
users.add(user2);
```

The SimpleRealm class provides the implementation of one of the four authenticate method overloads.

```
public Principal authenticate(String username, String credentials) {
  System.out.println("SimpleRealm.authenticate()");
  if (username==null || credentials==null)
    return null;
  User user = getUser(username, credentials);
  if (user==null)
```

```
      return null;
    return new GenericPrincipal(this, user.username,
      user.password, user.getRoles());
  }
```

This `authenticate` method is called by an authenticator. It returns `null` if the user whose user name and password are passed as arguments is not a valid user. Otherwise, it returns a `Principal` object representing the user.

The ex10.pyrmont.realm.SimpleUserDatabaseRealm Class

The `SimpleUserDatabaseRealm` class represents a more complex realm. It does not store the list of users in its body. Instead, it reads the tomcat-users.xml file in the conf directory and loads the content to the memory. Authentication is then conducted against this list. In the conf directory of the accompanying zip file, you can find a copy of the tomcat-users.xml file as follows:

```
<?xml version='1.0' encoding='utf-8'?>
<tomcat-users>
  <role rolename="tomcat"/>
  <role rolename="role1"/>
  <role rolename="manager"/>
  <role rolename="admin"/>
  <user username="tomcat" password="tomcat" roles="tomcat"/>
  <user username="role1" password="tomcat" roles="role1"/>
  <user username="both" password="tomcat" roles="tomcat,role1"/>
  <user username="admin" password="password" roles="admin,manager"/>
</tomcat-users>
```

The `SimpleUserDatabaseRealm` class is given in Listing 10.3.

Listing 10.3: The SimpleUserDatabaseRealm class

```
package ex10.pyrmont.realm;
// modification of org.apache.catalina.realm.UserDatabaseRealm
import java.security.Principal;
import java.util.ArrayList;
import java.util.Iterator;
import org.apache.catalina.Group;
import org.apache.catalina.Role;
import org.apache.catalina.User;
import org.apache.catalina.UserDatabase;
import org.apache.catalina.realm.GenericPrincipal;
import org.apache.catalina.realm.RealmBase;
import org.apache.catalina.users.MemoryUserDatabase;

public class SimpleUserDatabaseRealm extends RealmBase {
  protected UserDatabase database = null;
  protected static final String name = "SimpleUserDatabaseRealm";
```

```
protected String resourceName = "UserDatabase";
public Principal authenticate(String username, String credentials) {
  // Does a user with this username exist?
  User user = database.findUser(username);
  if (user == null) {
    return (null);
  }
  // Do the credentials specified by the user match?
  boolean validated = false;
  if (hasMessageDigest()) {
    // Hex hashes should be compared case-insensitive
    validated =
      (digest(credentials).equalsIgnoreCase(user.getPassword()));
  }
  else {
    validated = (digest(credentials).equals(user.getPassword()));
  }
  if (!validated) {
    return null;
  }

  ArrayList combined = new ArrayList();
  Iterator roles = user.getRoles();
  while (roles.hasNext()) {
    Role role = (Role) roles.next();
    String rolename = role.getRolename();
    if (!combined.contains(rolename)) {
      combined.add(rolename);
    }
  }
  Iterator groups = user.getGroups();
  while (groups.hasNext()) {
    Group group = (Group) groups.next();
    roles = group.getRoles();
    while (roles.hasNext()) {
      Role role = (Role) roles.next();
      String rolename = role.getRolename();
      if (!combined.contains(rolename)) {
        combined.add(rolename);
      }
    }
  }
  return (new GenericPrincipal(this, user.getUsername(),
    user.getPassword(), combined));
}

protected Principal getPrincipal(String username) {
  return (null);
}
protected String getPassword(String username) {
  return null;
}
protected String getName() {
  return this.name;
}
public void createDatabase(String path) {
```

```
    database = new MemoryUserDatabase(name);
    ((MemoryUserDatabase) database).setPathname(path);
    try {
      database.open();
    }
    catch (Exception e)  {
    }
  }
}
```

After instantiating the `SimpleUserDatabaseRealm` class, you must call its `createDatabase` method passing the path to the XML document containing the list of users. The `createDatabase` method instantiates the `org.apache.catalina.users.MemoryUserDatabase` class that performs the reading and parsing of the XML document.

The ex10.pyrmont.startup.Bootstrap1 Class

The `Bootstrap1` class starts the first application in this chapter. It is given in Listing 10.4.

Listing 10.4: The Bootstrap1 Class

```java
package ex10.pyrmont.startup;

import ex10.pyrmont.core.SimpleWrapper;
import ex10.pyrmont.core.SimpleContextConfig;
import ex10.pyrmont.realm.SimpleRealm;
import org.apache.catalina.Connector;
import org.apache.catalina.Context;
import org.apache.catalina.Lifecycle;
import org.apache.catalina.LifecycleListener;
import org.apache.catalina.Loader;
import org.apache.catalina.Realm;
import org.apache.catalina.Wrapper;
import org.apache.catalina.connector.http.HttpConnector;
import org.apache.catalina.core.StandardContext;
import org.apache.catalina.deploy.LoginConfig;
import org.apache.catalina.deploy.SecurityCollection;
import org.apache.catalina.deploy.SecurityConstraint;
import org.apache.catalina.loader.WebappLoader;

public final class Bootstrap1 {
  public static void main(String[] args) {
    System.setProperty("catalina.base",
      System.getProperty("user.dir"));
    Connector connector = new HttpConnector();
    Wrapper wrapper1 = new SimpleWrapper();
    wrapper1.setName("Primitive");
    wrapper1.setServletClass("PrimitiveServlet");
    Wrapper wrapper2 = new SimpleWrapper();
    wrapper2.setName("Modern");
```

```java
    wrapper2.setServletClass("ModernServlet");

    Context context = new StandardContext();
    // StandardContext's start method adds a default mapper
    context.setPath("/myApp");
    context.setDocBase("myApp");
    LifecycleListener listener = new SimpleContextConfig();
    ((Lifecycle) context).addLifecycleListener(listener);

    context.addChild(wrapper1);
    context.addChild(wrapper2);
    // for simplicity, we don't add a valve, but you can add
    // valves to context or wrapper just as you did in Chapter 6

    Loader loader = new WebappLoader();
    context.setLoader(loader);
    // context.addServletMapping(pattern, name);
    context.addServletMapping("/Primitive", "Primitive");
    context.addServletMapping("/Modern", "Modern");
    // add ContextConfig. This listener is important because it
    // configures StandardContext (sets configured to true), otherwise
    // StandardContext won't start

    // add constraint
    SecurityCollection securityCollection = new SecurityCollection();
    securityCollection.addPattern("/");
    securityCollection.addMethod("GET");

    SecurityConstraint constraint = new SecurityConstraint();
    constraint.addCollection(securityCollection);
    constraint.addAuthRole("manager");
    LoginConfig loginConfig = new LoginConfig();
    loginConfig.setRealmName("Simple Realm");
    // add realm
    Realm realm = new SimpleRealm();

    context.setRealm(realm);
    context.addConstraint(constraint);
    context.setLoginConfig(loginConfig);

    connector.setContainer(context);

    try {
      connector.initialize();
      ((Lifecycle) connector).start();
      ((Lifecycle) context).start();

      // make the application wait until we press a key.
      System.in.read();
      ((Lifecycle) context).stop();
    }
    catch (Exception e) {
      e.printStackTrace();
    }
  }
}
```

The `main` method of the `Bootstrap1` class creates two `SimpleWrapper` objects and calls their `setName` and `setServletClass` methods. To the first `SimpleWrapper` object, you pass `Primitive` to its `setName` method and `PrimitiveServlet` to its `setServletClass` method. The second `SimpleWrapper` object gets `Modern` and `ModernServlet`.

The `main` method then creates a `StandardContext` object, sets its path and document base, and adds a listener of type `SimpleContextConfig`. Remember that the latter will install a `BasicAuthenticator` in the `StandardContext` object. Next, it adds a loader to the `StandardContext` and two servlet mappings. You have seen the same code in the application in Chapter 9. The next lines of code are new.

```
// add constraint
SecurityCollection securityCollection = new SecurityCollection();
securityCollection.addPattern("/");
securityCollection.addMethod("GET");
```

The `main` method creates a `SecurityCollection` object and calls its `addPattern` and `addMethod` methods. The `addPattern` method specifies the URL to which security constraint will apply. The `addMethod` method adds a method that is subject to this constraint. The `addMethod` method gets `GET`, so HTTP requests with a GET method will be subject to the security constraint.

Next, the `main` method instantiates the `SecurityConstraint` class and adds it to the collection. It also sets the role that can have access to the restricted resources. By passing `manager`, those users in the manager role will be able to view the resources. Note that the `SimpleRealm` class has only one user with the manager role, `ken`. His password is `blackcomb`.

```
SecurityConstraint constraint = new SecurityConstraint();
constraint.addCollection(securityCollection);
constraint.addAuthRole("manager");
```

Next, the `main` method creates a `LoginConfig` object and a `SimpleRealm` object.

```
LoginConfig loginConfig = new LoginConfig();
loginConfig.setRealmName("Simple Realm");
// add realm
Realm realm = new SimpleRealm();
```

Then, it associates the realm, constraint, and login config objects with the `StandardContext` instance:

```
context.setRealm(realm);
context.addConstraint(constraint);
context.setLoginConfig(loginConfig);
```

Next, it starts the context. This part has been explained in the previous chapters.

In effect, access to `PrimitiveServlet` and `ModernServlet` are now restricted. If a user requests any of the servlets, he/she must be authenticated using basic authentication. Only after he/she types in the correct user name and password (in this case, ken and blackcomb), will he/she be allowed access.

The ex10.pyrmont.startup.Bootstrap2 Class

The `Bootstrap2` class starts up the second application. This class is similar to the `Bootstrap1` class, except that it uses an instance of `SimpleUserDatabase` as a realm associated to the `StandardContext`. To access `PrimitiveServlet` and `ModernServlet`, the correct user name and password would be admin and password, respectively.

The `Bootstrap2` class is given in Listing 10.5.

Listing 10.5: The Bootstrap2 class

```
package ex10.pyrmont.startup;

import ex10.pyrmont.core.SimpleWrapper;
import ex10.pyrmont.core.SimpleContextConfig;
import ex10.pyrmont.realm.SimpleUserDatabaseRealm;
import org.apache.catalina.Connector;
import org.apache.catalina.Context;
import org.apache.catalina.Lifecycle;
import org.apache.catalina.LifecycleListener;
import org.apache.catalina.Loader;
import org.apache.catalina.Realm;
import org.apache.catalina.Wrapper;
import org.apache.catalina.connector.http.HttpConnector;
import org.apache.catalina.core.StandardContext;
import org.apache.catalina.deploy.LoginConfig;
import org.apache.catalina.deploy.SecurityCollection;
import org.apache.catalina.deploy.SecurityConstraint;
import org.apache.catalina.loader.WebappLoader;

public final class Bootstrap2 {
  public static void main(String[] args) {
    System.setProperty("catalina.base",
      System.getProperty("user.dir"));
    Connector connector = new HttpConnector();
    Wrapper wrapper1 = new SimpleWrapper();
    wrapper1.setName("Primitive");
    wrapper1.setServletClass("PrimitiveServlet");
    Wrapper wrapper2 = new SimpleWrapper();
    wrapper2.setName("Modern");
    wrapper2.setServletClass("ModernServlet");

    Context context = new StandardContext();
```

```
    // StandardContext's start method adds a default mapper
    context.setPath("/myApp");
    context.setDocBase("myApp");
    LifecycleListener listener = new SimpleContextConfig();
    ((Lifecycle) context).addLifecycleListener(listener);

    context.addChild(wrapper1);
    context.addChild(wrapper2);
    // for simplicity, we don't add a valve, but you can add
    // valves to context or wrapper just as you did in Chapter 6

    Loader loader = new WebappLoader();
    context.setLoader(loader);
    // context.addServletMapping(pattern, name);
    context.addServletMapping("/Primitive", "Primitive");
    context.addServletMapping("/Modern", "Modern");
    // add ContextConfig. This listener is important because it
    // configures StandardContext (sets configured to true), otherwise
    // StandardContext won't start

    // add constraint
    SecurityCollection securityCollection = new SecurityCollection();
    securityCollection.addPattern("/");
    securityCollection.addMethod("GET");

    SecurityConstraint constraint = new SecurityConstraint();
    constraint.addCollection(securityCollection);
    constraint.addAuthRole("manager");
    LoginConfig loginConfig = new LoginConfig();
    loginConfig.setRealmName("Simple User Database Realm");
    // add realm
    Realm realm = new SimpleUserDatabaseRealm();
    ((SimpleUserDatabaseRealm) realm).
      createDatabase("conf/tomcat-users.xml");
    context.setRealm(realm);
    context.addConstraint(constraint);
    context.setLoginConfig(loginConfig);

    connector.setContainer(context);

    try {
      connector.initialize();
      ((Lifecycle) connector).start();
      ((Lifecycle) context).start();

      // make the application wait until we press a key.
      System.in.read();
      ((Lifecycle) context).stop();
    }
    catch (Exception e) {
      e.printStackTrace();
    }
  }
}
```

Running the Applications

To run the first application in Windows, from the working directory, type the following:

```
java -classpath ./lib/servlet.jar;./lib/commons-collections.jar;./
ex10.pyrmont.startup.Bootstrap1
```

In Linux, you use a colon to separate two libraries.

```
java -classpath ./lib/servlet.jar:./lib/commons-collections.jar:./
ex10.pyrmont.startup.Bootstrap1
```

To run the second application in Windows, from the working directory, type the following:

```
java -classpath ./lib/servlet.jar;./lib/commons-collections.jar;
./lib/commons-digester.jar;./lib/commons-logging.jar;./
ex10.pyrmont.startup.Bootstrap2
```

In Linux, you use a colon to separate two libraries.

```
java -classpath ./lib/servlet.jar:./lib/commons-collections.jar:
./lib/commons-digester.jar:./lib/commons-logging.jar:./
ex10.pyrmont.startup.Bootstrap2
```

To invoke the Primitive servlet in both the first and second applications, use the following URL in your browser.

```
http://localhost:8080/Primitive
```

To invoke the Modern servlet in both the first and second applications, use the following URL in your browser.

```
http://localhost:8080/Modern
```

Summary

Security is an important topic in servlet programming and the servlet specifications cater for the need for security by providing security-related objects such as principal, roles, security constraints, login configuration, etc. In this chapter you have learned how a servlet container addresses this issue.

Chapter 11
StandardWrapper

You have learned in Chapter 5 that there are four types of containers: engine, host, context, and wrapper. You have also built your own simple contexts and wrappers in previous chapters. A context normally has one or more wrappers, in which each wrapper represents a servlet definition. This chapter will now look at the standard implementation of the Wrapper interface in Catalina. It starts by explaining the sequence of methods that get invoked for each HTTP request and continues with the `javax.servlet.SingleThreadModel` interface. The chapter concludes by explaining the `StandardWrapper` and `StandardWrapperValve` classes. The application that accompanies this chapter uses `StandardWrapper` instances to represents servlets.

Sequence of Methods Invocation

For each incoming HTTP request, the connector calls the `invoke` method of the associated container. The container will then call the `invoke` methods of all its child containers. For example, if the connector is associated with an instance of `StandardContext`, the connector will call the `invoke` method of the `StandardContext` instance, which then call the `invoke` methods of all its child containers (in this case, the child containers will be of type `StandardWrapper`). Figure 11.1 explains what happens when the connector receives an HTTP request. (Recall from Chapter 5 that a container has a pipeline with one or more valves.)

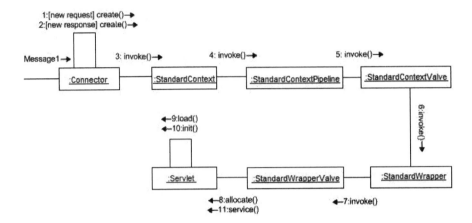

Figure 11.1: The collaboration diagram of methods invocation

- The connector creates the request and response objects
- The connector calls the `StandardContext` instance's `invoke` method.
- The `StandardContext`'s `invoke` method in turn calls the `invoke` method of the context's pipeline. The basic valve in a `StandardContext`'s pipeline is a `StandardContextValve`, therefore the `StandardContext`'s pipeline calls the `StandardContextValve`'s `invoke` method.
- The `StandardContextValve`'s `invoke` method obtains the appropriate wrapper to serve the request and calls the wrapper's `invoke` method.
- The `StandardWrapper` is the standard implementation of a wrapper. The `StandardWrapper` instance's `invoke` method calls its pipeline's `invoke` method.
- The basic valve in the `StandardWrapper`'s pipeline is a `StandardWrapperValve`. Therefore, the `invoke` method of the `StandardWrapperValve` is called. The `invoke` method of the `StandardWrapperValve` calls the wrapper's `allocate` method to obtain an instance of the servlet.
- The `allocate` method calls the `load` method to load the servlet, if the servlet needs to be loaded.
- The `load` method calls the servlet's `init` method.
- The `StandardWrapperValve` calls the servlet's `service` method.

Note

The `StandardContext` class's constructor sets an instance of `StandardContextValve` as its basic valve:

```
public StandardContext() {
```

```
super();
pipeline.setBasic(new StandardContextValve());
namingResources.setContainer(this);
}
```

Note
The StandardWrapper class's constructor sets an instance of
StandardWrapperValve as its basic valve:
```
public StandardWrapper() {
super();
pipeline.setBasic(new StandardWrapperValve());
}
```

In this chapter we are interested in the details on how a servlet is invoked. We
will therefore look at the StandardWrapper and StandardWrapperValve
classes. Before we do that, however, let's look at the
javax.servlet.SingleThreadModel interface first. Understanding this
interface is crucial in understanding how a wrapper loads a servlet.

SingleThreadModel

A servlet can implement the javax.servlet.SingleThreadModel
interface, and a servlet implementing this interface is colloquially called a
SingleThreadModel (STM) servlet. According to the Servlet specification,
the purpose of implementing this interface is to guarantee that the servlet
handles only one request at a time. Quoting the section SRV.14.2.24 of the
Servlet 2.4 specification (Servlet 2.3 has a similar explanation on the
SingleThreadModel interface):

If a servlet implements this interface, you are guaranteed *that no two threads will execute
concurrently in a servlet's* service *method. The servlet container can guarantee this by
synchronizing access to a single instance of the servlet, or by maintaining a pool of servlet
instances and dispatching each new request to a free servlet. This interface does not prevent
synchronization problems that result from servlets accessing shared resources such as static class
variables or classes outside the scope of the servlet.*

Many programmers do not read this carefully, and think that implementing
SingleThreadModel will make their servlet thread-safe. This is not the case.
Read the quotation above once again.

It is true that by implementing SingleThreadModel no two threads will
execute a servlet's service method at the same time. However, to enhance
performance the servlet container can create multiple instances of an STM
servlet. That means, the STM servlet's service method can be executed

concurrently in different instances. This will introduce synchronization problems if the servlet need to access static class variables or other resources outside the class.

False Sense of Multi-Thread Safety:
The SingleThreadModel interface is deprecated in Servlet 2.4 because it gives servlet programmers false sense of multi-thread safety. However, both Servlet 2.3 and Servlet 2.4 containers must still support this interface.

Note
You can find an interesting discussion about SingleThreadModel on http://w4.metronet.com/~wjm/tomcat/ToFeb11/msg02655.html.

StandardWrapper

The main responsibilities of a StandardWrapper object are to load the servlet it represents and allocates an instance of it. The StandardWrapper, however, does not call the servlet's service method. This task is left to the StandardWrapperValve object, the basic valve in the StandardWrapper instance's pipeline. The StandardWrapperValve object obtains the servlet instance from StandardWrapper by calling its allocate method. Upon receiving the servlet instance, the StandardWrapperValve calls the servlet's service method.

The StandardWrapper loads the servlet class when the servlet is requested the first time. The StandardWrapper instance loads a servlet dynamically, therefore it needs to know the fully qualified name of the servlet class. You tell the StandardWrapper this by passing the servlet class name to the setServletClass method of the StandardWrapper. In addition, you calls its setName method to pass the name the servlet will be referred to.

With regard to allocating the servlet instance when the StandardWrapperValve requests it, the StandardWrapper must take into account whether or not the servlet implements the SingleThreadModel interface.

For a servlet that does *not* implement the SingleThreadModel interface, StandardWrapper will load the servlet class once and keep returning the same instance for subsequent requests. The StandardWrapper instance does not need multiple instances of the servlet because it is assumed safe to call the servlet's service method from many threads. It is the responsibility of the servlet programmer to synchronize access to a common resource, if necessary.

For an STM servlet, things are different. The `StandardWrapper` instance must guarantee that no two threads will execute concurrently in the STM servlet's `service` method. If the `StandardWrapper` were to maintain a single instance of the STM servlet, here is how it would invoke the STM servlet's `service` method:

```
Servlet instance = <get an instance of the servlet>;
if ((servlet implementing SingleThreadModel>)  {
  synchronized (instance) {
    instance.service(request, response);
  }
}
else {
    instance.service(request, response);
}
```

However, for the sake of performance, `StandardWrapper` maintains a pool of STM servlet instances.

A wrapper is also responsible for preparing a `javax.servlet.ServletConfig` instance that can be obtained from inside the servlet. The two next sections discuss the allocation and loading of the servlet.

Allocating the servlet

As mentioned at the beginning of this section, the `StandardWrapperValve`'s `invoke` method calls the wrapper's `allocate` method to obtain an instance of the requested servlet. The `StandardWrapper` class therefore must have the implementation of this method.

The signature of the `allocate` method is as follows:

```
public javax.servlet.Servlet allocate() throws ServletException;
```

Notice that the `allocate` method returns an instance of the requested servlet.

The necessity for supporting STM servlets makes the `allocate` method a bit more complex. In fact, there are two parts in the `allocate` method, one to cater for non-STM servlets and the other for STM servlets. The first part has the following skeleton.

```
if (!singleThreadModel) {
  // returns a non-STM servlet instance
}
```

The singleThreadModel is a boolean that indicates whether the servlet represented by this StandardWrapper is an STM servlet. The initial value for singleThreadModel is false, but the loadServlet method tests the servlet it is loading and set this boolean if the servlet is a STM servlet. The loadServlet method is explained in the section "Loading the Servlet" below.

The second part of the allocate method is executed if singleThreadModel is true. The skeleton of the second part is as follows:

```
synchronized (instancePool) {
  // returns an instance of the servlet from the pool
}
```

We'll take a look at the first and the second parts now.

For non-STM servlets, the StandardWrapper defines a variable named instance of type javax.servlet.Servlet:

```
private Servlet instance = null;
```

The allocate method checks if instance is null. If it is, the allocate method calls the loadServlet method to load the servlet. It then increments the countAllocated integer and returns the instance.

```
if (!singleThreadModel) {
  // Load and initialize our instance if necessary
  if (instance == null) {
    synchronized (this) {
      if (instance == null) {
        try {
          instance = loadServlet();
        }
        catch (ServletException e) {
          throw e;
        }
        catch (Throwable e) {
          throw new ServletException
            (sm.getString("standardWrapper.allocate"), e);
        }
      }
    }
  }
  if (!singleThreadModel) {
    if (debug >= 2)
      log(" Returning non-STM instance");
    countAllocated++;
    return (instance);
  }
}
```

If the servlet represented by StandardWrapper is a STM servlet, the allocate method attempt to return an instance from a pool. The instancePool variable of type java.util.Stack references to a stack of STM servlet instances.

```
private Stack instancePool = null;
```

This variable is instantiated inside the loadServlet method, which we will discuss in the next section.

The allocate method will allocate an instance of the STM servlet as long as the number of instances does not exceed the specified maximum number. The maxInstances integer holds the maximum number of STM instances and by default its value is 20.

```
private int maxInstances = 20;
```

To track down the current number of STM instances, the StandardWrapper class uses the nInstances integer:

```
private int nInstances = 0;
```

Here is the second part of the allocate method .

```
synchronized (instancePool) {
  while (countAllocated >= nInstances) {
    // Allocate a new instance if possible, or else wait
    if (nInstances < maxInstances) {
      try {
        instancePool.push(loadServlet());
        nInstances++;
      }
      catch (ServletException e) {
        throw e;
      }
      catch (Throwable e) {
        throw new ServletException
          (sm.getString("standardWrapper.allocate"), e);
      }
    }
    else {
      try {
        instancePool.wait();
      }
      catch (InterruptedException e) {
        ;
      }
    }
  }
  if (debug >= 2)
    log(" Returning allocated STM instance");
  countAllocated++;
  return (Servlet) instancePool.pop();
```

```
}
```

The code above uses a `while` loop to wait until `nInstances` is less than or equal to the value of `countAllocated`. Inside the `while` loop, the `allocate` method checks the value of `nInstance`, and if it is lower than `maxInstances`, the `allocate` method calls the `loadServlet` method and pushes the new instance to the pool and increments `nInstances`. If the number of `nInstance` is equal to `maxInstance` or greater, it waits by calling the `instancePool` stack's `wait` method, waiting for an instance to be returned to the stack.

Loading the Servlet

The `StandardWrapper` class implements the `load` method of the `Wrapper` interface. The `load` method calls the `loadServlet` method that loads the servlet and calls its `init` method, passing a `javax.servlet.ServletConfig` instance. Here is how the `loadServlet` method works.

The `loadServlet` method starts by checking if the current `StandardWrapper` represents an STM servlet. If it does not and the variable `instance` is not `null` (which means the servlet has been previously loaded), it simply returns the instance.

```
// Nothing to do if we already have an instance or an instance pool
if (!singleThreadModel && (instance != null))
  return instance;
```

If instance is `null` or it is a STM servlet, it runs the rest of the method.

First, it captures the output of `System.out` and `System.err`, so that it can log any message later by using the `log` method of `javax.servlet.ServletContext`.

```
PrintStream out = System.out;
SystemLogHandler.startCapture();
```

It then defines the variable `servlet` of type `javax.servlet.Servlet`. This represents the instance of the loaded servlet that will be returned by the `loadServlet` method.

```
Servlet servlet = null;
```

The `loadServlet` method is responsible for loading the servlet class. The name of the class should have been assigned to the `servletClass` class variable. The method assigns the value of this variable to the `String` `actualClass`.

```
String actualClass = servletClass;
```

However, since Catalina is also a JSP container, the `loadServlet` method must also find out if the request servlet is a JSP page. If it is, the `loadServlet` method attempts to obtain the actual class for the JSP page.

```
if ((actualClass == null) && (jspFile != null)) {
  Wrapper jspWrapper = (Wrapper)
  ((Context) getParent()).findChild(Constants.JSP_SERVLET_NAME);
  if (jspWrapper != null)
    actualClass = jspWrapper.getServletClass();
}
```

If the name of the servlet for the JSP page cannot be found, the value of the `servletClass` variable will be used. However, if `servletClass` has not been set by calling the `StandardWrapper` class's `setServletClass` method, an exception will be thrown and the rest of the method will not be executed.

```
// Complain if no servlet class has been specified
if (actualClass == null) {
  unavailable(null);
  throw new ServletException
    (sm.getString("standardWrapper.notClass", getName()));
}
```

At this stage, the servlet class name has been resolved, so the `loadServlet` method obtains the loader. If no loader is found, it throws an exception and the method stops here.

```
// Acquire an instance of the class loader to be used
Loader loader = getLoader();
if (loader == null) {
  unavailable(null);
  throw new ServletException
    (sm.getString("standardWrapper.missingLoader", getName()));
}
```

If a loader can be found, the `loadServlet` method calls its `getClassLoader` method to obtain a `ClassLoader`.

```
ClassLoader classLoader = loader.getClassLoader();
```

Catalina provides special servlets that belong to the `org.apache.catalina` package. These special servlets have access to the internal body of the servlet container. If the servlet is a special servlet, i.e. if the `isContainerProvidedServlet` method returns `true`, the `classLoader` variable is assigned another `ClassLoader` instance, so access to the internal part of Catalina is possible.

```
// Special case class loader for a container provided servlet
if (isContainerProvidedServlet(actualClass)) {
  classLoader = this.getClass().getClassLoader();
  log(sm.getString
    ("standardWrapper.containerServlet", getName()));
}
```

Having a class loader and the servlet name to load, the `loadServlet` method can now load the servlet.

```
// Load the specified servlet class from the appropriate class
// loader
Class classClass = null;
try {
  if (classLoader != null) {
    System.out.println("Using classLoader.loadClass");
    classClass = classLoader.loadClass(actualClass);
  }
  else {
    System.out.println("Using forName");
    classClass = Class.forName(actualClass);
  }
}
catch (ClassNotFoundException e) {
  unavailable(null);
  throw new ServletException
    (sm.getString("standardWrapper.missingClass", actualClass), e);
}
if (classClass == null) {
  unavailable(null);
  throw new ServletException
    (sm.getString("standardWrapper.missingClass", actualClass));
}
```

Then, it can instantiate the servlet.

```
// Instantiate and initialize an instance of the servlet class
// itself
try {
  servlet = (Servlet) classClass.newInstance();
}
catch (ClassCastException e) {
  unavailable(null);
  // Restore the context ClassLoader
  throw new ServletException
    (sm.getString("standardWrapper.notServlet", actualClass), e);
}
catch (Throwable e) {
  unavailable(null);
  // Restore the context ClassLoader
  throw new ServletException
    (sm.getString("standardWrapper.instantiate", actualClass), e);
```

```
  }
```

However, before the `loadServlet` method initializes the servlet, it checks if loading this servlet is allowed by calling the `isServletAllowed` method.

```
// Check if loading the servlet in this web application should be
// allowed
if (!isServletAllowed(servlet)) {
  throw new SecurityException
    (sm.getString("standardWrapper.privilegedServlet",
      actualClass));
}
```

If the security check was passed, it checks if the servlet is a `ContainerServlet`. A `ContainerServlet` is a servlet that implements the `org.apache.catalina.ContainerServlet` interface and has access to Catalina internal functionality. If the servlet is a `ContainerServlet`, the `loadServlet` method calls the `ContainerServlet`'s `setWrapper` method, passing this `StandardWrapper` instance.

```
// Special handling for ContainerServlet instances
if ((servlet instanceof ContainerServlet) &&
  isContainerProvidedServlet(actualClass)) {
  ((ContainerServlet) servlet).setWrapper(this);
}
```

Next, the `loadServlet` method fires the `BEFORE_INIT_EVENT` and calls the servlet's `init` method.

```
try {
  instanceSupport.fireInstanceEvent(
    InstanceEvent.BEFORE_INIT_EVENT, servlet);
  servlet.init(facade);
```

Note that the `init` method is passed the `facade` variable that references a `javax.servlet.ServletConfig` object. Find out how the `ServletConfig` object is created in the section "Creating ServletConfig" later in this chapter.

If the `loadOnStartup` variable is assigned an integer value and the servlet is a JSP page, call the `service` method of the servlet as well.

```
// Invoke jspInit on JSP pages
if ((loadOnStartup > 0) && (jspFile != null)) {
  // Invoking jspInit
  HttpRequestBase req = new HttpRequestBase();
  HttpResponseBase res = new HttpResponseBase();
  req.setServletPath(jspFile);
  req.setQueryString("jsp_precompile=true");
  servlet.service(req, res);
}
```

Next, the loadServlet method fires the AFTER_INIT_EVENT event.

```
instanceSupport.fireInstanceEvent(InstanceEvent.AFTER_INIT_EVENT,
    servlet);
```

If the servlet represented by this StandardWrapper object is a STM servlet, the servlet instance will be added to the instance pool. Therefore, if the instancePool variable is still null, it is assigned a Stack object.

```
  // Register our newly initialized instance
  singleThreadModel = servlet instanceof SingleThreadModel;
  if (singleThreadModel) {
    if (instancePool == null)
      instancePool = new Stack();
  }
  fireContainerEvent("load", this);
}
```

In the finally block, the loadServlet stops the capturing of the System.out and System.err and logs any message during the loading process to the log method of the ServletContext.

```
finally {
  String log = SystemLogHandler.stopCapture();
  if (log != null && log.length() > 0) {
    if (getServletContext() != null) {
      getServletContext().log(log);
    }
    else {
      out.println(log);
    }
  }
}
```

And, finally, the loadServlet method returns the servlet instance.

```
return servlet;
```

The ServletConfig Object

The loadServlet method of the StandardWrapper class calls the servlet's init method after the servlet is loaded. The init method is passed an instance of javax.servlet.ServletConfig. You may be wondering how the StandardWrapper object obtains the ServletConfig object.

Look no further than the StandardWrapper class itself. This class implements the javax.servlet.ServletConfig interface, in addition to the Wrapper interface.

221

The `ServletConfig` interface has the following four methods: `getServletContext`, `getServletName`, `getInitParameter`, and `getInitParameterNames`. Let's now see how these methods are implemented in the `StandardWrapper` class.

> **Note**
>
> The `StandardWrapper` class does not pass itself to the servlet's `init` method, however. Instead, it wraps itself in a `StandardWrapperFacade` instance to hide most of its public method from a servlet programmer. See the section "StandardWrapperFacade" after this section.

getServletContext

The signature of this method is as follows:

```
public ServletContext getServletContext()
```

A `StandardWrapper` instance must be a child container of a `StandardContext`. This is to say, a `StandardWrapper`'s parent is a `StandardContext`. From the `StandardContext` object, you can obtain a `ServletContext` object by calling its `getServletContext` method. Here is the implementation of the `getServletContext` method in the `StandardWrapper` class:

```
public ServletContext getServletContext() {
  if (parent == null)
    return (null);
  else if (!(parent instanceof Context))
    return (null);
  else
    return (((Context) parent).getServletContext());
}
```

> **Note**
>
> Now you know that it is not possible to deploy a stand alone wrapper that represents a servlet definition. The wrapper must reside in a context so that the `ServletConfig` object can return a `ServletContext` instance when its `getServletContext` method is called.

getServletName

This method returns the name of the servlet. Its signature is as follows:

```
public java.lang.String getServletName()
```

Here is the implementation of the `getServletName` method in the `StandardWrapper` class:

```
public String getServletName() {
  return (getName());
}
```

It simply calls the getName method of the ContainerBase class, the parent class of StandardWrapper. The getName method is implemented as follows in ContainerBase:

```
public String getName() {
  return (name);
}
```

You can set the value of name by calling the setName method. Recall that you call the setName method of the StandardWrapper instance by passing the name of the servlet?

getInitParameter

This method returns the value of the specified initialization parameter. Its signature is as follows:

```
public java.lang.String getInitParameter(java.lang.String name)
```

In StandardWrapper, the initialization parameters are stored in a HashMap named parameters.

```
private HashMap parameters = new HashMap();
```

You populate parameters by calling the StandardWrapper class's addInitParameter method, passing the name and the value of the parameter:

```
public void addInitParameter(String name, String value) {
  synchronized (parameters) {
    parameters.put(name, value);
  }
  fireContainerEvent("addInitParameter", name);
}
```

Here is the implementation of getInitParameter in StandardWrapper:

```
public String getInitParameter(String name) {
  return (findInitParameter(name));
}
```

The findInitParameter method accepts the parameter name and calls the get method of the parameters HashMap. Here is the implementation of findInitParameter.

```
public String findInitParameter(String name) {
```

```
  synchronized (parameters) {
    return ((String) parameters.get(name));
  }
}
```

getInitParameterNames

This method returns an `Enumeration` containing all the names of the initialization parameters. Its signature is as follows:

```
public java.util.Enumeration getInitParameterNames()
```

Here is the implementation of the getInitParameterNames in StandardWrapper:

```
public Enumeration getInitParameterNames() {
  synchronized (parameters) {
    return (new Enumerator(parameters.keySet()));
  }
}
```

The Enumerator class implements java.util.Enumeration and is part of the org.apache.catalina.util package.

Parent and Children

A wrapper represents a container for each individual servlet. As such, a wrapper cannot have a child, and its `addChild` method should not be called. If you did, you would get a `java.lang.IllegalStateException`. Here is the implementation of the `addChild` method in the `StandardWrapper` class:

```
public void addChild(Container child) {
  throw new IllegalStateException
    (sm.getString("standardWrapper.notChild"));
}
```

A wrapper's parent can only be an implementation of `Context`. Its `setParent` method throws a `java.lang.IllegalArgumentException` if you pass a non-`Context` container to it.

```
public void setParent(Container container) {
  if ((container != null) && !(container instanceof Context))
    throw new IllegalArgumentException
      (sm.getString("standardWrapper.notContext"));
  super.setParent(container);
}
```

StandardWrapperFacade

The `StandardWrapper` instance calls the `init` method of the servlet it loads. The `init` method requires a `javax.servlet.ServletConfig` and the `StandardWrapper` class itself implements the `ServletConfig` interface, so in theory a `StandardWrapper` object could pass itself to the `init` method. However, the `StandardWrapper` class needs to hide most of its public method from the servlet. To achieve this, the `StandardWraper` class wraps itself in a `StandardWrapperFacade` instance. Figure 11.2 shows the relationship between `StandardWrapper` and `StandardWrapperFacade`. Both implement the `javax.servlet.ServletConfig` interface.

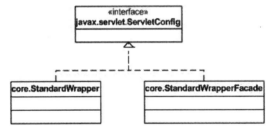

Figure 11.2: The relationship between `StandardWrapper` and `StandardWrapperFacade`

The following line can be found in the `StandardWrapper` class in which the `StandardWrapper` passes itself to the constructor of `StandardWrapperFacade`:

```
private StandardWrapperFacade facade = new StandardWrapperFacade(this);
```

The `StandardWrapperFacade` class provides the class-level variable `config` of type `ServletConfig`:

```
private ServletConfig config = null;
```

When an instance of `StandardWrapperFacade` is created from inside a `StandardWrapper` object, the `StandardWrapperFacade` class's constructor is passed the containing `StandardWrapper` object, which the constructor assigns to the `config` variable:

```
public StandardWrapperFacade(StandardWrapper config) {
  super();
  this.config = (ServletConfig) config;
}
```

Thus, when the StandardWrapper object calls the init method of a servlet instance, it passes an instance of StandardWrapperFacade. Calls to the ServletConfig's getServletName, getInitParameter, and getInitParameterNames methods from inside the servlet are simply passed to the corresponding methods implemented by the StandardWrapper class.

```
public String getServletName() {
  return config.getServletName();
}
public String getInitParameter(String name) {
  return config.getInitParameter(name);
}
public Enumeration getInitParameterNames() {
  return config.getInitParameterNames();
}
```

Calls to the getServletContext method is a bit more complex:

```
public ServletContext getServletContext() {
  ServletContext theContext = config.getServletContext();
  if ((theContext != null) && (theContext instanceof
ApplicationContext))
    theContext = ((ApplicationContext) theContext).getFacade();
  return (theContext);
}
```

The method calls the getServletContext method in the StandardWrapper class, but it returns the ServletContext's façade, instead of the ServletContext object itself.

StandardWrapperValve

The StandardWrapperValve class is the basic valve in a StandardWrapper instance. This valve does two things:

- Executes all filters associated with the servlet
- Calls the servlet's service method.

To do these, here are what the StandardWrapperValve must do in its invoke method implementation:

- Obtain an instance of the servlet that the containing StandardWrapper represents by calling the StandardWrapper's allocate method.
- Create a filter chain by calling the private createFilterChain method.
- Call the filter chain's doFilter method. This includes calling the servlet's service method.
- Release the filter chain.

- Call the wrapper's `deallocate` method.
- Call the wrapper's `unload` method if the servlet is permanently unavailable.

The following is the highlight of the `invoke` method:

```
// Allocate a servlet instance to process this request
try {
  if (!unavailable) {
    servlet = wrapper.allocate();
  }
}
...
// Acknowlege the request
try {
  response.sendAcknowledgement();
}
...
// Create the filter chain for this request
ApplicationFilterChain filterChain = createFilterChain(request,
  servlet);
// Call the filter chain for this request
// This also calls the servlet's service() method
try {
  String jspFile = wrapper.getJspFile();
  if (jspFile != null)
    sreq.setAttribute(Globals.JSP_FILE_ATTR, jspFile);
  else
    sreq.removeAttribute(Globals.JSP_FILE_ATTR);
  if ((servlet != null) && (filterChain != null)) {
    filterChain.doFilter(sreq, sres);
  }
  sreq.removeAttribute(Globals.JSP_FILE_ATTR);
}
...
// Release the filter chain (if any) for this request
try {
  if (filterChain != null)
    filterChain.release();
}
...
// Deallocate the allocated servlet instance
try {
  if (servlet != null) {
    wrapper.deallocate(servlet);
  }
}
...
// If this servlet has been marked permanently unavailable,
// unload it and release this instance
try {
  if ((servlet != null) && (wrapper.getAvailable() ==
    Long.MAX_VALUE)) {
    wrapper.unload();
  }
```

```
  }
  ...
```

Of utmost importance is the call to the `createFilterChain` method and the call to the `doFilter` method of the filter chain. The `createFilterChain` method creates an instance of `ApplicationFilterChain` and adds all filters that should be applied to the servlet represented by the `StandardWrapper`. The `ApplicationFilterChain` class is explained in detail in the section, "ApplicationFilterChain", later in this chapter. To fully understand this class, however, you need to understand the `FilterDef` and the `ApplicationFilterConfig` classes. Both are given in the sections "FilterDef" and "ApplicationFilterConfig", respectively.

FilterDef

The `org.apache.catalina.deploy.FilterDef` class represents a filter definition as defined by the `filter` element in the deployment descriptor. Listing 11.1 presents this class.

Listing 11.1: The FilterDef class

```java
package org.apache.catalina.deploy;

import java.util.HashMap;
import java.util.Map;

public final class FilterDef {
  /**
   * The description of this filter.
   */
  private String description = null;
  public String getDescription() {
    return (this.description);
  }
  public void setDescription(String description) {
    this.description = description;
  }

  /**
   * The display name of this filter.
   */
  private String displayName = null;
  public String getDisplayName() {
    return (this.displayName);
  }
  public void setDisplayName(String displayName) {
    this.displayName = displayName;
  }

  /**
```

```java
   * The fully qualified name of the Java class that implements this
   * filter.
   */
  private String filterClass = null;
  public String getFilterClass() {
    return (this.filterClass);
  }
  public void setFilterClass(String filterClass) {
    this.filterClass = filterClass;
  }

  /**
   * The name of this filter, which must be unique among the filters
   * defined for a particular web application.
   */
  private String filterName = null;
  public String getFilterName() {
    return (this.filterName);
  }
  public void setFilterName(String filterName) {
    this.filterName = filterName;
  }

  /**
   * The large icon associated with this filter.
   */
  private String largeIcon = null;
  public String getLargeIcon() {
    return (this.largeIcon);
  }
  public void setLargeIcon(String largeIcon) {
    this.largeIcon = largeIcon;
  }

  /**
   * The set of initialization parameters for this filter, keyed by
   * parameter name.
   */
  private Map parameters = new HashMap();
  public Map getParameterMap() {
    return (this.parameters);
  }

  /**
   * The small icon associated with this filter.
   */
  private String smallIcon = null;
  public String getSmallIcon() {
    return (this.smallIcon);
  }
  public void setSmallIcon(String smallIcon) {
    this.smallIcon = smallIcon;
  }

  public void addInitParameter(String name, String value) {
    parameters.put(name, value);
```

```
  }
  /**
   * Render a String representation of this object.
   */
  public String toString() {
    StringBuffer sb = new StringBuffer("FilterDef[");
    sb.append("filterName=");
    sb.append(this.filterName);
    sb.append(", filterClass=");
    sb.append(this.filterClass);
    sb.append("]");
    return (sb.toString());
  }
}
```

Each property in the `FilterDef` class represents a sub-element that can appear under the filter element. The class also has a `Map` named `parameters` that represents a `Map` containing all the initial parameters for this filter. The `addInitParameter` method adds a pair of initial parameter name/value.

ApplicationFilterConfig

The `org.apache.catalina.core.ApplicationFilterConfig` implements the `javax.servlet.FilterConfig` interface. `ApplicationFilterConfig` manages the filter instances that are created when the web application is first started.

You create an `ApplicationFilterConfig` object by passing an `org.apache.catalina.Context` object and a `FilterDef` object to the `ApplicationFilterConfig` class's constructor:

```
public ApplicationFilterConfig(Context context, FilterDef filterDef)
  throws ClassCastException, ClassNotFoundException,
    IllegalAccessException, InstantiationException, ServletException
```

The `Context` object represents a web application and the `FilterDef` object is the filter definition. The `ApplicationFilterConfig` class has the `getFilter` method that returns a `javax.servlet.Filter` object. This method loads the filter class and instantiates it.

```
Filter getFilter() throws ClassCastException, ClassNotFoundException,
  IllegalAccessException, InstantiationException, ServletException {

  // Return the existing filter instance, if any
  if (this.filter != null)
    return (this.filter);

  // Identify the class loader we will be using
```

```
    String filterClass = filterDef.getFilterClass();
    ClassLoader classLoader = null;
    if (filterClass.startsWith("org.apache.catalina."))
      classLoader = this.getClass().getClassLoader();
    else
      classLoader = context.getLoader().getClassLoader();

    ClassLoader oldCtxClassLoader =
      Thread.currentThread().getContextClassLoader();

    // Instantiate a new instance of this filter and return it
    Class clazz = classLoader.loadClass(filterClass);
    this.filter = (Filter) clazz.newInstance();
    filter.init(this);
    return (this.filter);
}
```

ApplicationFilterChain

The org.apache.catalina.core.ApplicationFilterChain class is
the implementation of the javax.servlet.FilterChain interface. The
invoke method in the StandardWrapperValve class creates an instance of
this class and calls its doFilter method. The ApplicationFilterChain
class's doFilter method calls the doFilter method of the first filter in the
chain. The Filter interface's doFilter method has the following signature:

```
public void doFilter(ServletRequest request, ServletResponse response,
  FilterChain chain) throws java.io.IOException, ServletException
```

The doFilter method of the ApplicationFilterChain class passes itself
as the third argument to the filter's doFilter method.

From its doFilter method, a filter can cause the invocation of another
filter by explicitly calling the doFilter method of the FilterChain object.
Here is an example of the doFilter method implementation in a filter.

```
public void doFilter(ServletRequest request, ServletResponse response,
  FilterChain chain) throws IOException, ServletException {
  // do something here
  ...
  chain.doFilter(request, response);
}
```

As you can see, the last line of the doFilter method is a call to the doFilter
method of the FilterChain. If the filter is the last filter in the chain, this will
cause the invocation of the requested servlet's service method. If the filter
does not call chain.doFilter, the next filter will not be invoked.

The Application

The application consists of two classes,
`ex11.pyrmont.core.SimpleContextConfig` and
`ex11.pyrmont.startup.Bootstrap`. The `SimpleContextConfig` class
is a copy of the previous chapter's application. The `Bootstrap` class is given in
Listing 11.2.

Listing 11.2: The Bootstrap class

```
package ex11.pyrmont.startup;
//use StandardWrapper
import ex11.pyrmont.core.SimpleContextConfig;
import org.apache.catalina.Connector;
import org.apache.catalina.Context;
import org.apache.catalina.Lifecycle;
import org.apache.catalina.LifecycleListener;
import org.apache.catalina.Loader;
import org.apache.catalina.Wrapper;
import org.apache.catalina.connector.http.HttpConnector;
import org.apache.catalina.core.StandardContext;
import org.apache.catalina.core.StandardWrapper;
import org.apache.catalina.loader.WebappLoader;

public final class Bootstrap {
  public static void main(String[] args) {
    System.setProperty("catalina.base",
      System.getProperty("user.dir"));
    Connector connector = new HttpConnector();
    Wrapper wrapper1 = new StandardWrapper();
    wrapper1.setName("Primitive");
    wrapper1.setServletClass("PrimitiveServlet");
    Wrapper wrapper2 = new StandardWrapper();
    wrapper2.setName("Modern");
    wrapper2.setServletClass("ModernServlet");

    Context context = new StandardContext();
    // StandardContext's start method adds a default mapper
    context.setPath("/myApp");
    context.setDocBase("myApp");
    LifecycleListener listener = new SimpleContextConfig();
    ((Lifecycle) context).addLifecycleListener(listener);
    context.addChild(wrapper1);
    context.addChild(wrapper2);
    // for simplicity, we don't add a valve, but you can add
    // valves to context or wrapper just as you did in Chapter 6
    Loader loader = new WebappLoader();
    context.setLoader(loader);
    // context.addServletMapping(pattern, name);
    context.addServletMapping("/Primitive", "Primitive");
    context.addServletMapping("/Modern", "Modern");
    // add ContextConfig. This listener is important because it
    // configures StandardContext (sets configured to true), otherwise
    // StandardContext won't start
```

```
    connector.setContainer(context);
    try {
      connector.initialize();
      ((Lifecycle) connector).start();
      ((Lifecycle) context).start();
      // make the application wait until we press a key.
      System.in.read();
      ((Lifecycle) context).stop();
    }
    catch (Exception e) {
      e.printStackTrace();
    }
  }
}
```

The `Bootstrap` class creates an instance of `StandardContext` and calls it myApp. To the `StandardContext`, the `Bootstrap` class adds two `StandardWrapper` instances: `Primitive` and `Modern`.

Running the Applications

To run the application in Windows, from the working directory, type the following:

```
java –classpath ./lib/servlet.jar;./lib/commons-collections.jar;./
ex11.pyrmont.startup.Bootstrap
```

In Linux, you use a colon to separate two libraries.

```
java –classpath ./lib/servlet.jar:./lib/commons-collections.jar:./
ex11.pyrmont.startup.Bootstrap
```

To invoke `PrimitiveServlet`, use the following URL in your browser.

```
http://localhost:8080/Primitive
```

To invoke `ModernServlet`, use the following URL.

```
http://localhost:8080/Modern
```

Summary

In this chapter you learned about the `StandardWrapper` class, the standard implementation of the `Wrapper` interface in Catalina. Also discussed was the filter and filter-related classes. An application that uses the `StandardWrapper` class was presented at the end of the chapter.

Chapter 12
StandardContext

As you have witnessed in the previous chapters, a context represents a web application and contains one or more wrappers, each of which represents a servlet definition. However, a context requires other components as well, notably a loader and a manager. This chapter explains the `org.apache.catalina.core.StandardContext` class, which represents Catalina's standard implementation of the `Context` interface.

We first have a look at the `StandardContext` object instantiation and configuration. We then discuss the related classes `StandardContextMapper` (in Tomcat 4) and `ContextConfig`. Next, we look at the sequence of method invocation for each incoming HTTP request. Then, we revisit the `StandardContext` class by discussing its important properties. Finally, the last section of this chapter discusses the `backgroundProcess` method in Tomcat 5.

Note
There is no application accompanying this chapter. StandardContext is used in Chapter 11 and previous chapters.

StandardContext Configuration

After a `StandardContext` instance is constructed, its `start` method must be called to make the instance available to service incoming HTTP requests. For one reason or another, a `StandardContext` object might fail to start. If this happens, the `available` property of the `StandardContext` object will be set to `false`. The `available` property of course indicates the availability of the `StandardContext`.

For the `start` method to succeed, the `StandardContext` object must be configured properly. In a Tomcat deployment, the configuration of `StandardContext` does a number of things. It prepares the `StandardContext` so that the context can read and parse the default web.xml file, which is located in the %CATALINA_HOME%/conf directory and applies to all applications deployed. It also makes sure that the StandardContext instance can process application-level web.xml files. In addition, the configuration installs an authenticator valve and a certificate valve.

Note:
More details on StandardContext configuration are discussed in Chapter 15.

One of the properties in the StandardContext class is the configured property, which is a boolean that indicates whether or not a StandardContext instance is configured properly. StandardContext uses an event listener as its configurator. When the start method on a StandardContext instance is called, one of the things it does is fire a lifecycle event. This event invokes the listener that in turn will configure the StandardContext instance. If configuration is successful, the listener will set the configured property to true. Otherwise, the StandardContext instance will refuse to start and thus will be unavailable to service HTTP requests.

In Chapter 11 you have seen an implementation of a lifecycle listener added to the StandardContext instance. Its type is ch11.pyrmont.core.SimpleContextConfig and it simply sets the configured property of the StandardContext to true without doing anything else, just to fool the StandardContext into thinking that it has been configured correctly. In a Tomcat deployment, the lifecycle listener that configures the StandardContext is of type org.apache.catalina.startup.ContextConfig, which will be explained in detail in Chapter 15.

Now that you understand the importance of configuring a StandardContext, let's look at the StandardContext class in more detail, starting from its constructor.

StandardContext Class's Constructor

Here is the StandardContext class's constructor:

```
public StandardContext() {
  super();
  pipeline.setBasic(new StandardContextValve());
  namingResources.setContainer(this);
}
```

The most important thing to note in the constructor is that the
StandardContext's pipeline is given a basic valve of type
org.apache.catalina.core.StandardContextValve. This valve will
handle every HTTP request that comes through the connector.

Starting StandardContext

The start method initializes the StandardContext instance and gives the
lifecycle listener a chance to configure the StandardContext instance. The
listener will set the configured property to true upon a successful
configuration. At the end of the day, the start method sets the available
property to either true or false. A value of true means the
StandardContext instance has been configured properly and all related child
containers and components have been started successfully and therefore the
StandardContext instance is ready to service incoming HTTP requests. A
value of false indicates otherwise.

The StandardContext class employs a boolean called configured
that is initially set to false. If the lifecycle listener is successful in performing
its tasks of configuring a StandardContext instance, it will set the
StandardContext's configured property to true. Towards the end of
the start method, the StandardContext checks the value of the
configured variable. If it is true, the StandardContext has started
successfully. Otherwise, the stop method is called to stop all the components
that have been started by the start method.

The start method of the StandardContext class in Tomcat 4 is given in
Listing 12.1.

Note
In Tomcat 5, the start method is similar to the one in Tomcat 4. However, it
includes some JMX-related coding, which will not make sense unless you
understand JMX. JMX is discussed in Chapter 20 and if you are new to JMX
you are welcomed to visit the start method in Tomcat 5 once you've read that
chapter.

**Listing 12.1: The start method of the StandardContext class in
Tomcat 4**

```
public synchronized void start() throws LifecycleException {
  if (started)
    throw new LifecycleException
      (sm.getString("containerBase.alreadyStarted", logName()));
  if (debug >= 1)
    log("Starting");
```

```
// Notify our interested LifecycleListeners
lifecycle.fireLifecycleEvent(BEFORE_START_EVENT, null);

if (debug >= 1)
  log("Processing start(), current available=" + getAvailable());
setAvailable(false);
setConfigured(false);
boolean ok = true;

// Add missing components as necessary
if (getResources() == null) {    // (1) Required by Loader
  if (debug >= 1)
    log("Configuring default Resources");
  try {
    if ((docBase != null) && (docBase.endsWith(".war")))
      setResources(new WARDirContext());
    else
      setResources(new FileDirContext());
  }
  catch (IllegalArgumentException e) {
    log("Error initializing resources: " + e.getMessage());
    ok = false;
  }
}

if (ok && (resources instanceof ProxyDirContext)) {
  DirContext dirContext =
    ((ProxyDirContext) resources).getDirContext();
  if ((dirContext != null)
    && (dirContext instanceof BaseDirContext)) {
    ((BaseDirContext) dirContext).setDocBase(getBasePath());
    ((BaseDirContext) dirContext).allocate();
  }
}
if (getLoader() == null) {        // (2) Required by Manager
  if (getPrivileged()) {
    if (debug >= 1)
      log("Configuring privileged default Loader");
    setLoader(new WebappLoader(this.getClass().getClassLoader()));
  }
  else {
    if (debug >= 1)
      log("Configuring non-privileged default Loader");
    setLoader(new WebappLoader(getParentClassLoader()));
  }
}
if (getManager() == null) {      // (3) After prerequisites
  if (debug >= 1)
    log("Configuring default Manager");
  setManager(new StandardManager());
}

// Initialize character set mapper
getCharsetMapper();
```

```
// Post work directory
postWorkDirectory();

// Reading the "catalina.useNaming" environment variable
String useNamingProperty = System.getProperty("catalina.useNaming");
if ((useNamingProperty != null)
  && (useNamingProperty.equals("false"))) {
  useNaming = false;
}

if (ok && isUseNaming()) {
  if (namingContextListener == null) {
    namingContextListener = new NamingContextListener();
    namingContextListener.setDebug(getDebug());
    namingContextListener.setName(getNamingContextName());
            addLifecycleListener(namingContextListener);
  }
}

// Binding thread
ClassLoader oldCCL = bindThread();

// Standard container startup
if (debug >= 1)
  log("Processing standard container startup");

if (ok) {
  try {
    addDefaultMapper(this.mapperClass);
    started = true;

    // Start our subordinate components, if any
    if ((loader != null) && (loader instanceof Lifecycle))
      ((Lifecycle) loader).start();
    if ((logger != null) && (logger instanceof Lifecycle))
      ((Lifecycle) logger).start();

    // Unbinding thread
    unbindThread(oldCCL);

    // Binding thread
    oldCCL = bindThread();

    if ((cluster != null) && (cluster instanceof Lifecycle))
      ((Lifecycle) cluster).start();
    if ((realm != null) && (realm instanceof Lifecycle))
      ((Lifecycle) realm).start();
    if ((resources != null) && (resources instanceof Lifecycle))
      ((Lifecycle) resources).start();

    // Start our Mappers, if any
    Mapper mappers[] = findMappers();
    for (int i = 0; i < mappers.length; i++) {
      if (mappers[i] instanceof Lifecycle)
      ((Lifecycle) mappers[i]).start();
    }
```

```
    // Start our child containers, if any
    Container children[] = findChildren();
    for (int i = 0; i < children.length; i++) {
      if (children[i] instanceof Lifecycle)
        ((Lifecycle) children[i]).start();
    }

    // Start the Valves in our pipeline (including the basic),
    // if any
    if (pipeline instanceof Lifecycle)
      ((Lifecycle) pipeline).start();

    // Notify our interested LifecycleListeners
    lifecycle.fireLifecycleEvent(START_EVENT, null);

    if ((manager != null) && (manager instanceof Lifecycle))
      ((Lifecycle) manager).start();
  }
  finally {
    // Unbinding thread
    unbindThread(oldCCL);
  }
}

if (!getConfigured())
  ok = false;

// We put the resources into the servlet context
if (ok)
  getServletContext().setAttribute
    (Globals.RESOURCES_ATTR, getResources());

// Binding thread
    oldCCL = bindThread();

// Create context attributes that will be required
if (ok) {
  if (debug >= 1)
    log("Posting standard context attributes");
  postWelcomeFiles();
}

// Configure and call application event listeners and filters
if (ok) {
  if (!listenerStart())
    ok = false;
}
if (ok) {
  if (!filterStart())
    ok = false;
}

// Load and initialize all "load on startup" servlets
if (ok)
  loadOnStartup(findChildren());
```

```
  // Unbinding thread
  unbindThread(oldCCL);

  // Set available status depending upon startup success
  if (ok) {
    if (debug >= 1)
      log("Starting completed");
    setAvailable(true);
  }
  else {
    log(sm.getString("standardContext.startFailed"));
    try {
      stop();
    }
    catch (Throwable t) {
      log(sm.getString("standardContext.startCleanup"), t);
    }
    setAvailable(false);
  }

  // Notify our interested LifecycleListeners
  lifecycle.fireLifecycleEvent(AFTER_START_EVENT, null);
}
```

As you can see in Listing 12.1, here is the list of things that the `start` method does:

- Fires the `BEFORE_START` event.
- Sets the `availability` property to `false`.
- Sets the `configured` property to `false`.
- Sets the resources.
- Sets a loader
- Sets a manager
- Initializes the character set mapper.
- Starts other components associated with this context
- Starts child containers (wrappers)
- Starts the pipeline
- Starts the manager
- Fires the `START` event. Here the listener (`ContextConfig`) will perform some configuration operations (discussed in Chapter 15). Upon a successful configuration, the `ContextConfig` will set the `StandardContext` instance's `configured` property to `true`.
- Checks the value of the `configured` property. If it is `true`, do the following: call the `postWelcomePages` method, load child wrappers that need to be loaded at start-up, and set the `availability` property to `true`. If the `configured` variable is false, call the `stop` method.
- Fire the `AFTER_START` event.

The Invoke Method

In Tomcat 4 the `StandardContext`'s invoke method is called by the associated connector or, if the `StandardContext` is a child container of a host, by the host's invoke method. The `StandardContext`'s invoke method first checks if reloading of the application is taking place, and, if so, waits until the application reloading has finished. It then calls the invoke method of its parent class, `ContainerBase`. Listing 12.2 presents the invoke method of the `StandardContext` class.

Listing 12.2: The `invoke` method of the `StandardContext` Class

```
public void invoke(Request request, Response response)
  throws IOException, ServletException {

  // Wait if we are reloading
  while (getPaused()) {
    try {
      Thread.sleep(1000);
    }
    catch (InterruptedException e) {
      ;
    }
  }
  // Normal request processing
  if (swallowOutput) {
    try {
      SystemLogHandler.startCapture();
      super.invoke(request, response);
    }
    finally {
      String log = SystemLogHandler.stopCapture();
      if (log != null && log.length() > 0) {
        log(log);
      }
    }
  }
  else {
    super.invoke(request, response);
  }
}
```

The `getPaused` method returns the value of the `paused` property, which is true if the application reloading is taking place. Application reloading is discussed in the next sub-section.

In Tomcat 5, the `StandardContext` class does not provide an implementation of the invoke method, therefore the `ContainerBase` class's invoke method is executed. The checking of application reloading has been moved to the invoke method of the `StandardContextValve` class.

StandardContextMapper

For each incoming request, the `invoke` method of the `StandardContext`'s pipeline's basic valve will be called. The basic valve for a `StandardContext` is represented by the `org.apache.catalina.core.StandardContextValve` class. The first thing that `StandardContextValve.invoke` needs to do is obtain a wrapper that will handle the request.

In Tomcat 4, the `StandardContextValve` instance looks in its containing `StandardContext`. The `StandardContextValve` uses the context's mapper to find a suitable wrapper. Once it obtains the wrapper, it calls the `invoke` method of the wrapper. Before delving into what the `StandardContextValve` does, this section presents an introduction to the mapper component.

The `ContainerBase` class, the parent class of `StandardContext`, defines the `addDefaultMapper` method to add a default mapper as follows:

```
protected void addDefaultMapper(String mapperClass) {
  // Do we need a default Mapper?
  if (mapperClass == null)
    return;
  if (mappers.size() >= 1)
    return;

  // Instantiate and add a default Mapper
  try {
    Class clazz = Class.forName(mapperClass);
    Mapper mapper = (Mapper) clazz.newInstance();
    mapper.setProtocol("http");
    addMapper(mapper);
  }
  catch (Exception e) {
    log(sm.getString("containerBase.addDefaultMapper", mapperClass),
      e);
  }
}
```

The `StandardContext` class calls the `addDefaultMapper` method from its `start` method, passing the `mapperClass` variable:

```
public synchronized void start() throws LifecycleException {
  ...
  if (ok) {
    try {
      addDefaultMapper(this.mapperClass);
  ...
}
```

The `StandardContext` class defines the `mapperClass` variable as follows:

```
private String mapperClass =
  "org.apache.catalina.core.StandardContextMapper";
```

You must then associate a mapper with a container by calling the mapper's `setContainer` method, passing the instance of the container. The implementation class of the `org.apache.catalina.Mapper` interface for `StandardContextMapper` is `org.apache.catalina.core.StandardContextMapper`. `StandardContextMapper` can only be associated with a context, as indicated by its `setContainer` method.

```
public void setContainer(Container container) {
  if (!(container instanceof StandardContext))
    throw new IllegalArgumentException
      (sm.getString("httpContextMapper.container"));
  context = (StandardContext) container;
}
```

The most important method in a mapper is `map`, which returns a child container to handle an HTTP request. The signature of this method is as follows:

```
public Container map(Request request, boolean update)
```

In `StandardContextMapper`, the `map` method returns a wrapper that will handle a request. If the appropriate wrapper cannot be found, the `map` method returns `null`.

Now back to the discussion at the beginning of this section, the `StandardContextValve` instance calls the context's `map` method for each incoming HTTP request, passing a `org.apache.catalina.Request` object. The `map` method (in the parent class `ContainerBase`) first obtains a mapper for a particular protocol by calling the `findMapper` method, and then calling the mapper's `map` method.

```
// Select the Mapper we will use
Mapper mapper = findMapper(request.getRequest().getProtocol());
if (mapper == null)
  return (null);
// Use this Mapper to perform this mapping
return (mapper.map(request, update));
```

The `map` method in `StandardContextMapper` first identifies the context-relative URI to be mapped:

```
// Identify the context-relative URI to be mapped
String contextPath =
  ((HttpServletRequest) request.getRequest()).getContextPath();
String requestURI = ((HttpRequest) request).getDecodedRequestURI();
```

```
String relativeURI = requestURI.substring(contextPath.length());
```

It then attempts to obtain a wrapper by applying four matching rules:

```
// Apply the standard request URI mapping rules from the specification
Wrapper wrapper = null;
String servletPath = relativeURI;
String pathInfo = null;
String name = null;

// Rule 1 -- Exact Match
if (wrapper == null) {
  if (debug >= 2)
    context.log("  Trying exact match");
  if (!(relativeURI.equals("/")))
    name = context.findServletMapping(relativeURI);
  if (name != null)
    wrapper = (Wrapper) context.findChild(name);
  if (wrapper != null) {
    servletPath = relativeURI;
    pathInfo = null;
  }
}

// Rule 2 -- Prefix Match
if (wrapper == null) {
  if (debug >= 2)
    context.log("  Trying prefix match");
  servletPath = relativeURI;
  while (true) {
    name = context.findServletMapping(servletPath + "/*");
    if (name != null)
      wrapper = (Wrapper) context.findChild(name);
    if (wrapper != null) {
      pathInfo = relativeURI.substring(servletPath.length());
      if (pathInfo.length() == 0)
        pathInfo = null;
      break;
    }
    int slash = servletPath.lastIndexOf('/');
    if (slash < 0)
      break;
    servletPath = servletPath.substring(0, slash);
  }
}

// Rule 3 -- Extension Match
if (wrapper == null) {
  if (debug >= 2)
    context.log("  Trying extension match");
  int slash = relativeURI.lastIndexOf('/');
  if (slash >= 0) {
    String last = relativeURI.substring(slash);
    int period = last.lastIndexOf('.');
    if (period >= 0) {
      String pattern = "*" + last.substring(period);
```

```
      name = context.findServletMapping(pattern);
      if (name != null)
        wrapper = (Wrapper) context.findChild(name);
      if (wrapper != null) {
        servletPath = relativeURI;
        pathInfo = null;
      }
    }
  }
}

// Rule 4 -- Default Match
if (wrapper == null) {
  if (debug >= 2)
    context.log("  Trying default match");
  name = context.findServletMapping("/");
  if (name != null)
    wrapper = (Wrapper) context.findChild(name);
  if (wrapper != null) {
    servletPath = relativeURI;
    pathInfo = null;
  }
}
```

You might ask, how does the context have such information as the servlet mappings? Recall that the `Bootstrap` class in Chapter 11 adds two servlet mappings to the `StandardContext`.

```
context.addServletMapping("/Primitive", "Primitive");
context.addServletMapping("/Modern", "Modern");
```

It also adds the wrappers as children of the context:

```
context.addChild(wrapper1);
context.addChild(wrapper2);
```

Tomcat 5 removed the `Mapper` interface and its related classes. In fact, the `StandardContextValve` class's invoke method obtains the suitable wrapper from the request object:

```
Wrapper wrapper = request.getWrapper();
```

which indicates that the mapping information is encapsulated in the request object.

Support for Reloading

The `StandardContext` class defines the `reloadable` property to indicate whether reloading of the application is enabled. When reloading is enabled, the application will be reloaded if the web.xml file changes or if one of the files in the WEB-INF/classes directory is recompiled.

The `StandardContext` class depends on its loader to reload the application. In Tomcat 4 the `WebappLoader` class, the implementation class of `Loader` in `StandardContext`, has a thread that checks the timestamps of all class and JAR files in the WEB-INF directory. All you need to do to start this thread is associate the `WebappLoader` with the `StandardContext` by calling its `setContainer` method. Here is the implementation of the `setContainer` method of the `WebappLoader` class in Tomcat 4:

```
public void setContainer(Container container) {
  // Deregister from the old Container (if any)
  if ((this.container != null) && (this.container instanceof Context))
    ((Context) this.container).removePropertyChangeListener(this);
  // Process this property change
  Container oldContainer = this.container;
  this.container = container;
  support.firePropertyChange("container", oldContainer,
    this.container);
  // Register with the new Container (if any)
  if ((this.container!=null) && (this.container instanceof Context)) {
    setReloadable( ((Context) this.container).getReloadable() );
    ((Context) this.container).addPropertyChangeListener(this);
  }
}
```

Take a look at the last `if` block. If the container is a context, the `setReloadable` method will be called. This means, the value of the `reloadable` property of the `WebappLoader` instance will be the same as the value of the `reloadable` property of the `StandardContext` instance.

Here is the `setReloadable` method implementation of the `WebappLoader` class:

```
public void setReloadable(boolean reloadable) {
  // Process this property change
  boolean oldReloadable = this.reloadable;
  this.reloadable = reloadable;
  support.firePropertyChange("reloadable",
    new Boolean(oldReloadable), new Boolean(this.reloadable));
  // Start or stop our background thread if required
  if (!started)
    return;
  if (!oldReloadable && this.reloadable)
    threadStart();
  else if (oldReloadable && !this.reloadable)
    threadStop();
}
```

If the `reloadable` property changes from `false` to `true`, the `threadStart` method is called. If it changes from `true` to `false`, the `threadStop` method is called. The `threadStart` method starts a dedicated thread that continuously checks the timestamps of the class and JAR files in WEB-INF. The `threadStop` method stops this thread.

In Tomcat 5, the checking of classes' timestamps for reloading is performed by the `backgroundProcess` method, which is the topic of the next section.

The backgroundProcess Method

A context needs the help of other components, such as a loader and a manager. Often these components require a separate thread that handles background processing. For instance, a loader that support auto reload needs a thread to periodically check the timestamps of all class and JAR files in WEB-INF. A manager needs to a thread to check the expiration time of the session objects it manages. In Tomcat 4 those components end up having their own threads.

To save resources, Tomcat 5 uses a different approach. All background processes share the same thread. If a component or a container needs to have an operation done periodically, all it needs to do is write the code in its `backgroundProcess` method.

The shared thread is created in a `ContainerBase` object. The `ContainerBase` class calls its `threadStart` method in its `start` method (i.e. when the container is started):

```
protected void threadStart() {
  if (thread != null)
    return;
  if (backgroundProcessorDelay <= 0)
    return;
  threadDone = false;
  String threadName = "ContainerBackgroundProcessor[" + toString() +
    "]";
  thread = new Thread(new ContainerBackgroundProcessor(), threadName);
  thread.setDaemon(true);
  thread.start();
}
```

The `threadStart` method constructs a new thread by passing an instance of `ContainerBackgroundProcessor` class that implements `java.lang.Runnable`. The `ContainerBackgroundProcessor` class is given in Listing 12.3.

Listing 12.3: The ContainerBackgroundProcessor class

```
protected class ContainerBackgroundProcessor implements Runnable {
  public void run() {
    while (!threadDone) {
      try {
        Thread.sleep(backgroundProcessorDelay * 1000L);
      }
      catch (InterruptedException e) {
        ;
      }
      if (!threadDone) {
        Container parent = (Container) getMappingObject();
        ClassLoader cl =
          Thread.currentThread().getContextClassLoader();
        if (parent.getLoader() != null) {
          cl = parent.getLoader().getClassLoader();
        }
        processChildren(parent, cl);
      }
    }
  }

  protected void processChildren(Container container, ClassLoader cl) {
    try {
      if (container.getLoader() != null) {
        Thread.currentThread().setContextClassLoader
          (container.getLoader().getClassLoader());
      }
      container.backgroundProcess();
    }
    catch (Throwable t) {
      log.error("Exception invoking periodic operation: ", t);
    }
    finally {
      Thread.currentThread().setContextClassLoader(cl);
    }
    Container[] children = container.findChildren();
    for (int i = 0; i < children.length; i++) {
      if (children[i].getBackgroundProcessorDelay() <= 0) {
        processChildren(children[i], cl);
      }
    }
  }
}
```

The `ContainerBackgroundProcessor` class is an inner class of
`ContainerBase`. Inside its run method is a `while` loop that periodically calls
its `processChildren` method. The `processChildren` method in turn calls
the `backgroundProcess` method and the `processChildren` method of
each of its children. By implementing the `backgroundProcess` method, a
child class of `ContainerBase` can have a dedicated thread for running periodic
tasks, such as checking classes' timestamps or the expiry times of session objects.

Listing 12.4 presents the `backgroundProcess` method in the `StandardContext` class in Tomcat 5.

Listing 12.4: The backgroundProcess method of the StandardContext class

```
public void backgroundProcess() {
  if (!started)
    return;
  count = (count + 1) % managerChecksFrequency;
  if ((getManager() != null) && (count == 0)) {
    try {
      getManager().backgroundProcess();
    }
    catch ( Exception x ) {
      log.warn("Unable to perform background process on manager",x);
    }
  }
  if (getLoader() != null) {
    if (reloadable && (getLoader().modified())) {
      try {
        Thread.currentThread().setContextClassLoader
          (StandardContext.class.getClassLoader());
        reload();
      }
      finally {
        if (getLoader() != null) {
          Thread.currentThread().setContextClassLoader
            (getLoader().getClassLoader());
        }
      }
    }
    if (getLoader() instanceof WebappLoader) {
      ((WebappLoader) getLoader()).closeJARs(false);
    }
  }
}
```

It should be clear how `StandardContext` helps its associated manager and loader with their periodic tasks.

Summary

In this chapter you have learned about the `StandardContext` class and its related classes. You have also seen how a `StandardContext` instance is configured and what happens inside it for each incoming HTTP request. The last section of this chapter discusses the `backgroundProcess` implementation in Tomcat 5.

Chapter 13
Host and Engine

Two topics of discussion in this chapter are hosts and engines. You use a host if you want to run more than one context in the same Tomcat deployment. In theory, you do not need a host if you only have one context, as stated in the description of the org.apache.catalina.Context interface:

The parent Container attached to a Context is generally a Host, but may be some other implementation, or may be omitted if it is not necessary.

In practice, however, a Tomcat deployment always needs a host. Why this is so is explained in the section, "Why You Cannot Live without a Host" later in this chapter.

An engine represents the entire Catalina servlet engine. If used, an engine is always the top level container. Child containers added to an engine are normally implementations of org.apache.catalina.Host or org.apache.catalina.Context. An engine is used in a Tomcat deployment by default. In this deployment, the engine has one host, the default host.

This chapter discusses classes related to the Host and Engine interfaces. It starts with the Host interface followed by the StandardHost, StandardHostMapper (in Tomcat 4) and StandardHostValve classes. Next, to conclude the discussion of Host, an application is presented that demonstrates the use of a host as a top level container. The Engine interface begins the second topic of discussion, followed by the StandardEngine and the StandardEngineValve classes. Then, comes the second application in this chapter, which illustrates the use of an engine as the top level container.

The Host Interface

A host is represented by the org.apache.catalina.Host interface. This interface extends the Container interface and is given in Listing 13.1.

Listing 13.1: The Host interface

```
package org.apache.catalina;

public interface Host extends Container {
  public static final String ADD_ALIAS_EVENT = "addAlias";
  public static final String REMOVE_ALIAS_EVENT = "removeAlias";
  /**
   * Return the application root for this Host.
   * This can be an absolute
   * pathname, a relative pathname, or a URL.
   */
  public String getAppBase();

  /**
   * Set the application root for this Host.  This can be an absolute
   * pathname, a relative pathname, or a URL.
   *
   * @param appBase The new application root
   */
  public void setAppBase(String appBase);

  /**
   * Return the value of the auto deploy flag.
   * If true, it indicates that
   * this host's child webapps should be discovred and automatically
   * deployed.
   */
  public boolean getAutoDeploy();

  /**
   * Set the auto deploy flag value for this host.
   *
   * @param autoDeploy The new auto deploy flag
   */
  public void setAutoDeploy(boolean autoDeploy);

  /**
   * Set the DefaultContext
   * for new web applications.
   *
   * @param defaultContext The new DefaultContext
   */
  public void addDefaultContext(DefaultContext defaultContext);

  /**
   * Retrieve the DefaultContext for new web applications.
   */
```

```
   public DefaultContext getDefaultContext();

  /**
   * Return the canonical, fully qualified, name of the virtual host
   * this Container represents.
   */
  public String getName();

  /**
   * Set the canonical, fully qualified, name of the virtual host
   * this Container represents.
   *
   * @param name Virtual host name
   *
   * @exception IllegalArgumentException if name is null
   */
  public void setName(String name);

  /**
   * Import the DefaultContext config into a web application context.
   *
   * @param context web application context to import default context
   */
  public void importDefaultContext(Context context);

  /**
   * Add an alias name that should be mapped to this same Host.
   *
   * @param alias The alias to be added
   */
  public void addAlias(String alias);

  /**
   * Return the set of alias names for this Host.  If none are defined,
   * a zero length array is returned.
   */
  public String[] findAliases();

  /**
   * Return the Context that would be used to process the specified
   * host-relative request URI, if any; otherwise return
   * <code>null</code>.
   *
   * @param uri Request URI to be mapped
   */
  public Context map(String uri);

  /**
   * Remove the specified alias name from the aliases for this Host.
   * @param alias Alias name to be removed
   */
  public void removeAlias(String alias);
}
```

Of particular importance is the map method that returns the right context to handle the incoming request. The implementation of this method can be found in the StandardHost class, discussed in the next section.

StandardHost

The org.apache.catalina.core.StandardHost class is the standard implementation of Host. This class extends the org.apache.catalina.core.ContainerBase class and implements the Host and Deployer interfaces. Deployer is discussed in Chapter 17.

Just like the StandardContext and the StandardWrapper classes, the StandardHost class's constructor adds the basic valve to its pipeline:

```
public StandardHost() {
  super();
  pipeline.setBasic(new StandardHostValve());
}
```

As you can see, the basic valve is an instance of org.apache.catalina.core.StandardHostValve.

When started, i.e. when its start method is called, the StandardHost adds two valves: ErrorReportValve and ErrorDispatcherValve. Both valves are part of the org.apache.catalina.valves package. The start method of StandardHost in Tomcat 4 is given in Listing 13.2:

Listing 13.2: The start method of StandardHost

```
public synchronized void start() throws LifecycleException {
  // Set error report valve
  if ((errorReportValveClass != null)
    && (!errorReportValveClass.equals(""))) {
    try {
      Valve valve =
        (Valve) Class.forName(errorReportValveClass).newInstance();
      addValve(valve);
    }
    catch (Throwable t) {
      log(sm.getString
        ("standardHost.invalidErrorReportValveClass",
          errorReportValveClass));
    }
  }
  // Set dispatcher valve
  addValve(new ErrorDispatcherValve());
  super.start();
}
```

Note
In Tomcat 5, the start method is similar, except for the fact that it includes code for constructing JXM object name, which will only be discussed in Chapter 20.

The value of `errorReportValveClass` is determined in the `StandardHost` class as follows:

```
private String errorReportValveClass =
  "org.apache.catalina.valves.ErrorReportValve";
```

For every incoming request, the `invoke` method of the host will be called. Since `StandardHost` does not have its own implementation of the `invoke` method, the `invoke` method of `ContainerBase`, its parent class, will be called. The `invoke` method in turn calls the `invoke` method of the `StandardHostValve`, the basic valve of `StandardHost`. The `invoke` method of the `StandardHostValve` is discussed in the section "StandardHostValve" below. Among others, the `StandardHostValve` class's `invoke` method calls the `StandardHost` class's `map` method to obtain the right context to handle the request. The implementation of the `map` method in StandardHost is given in Listing 13.3.

Listing 13.3: The `map` method in the `StandardHost` class

```
public Context map(String uri) {
  if (debug > 0)
    log("Mapping request URI '" + uri + "'");
  if (uri == null)
    return (null);

  // Match on the longest possible context path prefix
  if (debug > 1)
    log("  Trying the longest context path prefix");
  Context context = null;
  String mapuri = uri;
  while (true) {
    context = (Context) findChild(mapuri);
    if (context != null)
      break;
    int slash = mapuri.lastIndexOf('/');
    if (slash < 0)
      break;
    mapuri = mapuri.substring(0, slash);
  }

  // If no Context matches, select the default Context
  if (context == null) {
    if (debug > 1)
      log("  Trying the default context");
    context = (Context) findChild("");
  }

  // Complain if no Context has been selected
```

```
  if (context == null) {
    log(sm.getString("standardHost.mappingError", uri));
    return (null);
  }

  // Return the mapped Context (if any)
  if (debug > 0)
    log(" Mapped to context '" + context.getPath() + "'");
  return (context);
}
```

Note that the `ContainerBase` class in Tomcat 4 also defines a map method with the following signature:

```
public Container map(Request request, boolean update);
```

In Tomcat 4 the `invoke` method in `StandardHostValve` calls the map method in `ContainerBase`, which in turn calls the map method in `StandardHost`. Tomcat 5 does not use a mapper component, and the right context is obtained from the request object.

StandardHostMapper

In Tomcat 4 the `ContainerBase` class, the parent class of `StandardHost`, creates a default mapper by calling its `addDefaultMapper` method from the `start` method. The type of the default mapper is given by the `mapperClass` property. Here is the `addDefaultMapper` method of `ContainerBase`:

```
protected void addDefaultMapper(String mapperClass) {
  // Do we need a default Mapper?
  if (mapperClass == null)
    return;
  if (mappers.size() >= 1)
    return;

  // Instantiate and add a default Mapper
  try {
    Class clazz = Class.forName(mapperClass);
    Mapper mapper = (Mapper) clazz.newInstance();
    mapper.setProtocol("http");
    addMapper(mapper);
  }
  catch (Exception e) {
    log(sm.getString("containerBase.addDefaultMapper", mapperClass),
      e);
  }
}
```

The StandardHost class defines the mapperClass variable as follows:

```
private String mapperClass =
  "org.apache.catalina.core.StandardHostMapper";
```

Also, the `StandardHost` class's `start` method calls `super.start()` at the end of its body, thus ensuring the creation of a default mapper.

> **Note**
> The `StandardContext` class in Tomcat 4 uses a slightly different approach to creating a default mapper. Its `start` method does not call `supoer.start()`. Instead, the `StandardContext` class's `start` method calls the `addDefaultMapper` method passing the `mapperClass` variable.

The most important method in `StandardHostMapper` is, of course, `map`. Here it is.

```
public Container map(Request request, boolean update) {
  // Has this request already been mapped?
  if (update && (request.getContext() != null))
    return (request.getContext());

  // Perform mapping on our request URI
  String uri = ((HttpRequest) request).getDecodedRequestURI();
  Context context = host.map(uri);

  // Update the request (if requested) and return the selected Context
  if (update) {
    request.setContext(context);
    if (context != null)
      ((HttpRequest) request).setContextPath(context.getPath());
    else
      ((HttpRequest) request).setContextPath(null);
  }
  return (context);
}
```

Notice that the `map` method simply calls the Host's `map` method!

StandardHostValve

The `org.apache.catalina.core.StandardHostValve` class is the basic valve of `StandardHost`. Its `invoke` method (in Listing 13.4) is called when there is an incoming HTTP request.

Listing 13.4: The `invoke` method of `StandardHostValve`

```
public void invoke(Request request, Response response,
  ValveContext valveContext)
  throws IOException, ServletException {

  // Validate the request and response object types
```

```
if (!(request.getRequest() instanceof HttpServletRequest) ||
  !(response.getResponse() instanceof HttpServletResponse)) {
  return;      // NOTE - Not much else we can do generically
}

// Select the Context to be used for this Request
StandardHost host = (StandardHost) getContainer();
Context context = (Context) host.map(request, true);
if (context == null) {
  ((HttpServletResponse) response.getResponse()).sendError
  (HttpServletResponse.SC_INTERNAL_SERVER_ERROR,
  sm.getString("standardHost.noContext"));
  return;
}

// Bind the context CL to the current thread
Thread.currentThread().setContextClassLoader
  (context.getLoader().getClassLoader());

// Update the session last access time for our session (if any)
HttpServletRequest hreq = (HttpServletRequest) request.getRequest();
String sessionId = hreq.getRequestedSessionId();
if (sessionId != null) {
  Manager manager = context.getManager();
  if (manager != null) {
    Session session = manager.findSession(sessionId);
    if ((session != null) && session.isValid())
      session.access();
    }
  }

// Ask this Context to process this request
context.invoke(request, response);
}
```

The invoke method in Tomcat 4 obtains the appropriate context by calling the map method of StandardHost.

```
// Select the Context to be used for this Request
StandardHost host = (StandardHost) getContainer();
Context context = (Context) host.map(request, true);
```

Note

There is a round trip when obtaining the Context object above. The map method above accepts two arguments. This is the map method defined in the ContainerBase class. The map method in the ContainerBase class then finds the appropriate mapper in the child object (i.e. the StandardHost instance in this case) and calls its map method.

The invoke method then obtains the session object associated with the request object and calls its access method. The access method updates the last access time. Here is the access method in the org.apache.catalina.session.StandardSession class:

```
public void access() {
  this.isNew = false;
  this.lastAccessedTime = this.thisAccessedTime;
  this.thisAccessedTime = System.currentTimeMillis();
}
```

Finally, the `invoke` method calls the `invoke` method of the context, letting the context handle the request.

Why You Cannot Live without a Host

A Tomcat deployment (Tomcat 4 and 5) must have a host if each context is to be configured using `ContextConfig`. The reason is this.

`ContextConfig` needs the location of the application web.xml file. It attempts to open the web.xml file in its `applicationConfig` method. Here is the fragment of the `applicationConfig` method:

```
synchronized (webDigester) {
  try {
    URL url =
      servletContext.getResource(Constants.ApplicationWebXml);
    InputSource is = new InputSource(url.toExternalForm());
    is.setByteStream(stream);
    ...
    webDigester.parse(is);
    ...
```

where `Constants.ApplicationWebXml` is `/WEB-INF/web.xml`, the relative path to the web.xml file, and `servletContext` is an object of type `org.apache.catalina.core.ApplicationContext` (implements `javax.servlet.ServletContext`).

Here is the `getResource` method of `ApplicationContext`:

```
public URL getResource(String path)
  throws MalformedURLException {

  DirContext resources = context.getResources();
  if (resources != null) {
    String fullPath = context.getName() + path;
    // this is the problem. Host must not be null
    String hostName = context.getParent().getName();
```

The last line shows clearly that a context must have a parent (a host) if it is to be configured by a `ContextConfig`. You will learn how the web.xml file is parsed in Chapter 15, "Digester". In short, you must have a host unless you write your own `ContextConfig` class.

Application 1

The first application in this chapter demonstrates the use of a host as the top
level container. This application uses two classes,
ex13.pyrmont.core.SimpleContextConfig and
ex13.pyrmont.startup.Bootstrap1 class. The
SimpleContextConfig class is copied from Chapter 11 and the
Bootstrap2 class is given in Listing 13.5:

Listing 13.5: The **Bootstrap1** Class

```
package ex13.pyrmont.startup;

import ex13.pyrmont.core.SimpleContextConfig;
import org.apache.catalina.Connector;
import org.apache.catalina.Context;
import org.apache.catalina.Host;
import org.apache.catalina.Lifecycle;
import org.apache.catalina.LifecycleListener;
import org.apache.catalina.Loader;
import org.apache.catalina.Wrapper;
import org.apache.catalina.connector.http.HttpConnector;
import org.apache.catalina.core.StandardContext;
import org.apache.catalina.core.StandardHost;
import org.apache.catalina.core.StandardWrapper;
import org.apache.catalina.loader.WebappLoader;

public final class Bootstrap1 {
  public static void main(String[] args) {
    System.setProperty("catalina.base",
      System.getProperty("user.dir"));
    Connector connector = new HttpConnector();
    Wrapper wrapper1 = new StandardWrapper();
    wrapper1.setName("Primitive");
    wrapper1.setServletClass("PrimitiveServlet");
    Wrapper wrapper2 = new StandardWrapper();
    wrapper2.setName("Modern");
    wrapper2.setServletClass("ModernServlet");
    Context context = new StandardContext();
    // StandardContext's start method adds a default mapper
    context.setPath("/app1");
    context.setDocBase("app1");
    context.addChild(wrapper1);
    context.addChild(wrapper2);
    LifecycleListener listener = new SimpleContextConfig();
    ((Lifecycle) context).addLifecycleListener(listener);
    Host host = new StandardHost();
    host.addChild(context);
    host.setName("localhost");
    host.setAppBase("webapps");
    Loader loader = new WebappLoader();
    context.setLoader(loader);
    // context.addServletMapping(pattern, name);
```

```
    context.addServletMapping("/Primitive", "Primitive");
    context.addServletMapping("/Modern", "Modern");
    connector.setContainer(host);
    try {
      connector.initialize();
      ((Lifecycle) connector).start();
      ((Lifecycle) host).start();
      // make the application wait until we press a key.
      System.in.read();
      ((Lifecycle) host).stop();
    }
    catch (Exception e) {
      e.printStackTrace();
    }
  }
}
```

Running the Applications

To run the application in Windows, from the working directory, type the following:

```
java -classpath ./lib/servlet.jar;./lib/commons-
collections.jar;./lib/commons-digester.jar;./
ex13.pyrmont.startup.Bootstrap1
```

In Linux, you use a colon to separate two libraries.

```
java -classpath ./lib/servlet.jar:./lib/commons-
collections.jar:./lib/commons-digester.jar:./
ex13.pyrmont.startup.Bootstrap1
```

To invoke `PrimitiveServlet`, use the following URL in your browser.

```
http://localhost:8080/app1/Primitive
```

To invoke `ModernServlet`, use the following URL.

```
http://localhost:8080/app1/Modern
```

The Engine Interface

The `org.apache.catalina.Engine` interface represents an engine. An engine represents the entire Catalina servlet engine. You would want to use an engine if you want to support multiple virtual hosts. In fact, a Tomcat deployment normally uses an engine.

The `Engine` interface is shown in Listing 13.6:

Listing 13.6: The Engine Interface

```
package org.apache.catalina;

public interface Engine extends Container {
  /**
   * Return the default hostname for this Engine.
   */
  public String getDefaultHost();
  /**
   * Set the default hostname for this Engine.
   *
   * @param defaultHost The new default host
   */
  public void setDefaultHost(String defaultHost);
  /**
   * Retrieve the JvmRouteId for this engine.
   */
  public String getJvmRoute();
  /**
   * Set the JvmRouteId for this engine.
   *
   * @param jvmRouteId the (new) JVM Route ID. Each Engine within a
   * cluster must have a unique JVM Route ID.
   */
  public void setJvmRoute(String jvmRouteId);
  /**
   * Return the <code>Service</code> with which we are associated (if
   * any).
   */
  public Service getService();
  /**
   * Set the <code>Service</code> with which we are associated (if
   * any).
   *
   * @param service The service that owns this Engine
   */
  public void setService(Service service);
  /**
   * Set the DefaultContext
   * for new web applications.
   *
   * @param defaultContext The new DefaultContext
   */
  public void addDefaultContext(DefaultContext defaultContext);
  /**
   * Retrieve the DefaultContext for new web applications.
   */
  public DefaultContext getDefaultContext();
  /**
   * Import the DefaultContext config into a web application context.
   *
   * @param context web application context to import default context
   */
  public void importDefaultContext(Context context);
}
```

You can set a default host or add a default context to an Engine. Note also that an engine can be associated with a service. Services are discussed in Chapter 14.

StandardEngine

The `org.apache.catalina.core.StandardEngine` is the standard implementation of the `Engine` interface. Compared to `StandardContext` and `StandardHost`, the `StandardEngine` class is relatively small. When instantiated, the `StandardEngine` class adds a basic valve, as indicated in its constructor:

```
public StandardEngine() {
  super();
  pipeline.setBasic(new StandardEngineValve());
}
```

As the top level container, a `StandardEngine` will have child containers. A child container of a `StandardEngine` must be a host. An exception will be thrown if you try to add a non-host container. Here is the `addChild` method of `StandardEngine`.

```
public void addChild(Container child) {
  if (!(child instanceof Host))
    throw new IllegalArgumentException
      (sm.getString("standardEngine.notHost"));
  super.addChild(child);
}
```

As a top level container, it is impossible for an engine to have a parent. An exception will be thrown if you try to set a parent, as displayed by the `StandardEngine` class's `setParent` method:

```
public void setParent(Container container) {
  throw new IllegalArgumentException
    (sm.getString("standardEngine.notParent"));
}
```

StandardEngineValve

The `org.apache.catalina.core.StandardEngineValve` is the basic valve of `StandardEngine`. The `invoke` method of `StandardEngineValve` is presented in Listing 13.7.

Listing 13.7: The invoke method of StandardEngineValve

```
public void invoke(Request request, Response response,
  ValveContext valveContext)
  throws IOException, ServletException {
  // Validate the request and response object types
  if (!(request.getRequest() instanceof HttpServletRequest) ||
    !(response.getResponse() instanceof HttpServletResponse)) {
    return;      // NOTE - Not much else we can do generically
  }
  // Validate that any HTTP/1.1 request included a host header
  HttpServletRequest hrequest = (HttpServletRequest) request;
  if ("HTTP/1.1".equals(hrequest.getProtocol()) &&
    (hrequest.getServerName() == null)) {
    ((HttpServletResponse) response.getResponse()).sendError
    (HttpServletResponse.SC_BAD_REQUEST,
      sm.getString("standardEngine.noHostHeader",
    request.getRequest().getServerName())));
    return;
  }
  // Select the Host to be used for this Request
  StandardEngine engine = (StandardEngine) getContainer();
  Host host = (Host) engine.map(request, true);
  if (host == null) {
    ((HttpServletResponse) response.getResponse()).sendError
      (HttpServletResponse.SC_BAD_REQUEST,
      sm.getString("standardEngine.noHost",
      request.getRequest().getServerName())));
    return;
  }
  // Ask this Host to process this request
  host.invoke(request, response);
}
```

After validating the type of the request and response objects, the invoke
method obtains the Host instance used for processing the request. It obtains the
Host by calling the Engine's map method. Once the Host is obtained, its
invoke method is called.

Application 2

The second application in this chapter demonstrates the use of an engine as the
top level container. This application uses two classes,
ex13.pyrmont.core.SimpleContextConfig and
ex13.pyrmont.startup.Bootstrap2 class. The Bootstrap2 class is
given in Listing 13.8:

Listing 13.8: The Bootstrap2 class

```
package ex13.pyrmont.startup;
```

```java
//Use engine
import ex13.pyrmont.core.SimpleContextConfig;
import org.apache.catalina.Connector;
import org.apache.catalina.Context;
import org.apache.catalina.Engine;
import org.apache.catalina.Host;
import org.apache.catalina.Lifecycle;
import org.apache.catalina.LifecycleListener;
import org.apache.catalina.Loader;
import org.apache.catalina.Wrapper;
import org.apache.catalina.connector.http.HttpConnector;
import org.apache.catalina.core.StandardContext;
import org.apache.catalina.core.StandardEngine;
import org.apache.catalina.core.StandardHost;
import org.apache.catalina.core.StandardWrapper;
import org.apache.catalina.loader.WebappLoader;

public final class Bootstrap2 {
  public static void main(String[] args) {
    System.setProperty("catalina.base",
      System.getProperty("user.dir"));
    Connector connector = new HttpConnector();
    Wrapper wrapper1 = new StandardWrapper();
    wrapper1.setName("Primitive");
    wrapper1.setServletClass("PrimitiveServlet");
    Wrapper wrapper2 = new StandardWrapper();
    wrapper2.setName("Modern");
    wrapper2.setServletClass("ModernServlet");
    Context context = new StandardContext();
    // StandardContext's start method adds a default mapper
    context.setPath("/app1");
    context.setDocBase("app1");
    context.addChild(wrapper1);
    context.addChild(wrapper2);
    LifecycleListener listener = new SimpleContextConfig();
    ((Lifecycle) context).addLifecycleListener(listener);
    Host host = new StandardHost();
    host.addChild(context);
    host.setName("localhost");
    host.setAppBase("webapps");
    Loader loader = new WebappLoader();
    context.setLoader(loader);
    // context.addServletMapping(pattern, name);
    context.addServletMapping("/Primitive", "Primitive");
    context.addServletMapping("/Modern", "Modern");
    Engine engine = new StandardEngine();
    engine.addChild(host);
    engine.setDefaultHost("localhost");
    connector.setContainer(engine);
    try {
      connector.initialize();
      ((Lifecycle) connector).start();
      ((Lifecycle) engine).start();
      // make the application wait until we press a key.
      System.in.read();
      ((Lifecycle) engine).stop();
```

```
    }
    catch (Exception e) {
      e.printStackTrace();
    }
  }
}
```

Running the Applications

To run the application in Windows, from the working directory, type the following:

```
java -classpath ./lib/servlet.jar;./lib/commons-
collections.jar;./lib/commons-digester.jar;./
ex13.pyrmont.startup.Bootstrap2
```

In Linux, you use a colon to separate two libraries.

```
java -classpath ./lib/servlet.jar:./lib/commons-
collections.jar:./lib/commons-digester.jar:./
ex13.pyrmont.startup.Bootstrap2
```

To invoke PrimitiveServlet, use the following URL in your browser.

```
http://localhost:8080/app1/Primitive
```

To invoke ModernServlet, use the following URL.

```
http://localhost:8080/app1/Modern
```

Summary

In this chapter you have learned about two types of containers: host and engine. This chapter also explained the classes related to both containers. Two applications are also presented that show the use of a host and an engine as top level containers.

Chapter 14
Server and Service

In previous chapters you have seen how you can have a servlet container by instantiating a connector and a container and then associating them with each other. Only one connector could be used, and that was to serve HTTP requests on port 8080. You could not add another connector to service HTTPS requests, for example.

In addition, all applications accompanying the previous chapters lack one thing: a good mechanism for starting and stopping the servlet container. In this chapter, we'll look at two other components that offer this mechanism as well as offer many other features: server and service.

Server

The `org.apache.catalina.Server` interface represents the entire Catalina servlet container and engulfs all other components. A server is particularly useful because it provides an elegant mechanism for starting and stopping the whole system. There is no need to start the connector and the container individually any longer.

Here is how the `start` and `stop` mechanism works. When you start a server, it starts all components inside it. It then waits indefinitely for a shutdown command. If you want to shut the system down, you send a shutdown command to a designated port. This will reach the server and if it receives the right shutdown command, it will obey by stopping all its components.

A server uses another component, a service, to contain components such as a container and one or more connectors. Service is explained in the section "Service" later in this chapter.

The `Server` interface is given in Listing 14.1.

Listing 14.1: The `Server` interface

```
package org.apache.catalina;
```

```
import org.apache.catalina.deploy.NamingResources;

public interface Server {
  /**
   * Return descriptive information about this Server implementation
   * and the corresponding version number, in the format
   * <code>&lt;description&gt;/&lt;version&gt;</code>.
   */
  public String getInfo();
  /**
   * Return the global naming resources.
   */
  public NamingResources getGlobalNamingResources();
  /**
   * Set the global naming resources.
   *
   * @param namingResources The new global naming resources
   */
  public void setGlobalNamingResources
    (NamingResources globalNamingResources);
  /**
   * Return the port number we listen to for shutdown commands.
   */
  public int getPort();
  /**
   * Set the port number we listen to for shutdown commands.
   *
   * @param port The new port number
   */
  public void setPort(int port);
  /**
   * Return the shutdown command string we are waiting for.
   */
  public String getShutdown();
  /**
   * Set the shutdown command we are waiting for.
   *
   * @param shutdown The new shutdown command
   */
  public void setShutdown(String shutdown);
  /**
   * Add a new Service to the set of defined Services.
   *
   * @param service The Service to be added
   */
  public void addService(Service service);
  /**
   * Wait until a proper shutdown command is received, then return.
   */
  public void await();
  /**
   * Return the specified Service (if it exists); otherwise return
   * <code>null</code>.
   *
   * @param name Name of the Service to be returned
```

```
    */
   public Service findService(String name);
   /**
    * Return the set of Services defined within this Server.
    */
   public Service[] findServices();
   /**
    * Remove the specified Service from the set associated from this
    * Server.
    *
    * @param service The Service to be removed
    */
   public void removeService(Service service);
   /**
    * Invoke a pre-startup initialization. This is used to allow
    * onnectors to bind to restricted ports under Unix operating
    * environments.
    *
    * @exception LifecycleException If this server was already
    * initialized.
    */
   public void initialize() throws LifecycleException;
}
```

The shutdown property holds the string that must be sent to a Server instance to shut it down. The port property defines the port the server waits for a shutdown command. You can add Service objects to a server by calling its addService method. Later, a service can be removed by invoking the removeService method. The findServices method returns all services added to the server. The initialize method contains code that needs to be executed before start-up.

StandardServer

The org.apache.catalina.core.StandardServer class is the standard implementation of Server. We're particularly interested in the shutdown mechanism offered by this class, which is also the most important feature in this class. Many methods are related to the storing of the server configuration into a new server.xml file, but they will not be discussed here. For those interested, these methods are not difficult to understand, though.

A Server can have zero or more services. The StandardServer provides the implementations of the addService, removeService, and findServices methods.

Four methods are related to the lifecycle of the StandardServer: initialize, start, stop, and await. Just like any other components, you initialize and start a server. You then call the `await` method followed by the `stop` method. The `await` method does not return until it receives a shutdown command on port 8085 (or some other port). When the `await` method returns, the `stop` method is run to stop all the sub-components. In the accompanying application of this chapter, you will learn how you can implement this shutdown mechanism.

The `initialize`, `start`, `stop`, and `await` methods are discussed in the following sub-sections.

The `initialize` Method

The `initialize` method is used to initialize services added to the `Server` instance. The `initialize` method in the `StandardServer` class in Tomcat 4 is given in Listing 14.2.

Listing 14.2: The `initialize` method

```
public void initialize() throws LifecycleException {
  if (initialized)
    throw new LifecycleException (
      sm.getString("standardServer.initialize.initialized"));
  initialized = true;

  // Initialize our defined Services
  for (int i = 0; i < services.length; i++) {
    services[i].initialize();
  }
}
```

Note that the `initialize` method employs a `boolean` named `initialized` that prevents the server from being initialized twice. In Tomcat 5, the `initialize` method is similar, but it also includes code related to JMX (discussed in Chapter 20). The `stop` method does not reset the value of `initialized`, so that if the server is stopped and started again, its `initialized` method is not called again.

The `start` Method

You call the `start` method to start a Server. The implementation of this method in `StandardServer` starts all services which in turn starts all other components, such as the connector(s) and the container. Listing 14.3 presents the `start` method.

Listing 14.3: The `start` method

```
public void start() throws LifecycleException {
  // Validate and update our current component state
  if (started)
    throw new LifecycleException
      (sm.getString("standardServer.start.started"));
  // Notify our interested LifecycleListeners
  lifecycle.fireLifecycleEvent(BEFORE_START_EVENT, null);
  lifecycle.fireLifecycleEvent(START_EVENT, null);
  started = true;
  // Start our defined Services
  synchronized (services) {
    for (int i = 0; i < services.length; i++) {
      if (services[i] instanceof Lifecycle)
        ((Lifecycle) services[i]).start();
    }
  // Notify our interested LifecycleListeners
  lifecycle.fireLifecycleEvent(AFTER_START_EVENT, null);
}
```

The `start` method employs the `start boolean` variable to prevent a server from being started twice. The `stop` method resets this variable.

The `stop` Method

The `stop` method stops the server. This method is given in Listing 14.4.

Listing 14.4: The `stop` method

```
public void stop() throws LifecycleException {
  // Validate and update our current component state
  if (!started)
    throw new LifecycleException
      (sm.getString("standardServer.stop.notStarted"));
  // Notify our interested LifecycleListeners
  lifecycle.fireLifecycleEvent(BEFORE_STOP_EVENT, null);
  lifecycle.fireLifecycleEvent(STOP_EVENT, null);
  started = false;

  // Stop our defined Services
  for (int i = 0; i < services.length; i++) {
    if (services[i] instanceof Lifecycle)
      ((Lifecycle) services[i]).stop();
  }
  // Notify our interested LifecycleListeners
  lifecycle.fireLifecycleEvent(AFTER_STOP_EVENT, null);
}
```

Calling the `stop` method stops all the services and resets the `started` `boolean`, so that the server can be started again.

The `await` Method

The `await` method is responsible for the stop mechanism of the whole Tomcat deployment. It is given in Listing 14.5.

Listing 14.4: The `await` method

```
/**
 * Wait until a proper shutdown command is received, then return.
 */
public void await() {
  // Set up a server socket to wait on
  ServerSocket serverSocket = null;
  try {
    serverSocket = new ServerSocket(port, 1,
      InetAddress.getByName("127.0.0.1"));
  }
  catch (IOException e) {
    System.err.println("StandardServer.await: create[" +
      port + "]: " + e);
    e.printStackTrace();
    System.exit(1);
  }
  // Loop waiting for a connection and a valid command
  while (true) {
    // Wait for the next connection
    Socket socket = null;
    InputStream stream = null;
    try {
      socket = serverSocket.accept();
      socket.setSoTimeout(10 * 1000);  // Ten seconds
      stream = socket.getInputStream();
    }
    catch (AccessControlException ace) {
      System.err.println("StandardServer.accept security exception: "
        + ace.getMessage());
      continue;
    }
    catch (IOException e) {
      System.err.println("StandardServer.await: accept: " + e);
      e.printStackTrace();
      System.exit(1);
    }

    // Read a set of characters from the socket
    StringBuffer command = new StringBuffer();
    int expected = 1024; // Cut off to avoid DoS attack
    while (expected < shutdown.length()) {
      if (random == null)
        random = new Random(System.currentTimeMillis());
      expected += (random.nextInt() % 1024);
    }
    while (expected > 0) {
      int ch = -1;
      try {
```

```
      ch = stream.read();
    }
    catch (IOException e) {
      System.err.println("StandardServer.await: read: " + e);
      e.printStackTrace();
      ch = -1;
    }
    if (ch < 32)  // Control character or EOF terminates loop
      break;
    command.append((char) ch);
    expected--;
  }

  // Close the socket now that we are done with it
  try {
    socket.close();
  }
  catch (IOException e) {
    ;
  }

  // Match against our command string
  boolean match = command.toString().equals(shutdown);
  if (match) {
    break;
  }
  else
    System.err.println("StandardServer.await: Invalid command '" +
      command.toString() + "' received");
}

// Close the server socket and return
try {
  serverSocket.close();
}
catch (IOException e) {
  ;
}
}
```

The `await` method creates a `ServerSocket` object that waits on port 8085 and then calls its `accept` method in a `while` loop. The `accept` method will only return if there is an incoming message on the designated port (8085). Each message will then be matched against the shutdown string. If it matches, control breaks out of the `while` loop and the `SocketServer` is closed. If it does not match, control stays in the `while` loop waiting for another message.

Service

The `org.apache.catalina.Service` interface represents a service. A service can hold one container and multiple connectors. You can add as many

connectors as you want and all the connectors will be associated with the
container. The `Service` interface is given in Listing 14.6.

Listing 14.6: The `Service` interface

```
package org.apache.catalina;

public interface Service {

  /**
   * Return the <code>Container</code> that handles requests for all
   * <code>Connectors</code> associated with this Service.
   */
  public Container getContainer();

  /**
   * Set the <code>Container</code> that handles requests for all
   * <code>Connectors</code> associated with this Service.
   *
   * @param container The new Container
   */
  public void setContainer(Container container);

  /**
   * Return descriptive information about this Service implementation
   * and the corresponding version number, in the format
   * <code>&lt;description&gt;/&lt;version&gt;</code>.
   */
  public String getInfo();

  /**
   * Return the name of this Service.
   */
  public String getName();

  /**
   * Set the name of this Service.
   *
   * @param name The new service name
   */
  public void setName(String name);

  /**
   * Return the <code>Server</code> with which we are associated
   * (if any).
   */
  public Server getServer();

  /**
   * Set the <code>Server</code> with which we are associated (if any).
   *
   * @param server The server that owns this Service
   */
  public void setServer(Server server);

  /**
```

```
   * Add a new Connector to the set of defined Connectors,
   * and associate it with this Service's Container.
   *
   * @param connector The Connector to be added
   */
  public void addConnector(Connector connector);

  /**
   * Find and return the set of Connectors associated with
   * this Service.
   */
  public Connector[] findConnectors();

  /**
   * Remove the specified Connector from the set associated from this
   * Service.  The removed Connector will also be disassociated
   * from our Container.
   *
   * @param connector The Connector to be removed
   */
  public void removeConnector(Connector connector);

  /**
   * Invoke a pre-startup initialization. This is used to
   * allow connectors to bind to restricted ports under
   * Unix operating environments.
   *
   * @exception LifecycleException If this server was
   * already initialized.
   */
  public void initialize() throws LifecycleException;
}
```

StandardService

The org.apache.catalina.core.StandardService class is the standard implementation of Service. The StandardService class's initialize method initializes all the connectors added to the service. StandardService implements Service as well as the org.apache.catalina.Lifecycle interface. Its start method starts the container and all the connectors.

Container and Connector(s)

A StandardService instance contains two types of components: a container and one or more connectors. Being able to have multiple connectors enable Tomcat to service multiple protocols. One connector can be used to service HTTP requests, and another for servicing HTTPS requests.

The StandardService class uses the container variable as an object reference for the the Container instance and the connectors array for all the connectors.

```
private Container container = null;
private Connector connectors[] = new Connector[0];
```

To associate a container with this service, you use the setContainer method, which is given in Listing 14.7.

Listing 14.7: The setContainer method

```
public void setContainer(Container container) {
  Container oldContainer = this.container;
  if ((oldContainer != null) && (oldContainer instanceof Engine))
    ((Engine) oldContainer).setService(null);
  this.container = container;
  if ((this.container != null) && (this.container instanceof Engine))
    ((Engine) this.container).setService(this);
  if (started && (this.container != null) &&
    (this.container instanceof Lifecycle)) {
    try {
      ((Lifecycle) this.container).start();
    }
    catch (LifecycleException e) {
      ;
    }
  }
  synchronized (connectors) {
    for (int i = 0; i < connectors.length; i++)
      connectors[i].setContainer(this.container);
  }
  if (started && (oldContainer != null) &&
    (oldContainer instanceof Lifecycle)) {
    try {
      ((Lifecycle) oldContainer).stop();
    }
    catch (LifecycleException e) {
      ;
    }
  }

  // Report this property change to interested listeners
  support.firePropertyChange("container", oldContainer,
    this.container);
}
```

The container associated with this service will be passed to the setContainer method on each Connector object that is available in this service to create the association between the container and each individual connector.

To add a connector to a Service object, use the addConnector method. To remove a connector, call the removeConnector method. The

addConnector method is given in Listing 14.8 and the removeConnector
method in Listing 14.9.

Listing 14.8: The `addConnector` method

```java
public void addConnector(Connector connector) {
  synchronized (connectors) {
    connector.setContainer(this.container);
    connector.setService(this);
    Connector results[] = new Connector[connectors.length + 1];
    System.arraycopy(connectors, 0, results, 0, connectors.length);
    results[connectors.length] = connector;
    connectors = results;

    if (initialized) {
      try {
        connector.initialize();
      }
      catch (LifecycleException e) {
        e.printStackTrace(System.err);
      }
    }

    if (started && (connector instanceof Lifecycle)) {
      try {
        ((Lifecycle) connector).start();
      }
      catch (LifecycleException e) {
        ;
      }
    }

    // Report this property change to interested listeners
    support.firePropertyChange("connector", null, connector);
  }
}
```

The addConnector method initializes and starts the added connector.

Listing 14.9: The `removeConnector` method

```java
public void removeConnector(Connector connector) {
  synchronized (connectors) {
    int j = -1;
    for (int i = 0; i < connectors.length; i++) {
      if (connector == connectors[i]) {
        j = i;
        break;
      }
    }
    if (j < 0)
      return;
    if (started && (connectors[j] instanceof Lifecycle)) {
      try {
```

```
      ((Lifecycle) connectors[j]).stop();
    }
    catch (LifecycleException e) {
      ;
    }
  }
  connectors[j].setContainer(null);
  connector.setService(null);
  int k = 0;
  Connector results[] = new Connector[connectors.length - 1];
  for (int i = 0; i < connectors.length; i++) {
    if (i != j)
      results[k++] = connectors[i];
  }
  connectors = results;

  // Report this property change to interested listeners
  support.firePropertyChange("connector", connector, null);
  }
}
```

Lifecycle Methods

The lifecycle methods are the `start` and the `stop` methods inherited from the `Lifecycle` interface plus the `initialize` method. The `initialize` method calls the `initialize` method of each connector in this service. This method is given in Listing 14.10.

Listing 14.10: The `initialize` method of `StandardService`

```
public void initialize() throws LifecycleException {
  if (initialized)
    throw new LifecycleException (
      sm.getString("standardService.initialize.initialized"));
  initialized = true;

  // Initialize our defined Connectors
  synchronized (connectors) {
    for (int i = 0; i < connectors.length; i++) {
      connectors[i].initialize();
    }
  }
}
```

The `start` method starts the associated container as well as all the connector added to this service. This method is presented in Listing 14.11.

Listing 14.11: The `start` method

```
public void start() throws LifecycleException {
  // Validate and update our current component state
  if (started) {
```

```
    throw new LifecycleException
      (sm.getString("standardService.start.started"));
  }

  // Notify our interested LifecycleListeners
  lifecycle.fireLifecycleEvent(BEFORE_START_EVENT, null);

  System.out.println
    (sm.getString("standardService.start.name", this.name));
  lifecycle.fireLifecycleEvent(START_EVENT, null);
  started = true;

  // Start our defined Container first
  if (container != null) {
    synchronized (container) {
      if (container instanceof Lifecycle) {
        ((Lifecycle) container).start();
      }
    }
  }

  // Start our defined Connectors second
  synchronized (connectors) {
    for (int i = 0; i < connectors.length; i++) {
      if (connectors[i] instanceof Lifecycle)
        ((Lifecycle) connectors[i]).start();
    }
  }

  // Notify our interested LifecycleListeners
  lifecycle.fireLifecycleEvent(AFTER_START_EVENT, null);
}
```

The stop method stops the associated container and all the connectors. The stop method is given in Listing 14.12.

Listing 14.12: The **stop** method

```
public void stop() throws LifecycleException {
  // Validate and update our current component state
  if (!started) {
    throw new LifecycleException
      (sm.getString("standardService.stop.notStarted"));
  }

  // Notify our interested LifecycleListeners
  lifecycle.fireLifecycleEvent(BEFORE_STOP_EVENT, null);

  lifecycle.fireLifecycleEvent(STOP_EVENT, null);

  System.out.println
    (sm.getString("standardService.stop.name", this.name));
  started = false;

  // Stop our defined Connectors first
  synchronized (connectors) {
```

```
    for (int i = 0; i < connectors.length; i++) {
      if (connectors[i] instanceof Lifecycle)
        ((Lifecycle) connectors[i]).stop();
    }
  }

  // Stop our defined Container second
  if (container != null) {
    synchronized (container) {
      if (container instanceof Lifecycle) {
        ((Lifecycle) container).stop();
      }
    }
  }

  // Notify our interested LifecycleListeners
  lifecycle.fireLifecycleEvent(AFTER_STOP_EVENT, null);
}
```

The Application

The application shows you how to use a server and a service. In particular, it demonstrates how to utilize the `start` and `stop` mechanisms in the `StandardServer` class. There are three classes in the application. The first is the `SimpleContextConfig`, which is a copy from the application in Chapter 13. The two other classes are `Bootstrap` and `Stopper`. The `Bootstrap` class is used to start the application, and the `Stopper` class to stop it.

The Bootstrap Class

The Bootstrap class is given in Listing 14.13.

Listing 14.13: The Bootstrap Class

```
package ex14.pyrmont.startup;

import ex14.pyrmont.core.SimpleContextConfig;
import org.apache.catalina.Connector;
import org.apache.catalina.Context;
import org.apache.catalina.Engine;
import org.apache.catalina.Host;
import org.apache.catalina.Lifecycle;
import org.apache.catalina.LifecycleException;
import org.apache.catalina.LifecycleListener;
import org.apache.catalina.Loader;
import org.apache.catalina.Server;
import org.apache.catalina.Service;
import org.apache.catalina.Wrapper;
import org.apache.catalina.connector.http.HttpConnector;
```

```
import org.apache.catalina.core.StandardContext;
import org.apache.catalina.core.StandardEngine;
import org.apache.catalina.core.StandardHost;
import org.apache.catalina.core.StandardServer;
import org.apache.catalina.core.StandardService;
import org.apache.catalina.core.StandardWrapper;
import org.apache.catalina.loader.WebappLoader;

public final class Bootstrap {
  public static void main(String[] args) {
    System.setProperty("catalina.base",
      System.getProperty("user.dir"));
    Connector connector = new HttpConnector();
    Wrapper wrapper1 = new StandardWrapper();
    wrapper1.setName("Primitive");
    wrapper1.setServletClass("PrimitiveServlet");
    Wrapper wrapper2 = new StandardWrapper();
    wrapper2.setName("Modern");
    wrapper2.setServletClass("ModernServlet");
    Context context = new StandardContext();
    // StandardContext's start method adds a default mapper
    context.setPath("/app1");
    context.setDocBase("app1");
    context.addChild(wrapper1);
    context.addChild(wrapper2);
    LifecycleListener listener = new SimpleContextConfig();
    ((Lifecycle) context).addLifecycleListener(listener);
    Host host = new StandardHost();
    host.addChild(context);
    host.setName("localhost");
    host.setAppBase("webapps");
    Loader loader = new WebappLoader();
    context.setLoader(loader);
    // context.addServletMapping(pattern, name);
    context.addServletMapping("/Primitive", "Primitive");
    context.addServletMapping("/Modern", "Modern");
    Engine engine = new StandardEngine();
    engine.addChild(host);
    engine.setDefaultHost("localhost");
    Service service = new StandardService();
    service.setName("Stand-alone Service");
    Server server = new StandardServer();
    server.addService(service);
    service.addConnector(connector);
    // StandardService class's setContainer method calls
    // its connectors' setContainer method
    service.setContainer(engine);
    // Start the new server
    if (server instanceof Lifecycle) {
      try {
        server.initialize();
        ((Lifecycle) server).start();
        server.await();
        // the program waits until the await method returns,
        // i.e. until a shutdown command is received.
      }
```

```
      catch (LifecycleException e) {
        e.printStackTrace(System.out);
      }
    }

    // Shut down the server
    if (server instanceof Lifecycle) {
      try {
        ((Lifecycle) server).stop();
      }
      catch (LifecycleException e) {
        e.printStackTrace(System.out);
      }
    }
  }
}
```

The beginning part of the `main` method of the `Bootstrap` class is similar to the one in Chapter 13. It creates a connector, two wrappers, a context, a host, and an engine. It then adds the wrappers to the context, the context to the host, and the host to the engine. It does not associate the connector with the top level container (the engine), however. Instead, the `main` method creates a `Service` object, sets its name, creates a `Server` object, and adds the service to the server:

```
Service service = new StandardService();
service.setName("Stand-alone Service");
Server server = new StandardServer();
server.addService(service);
```

The `main` method then adds the connector and the engine to the service:

```
service.addConnector(connector);
service.setContainer(engine);
```

By adding the connector to the service, the connector will be associated with the container in the service.

The `main` method then calls the `initialize` and `start` methods of the `Server`, thereby initializing the connector and starting the connector and the container:

```
if (server instanceof Lifecycle) {
  try {
    server.initialize();
    ((Lifecycle) server).start();
```

Next, it calls the server's `await` method that makes the server waits for a shutdown command on port 8085. Note that at this stage the connector is already running, waiting for HTTP requests on port 8080 (the default port).

```
server.await();
```

The await method will not return until the correct shutdown command is received. When that happens, the main method calls the server's stop method, in effect stopping all other components.

Let's now review the Stopper class that you can use to stop the Server.

The Stopper Class

In the application in previous chapters, you either stop the container either abruptly or by pressing a key. The Stopper class provides a more elegant way of stopping a Catalina server. It also makes sure that the stop method of all lifecycle components will be called.

The Stopper class is given in Listing 14.14.

Listing 14.14: The Stopper class

```
package ex14.pyrmont.startup;

import java.io.OutputStream;
import java.io.IOException;
import java.net.Socket;

public class Stopper {
  public static void main(String[] args) {
    // the following code is taken from the Stop method of
    // the org.apache.catalina.startup.Catalina class
    int port = 8005;
    try {
      Socket socket = new Socket("127.0.0.1", port);
      OutputStream stream = socket.getOutputStream();
      String shutdown = "SHUTDOWN";
      for (int i = 0; i < shutdown.length(); i++)
        stream.write(shutdown.charAt(i));
      stream.flush();
      stream.close();
      socket.close();
      System.out.println("The server was successfully shut down.");
    }
    catch (IOException e) {
      System.out.println("Error. The server has not been started.");
    }
  }
}
```

The main method of the Stopper class creates a Socket object and then flushes the string SHUTDOWN, which is the correct shutdown command, to port 8085. If a Catalina server is running, it will be shut down.

Running the Applications

To run the `Bootstrap` class in Windows, from the working directory, type the following:

```
java -classpath ./lib/servlet.jar;./lib/commons-
collections.jar;./lib/commons-digester.jar;./lib/naming-
factory.jar;./lib/naming-common.jar;./ ex14.pyrmont.startup.Bootstrap
```

In Linux, you use a colon to separate two libraries.

```
java -classpath ./lib/servlet.jar:./lib/commons-
collections.jar:./lib/commons-digester.jar:./lib/naming-
factory.jar:./lib/naming-common.jar:./ ex14.pyrmont.startup.Bootstrap
```

To invoke `PrimitiveServlet`, use the following URL in your browser.

```
http://localhost:8080/app1/Primitive
```

To invoke `ModernServlet`, use the following URL.

```
http://localhost:8080/app1/Modern
```

To run the stopper to stop the application in both Windows and Linux, from the working directory, type the following:

```
java ex14.pyrmont.startup.Stopper
```

Note that in a real Catalina deployment, the functionality offered by the `Stopper` class is encapsulated into the `Bootstrap` class.

Summary

This chapter explains two important components in Catalina: server and service . A server is particularly useful because it provides a gentle mechanism for starting and stopping a Catalina deployment. A service component encapsulates a container and one or many connectors. The application accompanying this chapter shows how to use the server and service components. It also demonstrates how you can use the stop mechanism in the `StandardServer` class.

Chapter 15
Digester

As you have seen in the previous chapters, we use a Bootstrap class to instantiate a connector, a context, wrappers, and other components. Once you have those objects, you then associate them with each other by calling the set methods of various objects. For example, to instantiate a connector and a context, use the following code:

```
Connector connector = new HttpConnector();
Context context = new StandardContext();
```

To associate the connector with the context, you then write the following code:

```
connector.setContainer(context);
```

You can also configure the properties of each object by calling the corresponding set methods. For instance, you can set the path and docBase properties of a Context object by calling its setPath and setDocBase methods:

```
context.setPath("/myApp");
context.setDocBase("myApp");
```

In addition, you can add various components to the Context object by instantiating the components and call the corresponding add method on the context. For instance, here is how you add a lifecycle listener and a loader to your context object:

```
LifecycleListener listener = new SimpleContextConfig();
((Lifecycle) context).addLifecycleListener(listener);
Loader loader = new WebappLoader();
context.setLoader(loader);
```

Once all necessary associations and additions have been performed, to complete the application start-up you call the initialize and start methods of the connector and the start method of the context:

```
connector.initialize();
((Lifecycle) connector).start();
((Lifecycle) context).start();
```

This approach to application configuration has one apparent drawback: everything is hard-coded. Changing a component or even the value of a property requires the recompilation of the Bootstrap class. Fortunately, the Tomcat designer has chosen a more elegant way of configuration, i.e. an XML document named server.xml. Each element in the server.xml file is converted to a Java object and an element's attribute is used to set a property. This way, you can simply edit the server.xml file to change Tomcat settings. For example, a Context element in the server.xml file represents a context:

```
<context/>
```

To set the path and docBase properties you use attributes in the XML element:

```
<context docBase="myApp" path="/myApp"/>
```

Tomcat uses the open source library Digester to convert XML elements into Java objects. Digester is explained in the first section of this chapter.

The next section explains the configuration of a web application. A context represents a Web application, therefore the configuration of a web application is achieved through configuring the instantiated Context instance. The XML file used for configuring a web application is named web.xml. This file must reside in the WEB-INF directory of the application.

Digester

Digester is an open source project under the subproject Commons under the Apache's Jakarta project. You can download Digester it from http://jakarta.apache.org/commons/digester/. The Digester API comes in three packages, which are packaged into the commons-digester.jar file:

- org.apache.commons.digester. This package provides for rules-based processing of arbitrary XML documents.
- org.apache.commons.digester.rss. Example usage of Digester to parse XML documents compatible with the *Rich Site Summary* format used by many newsfeeds.
- org.apache.commons.digester.xmlrules. This package provides for XML-based definition of rules for Digester.

We will not cover all members in the three packages. Instead, we will concentrate on several important types used by Tomcat. We will start this section by presenting the `Digester` class, the most important type in the Digester library.

The Digester Class

The `org.apache.commons.digester.Digester` class is the main class in the Digester library. You use it to parse an XML document. For each element in the document, the `Digester` object will check if it needs to do something. You, the programmer, decide what the `Digester` instance must do before you call its the parse method.

How do you tell the Digester object what to do when it encounters an XML element? Easy. You define patterns and associate each pattern with one or more rules. The root element in an XML document has a pattern that is the same as the name of the element. For example, consider the XML document in Listing 13.1.

Listing 13.1: The example.xml file

```
<?xml version="1.0" encoding="ISO-8859-1"?>
<employee firstName="Brian" lastName="May">
  <office>
    <address streeName="Wellington Street" streetNumber="110"/>
  </office>
</employee>
```

The root document of the XML document is `employee`. The `employee` element has the pattern **employee**. The `office` element is a subelement of `<employee>`. The pattern of a subelement is the name of the subelement prefixed by the pattern of its containing element plus /. Therefore, the pattern for the `office` element is `employee/office`. The pattern for the `address` element is equal to:

```
the parent element's pattern + "/" + the name of the element
```

The parent of the address element is `<office>`, and the pattern for `<office>` is **employee/office**. Therefore, the pattern for `<address>` is **employee/office/address**.

Now that you understand how a pattern derives from an XML element, let's talk about rules.

A rule specifies an action or a couple of actions that the Digester must do upon encountering a particular pattern. A rule is represented by the `org.apache.commons.digester.Rule` class. The `Digester` class contains zero or more `Rule` objects. Inside a `Digester` instance, these rules and their corresponding patterns are stored in a type of storage represented by the `org.apache.commons.digester.Rules` interface. Every time you add a rule to a `Digester` instance, the `Rule` object is added to the `Rules` object.

Among others, the `Rule` class has the `begin` and `end` methods. When parsing an XML document, a `Digester` instance calls the `begin` method of the `Rule` object(s) added to it when it encounters the start element with a matching pattern. The `end` method of the `Rule` object is called when the `Digester` sees an end element.

When parsing the example.xml document in Listing 13.1, here is what the `Digester` object does:

- It first encounters the `employee` start element, therefore it checks if there is a rule (rules) for the pattern **employee**. If there is, the Digester executes the `begin` method of the `Rule` object(s), starting from the `begin` method of the first rule added to the Digester.
- It then sees the `office` start element, so the `Digester` object checks if there is a rule (rules) for the pattern **employee/office**. If there is, it executes the `begin` method(s) implemented by the rule(s).
- Next, the `Digester` instance encounters the `address` start element. This makes it check if there is a rule (rules) for the pattern **employee/office/address**. If one or more rule is found, execute the `begin` method(s) of the rule(s).
- Next, the `Digester` encounters the `address` end element, causing the end method(s) of the matching rules to be executed.
- Next, the `Digester` encounters the `office` end element, causing the end method(s) of the matching rules to be run.
- Finally, the `Digester` encounters the `employee` end element, causing the end method(s) of the matching rules to be executed.

What rules can you use? Digester has predefined a number of rules. You can use these rules without even having to understand the `Rule` class. However, if these rules are not sufficient, you can make your own rules. The predefined rules include the rules for creating objects, setting the value of a property, etc.

Creating Objects

If you want your `Digester` instance to create an object upon seeing a particular pattern, call its `addObjectCreate` method. This method has four overloads. The signatures of the two more frequently used overloads are as follows:

```
public void addObjectCreate(java.lang.String pattern,
  java.lang.Class clazz)
```

```
public void addObjectCreate(java.lang.String pattern,
  java.lang.String className)
```

You pass the pattern and a `Class` object or a class name. For instance, if you want the `Digester` to create an `Employee` object (whose class is `ex15.pyrmont.digestertest.Employee`) upon encountering the pattern `employee`, you call one of the following lines of code:

```
digester.addObjectCreate("employee",
  ex15.pyrmont.digestertest.Employee.class);
```

or

```
digester.addObjectCreate("employee",
  "ex15.pyrmont.digestertest.Employee");
```

The other two overloads of `addObjectCreate` allow you to define the name of the class in the XML element, instead of as an argument to the method. This is a very powerful feature because the class name can be determined at runtime. Here are the signatures of those method overloads:

```
public void addObjectCreate(java.lang.String pattern,
  java.lang.String className, java.lang.String attributeName)
```

```
public void addObjectCreate(java.lang.String pattern,
  java.lang.String attributeName, java.lang.Class clazz)
```

In these two overloads, the `attributeName` argument specifies the name of the attribute of the XML element that contains the name of the class to be instantiated. For example, you can use the following line of code to add a rule for creating an object:

```
digester.addObjectCreate("employee", null, "className");
```

where the attribute name is `className`.

You then pass the class name in the XML element.

```
<employee firstName="Brian" lastName="May"
  className="ex15.pyrmont.digestertest.Employee">
```

Or, you can define the default class name in the `addObjectCreate` method as follows:

```
digester.addObjectCreate("employee",
  "ex15.pyrmont.digestertest.Employee", "className");
```

If the `employee` element contains a `className` attribute, the value specified by this attribute will be used as the name of the class to instantiate. If no `className` attribute is found, the default class name is used.

The object created by `addObjectCreate` is pushed to an internal stack. A number of methods are also provided for you to peek, push, and pop the created objects.

Setting Properties

Another useful method is `addSetProperties`, which you can use to make the `Digester` object set object properties. One of the overloads of this method has the following signature:

```
public void addSetProperties(java.lang.String pattern)
```

You pass a pattern to this method. For example, consider the following code:

```
digester.addObjectCreate("employee",
  "ex15.pyrmont.digestertest.Employee");
digester.addSetProperties("employee");
```

The `Digester` instance above has two rules, object create and set properties. Both are set to be triggered by the pattern **employee**. The rules are executed in the order they are added to the `Digester` instance. For the following `employee` element in an XML document (which corresponds to the pattern employee):

```
<employee firstName="Brian" lastName="May">
```

The `Digester` instance first creates an instance of `ex15.pyrmont.digestertest.Employee`, thanks to the first rule added to it. The `Digester` instance then responds to the second rule for the pattern **employee** by calling the `setFirstName` and `setLastName` properties of the instantiated `Employee` object, passing `Brian` and `May`, respectively. An attribute in the `employee` element corresponds to a property in the `Employee` object. An error will occur if the `Employee` class does not define any one of the properties.

Calling Methods

The `Digester` class allows you to add a rule that calls a method on the topmost object in the stack upon seeing a corresponding pattern. This method is `addCallMethod`. One of its overloads has the following signature:

```
public void addCallMethod(java.lang.String pattern,
  java.lang.String methodName)
```

Creating Relationships between Objects

A `Digester` instance has an internal stack for storing objects temporarily. When the `addObjectCreate` method instantiates a class, the result is pushed into this stack. Imagine the stack as a well. To push an object into the stack is like dropping a round object having the same diameter as the well into it. To pop an object means to lift the top most object from the well.

When two `addObjectCreate` methods are invoked, the first object is dropped to the well first, followed by the second object. The `addSetNext` method is used to create a relationship between the first and the second object by calling the specified method on the first object and passing the second object as an argument to the method. Here is the signature of the `addSetNext` method:

```
public void addSetNext(java.lang.String pattern,
  java.lang.String methodName)
```

The `pattern` argument specifies the pattern that triggers this rule, the `methodName` argument is the name of the method on the first object that will be called. The pattern should be of the form **firstObject/secondObject**.

For example, an employee can have an office. To create a relationship between an employee and his/her office, you will first need to use two `addObjectCreate` methods, such as the following:

```
digester.addObjectCreate("employee",
  "ex15.pyrmont.digestertest.Employee");
digester.addObjectCreate("employee/office",
  "ex15.pyrmont.digestertest.Office");
```

The first `addObjectCreate` method creates an instance of the `Employee` class upon seeing an `employee` element. The second `addObjectCreate` method creates an instance of `Office` on seeing `<office>` under `<employee>`.

The two `addObjectCreate` methods push two objects to the stack. Now, the `Employee` object is at the bottom and the `Office` object on top. To create a relationship between them, you define another rule using the `addSetNext` method, such as the following:

```
digester.addSetNext("employee/office", "addOffice");
```

in which `addOffice` is a method in the `Employee` class. This method must accept an `Office` object as an argument. The second `Digester` example in this section will clarify the use of `addSetNext`.

Validating the XML Document

The XML document a `Digester` parses can be validated against a schema. Whether or not the XML document will be validated is determined by the validating property of the `Digester`. By default, the value of this property is `false`.

The `setValidating` method is used to indicate if you want validation to be performed. The `setValidating` method has the following signature:

```
public void setValidating(boolean validating)
```

If you want the well-formedness of your XML document to be validated, pass `true` to the `setValidating` method.

Digester Example 1

The first example explains how to use Digester to create an object dynamically and set its properties. Consider the `Employee` class in Listing 15.2 that we will instantiate using Digester.

Listing 15.2: The Employee Class

```java
package ex15.pyrmont.digestertest;

import java.util.ArrayList;

public class Employee {
  private String firstName;
  private String lastName;
  private ArrayList offices = new ArrayList();

  public Employee() {
    System.out.println("Creating Employee");
  }
  public String getFirstName() {
    return firstName;
  }
  public void setFirstName(String firstName) {
    System.out.println("Setting firstName : " + firstName);
    this.firstName = firstName;
  }
  public String getLastName() {
    return lastName;
  }
  public void setLastName(String lastName) {
    System.out.println("Setting lastName : " + lastName);
    this.lastName = lastName;
  }
  public void addOffice(Office office) {
```

```
      System.out.println("Adding Office to this employee");
      offices.add(office);
    }
    public ArrayList getOffices() {
      return offices;
    }
    public void printName() {
      System.out.println("My name is " + firstName + " " + lastName);
    }
}
```

The Employee class has three properties: firstName, lastName, and office. The firstName and lastName properties are strings, and office is of type ex15.pyrmont.digester.Office. The office property will be used in the second example of Digester.

The Employee class also has one method: printName that simply prints the first name and last name properties to the console.

We will now write a test class that uses a Digester and adds rules for creating an Employee object and setting its properties. The Test01 class in Listing 15.3 can be used for this purpose.

Listing 15.3: The Test01 Class

```
package ex15.pyrmont.digestertest;

import java.io.File;
import org.apache.commons.digester.Digester;

public class Test01 {

  public static void main(String[] args) {
    String path = System.getProperty("user.dir") + File.separator +
      "etc";
    File file = new File(path, "employee1.xml");
    Digester digester = new Digester();
    // add rules
    digester.addObjectCreate("employee",
      "ex15.pyrmont.digestertest.Employee");
    digester.addSetProperties("employee");
    digester.addCallMethod("employee", "printName");

    try {
      Employee employee = (Employee) digester.parse(file);
      System.out.println("First name : " + employee.getFirstName());
      System.out.println("Last name : " + employee.getLastName());
    }
    catch(Exception e) {
      e.printStackTrace();
    }
  }
}
```

You first define the path containing the location of your XML document and pass it the `File` class's constructor. You then create a `Digester` object and add three rules having the pattern **employee**:

```
digester.addObjectCreate("employee",
  "ex15.pyrmont.digestertest.Employee");
digester.addSetProperties("employee");
digester.addCallMethod("employee", "printName");
```

Next, you call the `parse` method on the `Digester` object passing the `File` object referencing the XML document. The return value of the `parse` method is the first object in the `Digester`'s internal stack:

```
Employee employee = (Employee) digester.parse(file);
```

This gives you an `Employee` object instantiated by the `Digester`. To see if the `Employee` object's properties have been set, call the `getFirstName` and `getLastName` methods of the `Employee` object:

```
System.out.println("First name : " + employee.getFirstName());
System.out.println("Last name : " + employee.getLastName());
```

Now, Listing 15.4 offers the employee1.xml document with the root element `employee`. The element has two attributes, `firstName` and `lastName`.

Listing 15.4: The employee1.xml file

```
<?xml version="1.0" encoding="ISO-8859-1"?>
<employee firstName="Brian" lastName="May">
</employee>
```

The result of running the `Test01` class is as follows:

```
Creating Employee
Setting firstName : Brian
Setting lastName : May
My name is Brian May
First name : Brian
Last name : May
```

Here is what happened.

When you call the `parse` method on the `Digester` object, it opens the XML document and starts parsing it. First, the `Digester` sees the `employee` start element. This triggers the three rules for the pattern **employee** in the order the rules were added. The first rule is for creating an object. Therefore, the Digester instantiates the `Employee` class, resulting the calling of the `Employee` class's constructor. This constructor prints the string `Creating Employee`.

The second rule sets the attribute of the `Employee` object. There are two attributes in the `employee` element, `firstName` and `lastName`. This rule causes the set methods of the `firstName` and `lastName` properties to be invoked. The set methods print the following strings:

```
Setting firstName : Brian
Setting lastName : May
```

The third rule calls the `printName` method, which prints the following text:

```
My name is Brian May
```

Then, the last two lines are the result of calling the `getFirstName` and `getLastName` methods on the `Employee` object:

```
First name : Brian
Last name : May
```

Digester Example 2

The second Digester example demonstrates how to create two objects and create a relationship between them. You define the type of relationship created. For example, an employee works in one or more office. An office is represented by the `Office` class. You can create an `Employee` and an `Office` object, and create a relationship between the Employee and Office objects. The `Office` class is given in Listing 15.5.

Listing 15.5: The Office Class

```java
package ex15.pyrmont.digestertest;

public class Office {
  private Address address;
  private String description;
  public Office() {
    System.out.println("..Creating Office");
  }
  public String getDescription() {
    return description;
  }
  public void setDescription(String description) {
    System.out.println("..Setting office description : " +
description);
    this.description = description;
  }
  public Address getAddress() {
    return address;
  }
  public void setAddress(Address address) {
    System.out.println("..Setting office address : " + address);
```

```
    this.address = address;
  }
}
```

You create a relationship by calling a method on the parent object. Note that this example uses the `Employee` class in Listing 15.2. The `Employee` class has the `addOffice` method to add an `Office` object to its `offices` collection.

Without the Digester, your Java code would look like this:

```
Employee employee = new Employee();
Office office = new Office();
employee.addOffice(office);
```

An office has an address and an address is represented by the `Address` class, given in Listing 15.6.

Listing 15.6: The Address Class

```
package ex15.pyrmont.digestertest;

public class Address {
  private String streetName;
  private String streetNumber;
  public Address() {
    System.out.println("....Creating Address");
  }
  public String getStreetName() {
    return streetName;
  }
  public void setStreetName(String streetName) {
    System.out.println("....Setting streetName : " + streetName);
    this.streetName = streetName;
  }
  public String getStreetNumber() {
    return streetNumber;
  }
  public void setStreetNumber(String streetNumber) {
    System.out.println("....Setting streetNumber : " + streetNumber);
    this.streetNumber = streetNumber;
  }
  public String toString() {
    return "...." + streetNumber + " " + streetName;
  }
}
```

To assign an address to an office, you can call the `setAddress` method of the `Office` class. With no help from Digester, you would have the following code:

```
Office office = new Office();
Address address = new Address();
office.setAddress(address);
```

The second Digester example shows how you can create objects and create relationships between them. We will use the Employee, Office, and Address classes. The Test02 class (in Listing 15.7) uses a Digester and adds rules to it.

Listing 15.7: The Test02 Class

```
package ex15.pyrmont.digestertest;

import java.io.File;
import java.util.*;
import org.apache.commons.digester.Digester;

public class Test02 {

  public static void main(String[] args) {
    String path = System.getProperty("user.dir") + File.separator +
      "etc";
    File file = new File(path, "employee2.xml");
    Digester digester = new Digester();
    // add rules
    digester.addObjectCreate("employee",
      "ex15.pyrmont.digestertest.Employee");
    digester.addSetProperties("employee");
    digester.addObjectCreate("employee/office",
      "ex15.pyrmont.digestertest.Office");
    digester.addSetProperties("employee/office");
    digester.addSetNext("employee/office", "addOffice");
    digester.addObjectCreate("employee/office/address",
      "ex15.pyrmont.digestertest.Address");
    digester.addSetProperties("employee/office/address");
    digester.addSetNext("employee/office/address", "setAddress");
    try {
      Employee employee = (Employee) digester.parse(file);
      ArrayList offices = employee.getOffices();
      Iterator iterator = offices.iterator();
      System.out.println(
        "----------------------------------------------");
      while (iterator.hasNext()) {
        Office office = (Office) iterator.next();
        Address address = office.getAddress();
        System.out.println(office.getDescription());
        System.out.println("Address : " +
          address.getStreetNumber() + " " + address.getStreetName());
        System.out.println("------------------------------");
      }
    }
    catch(Exception e) {
      e.printStackTrace();
    }
  }
}
```

To see the Digester in action, you can use the XML document employee2.xml in Listing 15.8.

Listing 15.8: The employee2.xml file

```xml
<?xml version="1.0" encoding="ISO-8859-1"?>
<employee firstName="Freddie" lastName="Mercury">
  <office description="Headquarters">
    <address streetName="Wellington Avenue" streetNumber="223"/>
  </office>
  <office description="Client site">
    <address streetName="Downing Street" streetNumber="10"/>
  </office>
</employee>
```

The result when the Test02 class is run is as follows:

```
Creating Employee
Setting firstName : Freddie
Setting lastName : Mercury
..Creating Office
..Setting office description : Headquarters
....Creating Address
....Setting streetName : Wellington Avenue
....Setting streetNumber : 223
..Setting office address : ....223 Wellington Avenue
Adding Office to this employee
..Creating Office
..Setting office description : Client site
....Creating Address
....Setting streetName : Downing Street
....Setting streetNumber : 10
..Setting office address : ....10 Downing Street
Adding Office to this employee
-------------------------------------------------
Headquarters
Address : 223 Wellington Avenue
------------------------------
Client site
Address : 10 Downing Street
------------------------------
```

The Rule Class

The Rule class has several methods, the two most important of which are begin and end. When a Digester instance encounters the beginning of an XML element, it calls the begin method of all matching Rule objects it contains. The begin method of the *Rule* class has the following signature:

```java
public void begin(org.xml.sax.Attributes attributes)
  throws java.lang.Exception
```

When the `Digester` instance encounters the end of an XML element, it calls the end method of all matching `Rule` instances it contains. The signature of the end method of the `Rule` class is as follows.

```
public void end() throws java.lang.Exception
```

How do the `Digester` objects in the preceding examples do the wonder? Every time you call the `addObjectCreate`, `addCallMethod`, `addSetNext`, and other methods of the `Digester`, you indirectly invoke the `addRule` method of the `Digester` class, which adds a `Rule` object and its matching pattern to the `Rules` collection inside the `Digester`.

The signature of the `addRule` method is as follows:

```
public void addRule(java.lang.String pattern, Rule rule)
```

The implementation of the `addRule` method in the `Digester` class is as follows:

```
public void addRule(String pattern, Rule rule) {
  rule.setDigester(this);
  getRules().add(pattern, rule);
}
```

Take a look at the `Digester` class source code for the `addObjectCreate` method overloads:

```
public void addObjectCreate(String pattern, String className) {
  addRule(pattern, new ObjectCreateRule(className));
}
public void addObjectCreate(String pattern, Class clazz) {
  addRule(pattern,  new ObjectCreateRule(clazz));
}
public void addObjectCreate(String pattern, String className,
  String attributeName) {
  addRule(pattern, new ObjectCreateRule(className, attributeName));
}
public void addObjectCreate(String pattern,
  String attributeName, Class clazz) {
  addRule(pattern, new ObjectCreateRule(attributeName, clazz));
}
```

The four overloads call the `addRule` method. The `ObjectCreateRule` class--whose instance gets created as the second argument to the `addRule` method--is a subclass of the `Rule` class. You may be interested in the `begin` and `end` method implementations in the `ObjectCreateRule` class:

```
public void begin(Attributes attributes) throws Exception {
  // Identify the name of the class to instantiate
  String realClassName = className;
  if (attributeName != null) {
    String value = attributes.getValue(attributeName);
```

```
    if (value != null) {
      realClassName = value;
    }
  }
  if (digester.log.isDebugEnabled()) {
    digester.log.debug("[ObjectCreateRule]{" + digester.match +
    "}New " + realClassName);
  }

  // Instantiate the new object and push it on the context stack
  Class clazz = digester.getClassLoader().loadClass(realClassName);
  Object instance = clazz.newInstance();
  digester.push(instance);
}
public void end() throws Exception {
  Object top = digester.pop();
  if (digester.log.isDebugEnabled()) {
    digester.log.debug("[ObjectCreateRule]{" + digester.match +
      "} Pop " + top.getClass().getName());
  }
}
```

The last three lines in the `begin` method creates an instance of the object and then pushes it to the internal stack inside the `Digester`. The `end` method pops the object from the stack.

The other subclass of the `Rule` class works similarly. You can open the source code if you are keen to know what is behind each rule.

Digester Example 3: Using RuleSet

Another way of adding rules to a Digester instance is by calling its `addRuleSet` method. The signature of this method is as follows:

```
public void addRuleSet(RuleSet ruleSet)
```

The `org.apache.commons.digester.RuleSet` interface represents a set of `Rule` objects. This interface defines two methods, `addRuleInstance` and `getNamespaceURI`. The signature of the `addRuleInstance` is as follows:

```
public void addRuleInstance(Digester digester)
```

The `addRuleInstance` method adds the set of `Rule` objects defined in the current `RuleSet` to the `Digester` instance passed as the argument to this method.

The `getNamespaceURI` returns the namespace URI that will be applied to all `Rule` objects created in this `RuleSet`. Its signature is as follows:

```
public java.lang.String getNamespaceURI()
```

Therefore, after you create a `Digester` object, you can create a `RuleSet` object and pass the `RuleSet` object to the `addRuleSet` method on the `Digester`.

A convenience base class, `RuleSetBase`, implements `RuleSet`. `RuleSetBase` is an abstract class that provides the implementation of the `getNamespaceURI`. You only need to provide the implementation of the `addRuleInstances` method.

As an example, let's modify the `Test02` class in the previous example by introducing the `EmployeeRuleSet` class in Listing 15.9.

Listing 15.9: The EmployeeRuleSet Class

```
package ex15.pyrmont.digestertest;

import org.apache.commons.digester.Digester;
import org.apache.commons.digester.RuleSetBase;

public class EmployeeRuleSet extends RuleSetBase  {
  public void addRuleInstances(Digester digester) {
    // add rules
    digester.addObjectCreate("employee",
      "ex15.pyrmont.digestertest.Employee");
    digester.addSetProperties("employee");
    digester.addObjectCreate("employee/office",
      "ex15.pyrmont.digestertest.Office");
    digester.addSetProperties("employee/office");
    digester.addSetNext("employee/office", "addOffice");
    digester.addObjectCreate("employee/office/address",
      "ex15.pyrmont.digestertest.Address");
    digester.addSetProperties("employee/office/address");
    digester.addSetNext("employee/office/address", "setAddress");
  }
}
```

Notice that the implementation of the `addRuleInstances` method in the `EmployeeRuleSet` class adds the same rules to the `Digester` as the `Test02` class does. The `Test03` class in Listing 15.10 creates an instance of the `EmployeeRuleSet` and then adds it to the `Digester` it created earlier.

Listing 15.10: The Test03 Class

```
package ex15.pyrmont.digestertest;

import java.io.File;
import java.util.ArrayList;
import java.util.Iterator;
import org.apache.commons.digester.Digester;

public class Test03 {
```

```
public static void main(String[] args) {
  String path = System.getProperty("user.dir") +
    File.separator  + "etc";
  File file = new File(path, "employee2.xml");
  Digester digester = new Digester();
  digester.addRuleSet(new EmployeeRuleSet());
  try {
    Employee employee = (Employee) digester.parse(file);
    ArrayList offices = employee.getOffices();
    Iterator iterator = offices.iterator();
    System.out.println(
      "-----------------------------------------------");
    while (iterator.hasNext()) {
      Office office = (Office) iterator.next();
      Address address = office.getAddress();
      System.out.println(office.getDescription());
      System.out.println("Address : " +
        address.getStreetNumber() + " " + address.getStreetName());
      System.out.println("-----------------------------");
    }
  }
  catch(Exception e) {
    e.printStackTrace();
  }
}
}
```

When run, the Test03 class produces the same output as the Test02 class. Note however, that the Test03 is shorter because the code for adding Rule objects is now hidden inside the EmployeeRuleSet class.

As you will see later, Catalina uses subclasses of RuleSetBase for initializing its server and other components. In the next sections, you will see how Digester plays a very important role in Catalina.

ContextConfig

Unlike other types of containers, a StandardContext must have a listener. This listener configures the StandardContext instance and upon successfully doing so sets the StandardContext's configured variable to true. In previous chapters, we used the SimpleContextConfig class as the StandardContext's listener. This class was a very simple one whose sole purpose is to set the configured variable so that the start method of StandardContext can continue.

In a real Tomcat deployment, the standard listener for StandardContext is an instance of org.apache.catalina.startup.ContextConfig class.

Unlike our humble `SimpleContextConfig` class, `ContextConfig` does a lot of useful stuff that the `StandardContext` instance cannot live without it. For example, a `ContextConfig` instance associated with a `StandardContext` installs an authenticator valve in the `StandardContext`'s pipeline. It also adds a certificate valve (of type `org.apache.catalina.valves.CertificateValve`) to the pipeline.

More importantly, however, the `ContextConfig` instance also reads and parses the default web.xml file and the application web.xml file and convert the XML elements to Java objects. The default web.xml file is located in the conf directory of CATALINE_HOME. It defines and maps default servlets, maps file extensions with MIME types, defines the default session timeout, and list welcome files. You should open the file now to see its contents.

The application web.xml file is the application configuration file, located in the WEB-INF directory of an application. Both files are not required. `ContextConfig` will continue even if none of these files is found.

The `ContextConfig` creates a `StandardWrapper` instance for each servlet element. Therefore, as you can see in the application accompanying this chapter, configuration is made easy. You are no longer required to instantiate a wrapper anymore.

Therefore, somewhere in your bootstrap class, you must instantiate the `ContextConfig` class and add it to the `StandardContext` by calling the `addLifecycleListener` method of the `org.apache.catalina.Lifecycle` interface.

```
LifecycleListener listener = new ContextConfig();
((Lifecycle) context).addLifecycleListener(listener);
```

The `StandardContext` fires the following events when it is started:

- BEFORE_START_EVENT
- START_EVENT
- AFTER_START_EVENT

When stopped, the `StandardContext` fires the following events:

- BEFORE_STOP_EVENT
- STOP_EVENT
- AFTER_STOP_EVENT

The `ContextConfig` class responds to two events: START_EVENT and STOP_EVENT. The `lifecycleEvent` method is invoked every time the `StandardContext` triggers an event. This method is given in Listing 15.11.

We have added comments to Listing 15.11 so that the stop method is easier to understand.

Listing 15.11: The `lifecycleEvent` method of `ContextConfig`

```java
public void lifecycleEvent(LifecycleEvent event) {
  // Identify the context we are associated with
  try {
    context = (Context) event.getLifecycle();
    if (context instanceof StandardContext) {
      int contextDebug = ((StandardContext) context).getDebug();
      if (contextDebug > this.debug)
        this.debug = contextDebug;
    }
  }
  catch (ClassCastException e) {
    log(sm.getString("contextConfig.cce", event.getLifecycle()), e);
    return;
  }
  // Process the event that has occurred
  if (event.getType().equals(Lifecycle.START_EVENT))
    start();
  else if (event.getType().equals(Lifecycle.STOP_EVENT))
    stop();
}
```

As you can see in the end of the lifecycleEvent method, it calls either its start method or its stop method. The start method is given in Listing 15.12. Notice that somewhere in its body the start method calls the defaultConfig and applicationConfig methods. Both are explained in the sections after this.

Listing 15.12: The `start` method of `ContextConfig`

```java
private synchronized void start() {
  if (debug > 0)
    log(sm.getString("contextConfig.start"));
  // reset the configured boolean
  context.setConfigured(false);
  // a flag that indicates whether the process is still
  // going smoothly
  ok = true;
  // Set properties based on DefaultContext
  Container container = context.getParent();
  if( !context.getOverride() ) {
    if( container instanceof Host ) {
      ((Host)container).importDefaultContext(context);
      container = container.getParent();
    }
    if( container instanceof Engine ) {
      ((Engine)container).importDefaultContext(context);
    }
  }
```

```
  // Process the default and application web.xml files
  defaultConfig();
  applicationConfig();
  if (ok) {
    validateSecurityRoles();
  }

  // Scan tag library descriptor files for additional listener classes
  if (ok) {
    try {
      tldScan();
    }
    catch (Exception e) {
      log(e.getMessage(), e);
      ok = false;
    }
  }
  // Configure a certificates exposer valve, if required
  if (ok)
    certificatesConfig();

  // Configure an authenticator if we need one
  if (ok)
    authenticatorConfig();
  // Dump the contents of this pipeline if requested
  if ((debug >= 1) && (context instanceof ContainerBase)) {
    log("Pipline Configuration:");
    Pipeline pipeline = ((ContainerBase) context).getPipeline();
    Valve valves[] = null;
    if (pipeline != null)
      valves = pipeline.getValves();
    if (valves != null) {
      for (int i = 0; i < valves.length; i++) {
        log("  " + valves[i].getInfo());
      }
    }
    log("======================");
  }
  // Make our application available if no problems were encountered
  if (ok)
    context.setConfigured(true);
  else {
    log(sm.getString("contextConfig.unavailable"));
    context.setConfigured(false);
  }
}
```

The defaultConfig Method

The defaultConfig method reads and parses the default web.xml file in the %CATALINA_HOME%/conf directory. The defaultConfig method is presented in Listing 15.13.

Listing 15.13: The defaultConfig method

```
private void defaultConfig() {
  // Open the default web.xml file, if it exists
  File file = new File(Constants.DefaultWebXml);
  if (!file.isAbsolute())
    file = new File(System.getProperty("catalina.base"),
      Constants.DefaultWebXml);
  FileInputStream stream = null;
  try {
    stream = new FileInputStream(file.getCanonicalPath());
    stream.close();
    stream = null;
  }
  catch (FileNotFoundException e) {
    log(sm.getString("contextConfig.defaultMissing"));
    return;
  }
  catch (IOException e) {
    log(sm.getString("contextConfig.defaultMissing"), e);
    return;
  }
  // Process the default web.xml file
  synchronized (webDigester) {
    try {
      InputSource is =
        new InputSource("file://" + file.getAbsolutePath());
      stream = new FileInputStream(file);
      is.setByteStream(stream);
      webDigester.setDebug(getDebug());
      if (context instanceof StandardContext)
        ((StandardContext) context).setReplaceWelcomeFiles(true);
      webDigester.clear();
      webDigester.push(context);
      webDigester.parse(is);
    }
    catch (SAXParseException e) {
      log(sm.getString("contextConfig.defaultParse"), e);
      log(sm.getString("contextConfig.defaultPosition",
        "" + e.getLineNumber(), "" + e.getColumnNumber()));
      ok = false;
    }
    catch (Exception e) {
      log(sm.getString("contextConfig.defaultParse"), e);
      ok = false;
    }
    finally {
      try {
        if (stream != null) {
          stream.close();
        }
      }
      catch (IOException e) {
        log(sm.getString("contextConfig.defaultClose"), e);
      }
    }
```

```
    }
}
```

The defaultConfig method begins by creating a File object that references the default web.xml file.

```
File file = new File(Constants.DefaultWebXml);
```

The value of DefaultWebXML can be found in the org.apache.catalina.startup.Constants class as follows:

```
public static final String DefaultWebXml = "conf/web.xml";
```

The defaultConfig method then processes the web.xml file. It locks the webDigester object variable, then parses the file.

```
    synchronized (webDigester) {
      try {
        InputSource is =
          new InputSource("file://" + file.getAbsolutePath());
        stream = new FileInputStream(file);
        is.setByteStream(stream);
        webDigester.setDebug(getDebug());
        if (context instanceof StandardContext)
          ((StandardContext) context).setReplaceWelcomeFiles(true);
        webDigester.clear();
        webDigester.push(context);
        webDigester.parse(is);
```

The webDigester object variable references a Digester instance that have been populated with rules for processing a web.xml file. It is discussed in the subsection, "Creating Web Digester" later in this section.

The applicationConfig Method

The applicationConfig method is similar to the defaultConfig method, except that it processes the application deployment descriptor. A deployment descriptor resides in the WEB-INF directory of the application directory.

The applicationConfig method is given in Listing 15.14.

Listing 15.14: The applicationConfig method of ContextConfig

```
private void applicationConfig() {
  // Open the application web.xml file, if it exists
  InputStream stream = null;
  ServletContext servletContext = context.getServletContext();
  if (servletContext != null)
    stream = servletContext.getResourceAsStream
  (Constants.ApplicationWebXml);
  if (stream == null) {
```

```
      log(sm.getString("contextConfig.applicationMissing"));
      return;
    }

    // Process the application web.xml file
    synchronized (webDigester) {
      try {
        URL url =
          servletContext.getResource(Constants.ApplicationWebXml);

        InputSource is = new InputSource(url.toExternalForm());
        is.setByteStream(stream);
        webDigester.setDebug(getDebug());
        if (context instanceof StandardContext) {
          ((StandardContext) context).setReplaceWelcomeFiles(true);
        }
        webDigester.clear();
        webDigester.push(context);
        webDigester.parse(is);
      }
      catch (SAXParseException e) {
        log(sm.getString("contextConfig.applicationParse"), e);
        log(sm.getString("contextConfig.applicationPosition",
          "" + e.getLineNumber(),
          "" + e.getColumnNumber())));
        ok = false;
      }
      catch (Exception e) {
        log(sm.getString("contextConfig.applicationParse"), e);
        ok = false;
      }
      finally {
        try {
          if (stream != null) {
            stream.close();
          }
        }
        catch (IOException e) {
          log(sm.getString("contextConfig.applicationClose"), e);
        }
      }
    }
  }
}
```

Creating Web Digester

A Digester object reference called webDigester exists in the
ContextConfig class:

```
private static Digester webDigester = createWebDigester();
```

This Digester is used to parse the default web.xml and application web.xml
files. The rules for processing the web.xml file are added when the

createWebDigester method is invoked. The createWebDigester method is given in Listing 15.15.

Listing 15.15: The createWebDigester method

```
private static Digester createWebDigester() {
  URL url = null;
  Digester webDigester = new Digester();
  webDigester.setValidating(true);
  url =  ContextConfig.class.getResource(
    Constants.WebDtdResourcePath_22);
  webDigester.register(Constants.WebDtdPublicId_22,
    url.toString());
  url = ContextConfig.class.getResource(
    Constants.WebDtdResourcePath_23);
  webDigester.register(Constants.WebDtdPublicId_23,
  url.toString());
  webDigester.addRuleSet(new WebRuleSet());
  return (webDigester);
}
```

Notice that createWebDigester method calls the addRuleSet on webDigester by passing an instance of org.apache.catalina.startup.WebRuleSet. The WebRuleSet is a subclass of the org.apache.commons.digester.RuleSetBase class. If you are familiar with the syntax of a servlet application deployment descriptor and you have read the Digester section at the beginning of this chapter, you sure can understand how it works.

The WebRuleSet class is given in Listing 15.16. Note that we have removed some parts of the addRuleInstances method to save space.

Listing 15.16: The WebRuleSet class

```
package org.apache.catalina.startup;

import java.lang.reflect.Method;
import org.apache.catalina.Context;
import org.apache.catalina.Wrapper;
import org.apache.catalina.deploy.SecurityConstraint;
import org.apache.commons.digester.Digester;
import org.apache.commons.digester.Rule;
import org.apache.commons.digester.RuleSetBase;
import org.xml.sax.Attributes;

/**
 * <p><strong>RuleSet</strong> for processing the contents of a web
application
 * deployment descriptor (<code>/WEB-INF/web.xml</code>) resource.</p>
 *
 * @author Craig R. McClanahan
 * @version $Revision: 1.1 $ $Date: 2001/10/17 00:44:02 $
 */
```

```java
public class WebRuleSet extends RuleSetBase {
  // --------------------------------- Instance Variables
  /**
   * The matching pattern prefix to use for recognizing our elements.
   */
  protected String prefix = null;

  // ----------------------------------------- Constructor
  /**
   * Construct an instance of this <code>RuleSet</code> with
   * the default matching pattern prefix.
   */
  public WebRuleSet() {
    this("");
  }

  /**
   * Construct an instance of this <code>RuleSet</code> with
   * the specified matching pattern prefix.
   *
   * @param prefix Prefix for matching pattern rules (including the
   *  trailing slash character)
   */
  public WebRuleSet(String prefix) {
    super();
    this.namespaceURI = null;
    this.prefix = prefix;
  }

  // ----------------------------------------- Public Methods
  /**
   * <p>Add the set of Rule instances defined in this RuleSet to the
   * specified <code>Digester</code> instance, associating them with
   * our namespace URI (if any).  This method should only be called
   * by a Digester instance.</p>
   *
   * @param digester Digester instance to which the new Rule instances
   *  should be added.
   */
  public void addRuleInstances(Digester digester) {
    digester.addRule(prefix + "web-app",
      new SetPublicIdRule(digester, "setPublicId"));
    digester.addCallMethod(prefix + "web-app/context-param",
      "addParameter", 2);
    digester.addCallParam(prefix +
      "web-app/context-param/param-name", 0);
    digester.addCallParam(prefix +
      "web-app/context-param/param-value", 1);
    digester.addCallMethod(prefix + "web-app/display-name",
      "setDisplayName", 0);
    digester.addRule(prefix + "web-app/distributable",
      new SetDistributableRule(digester));
    ...
    digester.addObjectCreate(prefix + "web-app/filter",
      "org.apache.catalina.deploy.FilterDef");
    digester.addSetNext(prefix + "web-app/filter", "addFilterDef",
```

```
  "org.apache.catalina.deploy.FilterDef");
digester.addCallMethod(prefix + "web-app/filter/description",
  "setDescription", 0);
digester.addCallMethod(prefix + "web-app/filter/display-name",
  "setDisplayName", 0);
digester.addCallMethod(prefix + "web-app/filter/filter-class",
  "setFilterClass", 0);
digester.addCallMethod(prefix + "web-app/filter/filter-name",
  "setFilterName", 0);
digester.addCallMethod(prefix + "web-app/filter/large-icon",
  "setLargeIcon", 0);
digester.addCallMethod(prefix + "web-app/filter/small-icon",
  "setSmallIcon", 0);
digester.addCallMethod(prefix + "web-app/filter/init-param",
  "addInitParameter", 2);
digester.addCallParam(prefix +
  "web-app/filter/init-param/param-name", 0);
digester.addCallParam(prefix +
  "web-app/filter/init-param/param-value", 1);
digester.addObjectCreate(prefix + "web-app/filter-mapping",
  "org.apache.catalina.deploy.FilterMap");
digester.addSetNext(prefix + "web-app/filter-mapping",
  "addFilterMap", "org.apache.catalina.deploy.FilterMap");
digester.addCallMethod(prefix +
  "web-app/filter-mapping/filter-name", "setFilterName", 0);
digester.addCallMethod(prefix +
  "web-app/filter-mapping/servlet-name", "setServletName", 0);
digester.addCallMethod(prefix +
  "web-app/filter-mapping/url-pattern", "setURLPattern", 0);
digester.addCallMethod(prefix +
  "web-app/listener/listener-class", "addApplicationListener", 0);
...
digester.addRule(prefix + "web-app/servlet",
  new WrapperCreateRule(digester));
digester.addSetNext(prefix + "web-app/servlet",
  "addChild", "org.apache.catalina.Container");
digester.addCallMethod(prefix + "web-app/servlet/init-param",
  "addInitParameter", 2);
digester.addCallParam(prefix +
  "web-app/servlet/init-param/param-name", 0);
digester.addCallParam(prefix +
  "web-app/servlet/init-param/param-value", 1);
digester.addCallMethod(prefix + "web-app/servlet/jsp-file",
  "setJspFile", 0);
digester.addCallMethod(prefix +
  "web-app/servlet/load-on-startup", "setLoadOnStartupString", 0);
digester.addCallMethod(prefix +
  "web-app/servlet/run-as/role-name", "setRunAs", 0);
digester.addCallMethod(prefix +
  "web-app/servlet/security-role-ref", "addSecurityReference", 2);
digester.addCallParam(prefix +
  "web-app/servlet/security-role-ref/role-link", 1);
digester.addCallParam(prefix +
  "web-app/servlet/security-role-ref/role-name", 0);
digester.addCallMethod(prefix + "web-app/servlet/servlet-class",
  "setServletClass", 0);
```

```
    digester.addCallMethod(prefix + "web-app/servlet/servlet-name",
      "setName", 0);
    digester.addCallMethod(prefix + "web-app/servlet-mapping",
      "addServletMapping", 2);
    digester.addCallParam(prefix +
      "web-app/servlet-mapping/servlet-name", 1);
    digester.addCallParam(prefix +
      "web-app/servlet-mapping/url-pattern", 0);
    digester.addCallMethod(prefix +
      "web-app/session-config/session-timeout", "setSessionTimeout", 1,
      new Class[] { Integer.TYPE });
    digester.addCallParam(prefix +
      "web-app/session-config/session-timeout", 0);
    digester.addCallMethod(prefix + "web-app/taglib",
      "addTaglib", 2);
    digester.addCallParam(prefix + "web-app/taglib/taglib-location",
1);
    digester.addCallParam(prefix + "web-app/taglib/taglib-uri", 0);
    digester.addCallMethod(prefix +
      "web-app/welcome-file-list/welcome-file", "addWelcomeFile", 0);
  }
}
// ------------------------------------------- Private Classes

/**
 * A Rule that calls the <code>setAuthConstraint(true)</code> method of
 * the top item on the stack, which must be of type
 * <code>org.apache.catalina.deploy.SecurityConstraint</code>.
 */
final class SetAuthConstraintRule extends Rule {
  public SetAuthConstraintRule(Digester digester) {
    super(digester);
  }
  public void begin(Attributes attributes) throws Exception {
    SecurityConstraint securityConstraint =
      (SecurityConstraint) digester.peek();
    securityConstraint.setAuthConstraint(true);
    if (digester.getDebug() > 0)
      digester.log("Calling
SecurityConstraint.setAuthConstraint(true)");
  }
}

...
final class WrapperCreateRule extends Rule {
  public WrapperCreateRule(Digester digester) {
    super(digester);
  }
  public void begin(Attributes attributes) throws Exception {
    Context context =
      (Context) digester.peek(digester.getCount() - 1);
    Wrapper wrapper = context.createWrapper();
    digester.push(wrapper);
    if (digester.getDebug() > 0)
      digester.log("new " + wrapper.getClass().getName());
  }
```

```
  public void end() throws Exception {
    Wrapper wrapper = (Wrapper) digester.pop();
    if (digester.getDebug() > 0)
      digester.log("pop " + wrapper.getClass().getName());
  }
}
```

The Application

This chapter's application shows how to use a `ContextConfig` instance as a listener to configure the `StandardContext` object. It consists of only one class, `Bootstrap`, which is presented in Listing 15.17.

Listing 15.17: The `Bootstrap` class

```java
package ex15.pyrmont.startup;

import org.apache.catalina.Connector;
import org.apache.catalina.Container;
import org.apache.catalina.Context;
import org.apache.catalina.Host;
import org.apache.catalina.Lifecycle;
import org.apache.catalina.LifecycleListener;
import org.apache.catalina.Loader;
import org.apache.catalina.connector.http.HttpConnector;
import org.apache.catalina.core.StandardContext;
import org.apache.catalina.core.StandardHost;
import org.apache.catalina.loader.WebappLoader;
import org.apache.catalina.startup.ContextConfig;


public final class Bootstrap {

  // invoke: http://localhost:8080/app1/Modern or
  // http://localhost:8080/app2/Primitive
  // note that we don't instantiate a Wrapper here,
  // ContextConfig reads the WEB-INF/classes dir and loads all
  // servlets.
  public static void main(String[] args) {
    System.setProperty("catalina.base",
      System.getProperty("user.dir"));
    Connector connector = new HttpConnector();
    Context context = new StandardContext();
    // StandardContext's start method adds a default mapper
    context.setPath("/app1");
    context.setDocBase("app1");
    LifecycleListener listener = new ContextConfig();
    ((Lifecycle) context).addLifecycleListener(listener);
    Host host = new StandardHost();
    host.addChild(context);
    host.setName("localhost");
    host.setAppBase("webapps");
```

```
    Loader loader = new WebappLoader();
    context.setLoader(loader);
    connector.setContainer(host);
    try {
      connector.initialize();
      ((Lifecycle) connector).start();
      ((Lifecycle) host).start();
      Container[] c = context.findChildren();
      int length = c.length;
      for (int i=0; i<length; i++) {
        Container child = c[i];
        System.out.println(child.getName());
      }
      // make the application wait until we press a key.
      System.in.read();
      ((Lifecycle) host).stop();
    }
    catch (Exception e) {
      e.printStackTrace();
    }
  }
}
```

Running the Applications

To run the application in Windows, from the working directory, type the following:

```
java -classpath ./lib/servlet.jar;./lib/commons-
collections.jar;./lib/commons-digester.jar;./lib/commons-
logging.jar;./lib/commons-beanutils.jar;./
ex15.pyrmont.startup.Bootstrap
```

In Linux, you use a colon to separate two libraries.

```
java -classpath ./lib/servlet.jar:./lib/commons-
collections.jar:./lib/commons-digester.jar:./lib/commons-
logging.jar:./lib/commons-beanutils.jar:./
ex15.pyrmont.startup.Bootstrap
```

To invoke PrimitiveServlet, use the following URL in your browser.

```
http://localhost:8080/app1/Primitive
```

To invoke ModernServlet, use the following URL.

```
http://localhost:8080/app1/Modern
```

Summary

Tomcat is used in different configurations. Easy configuration using a server.xml file is achieved through the use of `Digester` objects that converts XML elements to Java objects. In addition, a web.xml document is used to configure a servlet/JSP application. Tomcat must be able to parse this web.xml document and configure a `Context` object based on the elements in the XML document. Again, Digester solves this problem elegantly.

314

Chapter 16
Shutdown Hook

In many circumstances, you need a chance to do clean-up when the user shuts down your application. The problem is, the user does not always follow the recommended procedure to exit. For example, in a Tomcat deployment you start the servlet container by instantiating a Server object and call its start method, which in turn calls the start method of other components. In a normal situation, to give a chance for the Server object to stop all other components, you should close it by sending the proper shutdown command, as explained in Chapter 14, "Server and Service". Something unexpected could happen if you simply exit abruptly, such as by closing the console on which the application is running.

Fortunately, Java provides an elegant way for programmers to execute code in the middle of a shutdown process, thus making sure your clean-up code is always executed. This chapter shows how to use a shutdown hook to guarantee the clean-up code is always run regardless how the user terminates the application.

In Java, the virtual machine shuts down itself in response to two types of events:

- the application exits normally as in the case where the System.exit method is called or when the last non-daemon thread exits.
- The user abruptly forces the virtual machine to terminate, for example by typing CTRL+C or logs off from the system before closing a running Java program.

Fortunately enough, when shutting down, the virtual machine follows this two-phase sequence:

1. The virtual machine starts all registered shutdown hooks, if any. Shutdown hooks are threads that are previously registered with the Runtime. All shutdown hooks are run concurrently until they finish.

2. The virtual machine calls all uninvoked finalizers if appropriate.

In this chapter, we are interested in the first phase because this allows programmers to tell the virtual machine to execute some clean up code in the program. A shutdown hook is simply an instance of a subclass of the `java.lang.Thread` class. Creating a shutdown hook is simple:

- Write a class extending the Thread class.
- Provide the implementation of your class's `run` method. This method is the code that needs to be run when the application is shut down, either normally or abruptly.
- In your application, instantiate your shutdown hook class.
- Register the shutdown hook with the current `Runtime`'s `addShutdownHook` method.

As you may have noticed, you do not start the shutdown hook as you would other threads. The virtual machine will start and run your shutdown hook when it runs its shutdown sequence.

The code in Listing 16.1 provides a simple class called `ShutdownHookDemo` and a subclass of Thread named `ShutdownHook`. Note that the run method of the `ShutdownHook` class simply prints the string `Shutting down` on the console. However, you can insert any code that needs to be run before the shutdown.

Listing 16.1: Using Shutdown Hook

```
package ex16.pyrmont.shutdownhook;
public class ShutdownHookDemo {

  public void start() {
    System.out.println("Demo");
    ShutdownHook shutdownHook = new ShutdownHook();
    Runtime.getRuntime().addShutdownHook(shutdownHook);
  }

  public static void main(String[] args) {
    ShutdownHookDemo demo = new ShutdownHookDemo();
    demo.start();
    try {
      System.in.read();
    }
    catch(Exception e) {
    }
  }
}

class ShutdownHook extends Thread {
  public void run() {
    System.out.println("Shutting down");
  }
}
```

After the instantiating the ShutdownHookDemo class, the `main` method calls the `start` method. The `start` method creates a shutdown hook and registers it with the current runtime.

```
ShutdownHook shutdownHook = new ShutdownHook();
Runtime.getRuntime().addShutdownHook(shutdownHook);
```

Then, the program waits for the user to press Enter.

```
System.in.read();
```

When the user presses Enter, the program exits. However, the virtual machine will run the shutdown hook, in effect printing the words `Shutting down`.

A Shutdown Hook Example

As another example, consider a simple Swing application whose class is called `MySwingApp` (See Figure 16.1). This application creates a temporary file when it is launched. When closed, the temporary file must be deleted.

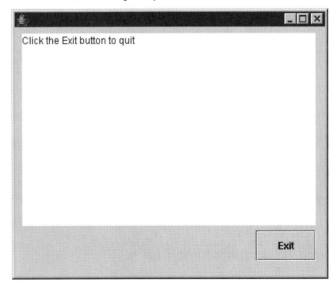

Figure 16.1: A Swing application

318

The code for this class is given in Listing 16.2.

Listing 16.2: A simple Swing application

```
package ex16.pyrmont.shutdownhook;
import java.awt.*;
import javax.swing.*;
import java.awt.event.*;
import java.io.File;
import java.io.IOException;

public class MySwingApp extends JFrame {
  JButton exitButton = new JButton();
  JTextArea jTextArea1 = new JTextArea();
  String dir = System.getProperty("user.dir");
  String filename = "temp.txt";

  public MySwingApp() {
    exitButton.setText("Exit");
    exitButton.setBounds(new Rectangle(304, 248, 76, 37));
    exitButton.addActionListener(new java.awt.event.ActionListener() {
      public void actionPerformed(ActionEvent e) {
        exitButton_actionPerformed(e);
      }
    });
    this.getContentPane().setLayout(null);
    jTextArea1.setText("Click the Exit button to quit");
    jTextArea1.setBounds(new Rectangle(9, 7, 371, 235));
    this.getContentPane().add(exitButton, null);
    this.getContentPane().add(jTextArea1, null);
    this.setDefaultCloseOperation(EXIT_ON_CLOSE);
    this.setBounds(0,0, 400, 330);
    this.setVisible(true);
    initialize();
  }

  private void initialize() {
    // create a temp file
    File file = new File(dir, filename);
    try {
      System.out.println("Creating temporary file");
      file.createNewFile();
    }
    catch (IOException e) {
      System.out.println("Failed creating temporary file.");
    }
  }

  private void shutdown() {
    // delete the temp file
    File file = new File(dir, filename);
    if (file.exists()) {
      System.out.println("Deleting temporary file.");
      file.delete();
    }
  }
```

```
  void exitButton_actionPerformed(ActionEvent e) {
    shutdown();
    System.exit(0);
  }

  public static void main(String[] args) {
    MySwingApp mySwingApp = new MySwingApp();
  }
}
```

When run, the application calls its `initialize` method. The `initialize` method in turn creates a temporary file called temp.txt in the user's directory:

```
private void initialize() {
  // create a temp file
  File file = new File(dir, filename);
  try {
    System.out.println("Creating temporary file");
    file.createNewFile();
  }
  catch (IOException e) {
    System.out.println("Failed creating temporary file.");
  }
}
```

When the user closes the application, the application must delete the temporary file. We hope that the user will always click the Exit button because by doing so the shutdown method (which deletes the temporary file) will always gets called. However, the temporary file will not be deleted if the user closes the application by clicking the X button of the frame or by some other means.

The class in Listing 16.3 offers a solution to this. It modifies the code in Listing 16.2 by providing a shutdown hook. The shutdown hook class is declared as an inner class so that it has access to all the main class's methods. In Listing 16.3, the shutdown hook's `run` method calls the `shutdown` method, guaranteeing that this method will be invoked when the virtual machine shuts down.

Listing 16.3: Using a shutdown hook in the Swing application

```
package ex16.pyrmont.shutdownhook;

import java.awt.*;
import javax.swing.*;
import java.awt.event.*;
import java.io.File;
import java.io.IOException;

public class MySwingAppWithShutdownHook extends JFrame {
  JButton exitButton = new JButton();
  JTextArea jTextArea1 = new JTextArea();
```

```java
    String dir = System.getProperty("user.dir");
    String filename = "temp.txt";

  public MySwingAppWithShutdownHook() {
    exitButton.setText("Exit");
    exitButton.setBounds(new Rectangle(304, 248, 76, 37));
    exitButton.addActionListener(new java.awt.event.ActionListener() {
      public void actionPerformed(ActionEvent e) {
        exitButton_actionPerformed(e);
      }
    });
    this.getContentPane().setLayout(null);
    jTextArea1.setText("Click the Exit button to quit");
    jTextArea1.setBounds(new Rectangle(9, 7, 371, 235));
    this.getContentPane().add(exitButton, null);
    this.getContentPane().add(jTextArea1, null);
    this.setDefaultCloseOperation(EXIT_ON_CLOSE);
    this.setBounds(0,0, 400, 330);
    this.setVisible(true);
    initialize();
  }

  private void initialize() {
    // add shutdown hook
    MyShutdownHook shutdownHook = new MyShutdownHook();
    Runtime.getRuntime().addShutdownHook(shutdownHook);

    // create a temp file
    File file = new File(dir, filename);
    try {
      System.out.println("Creating temporary file");
      file.createNewFile();
    }
    catch (IOException e) {
      System.out.println("Failed creating temporary file.");
    }
  }

  private void shutdown() {
    // delete the temp file
    File file = new File(dir, filename);
    if (file.exists()) {
      System.out.println("Deleting temporary file.");
      file.delete();
    }
  }

  void exitButton_actionPerformed(ActionEvent e) {
    shutdown();
    System.exit(0);
  }

  public static void main(String[] args) {
    MySwingAppWithShutdownHook mySwingApp = new
MySwingAppWithShutdownHook();
  }
```

```
  private class MyShutdownHook extends Thread {
    public void run() {
      shutdown();
    }
  }
}
```

Pay special attention to the `initialize` method in the class shown in Listing 16.3. The first thing it does is create an instance of the inner class `MyShutdownHook`, which extends a `java.lang.Thread`:

```
// add shutdown hook
MyShutdownHook shutdownHook = new MyShutdownHook();
```

Once you get an instance of `MyShutdownHook`, you pass it to the `addShutDownHook` method of the `Runtime`, as in the following line of code:

```
Runtime.getRuntime().addShutdownHook(shutdownHook);
```

The rest of the `initialize` method is similar to the `initialize` method in the class in Listing 16.2. It creates a temporary file and prints the string `Creating temporary file`.

```
// create a temp file
File file = new File(dir, filename);
try {
  System.out.println("Creating temporary file");
  file.createNewFile();
}
catch (IOException e) {
  System.out.println("Failed creating temporary file.");
}
```

Now, start the small application given in Listing 16.3. Check that the temporary file is always deleted even if you abruptly shut down the application.

Shutdown Hook in Tomcat

As you may expect, Tomcat equips itself with a shutdown hook. You can find it in the `org.apache.catalina.startup.Catalina` class, the class responsible for starting a `Server` object that manages other components. An inner class named `CatalinaShutdownHook` (See Listing 16.4) extends `java.lang.Thread` and provides the implementation of the `run` method that calls the `stop` method of the `Server` object.

Listing 16.4: Catalina shutdown hook

```
protected class CatalinaShutdownHook extends Thread {
  public void run() {
    if (server != null) {
      try {
        ((Lifecycle) server).stop();
      }
      catch (LifecycleException e) {
        System.out.println("Catalina.stop: " + e);
        e.printStackTrace(System.out);
        if (e.getThrowable() != null) {
          System.out.println("----- Root Cause -----");
          e.getThrowable().printStackTrace(System.out);
        }
      }
    }
  }
}
```

This shutdown hook is instantiated and added to the Runtime at one stage when the Catalina instance is started. You will learn more about the Catalina class in Chapter 17.

Summary

Sometimes we want our application to run some clean up code prior to shutting down. However, it is impossible to rely on the user to always quit properly. The shutdown hook described in this chapter offers a solution that guarantees that the clean up code is run regardless how the user closes the application.

Chapter 17
Tomcat Startup

This chapter focuses on Tomcat startup using two classes in the `org.apache.catalina.startup` package, `Catalina` and `Bootstrap`. The `Catalina` class is used to start and stop a `Server` object as well as parse the Tomcat configuration file, server.xml. The `Bootstrap` class is the entry point that creates an instance of `Catalina` and calls its `process` method. In theory, these two classes could have been merged. However, to support more than one mode of running Tomcat, a number of bootstrap classes are provided. For example, the aforementioned `Bootstrap` class is used for running Tomcat as a stand-alone application. Another class, `org.apache.catalina.startup.BootstrapService`, is used to run Tomcat as a Windows NT service.

For user's convenience, Tomcat also comes with the batch files and shell scripts to start and stop the servlet container easily. With the help of these batch files and shell scripts, the user does not need to remember the options for the java.exe program to run the `Bootstrap` class. Instead, he/she can just run the appropriate batch file or shell script.

The first section of this chapter discusses the `Catalina` class and the second the `Bootstrap` class. To understand the topic of discussion in this chapter, make sure you have read Chapter 14 on servers and services, Chapter 15 on Digester, and Chapter 16 on shutdown hooks. The chapter also discusses how to run Tomcat on Windows and Unix/Linux in two sections. One section is dedicated to the discussion of batch files to start and stop Tomcat on Windows. The other section explains the shell scripts on Unix/Linux.

The Catalina Class

The `org.apache.catalina.startup.Catalina` class is the startup class. It contains a Digester that parses the server.xml file in the

%CATALINE_HOME%/conf directory. By understanding the rules added to this Digester, you can configure Tomcat the way you want it to be.

The Catalina class also encapsulates a Server object that will have a Service. As mentioned in Chapter 15, a Service object contains a container and one or more connectors. You use Catalina to start and stop the Server object.

You run Tomcat by instantiating the Catalina class and then calling its process method. You must pass the appropriate argument when calling this method. The first argument is start if you want to start Tomcat and stop if you want to send a shutdown command to stop it. There are also other acceptable arguments, such as -help, -config, -debug, and -nonaming.

Note

The nonaming argument, when present, specifies that JNDI naming should not be supported. See the org.apache.naming package for more information on how JNDI naming is supported in Tomcat.

Normally, you will need a Bootstrap class to instantiate Catalina and call its process method, even though the Catalina class has its own main method that provides an entry point. One of the Bootstrap classes is explained in the next section. You will also find out what the Bootstrap does in this section.

The process method in the Catalina class in Tomcat 4 is given in Listing 17.1.

Listing 17.1: The **process** method of the **Catalina** class

```
public void process(String args[]) {
  setCatalinaHome();
  setCatalinaBase();
  try {
    if (arguments(args))
      execute();
  }
  catch (Exception e) {
    e.printStackTrace(System.out);
  }
}
```

The process method sets two system properties, catalina.home and catalina.base. catalina.home defaults to the value of the user.dir property. The catalina.base property is assigned the value of catalina.home. Therefore, both properties have the value of the user.dir property.

Note
The user.dir system property refers to the user's working directory, i.e. the directory from which the java command is invoked. For the list of system properties, see the getProperties method of the java.lang.System class in the J2SE 1.4 API Specification documentation.

The process method then calls the arguments method, passing the list of arguments. The arguments method, given in Listing 17.2, processes the command line arguments and returns true if the Catalina object should continue processing.

Listing 17.2: The arguments method

```
protected boolean arguments(String args[]) {
  boolean isConfig = false;
  if (args.length < 1) {
    usage();
    return (false);
  }
  for (int i = 0; i < args.length; i++) {
    if (isConfig) {
      configFile = args[i];
      isConfig = false;
    }
    else if (args[i].equals("-config")) {
      isConfig = true;
    }
    else if (args[i].equals("-debug")) {
      debug = true;
    }
    else if (args[i].equals("-nonaming")) {
      useNaming = false;
    }
    else if (args[i].equals("-help")) {
      usage();
      return (false);
    }
    else if (args[i].equals("start")) {
      starting = true;
    }
    else if (args[i].equals("stop")) {
      stopping = true;
    }
    else {
      usage();
      return (false);
    }
  }
  return (true);
}
```

The `process` method examines the return value of the `arguments` method and calls the `execute` method if the arguments method returns `true`. The `execute` method is given in Listing 17.3.

Listing 17.3: The execute method

```
protected void execute() throws Exception {
  if (starting)
    start();
  else if (stopping)
    stop();
}
```

The `execute` method either calls the `start` method to start Tomcat or the `stop` method to stop Tomcat. The two methods are discussed in the following subsections.

> **Note**
> In Tomcat 5, there is no more the `execute` method. The `start` or `stop` method is called from the `process` method.

The **start** Method

The `start` method creates a Digester instance to process the server.xml file (Tomcat configuration file). Prior to parsing the XML file, the `start` method calls the `push` method on the Digester, passing the current `Catalina` object. This will cause the `Catalina` object to be the first object in the Digester's internal object stack. The parsing will result in the server variable to reference a `Server` object, which is by default will be of type `org.apache.catalina.core.StandardServer`. The `start` method will then call the `initialize` and `start` methods of the `Server` object. The `start` method in `Catalina` then continues by calling the `await` method on the `Server` object, causing the `Server` object to dedicate a thread to wait for a shutdown command. The `await` method does not return until a shutdown command is received. When the `await` method does return, the `start` method in `Catalina` calls the `stop` method of the `Server` object, which in effect stops the `Server` object and all other components. The `start` method also employs a shutdown hook to make sure the `stop` method of the `Server` object is executed should the user exit the application abruptly.

The `start` method is given in Listing 17.4.

Listing 17.4: The start method

```
protected void start() {
```

```
// Create and execute our Digester
Digester digester = createStartDigester();
File file = configFile();
try {
  InputSource is =
    new InputSource("file://" + file.getAbsolutePath());
  FileInputStream fis = new FileInputStream(file);
  is.setByteStream(fis);
  digester.push(this);
  digester.parse(is);
  fis.close();
}
catch (Exception e) {
  System.out.println("Catalina.start: " + e);
  e.printStackTrace(System.out);
  System.exit(1);
}

// Setting additional variables
if (!useNaming) {
  System.setProperty("catalina.useNaming", "false");
}
else {
  System.setProperty("catalina.useNaming", "true");
  String value = "org.apache.naming";
  String oldValue =
    System.getProperty(javax.naming.Context.URL_PKG_PREFIXES);
  if (oldValue != null) {
    value = value + ":" + oldValue;
  }
  System.setProperty(javax.naming.Context.URL_PKG_PREFIXES, value);
  value = System.getProperty
    (javax.naming.Context.INITIAL_CONTEXT_FACTORY);
  if (value == null) {
    System.setProperty
      (javax.naming.Context.INITIAL_CONTEXT_FACTORY,
      "org.apache.naming.java.javaURLContextFactory");
  }
}

// If a SecurityManager is being used, set properties for
// checkPackageAccess() and checkPackageDefinition
if( System.getSecurityManager() != null ) {
  String access = Security.getProperty("package.access");
  if( access != null && access.length() > 0 )
    access += ",";
  else
    access = "sun.,";
  Security.setProperty("package.access",
  access + "org.apache.catalina.,org.apache.jasper.");
  String definition = Security.getProperty("package.definition");
  if( definition != null && definition.length() > 0 )
    definition += ",";
  else
    definition = "sun.,";
  Security.setProperty("package.definition",
```

```
  // FIX ME package "javax." was removed to prevent HotSpot
  // fatal internal errors
  definition + "java.,org.apache.catalina.,org.apache.jasper.");
}

// Replace System.out and System.err with a custom PrintStream
SystemLogHandler log = new SystemLogHandler(System.out);
System.setOut(log);
System.setErr(log);

Thread shutdownHook = new CatalinaShutdownHook();

// Start the new server
if (server instanceof Lifecycle) {
  try {
    server.initialize();
    ((Lifecycle) server).start();
    try {
      // Register shutdown hook
      Runtime.getRuntime().addShutdownHook(shutdownHook);
    }
    catch (Throwable t) {
      // This will fail on JDK 1.2. Ignoring, as Tomcat can run
      // fine without the shutdown hook.
    }
    // Wait for the server to be told to shut down
    server.await();
  }
  catch (LifecycleException e) {
    System.out.println("Catalina.start: " + e);
    e.printStackTrace(System.out);
    if (e.getThrowable() != null) {
      System.out.println("----- Root Cause -----");
      e.getThrowable().printStackTrace(System.out);
    }
  }
}

// Shut down the server
if (server instanceof Lifecycle) {
  try {
    try {
      // Remove the ShutdownHook first so that server.stop()
      // doesn't get invoked twice
      Runtime.getRuntime().removeShutdownHook(shutdownHook);
    }
    catch (Throwable t) {
      // This will fail on JDK 1.2. Ignoring, as Tomcat can run
      // fine without the shutdown hook.
    }
    ((Lifecycle) server).stop();
  }
  catch (LifecycleException e) {
    System.out.println("Catalina.stop: " + e);
    e.printStackTrace(System.out);
    if (e.getThrowable() != null) {
```

```
        System.out.println("----- Root Cause -----");
        e.getThrowable().printStackTrace(System.out);
      }
    }
  }
}
```

The **stop** Method

The stop method stops the Catalina and causes the Server object to stop. The stop method is given in Listing 17.5.

Listing 17.5: The stop Method

```
protected void stop() {
  // Create and execute our Digester
  Digester digester = createStopDigester();
  File file = configFile();
  try {
    InputSource is =
      new InputSource("file://" + file.getAbsolutePath());
    FileInputStream fis = new FileInputStream(file);
    is.setByteStream(fis);
    digester.push(this);
    digester.parse(is);
    fis.close();
  }
  catch (Exception e) {
    System.out.println("Catalina.stop: " + e);
    e.printStackTrace(System.out);
    System.exit(1);
  }

  // Stop the existing server
  try {
    Socket socket = new Socket("127.0.0.1", server.getPort());
    OutputStream stream = socket.getOutputStream();
    String shutdown = server.getShutdown();
    for (int i = 0; i < shutdown.length(); i++)
      stream.write(shutdown.charAt(i));
    stream.flush();
    stream.close();
    socket.close();
  }
  catch (IOException e) {
    System.out.println("Catalina.stop: " + e);
    e.printStackTrace(System.out);
    System.exit(1);
  }
}
```

Notice that the `stop` method creates a Digester instance by calling the `createStopDigester` method, pushes the current `Catalina` object to the Digester internal stack by calling the `push` method on the Digester and parses the configuration file. The rules added to the Digester are discussed in the subsection, "Stop Digester."

The `stop` method then stops the running `Server` object by sending a shutdown command.

Start Digester

The `createStartDigester` in `Catalina` method creates a Digester instance and then adds to it rules for parsing the server.xml file. This XML document is used for Tomcat configuration and located in the %CATALINE_HOME%/conf directory. The rules added to the Digester are key to understanding Tomcat configuration.

The createStartDigester method is presented in Listing 17.6.

Listing 17.6: The createStartDigester method

```
protected Digester createStartDigester() {

  // Initialize the digester
  Digester digester = new Digester();
  if (debug)
    digester.setDebug(999);
  digester.setValidating(false);

  // Configure the actions we will be using
  digester.addObjectCreate("Server",
    "org.apache.catalina.core.StandardServer", "className");
  digester.addSetProperties("Server");
  digester.addSetNext("Server", "setServer",
    "org.apache.catalina.Server");

  digester.addObjectCreate("Server/GlobalNamingResources",
    "org.apache.catalina.deploy.NamingResources");
  digester.addSetProperties("Server/GlobalNamingResources");
  digester.addSetNext("Server/GlobalNamingResources",
    "setGlobalNamingResources",
    "org.apache.catalina.deploy.NamingResources");

  digester.addObjectCreate("Server/Listener", null, "className");
  digester.addSetProperties("Server/Listener");
  digester.addSetNext("Server/Listener",
    "addLifecycleListener",
    "org.apache.catalina.LifecycleListener");

  digester.addObjectCreate("Server/Service",
```

```
      "org.apache.catalina.core.StandardService", "className");
    digester.addSetProperties("Server/Service");
    digester.addSetNext("Server/Service", "addService",
     "org.apache.catalina.Service");

    digester.addObjectCreate("Server/Service/Listener",
      null, "className");
    digester.addSetProperties("Server/Service/Listener");
    digester.addSetNext("Server/Service/Listener",
      "addLifecycleListener", "org.apache.catalina.LifecycleListener");

    digester.addObjectCreate("Server/Service/Connector",
      "org.apache.catalina.connector.http.HttpConnector",
      "className");
    digester.addSetProperties("Server/Service/Connector");
    digester.addSetNext("Server/Service/Connector",
      "addConnector", "org.apache.catalina.Connector");

    digester.addObjectCreate("Server/Service/Connector/Factory",
      "org.apache.catalina.net.DefaultServerSocketFactory",
      "className");
    digester.addSetProperties("Server/Service/Connector/Factory");
    digester.addSetNext("Server/Service/Connector/Factory",
      "setFactory", "org.apache.catalina.net.ServerSocketFactory");

    digester.addObjectCreate("Server/Service/Connector/Listener",
      null, "className");
    digester.addSetProperties("Server/Service/Connector/Listener");
    digester.addSetNext("Server/Service/Connector/Listener",
      "addLifecycleListener", "org.apache.catalina.LifecycleListener");

    // Add RuleSets for nested elements
    digester.addRuleSet(
      new NamingRuleSet("Server/GlobalNamingResources/"));
    digester.addRuleSet(new EngineRuleSet("Server/Service/"));
    digester.addRuleSet(new HostRuleSet("Server/Service/Engine/"));
    digester.addRuleSet(new
      ContextRuleSet("Server/Service/Engine/Default"));
    digester.addRuleSet(
      new NamingRuleSet("Server/Service/Engine/DefaultContext/"));
    digester.addRuleSet(
      new ContextRuleSet("Server/Service/Engine/Host/Default"));
    digester.addRuleSet(
      new NamingRuleSet("Server/Service/Engine/Host/DefaultContext/"));
    digester.addRuleSet(
      new ContextRuleSet("Server/Service/Engine/Host/"));
    digester.addRuleSet(
      new NamingRuleSet("Server/Service/Engine/Host/Context/"));
    digester.addRule("Server/Service/Engine",
      new SetParentClassLoaderRule(digester, parentClassLoader));

    return (digester);
}
```

The createStartDigester method creates an instance of
org.apache.commons.digester.Digester class, and then adds rules.

The first three rules are for the server element in the server.xml file. As you may already know, the server element is the root element. Here are the rules for the pattern **server**.

```
digester.addObjectCreate("Server",
   "org.apache.catalina.core.StandardServer", "className");
digester.addSetProperties("Server");
digester.addSetNext("Server", "setServer",
   "org.apache.catalina.Server");
```

The first rule states that upon encountering the server element, the Digester must create an instance of org.apache.catalina.core.StandardServer. The exception is if the server element has a className attribute, in which case the value of the className attribute is the name of the class that must be instantiated instead.

The second rule populates the properties of the Server object with the values of the attributes having identical names.

The third rule causes the Server object to be pushed to the stack and associated with the next object in the stack, which is an instance of Catalina, and its setServer method to be called. How can an instance of Catalina be in the Digester's object stack? Remember that the start method calls the push method of the Digester prior to parsing the server.xml file:

```
digester.push(this);
```

The line of code above causes the Catalina object to be pushed to the internal object stack in the Digester.

You should be able to figure out the next rules by reading the method yourself. If you cannot, you should read Chapter 15 again.

Stop Digester

The createStopDigester method returns a Digester object that stops the Server object gracefully. This method is given in Listing 17.7.

Listing 17.7: The stop method

```
protected Digester createStopDigester() {
  // Initialize the digester
  Digester digester = new Digester();
  if (debug)
    digester.setDebug(999);

  // Configure the rules we need for shutting down
```

```
  digester.addObjectCreate("Server",
    "org.apache.catalina.core.StandardServer", "className");
  digester.addSetProperties("Server");
  digester.addSetNext("Server", "setServer",
    "org.apache.catalina.Server");
  return (digester);
}
```

Unlike the start Digester, the stop Digester is only interested in the root element.

The Bootstrap Class

The org.apache.catalina.startup.Bootstrap class is one of the classes that provide an entry point to start Tomcat. When you run the startup.bat or startup.sh file, you actually call the main method in this class. The main method creates three class loaders and instantiates the Catalina class. It then calls the process method on Catalina.

The Bootstrap class is given n Listing 17.8.

Listing 17.8: The Bootstrap class

```
package org.apache.catalina.startup;

import java.io.File;
import java.lang.reflect.Method;

/**
 * Boostrap loader for Catalina.  This application constructs a
 * class loader for use in loading the Catalina internal classes
 * (by accumulating all of the JAR files found in the "server"
 * directory under "catalina.home"), and starts the regular execution
 * of the container.  The purpose of this roundabout approach is to
 * keep the Catalina internal classes (and any other classes they
 * depend on, such as an XML parser) out of the system
 * class path and therefore not visible to application level classes.
 *
 * @author Craig R. McClanahan
 * @version $Revision: 1.36 $ $Date: 2002/04/01 19:51:31 $
 */

public final class Bootstrap {
  /**
   * Debugging detail level for processing the startup.
   */
  private static int debug = 0;

  /**
   * The main program for the bootstrap.
   *
   * @param args Command line arguments to be processed
   */
```

```
public static void main(String args[]) {

  // Set the debug flag appropriately
  for (int i = 0; i < args.length; i++)  {
    if ("-debug".equals(args[i]))
      debug = 1;
  }

  // Configure catalina.base from catalina.home if not yet set
  if (System.getProperty("catalina.base") == null)
    System.setProperty("catalina.base", getCatalinaHome());

  // Construct the class loaders we will need
  ClassLoader commonLoader = null;
  ClassLoader catalinaLoader = null;
  ClassLoader sharedLoader = null;
  try {
    File unpacked[] = new File[1];
    File packed[] = new File[1];
    File packed2[] = new File[2];
    ClassLoaderFactory.setDebug(debug);

    unpacked[0] = new File(getCatalinaHome(),
      "common" + File.separator + "classes");
    packed2[0] = new File(getCatalinaHome(),
      "common" + File.separator + "endorsed");
    packed2[1] = new File(getCatalinaHome(),
      "common" + File.separator + "lib");
    commonLoader =
      ClassLoaderFactory.createClassLoader(unpacked, packed2, null);

    unpacked[0] = new File(getCatalinaHome(),
      "server" + File.separator + "classes");
    packed[0] = new File(getCatalinaHome(),
      "server" + File.separator + "lib");
    catalinaLoader =
      ClassLoaderFactory.createClassLoader(unpacked, packed,
      commonLoader);

    unpacked[0] = new File(getCatalinaBase(),
      "shared" + File.separator + "classes");
    packed[0] = new File(getCatalinaBase(),
      "shared" + File.separator + "lib");
    sharedLoader =
      ClassLoaderFactory.createClassLoader(unpacked, packed,
      commonLoader);
  }
  catch (Throwable t) {
    log("Class loader creation threw exception", t);
    System.exit(1);
  }

  Thread.currentThread().setContextClassLoader(catalinaLoader);

  // Load our startup class and call its process() method
  try {
```

```java
      SecurityClassLoad.securityClassLoad(catalinaLoader);
      // Instantiate a startup class instance
      if (debug >= 1)
        log("Loading startup class");
      Class startupClass =
        catalinaLoader.loadClass
          ("org.apache.catalina.startup.Catalina");
      Object startupInstance = startupClass.newInstance();

      // Set the shared extensions class loader
      if (debug >= 1)
        log("Setting startup class properties");
      String methodName = "setParentClassLoader";
      Class paramTypes[] = new Class[1];
      paramTypes[0] = Class.forName("java.lang.ClassLoader");
      Object paramValues[] = new Object[1];
      paramValues[0] = sharedLoader;
      Method method =
        startupInstance.getClass().getMethod(methodName, paramTypes);
      method.invoke(startupInstance, paramValues);

      // Call the process() method
      if (debug >= 1)
        log("Calling startup class process() method");
      methodName = "process";
      paramTypes = new Class[1];
      paramTypes[0] = args.getClass();
      paramValues = new Object[1];
      paramValues[0] = args;
      method =
        startupInstance.getClass().getMethod(methodName, paramTypes);
      method.invoke(startupInstance, paramValues);
    }
    catch (Exception e) {
      System.out.println("Exception during startup processing");
      e.printStackTrace(System.out);
      System.exit(2);
    }
  }

  /**
   * Get the value of the catalina.home environment variable.
   */
  private static String getCatalinaHome() {
    return System.getProperty("catalina.home",
      System.getProperty("user.dir"));
  }

  /**
   * Get the value of the catalina.base environment variable.
   */
  private static String getCatalinaBase() {
    return System.getProperty("catalina.base", getCatalinaHome());
  }

  /**
```

```
 * Log a debugging detail message.
 *
 * @param message The message to be logged
 */
private static void log(String message) {
  System.out.print("Bootstrap: ");
  System.out.println(message);
}

/**
 * Log a debugging detail message with an exception.
 *
 * @param message The message to be logged
 * @param exception The exception to be logged
 */
private static void log(String message, Throwable exception) {
  log(message);
  exception.printStackTrace(System.out);
}

}
```

The Bootstrap class has four static methods, i.e. two log methods, the getCatalinaHome method, and the getCatalinaBase method. The getCatalinaHome method has the following implementation:

```
return System.getProperty("catalina.home",
  System.getProperty("user.dir"));
```

which basically means, if no value has been previously set for catalina.home, it returns the value of the user.dir property.

The getCatalinaBase method has the following implementation:

```
return System.getProperty("catalina.base", getCatalinaHome());
```

which means, it returns the value of catalina.home if there is no such property as catalina.base.

Both getCatalinaHome and getCatalinaBase are called from the main method of the Bootstrap class.

The main method of the Bootstrap class also constructs three class loaders for different purposes. The main reason for having different class loaders is to prevent application classes (servlets and other helper classes in a web application) from running classes outside the WEB-INF/classes and WEB-INF/lib directories. Jarred classes deployed to the %CATALINE_HOME%/common/lib directory are also allowed.

The three class loaders are defined as follows.

```
// Construct the class loaders we will need
```

```
ClassLoader commonLoader = null;
ClassLoader catalinaLoader = null;
ClassLoader sharedLoader = null;
```

Each class loader is then given a path it is allowed access to. The
commonLoader class loader is allowed to load Java classes in three directories:
%CATALINA_HOME%/common/classes,
%CATALINA_HOME%/common/endorsed, and
%CATALINA_HOME%/common/lib.

```
try {
  File unpacked[] = new File[1];
  File packed[] = new File[1];
  File packed2[] = new File[2];
  ClassLoaderFactory.setDebug(debug);

  unpacked[0] = new File(getCatalinaHome(),
    "common" + File.separator + "classes");
  packed2[0] = new File(getCatalinaHome(),
    "common" + File.separator + "endorsed");
  packed2[1] = new File(getCatalinaHome(),
    "common" + File.separator + "lib");
  commonLoader =
    ClassLoaderFactory.createClassLoader(unpacked, packed2, null);
```

The catalinaLoader class loader is responsible for loading classes required
by the Catalina servlet container to run. It can load Java classes in the
%CATALINA_HOME%/server/classes and
%CATALINA_HOME%/server/lib directories, as well as all directories that
the commonLoader class loader can access.

```
  unpacked[0] = new File(getCatalinaHome(),
    "server" + File.separator + "classes");
  packed[0] = new File(getCatalinaHome(),
    "server" + File.separator + "lib");
  catalinaLoader =
    ClassLoaderFactory.createClassLoader(unpacked, packed,
    commonLoader);
```

The sharedLoader class loader can access the
%CATALINA_HOME%/shared/classes and
%CATALINA_HOME%/shared/lib directories, as well as all directories
available to the commonLoader class loader. The sharedLoader class
loader is then assigned to be the parent class loader of every class loader of each
Web application associated with a Context deployed in Tomcat.

```
  unpacked[0] = new File(getCatalinaBase(),
    "shared" + File.separator + "classes");
  packed[0] = new File(getCatalinaBase(),
    "shared" + File.separator + "lib");
  sharedLoader =
```

```
    ClassLoaderFactory.createClassLoader(unpacked, packed,
    commonLoader);
  }
catch (Throwable t) {
  log("Class loader creation threw exception", t);
  System.exit(1);
}
```

Notice that the sharedLoader class loader does not have access to the Catalina internal classes nor to the class paths defined in the CLASSPATH environment variable. See Chapter 8 for more details on how a class loader works.

After creating the three class loaders, the main method then loads the Catalina class and creates an instance of it and assigns it to the startupInstance variable.

```
Class startupClass =
  catalinaLoader.loadClass
    ("org.apache.catalina.startup.Catalina");
Object startupInstance = startupClass.newInstance();
```

Afterwards, it calls the setParentClassLoader method by passing the sharedLoader class loader.

```
// Set the shared extensions class loader
if (debug >= 1)
  log("Setting startup class properties");
String methodName = "setParentClassLoader";
Class paramTypes[] = new Class[1];
paramTypes[0] = Class.forName("java.lang.ClassLoader");
Object paramValues[] = new Object[1];
paramValues[0] = sharedLoader;
Method method =
  startupInstance.getClass().getMethod(methodName, paramTypes);
method.invoke(startupInstance, paramValues);
```

Finally, the main method calls the process method on the Catalina object.

```
// Call the process() method
if (debug >= 1)
  log("Calling startup class process() method");
methodName = "process";
paramTypes = new Class[1];
paramTypes[0] = args.getClass();
paramValues = new Object[1];
paramValues[0] = args;
method =
  startupInstance.getClass().getMethod(methodName, paramTypes);
method.invoke(startupInstance, paramValues);
```

Running Tomcat on Windows

As you have learned in the previous sections, you call the `Bootstrap` class to run Tomcat as a stand-alone application. On a Windows platform, you do this by invoking the startup.bat batch file to start Tomcat and the shutdown.bat batch file to stop it. Both batch files can be found in the %CATALINA_HOME%/bin directory. This section discusses the batch files. For those not familiar with the DOS command lines that can appear in a batch file, read the first subsection, "Introduction to Writing Batch Files".

Introduction to Writing Batch Files

This section offers an introduction to batch files so that you can understand the batch files for starting and stopping Tomcat. In particular, it explains the following commands: `rem`, `if`, `echo`, `goto`, `label`, etc. It does not pretend to provide a comprehensive coverage of the topic, however, for which you should consult other resources.

First and foremost, a batch file must have a .bat extension. You can invoke a batch file by double-clicking it from Windows Explorer or by typing the command from a DOS console. Once invoked, each line of instruction will be interpreted from the first line to the last. The language elements used in the batch files in Tomcat are explained in the following subsections.

> **Note**
> DOS commands and environment variables are case-insensitive.

rem

The `rem` command is used for comments. A line beginning with `rem` is ignored and not processed.

pause

The `pause` command halts the processing of a batch file and prompts the user to press a key. The processing continues upon the user pressing a key.

echo

This command displays the text after it to the DOS console. For example, the following line prints `Hello World` on the console and pauses. You need the `pause` command so that the console does not close as soon as it displays it.

```
echo Hello World
pause
```

To echo the value of an environment variable, enclose the variable with `%`. For example, the following command prints the value of `myVar`.

```
echo %myVar%.
```

To print the name of the operating system, use the following command:

```
cho %OS%
```

echo off

`echo off` prevents the command lines in the batch file from being displayed. Only the result of the execution is displayed. However, the `echo off` command will still be displayed. To suppress the `echo off` command as well, use `@echo off`.

@echo off

`@echo off` is similar to `echo off`, but it also suppresses the `echo off` command itself.

set

This command is used to set user defined or named environment variables. The environment variables set in a batch file live temporarily in memory and is destroyed as soon as the batch file finishes executing.

For example, the following `set` command creates an environment variable named `THE_KING` with a value of `Elvis` and displays it on the console.

```
set THE_KING=Elvis
echo %THE_KING%
pause
```

Note
To refer to the value of a variable, enclose the variable name with the `%` characters. For instance, `echo %THE_KING%` means display the value of the `THE_KING` variable.

label

You use a colon to denote a label. You can then pass the label to the `goto` command to instruct the processing to jump to the line next to the label. Here is a label called `end`:

```
:end
```

See the `goto` command for a more descriptive example.

goto

The `goto` command forces the batch file processing to jump to the line after the specified label. Consider the following example.

```
echo Start
goto end
echo I can guarantee this line will not be executed
:end
echo End
pause
```

After printing `Start` on the first line, the batch file executes the `goto` command, which makes control jump to the line right after the `end` label. As a result, the third line is skipped.

if

`if` is used to test a statement. It can be used in three different ways:

1. To test the value of a variable.
2. To test the existence of a file
3. To test the error value.

To test a variable's value, use if in the following format:

```
if variable==value nextCommand
```

For example, the following `if` statement tests if the value of `myVar` is 3. If it is, it prints `Correct` on the console.

```
set myVar=3
if %myVar%==3 echo Correct
```

When run, the commands above evaluate the value of the variable `myVar` and prints `Correct`.

To use an `if` statement to test the existence of a file, use it in the following format:

```
if exist c:\temp\myFile.txt goto start
```

If the myFile.txt file exists in the c:\temp directory, control will go to the next line after the label `start`.

You can also use the `not` keyword to negate a statement.

not

The `not` keyword is used to negate a statement. For example, the following command prints `Correct` if the value of `myVar` is not 3.

```
set myVar=3
if not %myVar%==3 echo Correct
pause
```

The following command makes processing jump to `end` if the myFile.txt file does not exists in the c:\temp directory.

```
if not exist c:\temp\myFile.txt goto end
```

exist

The `exist` keyword is used in conjunction with the `if` statement to test the existence of a file. See the `if` statement for an example.

Accepting parameters

You can pass parameters to a batch file. You use `%1` to refer to the first parameter, `%2` to the second, and so forth.

For example, the following command prints the first parameter on the console.

```
echo %1
```

If your batch file is named test.bat and you invoke it by using `test Hello`, the word `Hello` will be displayed on the console.

The following batch file checks the value of the first parameter. If it is start, it will print `Starting application`. If it is stop, `Stopping application` will be printed. Otherwise, `Invalid parameter` is printed.

```
echo off
if %1==start goto start
```

```
if %1==stop goto stop
goto invalid

:start
echo Starting application
goto end

:stop
echo Stopping application
goto end

:invalid
echo Invalid parameter

:end
```

To check whether a parameter has been passed to the batch file, compare `"%1"` with a blank string. For example, if no parameter is passed to the following batch file, `No parameter` will be printed on the console.

```
if "%1"=="" echo No parameter
```

The above is the same as

```
if ""%1""=="""" echo No parameter
```

shift

The `shift` command shifts the parameters one parameter backward. This means the value of `%2` is copied to `%1`, `%3` to `%2`, and so forth. For example, the following batch file uses a `shift` command.

```
echo off
shift
echo %1
echo %2
```

If you invoke the batch file by passing three parameters `a`, `b`, and `c`, you will get the following result:

```
b
c
```

The first parameter after `shift` can be referenced by using `%0`. The last parameter is now lost.

call

The `call` command is used to invoke another command.

setLocal

You use `setLocal` in a batch file to indicate that any change to environment variables during the current batch file should be local to the batch file. The values of any changed environment variables will be restored at the end of the batch file or if an `endLocal` command is encountered.

start

Open a new Windows console. You can pass a title for the new window, such as:

```
start "Title"
```

Additionally, you can pass a command that will be executed in the new console, right after the title:

```
start "Title" commandName
```

The catalina.bat Batch File

The catalina.bat batch file can be used to start and stop Tomcat. Two other files, startup.bat and shutdown.bat, are provided to start and stop Tomcat more easily. The startup.bat and shutdown.bat call the catalina.bat file by passing the appropriate parameter.

You must call catalina.bat from the bin directory under %CATALINA_HOME% by using the following syntax:

```
catalina command
```

or from the %CATALINE_HOME% by using the following

```
bin\catalina command
```

In both cases, possible values for *command* are as follows:

- `debug`. Start Catalina in a debugger
- `debug -security`. Debug Catalina with a security manager
- `embedded`. Start Catalina in embedded mode
- `jpda start`. Start Catalina under JPDA debugger
- `run`. Start Catalina in the current window
- `run -security`. Start Catalina in the current window with a security manager
- `start`. Start Catalina in a separate window

- `start -security.`   Start Catalina in a separate window with security manager
- `stop`. Stop Catalina

For example, to start Catalina in a separate window, use the following command:

```
catalina start
```

The catalina.bat batch file is given in Listing 17.9.

Listing 17.9: The catalina.bat File

```
@echo off
if "%OS%" == "Windows_NT" setlocal
rem ----------------------------------------------------------------
--------
rem Start/Stop Script for the CATALINA Server
rem
rem Environment Variable Prequisites
rem
rem   CATALINA_HOME   May point at your Catalina "build" directory.
rem
rem   CATALINA_BASE   (Optional) Base directory for resolving dynamic
portions
rem                   of a Catalina installation.  If not present,
resolves to
rem                   the same directory that CATALINA_HOME points to.
rem
rem   CATALINA_OPTS   (Optional) Java runtime options used when the
"start",
rem                   "stop", or "run" command is executed.
rem
rem   CATALINA_TMPDIR (Optional) Directory path location of temporary
directory
rem                   the JVM should use (java.io.tmpdir).  Defaults to
rem                   %CATALINA_BASE%\temp.
rem
rem   JAVA_HOME       Must point at your Java Development Kit
installation.
rem
rem   JAVA_OPTS       (Optional) Java runtime options used when the
"start",
rem                   "stop", or "run" command is executed.
rem
rem   JSSE_HOME       (Optional) May point at your Java Secure Sockets
Extension
rem                   (JSSE) installation, whose JAR files will be
added to the
rem                   system class path used to start Tomcat.
rem
rem   JPDA_TRANSPORT  (Optional) JPDA transport used when the "jpda
start"
rem                   command is executed. The default is "dt_shmem".
rem
```

```
rem    JPDA_ADDRESS    (Optional) Java runtime options used when the
"jpda start"
rem                    command is executed. The default is "jdbconn".
rem
rem $Id: catalina.bat,v 1.3 2002/08/04 18:19:43 patrickl Exp $
rem ----------------------------------------------------------------
--------

rem Guess CATALINA_HOME if not defined
if not "%CATALINA_HOME%" == "" goto gotHome
set CATALINA_HOME=.
if exist "%CATALINA_HOME%\bin\catalina.bat" goto okHome
set CATALINA_HOME=..
:gotHome
if exist "%CATALINA_HOME%\bin\catalina.bat" goto okHome
echo The CATALINA_HOME environment variable is not defined correctly
echo This environment variable is needed to run this program
goto end
:okHome

rem Get standard environment variables
if exist "%CATALINA_HOME%\bin\setenv.bat" call
"%CATALINA_HOME%\bin\setenv.bat"

rem Get standard Java environment variables
if exist "%CATALINA_HOME%\bin\setclasspath.bat" goto okSetclasspath
echo Cannot find %CATALINA_HOME%\bin\setclasspath.bat
echo This file is needed to run this program
goto end
:okSetclasspath
set BASEDIR=%CATALINA_HOME%
call "%CATALINA_HOME%\bin\setclasspath.bat"

rem Add on extra jar files to CLASSPATH
if "%JSSE_HOME%" == "" goto noJsse
set
CLASSPATH=%CLASSPATH%;%JSSE_HOME%\lib\jcert.jar;%JSSE_HOME%\lib\jnet.ja
r;%JSSE_HOME%\lib\jsse.jar
:noJsse
set CLASSPATH=%CLASSPATH%;%CATALINA_HOME%\bin\bootstrap.jar

if not "%CATALINA_BASE%" == "" goto gotBase
set CATALINA_BASE=%CATALINA_HOME%
:gotBase

if not "%CATALINA_TMPDIR%" == "" goto gotTmpdir
set CATALINA_TMPDIR=%CATALINA_BASE%\temp
:gotTmpdir

rem ----- Execute The Requested Command ----------------------------
--------

echo Using CATALINA_BASE:   %CATALINA_BASE%
echo Using CATALINA_HOME:   %CATALINA_HOME%
echo Using CATALINA_TMPDIR: %CATALINA_TMPDIR%
echo Using JAVA_HOME:       %JAVA_HOME%
```

```
set _EXECJAVA=%_RUNJAVA%
set MAINCLASS=org.apache.catalina.startup.Bootstrap
set ACTION=start
set SECURITY_POLICY_FILE=
set DEBUG_OPTS=
set JPDA=

if not ""%1"" == ""jpda"" goto noJpda
set JPDA=jpda
if not "%JPDA_TRANSPORT%" == "" goto gotJpdaTransport
set JPDA_TRANSPORT=dt_shmem
:gotJpdaTransport
if not "%JPDA_ADDRESS%" == "" goto gotJpdaAddress
set JPDA_ADDRESS=jdbconn
:gotJpdaAddress
shift
:noJpda

if ""%1"" == ""debug"" goto doDebug
if ""%1"" == ""embedded"" goto doEmbedded
if ""%1"" == ""run"" goto doRun
if ""%1"" == ""start"" goto doStart
if ""%1"" == ""stop"" goto doStop

echo Usage:  catalina ( commands ... )
echo commands:
echo    debug              Start Catalina in a debugger
echo    debug -security    Debug Catalina with a security manager
echo    embedded           Start Catalina in embedded mode
echo    jpda start         Start Catalina under JPDA debugger
echo    run                Start Catalina in the current window
echo    run -security      Start in the current window with security
manager
echo    start              Start Catalina in a separate window
echo    start -security    Start in a separate window with security
manager
echo    stop               Stop Catalina
goto end

:doDebug
shift
set _EXECJAVA=%_RUNJDB%
set DEBUG_OPTS=-sourcepath "%CATALINA_HOME%\..\..\jakarta-tomcat-
4.0\catalina\src\share"
if not ""%1"" == ""-security"" goto execCmd
shift
echo Using Security Manager
set SECURITY_POLICY_FILE=%CATALINA_BASE%\conf\catalina.policy
goto execCmd

:doEmbedded
shift
set MAINCLASS=org.apache.catalina.startup.Embedded
goto execCmd
```

```
:doRun
shift
if not ""%1"" == ""-security"" goto execCmd
shift
echo Using Security Manager
set SECURITY_POLICY_FILE=%CATALINA_BASE%\conf\catalina.policy
goto execCmd

:doStart
shift
if not "%OS%" == "Windows_NT" goto noTitle
set _EXECJAVA=start "Tomcat" %_RUNJAVA%
goto gotTitle
:noTitle
set _EXECJAVA=start %_RUNJAVA%
:gotTitle
if not ""%1"" == ""-security"" goto execCmd
shift
echo Using Security Manager
set SECURITY_POLICY_FILE=%CATALINA_BASE%\conf\catalina.policy
goto execCmd

:doStop
shift
set ACTION=stop
goto execCmd

:execCmd
rem Get remaining unshifted command line arguments and save them in the
set CMD_LINE_ARGS=
:setArgs
if ""%1""=="""" goto doneSetArgs
set CMD_LINE_ARGS=%CMD_LINE_ARGS% %1
shift
goto setArgs
:doneSetArgs

rem Execute Java with the applicable properties
if not "%JPDA%" == "" goto doJpda
if not "%SECURITY_POLICY_FILE%" == "" goto doSecurity
%_EXECJAVA% %JAVA_OPTS% %CATALINA_OPTS% %DEBUG_OPTS% -
Djava.endorsed.dirs="%JAVA_ENDORSED_DIRS%" -classpath "%CLASSPATH%" -
Dcatalina.base="%CATALINA_BASE%" -Dcatalina.home="%CATALINA_HOME%" -
Djava.io.tmpdir="%CATALINA_TMPDIR%" %MAINCLASS% %CMD_LINE_ARGS%
%ACTION%
goto end
:doSecurity
%_EXECJAVA% %JAVA_OPTS% %CATALINA_OPTS% %DEBUG_OPTS% -
Djava.endorsed.dirs="%JAVA_ENDORSED_DIRS%" -classpath "%CLASSPATH%" -
Djava.security.manager -Djava.security.policy=="%SECURITY_POLICY_FILE%"
-Dcatalina.base="%CATALINA_BASE%" -Dcatalina.home="%CATALINA_HOME%" -
Djava.io.tmpdir="%CATALINA_TMPDIR%" %MAINCLASS% %CMD_LINE_ARGS%
%ACTION%
goto end
:doJpda
if not "%SECURITY_POLICY_FILE%" == "" goto doSecurityJpda
```

```
%_EXECJAVA% %JAVA_OPTS% %CATALINA_OPTS% -Xdebug -
Xrunjdwp:transport=%JPDA_TRANSPORT%,address=%JPDA_ADDRESS%,server=y,sus
pend=n %DEBUG_OPTS% -Djava.endorsed.dirs="%JAVA_ENDORSED_DIRS%" -
classpath "%CLASSPATH%" -Dcatalina.base="%CATALINA_BASE%" -
Dcatalina.home="%CATALINA_HOME%" -Djava.io.tmpdir="%CATALINA_TMPDIR%"
%MAINCLASS% %CMD_LINE_ARGS% %ACTION%
goto end
:doSecurityJpda
%_EXECJAVA% %JAVA_OPTS% %CATALINA_OPTS% -
Xrunjdwp:transport=%JPDA_TRANSPORT%,address=%JPDA_ADDRESS%,server=y,sus
pend=n %DEBUG_OPTS% -Djava.endorsed.dirs="%JAVA_ENDORSED_DIRS%" -
classpath "%CLASSPATH%" -Djava.security.manager -
Djava.security.policy=="%SECURITY_POLICY_FILE%" -
Dcatalina.base="%CATALINA_BASE%" -Dcatalina.home="%CATALINA_HOME%" -
Djava.io.tmpdir="%CATALINA_TMPDIR%" %MAINCLASS% %CMD_LINE_ARGS%
%ACTION%
goto end
:end
```

The catalina.bat file starts off by calling @echo off to suppress the commands. It then checks if the value of OS environment variable is Windows_NT (meaning the user is using Windows NT, Windows 2000, or Windows XP). If it is, it calls setLocal to make any changes to the environment variables local to the batch file.

```
if "%OS%" == "Windows_NT" setlocal
```

It then sets the value of CATALINA_HOME if there is not yet a variable named CATALINA_HOME. By default, the CATALINA_HOME variable is non-existent because you are not required to set this variable to run Tomcat.

If the CATALINA_HOME variable is not found, the batch file guesses the directory from which the batch file is invoked. First, it speculates that the catalina.bat file is run from the install directory, in which case it must find the catalina.bat file in the bin directory.

```
if not "%CATALINA_HOME%" == "" goto gotHome
set CATALINA_HOME=.
if exist "%CATALINA_HOME%\bin\catalina.bat" goto okHome
```

If the catalina.bat file is not found in the subdirectory bin under the current directory, the catalina.bat file could not have been invoked from the install directory. The batch file then guesses again. This time it reckons that the catalina.bat file is invoked from the bin directory under the install directory by setting the parent directory of bin to CATALINA_HOME and then checking the existence of catalina.bat under the bin directory.

```
set CATALINA_HOME=..
:gotHome
if exist "%CATALINA_HOME%\bin\catalina.bat" goto okHome
```

If the guess was correct, it jumps to okHome. Otherwise, it prints an error message telling the user that CATALINA_HOME is not set correctly and jump to end, the label at the end of the batch file.

```
echo The CATALINA_HOME environment variable is not defined correctly
echo This environment variable is needed to run this program
goto end
```

If CATALINA_HOME is defined correctly, the batch file calls the setenv.bat to set the required environment variables, if the setenv.bat exists. If it does not exist, no error message will be raised.

```
:okHome
rem Get standard environment variables
if exist "%CATALINA_HOME%\bin\setenv.bat" call
"%CATALINA_HOME%\bin\setenv.bat"
```

Next, it checks if the setclasspath.bat file exists. If the file cannot be found, it displays an error message and jumps to end to quit the batch file.

```
if exist "%CATALINA_HOME%\bin\setclasspath.bat" goto okSetclasspath
echo Cannot find %CATALINA_HOME%\bin\setclasspath.bat
echo This file is needed to run this program
goto end
```

If setclaspath.bat file is found, it sets the BASEDIR variable with the value of CATALINA_HOME and then calls the setclasspath.bat file to set the class path.

```
:okSetclasspath
set BASEDIR=%CATALINA_HOME%
call "%CATALINA_HOME%\bin\setclasspath.bat"
```

The setclasspath.bat file checks if the environment variable JAVA_HOME is defined correctly and set the following variables to used by the rest of the catalina.bat file.

```
set JAVA_ENDORSED_DIRS=%BASEDIR%\common\endorsed
set CLASSPATH=%JAVA_HOME%\lib\tools.jar
set _RUNJAVA="%JAVA_HOME%\bin\java"
set _RUNJAVAW="%JAVA_HOME%\bin\javaw"
set _RUNJDB="%JAVA_HOME%\bin\jdb"
set _RUNJAVAC="%JAVA_HOME%\bin\javac"
```

The catalina.bat file then checks if Java Secure Socket Extension (JSSE) has been installed and the JSSE_HOME variable is set correctly. If JSSE_HOME variable is found, it is added to the CLASSPATH variable.

```
if "%JSSE_HOME%" == "" goto noJsse
set
CLASSPATH=%CLASSPATH%;%JSSE_HOME%\lib\jcert.jar;%JSSE_HOME%\lib\jnet.ja
r;%JSSE_HOME%\lib\jsse.jar
```

If JSSE_HOME is not found, the batch file continues with the next line, which adds the bootstrap.jar in the bin directory to the CLASSPATH variable.

```
:noJsse
set CLASSPATH=%CLASSPATH%;%CATALINA_HOME%\bin\bootstrap.jar
```

Next, the catalina.bat file checks the value of CATALINA_BASE. If CATALINA_BASE is not found, it is created and the value of CATALINA_HOME is assigned to it.

```
if not "%CATALINA_BASE%" == "" goto gotBase
set CATALINA_BASE=%CATALINA_HOME%
:gotBase
```

Then, it checks the value of CATALINA_TMPDIR, which represents the temporary directory under CATALINA_BASE.

```
if not "%CATALINA_TMPDIR%" == "" goto gotTmpdir
set CATALINA_TMPDIR=%CATALINA_BASE%\temp
:gotTmpdir
```

Next, it echoes the values of several variables:

```
echo Using CATALINA_BASE:    %CATALINA_BASE%
echo Using CATALINA_HOME:    %CATALINA_HOME%
echo Using CATALINA_TMPDIR:  %CATALINA_TMPDIR%
echo Using JAVA_HOME:        %JAVA_HOME%
```

Then, it assigns the value of _RUNJAVA, a variable set in the setclaspath.bin to _EXECJAVA. The value of _RUNJAVA is "%JAVA_HOME%\bin\java". In other words, it refers to the java.exe program in the bin directory under JAVA_HOME.

```
set _EXECJAVA=%_RUNJAVA%
```

It then sets the following variables:

```
set MAINCLASS=org.apache.catalina.startup.Bootstrap
set ACTION=start
set SECURITY_POLICY_FILE=
set DEBUG_OPTS=
set JPDA=
```

The catalina.bat file then checks whether the first parameter passed to it is jpda (for Java Platform Debugger Architecture). If it is, it sets the JPDA variable to jpda, then checks the JPDA_TRANSPORT and JPDA_ADDRESS variables, and shifts the parameters.

```
if not ""%1"" == ""jpda"" goto noJpda
set JPDA=jpda
if not "%JPDA_TRANSPORT%" == "" goto gotJpdaTransport
set JPDA_TRANSPORT=dt_shmem
```

```
:gotJpdaTransport
if not "%JPDA_ADDRESS%" == "" goto gotJpdaAddress
set JPDA_ADDRESS=jdbconn
:gotJpdaAddress
shift
```

In most cases you will not use JPDA, therefore the value of the first parameters must be one of the following: debug, embedded, run, start, or stop.

```
:noJpda
if ""%1"" == ""debug"" goto doDebug
if ""%1"" == ""embedded"" goto doEmbedded
if ""%1"" == ""run"" goto doRun
if ""%1"" == ""start"" goto doStart
if ""%1"" == ""stop"" goto doStop
```

If the first parameter is not correct or no parameter exists, the batch file displays the usage instruction and exits.

```
echo Usage:  catalina ( commands ... )
echo commands:
echo    debug              Start Catalina in a debugger
echo    debug -security    Debug Catalina with a security manager
echo    embedded           Start Catalina in embedded mode
echo    jpda start         Start Catalina under JPDA debugger
echo    run                Start Catalina in the current window
echo    run -security      Start in the current window with security
manager
echo    start              Start Catalina in a separate window
echo    start -security    Start in a separate window with security
manager
echo    stop               Stop Catalina
goto end
```

If the first parameter is start, it goes to doStart. If it is stop, control jumps to doStop, etc.

After the doStart label, the catalina.bat file calls the shift command to check the next parameter, if any. If present, the next parameter must be -security. Otherwise, it will be ignored. If the next parameter is -security, the shift command is called again and the SECURITY_POLICY_FILE variable is set to %CATALINA_BASE%\conf\catalina.policy.

```
:doStart
shift
if not "%OS%" == "Windows_NT" goto noTitle
set _EXECJAVA=start "Tomcat" %_RUNJAVA%
goto gotTitle
:noTitle
set _EXECJAVA=start %_RUNJAVA%
:gotTitle
if not ""%1"" == ""-security"" goto execCmd
shift
```

```
echo Using Security Manager
set SECURITY_POLICY_FILE=%CATALINA_BASE%\conf\catalina.policy
```

At this stage, the value of _EXECJAVA is either one of the following:

```
start "Tomcat" "%JAVA_HOME%\bin\java"
start "%JAVA_HOME%\bin\java"
```

It then jumps to execCmd

```
goto execCmd
```

The commands below the execCmd label obtains the remaining unshifted command line arguments and save them to CMD_LINE_ARGS and then jump to doneSetArgs.

```
:execCmd
set CMD_LINE_ARGS=
:setArgs
if ""%1""=="""" goto doneSetArgs
set CMD_LINE_ARGS=%CMD_LINE_ARGS% %1
shift
goto setArgs
```

Here are the command lines next to doneSetArgs.

```
:doneSetArgs
rem Execute Java with the applicable properties
if not "%JPDA%" == "" goto doJpda
if not "%SECURITY_POLICY_FILE%" == "" goto doSecurity
%_EXECJAVA% %JAVA_OPTS% %CATALINA_OPTS% %DEBUG_OPTS% -
Djava.endorsed.dirs="%JAVA_ENDORSED_DIRS%" -classpath "%CLASSPATH%" -
Dcatalina.base="%CATALINA_BASE%" -Dcatalina.home="%CATALINA_HOME%" -
Djava.io.tmpdir="%CATALINA_TMPDIR%" %MAINCLASS% %CMD_LINE_ARGS%
%ACTION%
```

For example, in my computer, on calling catalina start the above long preceding command line (starting with %_EXECJAVA% and ends with %ACTION%) translates into the following:

```
start "Tomcat" "C:\j2sdk1.4.2_02\bin\java" -
Djava.endorsed.dirs="..\common\endorsed" -classpath
"C:\j2sdk1.4.2_02\lib\tools.jar;..\bin\bootstrap.jar" -
Dcatalina.base=".." -Dcatalina.home=".." -Djava.io.tmpdir="..\temp"
org.apache.catalina.startup.Bootstrap start
```

You should be able to figure out what the command is when the catalina.bat file is called by passing different parameters.

Starting Tomcat on Windows

The startup.bat file, given in Listing 17.10, is provided as the shortcut to call the catalina.bat file. It calls the catalina.bat file by passing one argument, start.

Listing 17.10: The startup.bat file

```
@echo off
if "%OS%" == "Windows_NT" setlocal
rem ---------------------------------------------------------------
rem Start script for the CATALINA Server
rem
rem $Id: startup.bat,v 1.4 2002/08/04 18:19:43 patrickl Exp $
rem ---------------------------------------------------------------

rem Guess CATALINA_HOME if not defined
if not "%CATALINA_HOME%" == "" goto gotHome
set CATALINA_HOME=.
if exist "%CATALINA_HOME%\bin\catalina.bat" goto okHome
set CATALINA_HOME=..
:gotHome
if exist "%CATALINA_HOME%\bin\catalina.bat" goto okHome
echo The CATALINA_HOME environment variable is not defined correctly
echo This environment variable is needed to run this program
goto end
:okHome

set EXECUTABLE=%CATALINA_HOME%\bin\catalina.bat

rem Check that target executable exists
if exist "%EXECUTABLE%" goto okExec
echo Cannot find %EXECUTABLE%
echo This file is needed to run this program
goto end
:okExec

rem Get remaining unshifted command line arguments and save them in the
set CMD_LINE_ARGS=
:setArgs
if ""%1""=="""" goto doneSetArgs
set CMD_LINE_ARGS=%CMD_LINE_ARGS% %1
shift
goto setArgs
:doneSetArgs

call "%EXECUTABLE%" start %CMD_LINE_ARGS%

:end
```

Stripping all rem and echo commands, you get the following:

```
if "%OS%" == "Windows_NT" setlocal
if not "%CATALINA_HOME%" == "" goto gotHome
set CATALINA_HOME=.
if exist "%CATALINA_HOME%\bin\catalina.bat" goto okHome
set CATALINA_HOME=..
:gotHome
```

```
if exist "%CATALINA_HOME%\bin\catalina.bat" goto okHome
goto end
:okHome
set EXECUTABLE=%CATALINA_HOME%\bin\catalina.bat
if exist "%EXECUTABLE%" goto okExec
goto end
:okExec

rem Get remaining unshifted command line arguments and save them in the
set CMD_LINE_ARGS=
:setArgs
if ""%1""=="""" goto doneSetArgs
set CMD_LINE_ARGS=%CMD_LINE_ARGS% %1
shift
goto setArgs
:doneSetArgs

call "%EXECUTABLE%" start %CMD_LINE_ARGS%

:end
```

Stopping Tomcat on Windows

The shutdown.bat file is provided as a shortcut to call catalina.bat by passing the stop argument. The shutdown.bat file is given in Listing 17.11.

Listing 17.11: The shutdown.bat file

```
@echo off
if "%OS%" == "Windows_NT" setlocal
rem ---------------------------------------------------------------
--------
rem Stop script for the CATALINA Server
rem
rem $Id: shutdown.bat,v 1.3 2002/08/04 18:19:43 patrickl Exp $
rem ---------------------------------------------------------------
--------

rem Guess CATALINA_HOME if not defined
if not "%CATALINA_HOME%" == "" goto gotHome
set CATALINA_HOME=.
if exist "%CATALINA_HOME%\bin\catalina.bat" goto okHome
set CATALINA_HOME=..
:gotHome
if exist "%CATALINA_HOME%\bin\catalina.bat" goto okHome
echo The CATALINA_HOME environment variable is not defined correctly
echo This environment variable is needed to run this program
goto end
:okHome

set EXECUTABLE=%CATALINA_HOME%\bin\catalina.bat

rem Check that target executable exists
if exist "%EXECUTABLE%" goto okExec
```

```
echo Cannot find %EXECUTABLE%
echo This file is needed to run this program
goto end
:okExec

rem Get remaining unshifted command line arguments and save them in the
set CMD_LINE_ARGS=
:setArgs
if ""%1""=="""" goto doneSetArgs
set CMD_LINE_ARGS=%CMD_LINE_ARGS% %1
shift
goto setArgs
:doneSetArgs

call "%EXECUTABLE%" stop %CMD_LINE_ARGS%
:end
```

Running Tomcat on Unix/Linux

Tomcat comes with shell scripts for starting and stopping Tomcat in Unix/Linux. These shell scripts have an .sh extension and reside in the bin directory of %CATALINA_HOME%. Four of them--catalina.sh, startup.sh, shutdown.sh, and setclasspath.sh--will be the topic of this section.

This section starts by offering an introduction to shell scripts for those not familiar with or need to brush up their knowledge of shell scripts. It then covers catalina.sh, startup.sh, and shutdown.sh. setclasspath.sh is called by catalina.sh and therefore is explained briefly in the subsection that discusses catalina.sh.

Introduction to Writing Unix/Linux Shell Scripts

This introduction to shell scripts is meant to give you enough information to be able to read the shell scripts accompanying Tomcat, especially the catalina.sh, startup.sh, shutdown.sh, and setclasspath.sh files. It is far from a complete coverage of the topic, for which you have to find another resource.

Physically, a shell file is a text file. You can use vi or other text editors to write it. Make sure you change the permission mode of the file to give it the permission to run, using the following syntax.

```
$ chmod +x scriptName
$ chmod 755 scriptName
```

This will set read, write, and execute permissions for the owner of the file, and read and execute permissions for group and other users.

```
You can then execute your script using one of the following commands:
bash scriptName
sh scriptName
./scriptName
```

The script is executed line by line by the interpreter. Your shell script can have any extension or no extension. However, the .sh extension is the most common.

The following are some common commands that are sufficient for you to understand Tomcat shell scripts.

comment

Use # to indicate that a piece of text is a comment and is not to be interpreted. The # character can appear at the beginning of a line, in which case the whole line is a comment.

```
# This is a comment
```

It can also appear in the middle of a line. In this case, the text to the right of the # character is a comment. For example:

```
echo Hello # print Hello
```

clear

Use clear to clear the screen. For example, the following script starts by clearing the screen and then prints a string.

```
clear
echo Shell scripts are useful
```

exit

Use the exit command to exit the shell script. exit is normally followed by an exit status, where 0 means a successful execution of the shell script and a non-zero value means an abnormal exit (possibly because there is an error). Therefore, if you want to exit because your shell has encountered a problem, write this:

```
exit 1
```

echo

Use echo to print a string to the screen. For example, the following command prints Hello World on the console.

```
echo Hello World
```

Calling A Function

You can use a period (.) to call a function or run another shell script. For example, the following command calls the test.sh script in the same directory as the running script.

```
. ./test.sh
```

System and User Defined Variables

Variable names must begin with an alphanumeric character or an underscore. You set the value of a variable by using the equal sign. For example, the following line sets the variable myVar with Tootsie.

```
myVar=Tootsie
```

Note that there must not be a space before and after the equal sign. Also note that variable names are case sensitive.

To define a NULL for a variable, use a blank string or simply leave out the right hand side of the equation:

```
myVar=
myVar=""
```

To access the value of a variable, use the dollar sign ($) before the name of the variable. For example, here is how you print the value of myVar on the screen.

```
echo $myVar
```

The Unix/Linux operating systems provide a number of system variables. For example, HOME contains the current user's home directory, PWD contains the user's current location, PATH contains the path that will be searched to find an invoked command, and so on.

Warning
You should not change a system variable without knowing exactly the effect of doing so.

expr

Use expr to evaluate an expression. An expression must be enclosed in back quote characters. The back quote key is normally located to the left of the 1 key on your keyboard. Here is a shell script that uses arithmetic expressions:

```
sum=`expr 100 + 200`
echo $sum
```

This will create a user defined variable named `sum` and assigns 300 (the result of adding 100 to 200) to it. Running this script gives you `300` on the console.

Here is another example:

```
echo `expr 200 + 300`
```

This prints the following result on the screen:

```
500
```

The special `uname` expression evaluates to the name of the operating system. For example, if you're using Linux, the following command prints `Linux` on the console.

```
echo `uname`
```

The special `dirname filePath` returns the directory of the file. For example, `dirname /home/user1/test.sh` returns `/home/user1`.

Accessing parameters

Just like you can pass arguments to a function, you can pass parameters to a shell script. You use `$1` to refer to the first parameter, `$2` to the second, and so forth. `$#` returns the number of parameters. `$@` returns all the parameters.

shift

This command shifts all parameters down by one. `$1` gets the value of `$2`, `$2` gets the value of `$3`, and so on.

if ... then ... [else ...] fi

An `if` statement tests a condition and executes the appropriate list of commands. Its syntax is as follows.

```
if condition then
  list of commands
[else
  list of commands
]
fi
```

Note:
You can also use `elif` for `else if`.

For example, the following script will print `Starting the application` if you pass `start` as the first argument and `Stopping the application` if you pass `stop` as the first argument.

```
if [ "$1" = "start" ]; then
  echo Starting the application
fi
if [ "$1" = "stop" ]; then
  echo Stopping the application
fi
```

Note
With the condition, there must be a space after [and a space before]

The `$1` is enclosed in double quotes so that the interpreter won't throw an exception if there is no parameter used to call the script.

`$0` refers to the command that is used to invoke the script. For example, if you invoke the following a script named test.sh by typing the following:

```
./test.sh
```

`$0` will then contain `./test.sh`.

The following can be used as a condition:

- `-f file`, true is `file` exists
- `-r file`, true if you have read access to `file`
- `-z string`, true if `string` is empty.
- `-n string`, true if `string` is not empty
- `string1 = string2`, true if `string1` equals `string2`.
- `string1 != string2`, true if `string1` is not equal to `string2`.

for Loop

Use the `for` loop to repeatedly run the same piece of code. The syntax is as follows:

```
for { var } in {list}
do
  list of commands
done
```

For example:

```
for i in 1 2 3
do
  echo iteration $i
done
```

prints

```
iteration 1
iteration 2
iteration 3
```

while Loop

The while loop has the following syntax.

```
while [ condition ]
do
  list of commands
done
```

For example

```
n=1
while [ $n -lt 3 ];
do
  echo iteration $n
  n=$((n + 1))
done
```

The output is

```
iteration 1
iteration 2
```

The -lt in [$n -lt 3]; means less than, so the condition says if the value of *n* is less than 3.

case

case lets you write alternatives of program execution. The syntax is as follows.

```
case $variable-name in
pattern1)
  list of commands
  ;;
pattern2)
  list of commands
  ;;

*)
  list of commands
  ;;
esac
```

The ;; ends the list of commands. The *) pattern will be executed if no other patterns match.

For example, the following script evaluates the name of the operating system and prints it on the console. If you are not using cygwin, OS400 or Linux, the `Operating system not recognized` will be printed.

```
case "`uname`" in
  CYGWIN*) echo cygwin;;
  OS400*) echo OS400;;
  Linux*) echo Linux;;
  *) echo Operating system not recognized
esac
```

Output Redirection

Use > to redirect the output to a file. For example, the following command

```
echo Hello > myFile.txt
```

creates a file named myFile.txt and write `Hello` to it. No output is displayed to the screen.

Also note that `1>&2` redirects error message on stdout to stderr and `2>&1` redirects output on stderr to stdout.

Conditional Executions

You can write a command or condition that determines the execution of another command. In this case, you use `&&` and `||`.

```
command1 && command2
```

`command2` is executed if `command1` returns a 0 exit status. `command1` can also be replaced by a condition. If the condition evaluates to true, `command2` will be executed. Otherwise, `command2` will not be executed.

```
command1 || command2
```

`command2` is executed if `command1` returns a non-zero exit status.

```
command1 && command2 || command3
```

if `command1` returns a 0 exit status, execute `command2`. Otherwise, execute `command3`.

The catalina.sh File

The catalina.sh file is used to start and stop Tomcat on Unix/Linux. To start Tomcat, you pass `start` as the first parameter to catalina.sh. To stop Tomcat, pass `stop` as the first parameter, instead. Here is the list of valid argument(s):

- `debug`. Start Catalina in a debugger (not available on OS400)
- `debug -security`. Debug Catalina with a security manager (not available on OS400)
- `embedded`. Start Catalina in embedded mode
- `jpda start`. Start Catalina under JPDA debugger
- `run`. Start Catalina in the current window
- `run -security`. Start in the current window with security manager
- `start`. Start Catalina in a separate window
- `start -security`. Start in a separate window with security manager
- `stop`. Stop Catalina

The catalina.sh file is given in Listing 17.12. Based on the introduction given in the preceding subsection, you should be able to figure out what it does.

Listing 17.12: The catalina.sh file

```
#!/bin/sh
# -----------------------------------------------------------------
--------
# Start/Stop Script for the CATALINA Server
#
# Environment Variable Prequisites
#
#   CATALINA_HOME    May point at your Catalina "build" directory.
#
#   CATALINA_BASE    (Optional) Base directory for resolving dynamic
portions
#                    of a Catalina installation.  If not present,
resolves to
#                    the same directory that CATALINA_HOME points to.
#
#   CATALINA_OPTS    (Optional) Java runtime options used when the
"start",
#                    "stop", or "run" command is executed.
#
#   CATALINA_TMPDIR (Optional) Directory path location of temporary
directory
#                    the JVM should use (java.io.tmpdir).  Defaults to
#                    $CATALINA_BASE/temp.
#
#   JAVA_HOME        Must point at your Java Development Kit
installation.
#
```

```
#   JAVA_OPTS        (Optional) Java runtime options used when the
"start",
#                    "stop", or "run" command is executed.
#
#   JPDA_TRANSPORT   (Optional) JPDA transport used when the "jpda
start"
#                    command is executed. The default is "dt_socket".
#
#   JPDA_ADDRESS     (Optional) Java runtime options used when the "jpda
start"
#                    command is executed. The default is 8000.
#
#   JSSE_HOME        (Optional) May point at your Java Secure Sockets
Extension
#                    (JSSE) installation, whose JAR files will be added
to the
#                    system class path used to start Tomcat.
#
#   CATALINA_PID     (Optional) Path of the file which should contains
the pid
#                    of catalina startup java process, when start (fork)
is used
#
# $Id: catalina.sh,v 1.8 2003/09/02 12:23:13 remm Exp $
# ---------------------------------------------------------------------
--------

# OS specific support.  $var _must_ be set to either true or false.
cygwin=false
os400=false
case "`uname`" in
CYGWIN*) cygwin=true;;
OS400*) os400=true;;
esac

# resolve links - $0 may be a softlink
PRG="$0"

while [ -h "$PRG" ]; do
  ls=`ls -ld "$PRG"`
  link=`expr "$ls" : '.*-> \(.*\)$'`
  if expr "$link" : '.*/.*' > /dev/null; then
    PRG="$link"
  else
    PRG=`dirname "$PRG"`/"$link"
  fi
done

# Get standard environment variables
PRGDIR=`dirname "$PRG"`
CATALINA_HOME=`cd "$PRGDIR/.." ; pwd`
if [ -r "$CATALINA_HOME"/bin/setenv.sh ]; then
  . "$CATALINA_HOME"/bin/setenv.sh
fi
```

```
# For Cygwin, ensure paths are in UNIX format before anything is
touched
if $cygwin; then
  [ -n "$JAVA_HOME" ] && JAVA_HOME=`cygpath --unix "$JAVA_HOME"`
  [ -n "$CATALINA_HOME" ] && CATALINA_HOME=`cygpath --unix
"$CATALINA_HOME"`
  [ -n "$CATALINA_BASE" ] && CATALINA_BASE=`cygpath --unix
"$CATALINA_BASE"`
  [ -n "$CLASSPATH" ] && CLASSPATH=`cygpath --path --unix "$CLASSPATH"`
  [ -n "$JSSE_HOME" ] && JSSE_HOME=`cygpath --path --unix "$JSSE_HOME"`
fi

# For OS400
if $os400; then
  # Set job priority to standard for interactive (interactive - 6) by
using
  # the interactive priority - 6, the helper threads that respond to
requests
  # will be running at the same priority as interactive jobs.
  COMMAND='chgjob job('$JOBNAME') runpty(6)'
  system $COMMAND

  # Enable multi threading
  export QIBM_MULTI_THREADED=Y
fi

# Get standard Java environment variables
if [ -r "$CATALINA_HOME"/bin/setclasspath.sh ]; then
  BASEDIR="$CATALINA_HOME"
  . "$CATALINA_HOME"/bin/setclasspath.sh
else
  echo "Cannot find $CATALINA_HOME/bin/setclasspath.sh"
  echo "This file is needed to run this program"
  exit 1
fi

# Add on extra jar files to CLASSPATH
if [ -n "$JSSE_HOME" ]; then

CLASSPATH="$CLASSPATH":"$JSSE_HOME"/lib/jcert.jar:"$JSSE_HOME"/lib/jnet
.jar:"$JSSE_HOME"/lib/jsse.jar
fi
CLASSPATH="$CLASSPATH":"$CATALINA_HOME"/bin/bootstrap.jar

if [ -z "$CATALINA_BASE" ] ; then
  CATALINA_BASE="$CATALINA_HOME"
fi

if [ -z "$CATALINA_TMPDIR" ] ; then
  # Define the java.io.tmpdir to use for Catalina
  CATALINA_TMPDIR="$CATALINA_BASE"/temp
fi

# For Cygwin, switch paths to Windows format before running java
if $cygwin; then
  JAVA_HOME=`cygpath --path --windows "$JAVA_HOME"`
```

```
    CATALINA_HOME=`cygpath --path --windows "$CATALINA_HOME"`
    CATALINA_BASE=`cygpath --path --windows "$CATALINA_BASE"`
    CATALINA_TMPDIR=`cygpath --path --windows "$CATALINA_TMPDIR"`
    CLASSPATH=`cygpath --path --windows "$CLASSPATH"`
    JSSE_HOME=`cygpath --path --windows "$JSSE_HOME"`
fi

# ----- Execute The Requested Command ---------------------------------
--------

echo "Using CATALINA_BASE:   $CATALINA_BASE"
echo "Using CATALINA_HOME:   $CATALINA_HOME"
echo "Using CATALINA_TMPDIR: $CATALINA_TMPDIR"
echo "Using JAVA_HOME:       $JAVA_HOME"

if [ "$1" = "jpda" ] ; then
  if [ -z "$JPDA_TRANSPORT" ]; then
    JPDA_TRANSPORT="dt_socket"
  fi
  if [ -z "$JPDA_ADDRESS" ]; then
    JPDA_ADDRESS="8000"
  fi
  if [ -z "$JPDA_OPTS" ]; then
    JPDA_OPTS="-Xdebug -
Xrunjdwp:transport=$JPDA_TRANSPORT,address=$JPDA_ADDRESS,server=y,suspe
nd=n"
  fi
  CATALINA_OPTS="$CATALINA_OPTS $JPDA_OPTS"
  shift
fi

if [ "$1" = "debug" ] ; then

  if $os400; then
    echo "Debug command not available on OS400"
    exit 1
  else
    shift
    if [ "$1" = "-security" ] ; then
      echo "Using Security Manager"
      shift
      exec "$_RUNJDB" $JAVA_OPTS $CATALINA_OPTS \
        -Djava.endorsed.dirs="$JAVA_ENDORSED_DIRS" -classpath
"$CLASSPATH" \
        -sourcepath "$CATALINA_HOME"/../../jakarta-tomcat-
4.0/catalina/src/share \
        -Djava.security.manager \
        -Djava.security.policy=="$CATALINA_BASE"/conf/catalina.policy \
        -Dcatalina.base="$CATALINA_BASE" \
        -Dcatalina.home="$CATALINA_HOME" \
        -Djava.io.tmpdir="$CATALINA_TMPDIR" \
        org.apache.catalina.startup.Bootstrap "$@" start
    else
      exec "$_RUNJDB" $JAVA_OPTS $CATALINA_OPTS \
        -Djava.endorsed.dirs="$JAVA_ENDORSED_DIRS" -classpath
"$CLASSPATH" \
```

```
            -sourcepath "$CATALINA_HOME"/../../jakarta-tomcat-
4.0/catalina/src/share \
            -Dcatalina.base="$CATALINA_BASE" \
            -Dcatalina.home="$CATALINA_HOME" \
            -Djava.io.tmpdir="$CATALINA_TMPDIR" \
            org.apache.catalina.startup.Bootstrap "$@" start
      fi
   fi

elif [ "$1" = "embedded" ] ; then

   shift
   echo "Embedded Classpath: $CLASSPATH"
   exec "$_RUNJAVA" $JAVA_OPTS $CATALINA_OPTS \
      -Djava.endorsed.dirs="$JAVA_ENDORSED_DIRS" -classpath "$CLASSPATH"
\
      -Dcatalina.base="$CATALINA_BASE" \
      -Dcatalina.home="$CATALINA_HOME" \
      -Djava.io.tmpdir="$CATALINA_TMPDIR" \
      org.apache.catalina.startup.Embedded "$@"

elif [ "$1" = "run" ]; then

   shift
   if [ "$1" = "-security" ] ; then
     echo "Using Security Manager"
     shift
     exec "$_RUNJAVA" $JAVA_OPTS $CATALINA_OPTS \
        -Djava.endorsed.dirs="$JAVA_ENDORSED_DIRS" -classpath
"$CLASSPATH" \
        -Djava.security.manager \
        -Djava.security.policy=="$CATALINA_BASE"/conf/catalina.policy \
        -Dcatalina.base="$CATALINA_BASE" \
        -Dcatalina.home="$CATALINA_HOME" \
        -Djava.io.tmpdir="$CATALINA_TMPDIR" \
        org.apache.catalina.startup.Bootstrap "$@" start
   else
     exec "$_RUNJAVA" $JAVA_OPTS $CATALINA_OPTS \
        -Djava.endorsed.dirs="$JAVA_ENDORSED_DIRS" -classpath
"$CLASSPATH" \
        -Dcatalina.base="$CATALINA_BASE" \
        -Dcatalina.home="$CATALINA_HOME" \
        -Djava.io.tmpdir="$CATALINA_TMPDIR" \
        org.apache.catalina.startup.Bootstrap "$@" start
   fi

elif [ "$1" = "start" ] ; then

   shift
   touch "$CATALINA_BASE"/logs/catalina.out
   if [ "$1" = "-security" ] ; then
     echo "Using Security Manager"
     shift
     "$_RUNJAVA" $JAVA_OPTS $CATALINA_OPTS \
        -Djava.endorsed.dirs="$JAVA_ENDORSED_DIRS" -classpath
"$CLASSPATH" \
```

```
      -Djava.security.manager \
      -Djava.security.policy=="$CATALINA_BASE"/conf/catalina.policy \
      -Dcatalina.base="$CATALINA_BASE" \
      -Dcatalina.home="$CATALINA_HOME" \
      -Djava.io.tmpdir="$CATALINA_TMPDIR" \
      org.apache.catalina.startup.Bootstrap "$@" start \
      >> "$CATALINA_BASE"/logs/catalina.out 2>&1 &

      if [ ! -z "$CATALINA_PID" ]; then
        echo $! > $CATALINA_PID
      fi
  else
    "$_RUNJAVA" $JAVA_OPTS $CATALINA_OPTS \
      -Djava.endorsed.dirs="$JAVA_ENDORSED_DIRS" -classpath
"$CLASSPATH" \
      -Dcatalina.base="$CATALINA_BASE" \
      -Dcatalina.home="$CATALINA_HOME" \
      -Djava.io.tmpdir="$CATALINA_TMPDIR" \
      org.apache.catalina.startup.Bootstrap "$@" start \
      >> "$CATALINA_BASE"/logs/catalina.out 2>&1 &

      if [ ! -z "$CATALINA_PID" ]; then
        echo $! > $CATALINA_PID
      fi
  fi

elif [ "$1" = "stop" ] ; then

  shift
  "$_RUNJAVA" $JAVA_OPTS $CATALINA_OPTS \
    -Djava.endorsed.dirs="$JAVA_ENDORSED_DIRS" -classpath "$CLASSPATH"
\
    -Dcatalina.base="$CATALINA_BASE" \
    -Dcatalina.home="$CATALINA_HOME" \
    -Djava.io.tmpdir="$CATALINA_TMPDIR" \
    org.apache.catalina.startup.Bootstrap "$@" stop

  if [ "$1" = "-force" ] ; then
    shift
    if [ ! -z "$CATALINA_PID" ]; then
      echo "Killing: `cat $CATALINA_PID`"
      kill -9 `cat $CATALINA_PID`
    fi
  fi

else

  echo "Usage: catalina.sh ( commands ... )"
  echo "commands:"
  if $os400; then
    echo " debug               Start Catalina in a debugger (not
available on OS400)"
    echo " debug -security     Debug Catalina with a security manager
(not available on OS400)"
  else
    echo " debug               Start Catalina in a debugger"
```

```
      echo "  debug -security   Debug Catalina with a security manager"
   fi
   echo "  embedded          Start Catalina in embedded mode"
   echo "  jpda start        Start Catalina under JPDA debugger"
   echo "  run               Start Catalina in the current window"
   echo "  run -security     Start in the current window with security
manager"
   echo "  start             Start Catalina in a separate window"
   echo "  start -security   Start in a separate window with security
manager"
   echo "  stop              Stop Catalina"
   exit 1
fi
```

Starting Tomcat on Linux/Unix

To make your life even easier, you can use the startup.sh to start Tomcat.
startup.sh sets the correct environment variables and calls catalina.sh by passing
`start`. The startup.sh is given in Listing 17.13.

Listing 17.13: The startup.sh file

```
#!/bin/sh
# -----------------------------------------------------------------------
--------
# Start Script for the CATALINA Server
#
# $Id: startup.sh,v 1.3 2002/08/04 18:19:43 patrickl Exp $
# -----------------------------------------------------------------------
--------

# resolve links - $0 may be a softlink
PRG="$0"

while [ -h "$PRG" ] ; do
  ls=`ls -ld "$PRG"`
  link=`expr "$ls" : '.*-> \(.*\)$'`
  if expr "$link" : '.*/.*' > /dev/null; then
    PRG="$link"
  else
    PRG=`dirname "$PRG"`/"$link"
  fi
done

PRGDIR=`dirname "$PRG"`
EXECUTABLE=catalina.sh

# Check that target executable exists
if [ ! -x "$PRGDIR"/"$EXECUTABLE" ]; then
  echo "Cannot find $PRGDIR/$EXECUTABLE"
  echo "This file is needed to run this program"
  exit 1
fi
```

```
exec "$PRGDIR"/"$EXECUTABLE" start "$@"
```

Stopping Tomcat on Linux/Unix

You can easily stop Tomcat by running the shutdown.sh script. This script calls catalina.sh and passes stop as an argument to it.

Listing 17.14 presents shutdown.sh.

Listing 17.14: The shutdown.sh File

```sh
#!/bin/sh
# -----------------------------------------------------------------------
# Stop script for the CATALINA Server
#
# $Id: shutdown.sh,v 1.3 2002/08/04 18:19:43 patrickl Exp $
# -----------------------------------------------------------------------
# resolve links - $0 may be a softlink
PRG="$0"

while [ -h "$PRG" ] ; do
  ls=`ls -ld "$PRG"`
  link=`expr "$ls" : '.*-> \(.*\)$'`
  if expr "$link" : '.*/.*' > /dev/null; then
    PRG="$link"
  else
    PRG=`dirname "$PRG"`/"$link"
  fi
done
PRGDIR=`dirname "$PRG"`
EXECUTABLE=catalina.sh

# Check that target executable exists
if [ ! -x "$PRGDIR"/"$EXECUTABLE" ]; then
  echo "Cannot find $PRGDIR/$EXECUTABLE"
  echo "This file is needed to run this program"
  exit 1
fi
exec "$PRGDIR"/"$EXECUTABLE" stop "$@"
```

Summary

This chapter explains the two classes for starting up the application, `Catalina` and `Bootstrap`, both of which are members of the `org.apache.catalina.startup` package. You have also learned about batch files and shell scripts that provides easy ways to start and stop Tomcat on Windows and Unix/Linux.

Chapter 18
Deployer

For a web application to be available, the context representing it must first be deployed to a host. In Tomcat, a context can be deployed as a WAR file or by copying the whole application to the webapps directory under the Tomcat installation directory. For each application you deploy, you can optionally have a descriptor file that contains the configuration settings for the context. A descriptor file takes the form of an XML document.

Note
Tomcat 4 and 5 come with two applications for managing Tomcat and applications deployed to it, the manager application and the admin application. The class files for both applications are in the %CATALINA_HOME%/server/webapps directory. Both applications come with descriptor files, which are manager.xml and admin.xml, respectively. In Tomcat 4, these descriptors reside in the %CATALINA_HOME%/webapps directory; in Tomcat 5 they live in the corresponding application directories, i.e. in the %CATALINA_HOME%/server/webapps/admin and %CATALINA_HOME%/server/webapps/manager, respectively.

This chapter discusses web application deployment using a deployer, which is represented by the `org.apache.catalina.Deployer` interface. A deployer is associated with a host and is used to install child contexts. Installing a context to a host means creating an instance of the `StandardContext` class and adding that instance to the host. A child context is started when the parent host is started (because a container's `start` method always calls the start method of its child containers, except for a wrapper). However, a deployer can also be used to start and stop each context individually.

In this chapter you will first learn how a Tomcat deployment deploys web applications in a host. This chapter will then explain about the `Deployer` interface and its standard implementation, the `org.apache.catalina.core.StandardHostDeployer` class.

Deploying A Web Context

In Chapter 15, you used the following code to instantiate the `StandardHost` class and add a `Context` instance as the host's child container.

```
Context context = new StandardContext();
context.setPath("/app1");
context.setDocBase("app1");
LifecycleListener listener = new ContextConfig();
((Lifecycle) context).addLifecycleListener(listener);

Host host = new StandardHost();
host.addChild(context);
```

That was how we deployed our application. However, such code does not exist in Tomcat. Then, how does a context get added to a host in a real life deployment? The answer lies in a lifecycle listener of type `org.apache.catalina.startup.HostConfig` in the `StandardHost` instance.

When the `start` method on the `StandardHost` instance is called, it triggers a `START` event. The `HostConfig` instance responds to it by calling its own `start` method, which in turn deploys and installs all web applications available in the specified directories. Here are the details.

Recall that Chapter 15, "Digester", explained how you could use a Digester object to parse an XML file. However it did not discuss all the rules in the Digester object. One subject of discussion that it skipped was deployer, which is the topic of this chapter.

The `org.apache.catalina.startup.Catalina` class is a startup class that employs a Digester to convert XML elements in the server.xml file to Java objects. The `Catalina` class defines the `createStartDigester` method for adding rules to the Digester. One line in the `createStartDigester` method is this:

```
digester.addRuleSet(new HostRuleSet("Server/Service/Engine/"));
```

The **org.apache.catalina.startup.HostRuleSet** class extends the `org.apache.commons.digester.RuleSetBase` class (also discussed in Chapter 15). As a subclass of `RuleSetBase`, the `HostRuleSet` class must provide the implementation of the `addRuleInstances` method, which defines the rule(s) for the `RuleSet`. Here is a fragment of the `HostRuleSet` class's `addRuleInstances` method.

```
public void addRuleInstances(Digester digester) {
  digester.addObjectCreate(prefix + "Host",
```

```
  "org.apache.catalina.core.StandardHost", "className");
digester.addSetProperties(prefix + "Host");
digester.addRule(prefix + "Host",
  new CopyParentClassLoaderRule(digester));
digester.addRule(prefix + "Host",
  new LifecycleListenerRule (digester,
  "org.apache.catalina.startup.HostConfig", "hostConfigClass"));
```

What the code says is, the occurrence of the **Server/Service/Engine/Host** pattern in the server.xml file creates an instance of org.apache.catalina.startup.HostConfig class and adds it to the host as a lifecycle listener. In other words, the HostConfig class handles the events fired by the StandardHost's start and stop methods.

Listing 18.1 offers the lifecycleEvent method of the HostConfig class. This method is an event handler. Because the HostConfig is a listener for a StandardHost instance, every time the StandardHost is started or stopped, the lifecycleEvent method will be invoked.

Listing 18.1: The lifecycleEvent method of the HostConfig class.

```
public void lifecycleEvent(LifecycleEvent event) {
  // Identify the host we are associated with
  try {
    host = (Host) event.getLifecycle();
    if (host instanceof StandardHost) {
      int hostDebug = ((StandardHost) host).getDebug();
      if (hostDebug > this.debug) {
        this.debug = hostDebug;
      }
      setDeployXML(((StandardHost) host).isDeployXML());
      setLiveDeploy(((StandardHost) host).getLiveDeploy());
      setUnpackWARs(((StandardHost) host).isUnpackWARs());
    }
  }
  catch (ClassCastException e) {
    log(sm.getString("hostConfig.cce", event.getLifecycle()), e);
    return;
  }

  // Process the event that has occurred
  if (event.getType().equals(Lifecycle.START_EVENT))
    start();
  else if (event.getType().equals(Lifecycle.STOP_EVENT))
    stop();
}
```

If the host is an instance of org.apache.catalina.core.StandardHost, the setDeployXML, setLiveDeploy, and setUnpackWARs methods are called.

```
setDeployXML(((StandardHost) host).isDeployXML());
setLiveDeploy(((StandardHost) host).getLiveDeploy());
```

```
    setUnpackWARs(((StandardHost) host).isUnpackWARs());
```

The isDeployXML method of the StandardHost class indicates whether or not the host should deploy a context's descriptor file. By default the value of the deployXML property is true. The liveDeploy property indicates whether or not the host should periodically check for a new deployment, and the unpackWARs property specifies whether or not to unpack applications deployed as WAR files.

Upon receiving a START event notification, the HostConfig object's lifecycleEvent method calls the start method to deploy applications. This method is given in Listing 18.2.

Listing 18.2: The start method of the HostConfig class

```
protected void start() {
  if (debug >= 1)
    log(sm.getString("hostConfig.start"));
  if (host.getAutoDeploy()) {
    deployApps();
  }
  if (isLiveDeploy()) {
    threadStart();
  }
}
```

The start method calls the deployApps method if the autoDeploy property is true (by default, its value is true). Also, it spawns a new thread by calling the threadStart method if liveDeploy is true (which it is, by default). Live deploy is discussed further in the subsection "Live Deploy" later in this section.

The deployApps method obtains the appBase property of the host. appBase by default has the value of webapps (See Tomcat's server.xml file). The deployment process regards all directories under the %CATALINE_HOME%/webapps directory as application directories to be deployed. In addition, all WAR and descriptor files found in this directory are to be deployed as well.

The deployApps method is given in Listing 18.3.

Listing 18.3: The deployApps method

```
protected void deployApps() {
  if (!(host instanceof Deployer))
    return;
  if (debug >= 1)
    log(sm.getString("hostConfig.deploying"));
  File appBase = appBase();
  if (!appBase.exists() || !appBase.isDirectory())
```

```
    return;
  String files[] = appBase.list();
  deployDescriptors(appBase, files);
  deployWARs(appBase, files);
  deployDirectories(appBase, files);
}
```

The deployApps method calls three other methods, deployDescriptors, deployWARs, and deployDirectories. To all methods, deployApps passes the appBase File and the array of files in the webapps directory. A context is identified by its path, and all deployed contexts must have unique paths. A context that has been deployed is added to the deployed ArrayList in the HostConfig object. Therefore, before deploying a context, the deployDescriptors, deployWARs, and deployDirectories methods make sure that the deployed ArrayList does not contain a context having an identical path.

We now look at each of the three deployment methods in turn. After reading the three subsections below, you should be able to answer this question: Is the order the three methods are called important? (The answer is yes)

Deploying a Descriptor

You can write an XML file that describes the context object. For instance, the admin and manager applications that accompany Tomcat 4 and 5 have the descriptors given in Listings 18.4 and 18.5, respectively.

Listing 18.4: The descriptor for the admin application (admin.xml)

```
<Context path="/admin" docBase="../server/webapps/admin"
  debug="0" privileged="true">
  <!-- Uncomment this Valve to limit access to the Admin app to
   localhost for obvious security reasons. Allow may be a comma-
   separated list of hosts (or even regular expressions).
  <Valve className="org.apache.catalina.valves.RemoteAddrValve"
   allow="127.0.0.1"/>
  -->
  <Logger className="org.apache.catalina.logger.FileLogger"
    prefix="localhost_admin_log." suffix=".txt"
    timestamp="true"/>
</Context>
```

Listing 18.5: The descriptor for the manager application (manager.xml)

```
<Context path="/manager" docBase="../server/webapps/manager"
  debug="0" privileged="true">
  <!-- Link to the user database we will get roles from -->
  <ResourceLink name="users" global="UserDatabase"
    type="org.apache.catalina.UserDatabase"/>
```

```
</Context>
```

Note that both descriptors have a Context element and the docBase attributes refer to %CATALINA_HOME%/server/webapps/admin and %CATALINA_HOME%/server/webapps/manager, respectively, which indicate that the admin and manager applications are not deployed to the usual place.

The HostConfig class uses the deployDescriptors method in Listing 18.6 to deploy all XML files found in %CATALINA_HOME%/webapps in Tomcat 4 and in the subdirectories of %CATALINA_HOME%/server/webapps/ in Tomcat 5.

Listing 18.6: The deployDescriptors method in HostConfig

```
protected void deployDescriptors(File appBase, String[] files) {
  if (!deployXML)
    return;

  for (int i = 0; i < files.length; i++) {
    if (files[i].equalsIgnoreCase("META-INF"))
      continue;
    if (files[i].equalsIgnoreCase("WEB-INF"))
      continue;
    if (deployed.contains(files[i]))
      continue;
    File dir = new File(appBase, files[i]);
    if (files[i].toLowerCase().endsWith(".xml")) {
      deployed.add(files[i]);

      // Calculate the context path and make sure it is unique
      String file = files[i].substring(0, files[i].length() - 4);
      String contextPath = "/" + file;
      if (file.equals("ROOT")) {
        contextPath = "";
      }
      if (host.findChild(contextPath) != null) {
        continue;
      }

      // Assume this is a configuration descriptor and deploy it
      log(sm.getString("hostConfig.deployDescriptor", files[i]));
      try {
        URL config =
          new URL("file", null, dir.getCanonicalPath());
          ((Deployer) host).install(config, null);
      }
      catch (Throwable t) {
        log(sm.getString("hostConfig.deployDescriptor.error",
          files[i]), t);
      }
    }
  }
}
```

Deploying a WAR File

You can deploy a web application as a WAR file. The `HostConfig` class employs the `deployWARs` method in Listing 18.7 to deploy any WAR files in the %CATALINA_HOME%/webapps directory.

Listing 18.7: The deployWARs method in HostConfig

```
protected void deployWARs(File appBase, String[] files) {
  for (int i = 0; i < files.length; i++) {
    if (files[i].equalsIgnoreCase("META-INF"))
      continue;
    if (files[i].equalsIgnoreCase("WEB-INF"))
      continue;
    if (deployed.contains(files[i]))
      continue;
    File dir = new File(appBase, files[i]);

    if (files[i].toLowerCase().endsWith(".war")) {
      deployed.add(files[i]);
      // Calculate the context path and make sure it is unique
      String contextPath = "/" + files[i];
      int period = contextPath.lastIndexOf(".");
      if (period >= 0)
      contextPath = contextPath.substring(0, period);
      if (contextPath.equals("/ROOT"))
        contextPath = "";
      if (host.findChild(contextPath) != null)
        continue;

      if (isUnpackWARs()) {
        // Expand and deploy this application as a directory
        log(sm.getString("hostConfig.expand", files[i]));
        try {
          URL url = new URL("jar:file:" +
            dir.getCanonicalPath() + "!/");
          String path = expand(url);
          url = new URL("file:" + path);
          ((Deployer) host).install(contextPath, url);
        }
        catch (Throwable t) {
          log(sm.getString("hostConfig.expand.error", files[i]), t);
        }
      }
      else {
        // Deploy the application in this WAR file
        log(sm.getString("hostConfig.deployJar", files[i]));
        try {
          URL url = new URL("file", null,
            dir.getCanonicalPath());
          url = new URL("jar:" + url.toString() + "!/");
          ((Deployer) host).install(contextPath, url);
        }
        catch (Throwable t) {
          log(sm.getString("hostConfig.deployJar.error",
```

```
        files[i]), t);
      }
    }
  }
 }
}
```

Deploying a Directory

Alternatively, you can deploy an application as it is by copying the whole directory to the %CATALINA_HOME%/webapps directory. HostConfig uses the deployDirectories in Listing 18.8 to deploy these applications.

Listing 18.8: The deployDirectories method in HostConfig

```
protected void deployDirectories(File appBase, String[] files) {
  for (int i = 0; i < files.length; i++) {
    if (files[i].equalsIgnoreCase("META-INF"))
      continue;
    if (files[i].equalsIgnoreCase("WEB-INF"))
      continue;
    if (deployed.contains(files[i]))
      continue;
    File dir = new File(appBase, files[i]);
    if (dir.isDirectory()) {
      deployed.add(files[i]);

      // Make sure there is an application configuration directory
      // This is needed if the Context appBase is the same as the
      // web server document root to make sure only web applications
      // are deployed and not directories for web space.
      File webInf = new File(dir, "/WEB-INF");
      if (!webInf.exists() || !webInf.isDirectory() ||
        !webInf.canRead())
        continue;

      // Calculate the context path and make sure it is unique
      String contextPath = "/" + files[i];
      if (files[i].equals("ROOT"))
        contextPath = "";
      if (host.findChild(contextPath) != null)
        continue;

      // Deploy the application in this directory
      log(sm.getString("hostConfig.deployDir", files[i]));
      try {
        URL url = new URL("file", null, dir.getCanonicalPath());
        ((Deployer) host).install(contextPath, url);
      }
      catch (Throwable t) {
        log(sm.getString("hostConfig.deployDir.error", files[i]), t);
      }
    }
```

```
    }
  }
```

Live Deploy

As mentioned previously, a `StandardHost` instance uses a `HostConfig` object as a lifecycle listener. When the `StandardHost` object is started, its `start` method fires a `START` event. In response to this `START` event, the `lifecycleEvent` method in `HostConfig`, the event handler in `HostConfig`, calls the `start` method. In Tomcat 4 the last line of this `start` method calls the `threadStart` method if the `liveDeploy` property is `true` (by default, this property is `true`).

```
if (isLiveDeploy()) {
  threadStart();
}
```

The `threadStart` method spawns a new thread that invokes the `run` method. The `run` method regularly checks for a new deployment and if any of the web.xml files of the existing deployed applications has been modified. The `run` method is presented in Listing 18.9.

Listing 18.9: The run method in HostConfig in Tomcat 4

```
/**
 * The background thread that checks for web application autoDeploy
 * and changes to the web.xml config.
 */
public void run() {
  if (debug >= 1)
    log("BACKGROUND THREAD Starting");
  // Loop until the termination semaphore is set
  while (!threadDone) {
    // Wait for our check interval
    threadSleep();
    // Deploy apps if the Host allows auto deploying
    deployApps();
    // Check for web.xml modification
    checkWebXmlLastModified();
  }
  if (debug >= 1)
    log("BACKGROUND THREAD Stopping");
}
```

The `threadSleep` method sends the thread to sleep for the duration indicated by the `checkInterval` property. By default, the value of this property is 15, meaning that checking is conducted every 15 seconds.

380

In Tomcat 5, the `HostConfig` class does not utilize a special thread. Instead, the `backgroundProcess` method of the `StandardHost` class fires a "check" event periodically:

```
public void backgroundProcess() {
  lifecycle.fireLifecycleEvent("check", null);
}
```

Note
The `backgroundProcess` method is periodically invoked by a special thread that serves all background processings in the containers.

Upon receiving a "check" event, the lifecycle listener (the `HostConfig` object) calls its `check` method that performs the checking.

```
public void lifecycleEvent(LifecycleEvent event) {
  if (event.getType().equals("check"))
    check();
  ...
```

The `check` method in the `HostConfig` class in Tomcat 5 is given in Listing 18.10.

Listing 18.10: The check method in HostConfig in Tomcat 5

```
protected void check() {
  if (host.getAutoDeploy()) {
    // Deploy apps if the Host allows auto deploying
    deployApps();
    // Check for web.xml modification
    checkContextLastModified();
  }
}
```

As you can see, the `check` method calls the `deployApps` method. The `deployApps` method in both Tomcat 4 and Tomcat 5 deploys the web applications and was given in Listing 18.3. As previously discussed, this method calls the `deployDescriptors`, `deployWARs`, and `deployDirectories` methods.

The `check` method in Tomcat 5 also calls the `checkContextLastModified` method that iterates all deployed contexts and checks the timestamps of the web.xml file and the contents of the WEB-INF directory in each context. If any of the checked resources has changed, the context is restarted. In addition, the `checkContextLastModified` method also checks the timestamps of all deployed WAR files and redeploys an application whose WAR file has been modified.

In Tomcat 4, the `run` method of the background thread calls the `checkWebXmlLastModified` method that performs a similar task to the `checkContextLastModified` method in Tomcat 5.

The Deployer Interface

A deployer is represented by the `org.apache.catalina.Deployer` interface. The `StandardHost` class implements the `Deployer` interface. Therefore, a `StandardHost` instance is also a deployer and it is a container into which web applications can be deployed and undeployed. The `Deployer` interface is presented in Listing 18.11.

Listing 18.11: The Deployer interface

```
package org.apache.catalina;

import java.io.IOException;
import java.net.URL;

/**
 * A <b>Deployer</b> is a specialized Container into which web
 * applications can be deployed and undeployed.  Such a Container
 * will create and install child Context instances for each deployed
 * application.  The unique key for each web application will be the
 * context path to which it is attached.
 *
 * @author Craig R. McClanahan
 * @version $Revision: 1.6 $ $Date: 2002/04/09 23:48:21 $
 */

public interface Deployer  {
  /**
   * The ContainerEvent event type sent when a new application is
   * being installed by <code>install()</code>, before it has been
   * started.
   */
  public static final String PRE_INSTALL_EVENT = "pre-install";

  /**
   * The ContainerEvent event type sent when a new application is
   * installed by <code>install()</code>, after it has been started.
   */
  public static final String INSTALL_EVENT = "install";

  /**
   * The ContainerEvent event type sent when an existing application is
   * removed by <code>remove()</code>.
   */
  public static final String REMOVE_EVENT = "remove";

  /**
```

```
 * Return the name of the Container with which this Deployer is
 * associated.
 */
public String getName();
/**
 * Install a new web application, whose web application archive is at
 * the specified URL, into this container with the specified context.
 * path. A context path of "" (the empty string) should be used for
 * the root application for this container.  Otherwise, the context
 * path must start with a slash.
 * <p>
 * If this application is successfully installed, a ContainerEvent of
 * type <code>INSTALL_EVENT</code> will be sent to all registered
 * listeners,
 * with the newly created <code>Context</code> as an argument.
 *
 * @param contextPath The context path to which this application
 *  should be installed (must be unique)
 * @param war A URL of type "jar:" that points to a WAR file, or type
 *  "file:" that points to an unpacked directory structure containing
 *  the web application to be installed
 *
 * @exception IllegalArgumentException if the specified context path
 *  is malformed (it must be "" or start with a slash)
 * @exception IllegalStateException if the specified context path
 *  is already attached to an existing web application
 * @exception IOException if an input/output error was encountered
 *  during installation
 */
public void install(String contextPath, URL war) throws IOException;

/**
 * <p>Install a new web application, whose context configuration file
 * (consisting of a <code>&lt;Context&gt;</code> element) and web
 * application archive are at the specified URLs.</p>
 *
 * <p>If this application is successfully installed, a ContainerEvent
 * of type <code>INSTALL_EVENT</code> will be sent to all registered
 * listeners, with the newly created <code>Context</code> as an
 * argument.
 * </p>
 *
 * @param config A URL that points to the context configuration file
 *  to be used for configuring the new Context
 * @param war A URL of type "jar:" that points to a WAR file, or type
 *  "file:" that points to an unpacked directory structure containing
 *  the web application to be installed
 *
 * @exception IllegalArgumentException if one of the specified URLs
 *  is null
 * @exception IllegalStateException if the context path specified in
 *  the context configuration file is already attached to an existing
 *  web application
 * @exception IOException if an input/output error was encountered
 *  during installation
 */
```

```
public void install(URL config, URL war) throws IOException;

/**
 * Return the Context for the deployed application that is associated
 * with the specified context path (if any); otherwise return
 * <code>null</code>.
 *
 * @param contextPath The context path of the requested web
 * application
 */
public Context findDeployedApp(String contextPath);

/**
 * Return the context paths of all deployed web applications in this
 * Container.  If there are no deployed applications, a zero-length
 * array is returned.
 */
public String[] findDeployedApps();

/**
 * Remove an existing web application, attached to the specified
 * context path. If this application is successfully removed, a
 * ContainerEvent of type <code>REMOVE_EVENT</code> will be sent to
 * all registered listeners, with the removed <code>Context</code> as
 * an argument.
 *
 * @param contextPath The context path of the application to be
 * removed
 *
 * @exception IllegalArgumentException if the specified context path
 *  is malformed (it must be "" or start with a slash)
 * @exception IllegalArgumentException if the specified context path
 *  does not identify a currently installed web application
 * @exception IOException if an input/output error occurs during
 *  removal
 */
public void remove(String contextPath) throws IOException;

/**
 * Start an existing web application, attached to the specified
 * context path. Only starts a web application if it is not running.
 *
 * @param contextPath The context path of the application to be
 *  started
 * @exception IllegalArgumentException if the specified context path
 *  is malformed (it must be "" or start with a slash)
 * @exception IllegalArgumentException if the specified context path
 *  does not identify a currently installed web application
 * @exception IOException if an input/output error occurs during
 *  startup
 */
public void start(String contextPath) throws IOException;

/**
 * Stop an existing web application, attached to the specified
 * context path.  Only stops a web application if it is running.
```

```
 *
 * @param contextPath The context path of the application to be
 *   stopped
 * @exception IllegalArgumentException if the specified context path
 *   is malformed (it must be "" or start with a slash)
 * @exception IllegalArgumentException if the specified context path
 *   does not identify a currently installed web application
 * @exception IOException if an input/output error occurs while
 *   stopping the web application
 */
  public void stop(String contextPath) throws IOException;
}
```

The StandardHost class employs a helper class
(org.apache.catalina.core.StandardHostDeployer) for performing
tasks related to deploying and installng a Web application. You can see in the
following fragment of StandardHost how it delegates the task of deploying
and installing web applications to an instance of StandardHostDeployer:

```
/**
 * The <code>Deployer</code> to whom we delegate application
 * deployment requests.
 */
private Deployer deployer = new StandardHostDeployer(this);

public void install(String contextPath, URL war) throws IOException {
  deployer.install(contextPath, war);
}
public synchronized void install(URL config, URL war) throws
IOException {
  deployer.install(config, war);
}
public Context findDeployedApp(String contextPath) {
  return (deployer.findDeployedApp(contextPath));
}
public String[] findDeployedApps() {
  return (deployer.findDeployedApps());
}
public void remove(String contextPath) throws IOException {
  deployer.remove(contextPath);
}
public void start(String contextPath) throws IOException {
  deployer.start(contextPath);
}
public void stop(String contextPath) throws IOException {
  deployer.stop(contextPath);
}
```

StandardHostDeployer is discussed in the next section.

The StandardHostDeployer Class

The org.apache.catalina.core.StandardHostDeployer class is a helper class that helps deploy and install web applications in a StandardHost. StandardHostDeployer was designed to be used by a StandardHost object, as indicated by its constructor that accepts a StandardHost instance.

```
public StandardHostDeployer(StandardHost host) {
  super();
  this.host = host;
}
```

The methods in this class are explained in the following sub-sections.

Installing a Descriptor

The StandardHostDeployer class has two install methods. The first one, which is the topic of this subsection, is used to install a descriptor. The second one, discussed in the next subsection, is used to install a WAR file or a directory.

The install method for installing descriptors is given in Listing 18.12. A StandardHost instance calls this method after its install method is called by the deployDescriptors method in a HostConfig object.

Listing 18.12: The install method for installing descriptors

```
public synchronized void install(URL config, URL war)
  throws IOException {
  // Validate the format and state of our arguments
  if (config == null)
    throw new IllegalArgumentException
      (sm.getString("standardHost.configRequired"));
  if (!host.isDeployXML())
    throw new IllegalArgumentException
      (sm.getString("standardHost.configNotAllowed"));
  // Calculate the document base for the new web application (if
  // needed)
  String docBase = null; // Optional override for value in config file
  if (war != null) {
    String url = war.toString();
    host.log(sm.getString("standardHost.installingWAR", url));
    // Calculate the WAR file absolute pathname
    if (url.startsWith("jar:")) {
      url = url.substring(4, url.length() - 2);
    }
    if (url.startsWith("file://"))
      docBase = url.substring(7);
    else if (url.startsWith("file:"))
```

```
      docBase = url.substring(5);
    else
      throw new IllegalArgumentException
        (sm.getString("standardHost.warURL", url));
  }

  // Install the new web application
  this.context = null;
  this.overrideDocBase = docBase;
  InputStream stream = null;
  try {
    stream = config.openStream();
    Digester digester = createDigester();
    digester.setDebug(host.getDebug());
    digester.clear();
    digester.push(this);
    digester.parse(stream);
    stream.close();
    stream = null;
  }
  catch (Exception e) {
    host.log
      (sm.getString("standardHost.installError", docBase), e);
        throw new IOException(e.toString());
  }
  finally {
    if (stream != null) {
      try {
        stream.close();
      }
      catch (Throwable t) {
        ;
        }
      }
    }
  }
}
```

Installing a WAR file and a Directory

The second `install` method accepts a String representation of a context path and a URL representing a WAR file. This `install` method is given in Listing 18.13.

Listing 18.13: The install **method** for installing a **WAR** file or a directory

```
public synchronized void install(String contextPath, URL war)
  throws IOException {
  // Validate the format and state of our arguments
  if (contextPath == null)
    throw new IllegalArgumentException
      (sm.getString("standardHost.pathRequired"));
  if (!contextPath.equals("") && !contextPath.startsWith("/"))
    throw new IllegalArgumentException
```

```
      (sm.getString("standardHost.pathFormat", contextPath));
  if (findDeployedApp(contextPath) != null)
    throw new IllegalStateException
      (sm.getString("standardHost.pathUsed", contextPath));
  if (war == null)
    throw new IllegalArgumentException
      (sm.getString("standardHost.warRequired"));

  // Calculate the document base for the new web application
  host.log(sm.getString("standardHost.installing",
  contextPath, war.toString())));
  String url = war.toString();
  String docBase = null;
  if (url.startsWith("jar:")) {
    url = url.substring(4, url.length() - 2);
  }
  if (url.startsWith("file://"))
    docBase = url.substring(7);
  else if (url.startsWith("file:"))
    docBase = url.substring(5);
  else
    throw new IllegalArgumentException
      (sm.getString("standardHost.warURL", url));

  // Install the new web application
  try {
    Class clazz = Class.forName(host.getContextClass());
    Context context = (Context) clazz.newInstance();
    context.setPath(contextPath);

    context.setDocBase(docBase);
    if (context instanceof Lifecycle) {
      clazz = Class.forName(host.getConfigClass());
      LifecycleListener listener =
        (LifecycleListener) clazz.newInstance();
      ((Lifecycle) context).addLifecycleListener(listener);
    }
    host.fireContainerEvent(PRE_INSTALL_EVENT, context);
    host.addChild(context);
    host.fireContainerEvent(INSTALL_EVENT, context);
  }
  catch (Exception e) {
    host.log(sm.getString("standardHost.installError", contextPath),
      e);
    throw new IOException(e.toString());
  }
}
```

Note that once a context is installed, it is added to the StandardHost.

Starting A Context

The start method in StandardHostDeployer is used to start a context. It is given in Listing 18.14.

Listing 18.14: The start method of the StandardHostDeployer class

```
public void start(String contextPath) throws IOException {
  // Validate the format and state of our arguments
  if (contextPath == null)
    throw new IllegalArgumentException
      (sm.getString("standardHost.pathRequired"));
  if (!contextPath.equals("") && !contextPath.startsWith("/"))
    throw new IllegalArgumentException
      (sm.getString("standardHost.pathFormat", contextPath));
  Context context = findDeployedApp(contextPath);
  if (context == null)
    throw new IllegalArgumentException
      (sm.getString("standardHost.pathMissing", contextPath));
  host.log("standardHost.start " + contextPath);
  try {
    ((Lifecycle) context).start();
  }
  catch (LifecycleException e) {
    host.log("standardHost.start " + contextPath + ": ", e);
      throw new IllegalStateException
    ("standardHost.start " + contextPath + ": " + e);
  }
}
```

Stopping A Context

To stop a context, you call the stop method of StandardHostDeployer in Listing 18.15.

Listing 18.15: The stop method in the StandardHostDeployer class

```
public void stop(String contextPath) throws IOException {
  // Validate the format and state of our arguments
  if (contextPath == null)
    throw new IllegalArgumentException
      (sm.getString("standardHost.pathRequired"));
  if (!contextPath.equals("") && !contextPath.startsWith("/"))
    throw new IllegalArgumentException
      (sm.getString("standardHost.pathFormat", contextPath));
  Context context = findDeployedApp(contextPath);
  if (context == null)
    throw new IllegalArgumentException
      (sm.getString("standardHost.pathMissing", contextPath));
  host.log("standardHost.stop " + contextPath);
  try {
```

```
    ((Lifecycle) context).stop();
  }
  catch (LifecycleException e) {
    host.log("standardHost.stop " + contextPath + ": ", e);
    throw new IllegalStateException
      ("standardHost.stop " + contextPath + ": " + e);
  }
}
```

Summary

Deployers are components for deploying and installing web applications. A deployer is represented by the org.apache.catalina.Deployer interface. The StandardHost class implements Deployer to make it a special container to which web applications can be deployed. The StandardHost class delegates the tasks of deploying and installing applications to a helper class, org.apache.catalina.core.StandardHostDeployer. The StandardHostDeployer class provides the code that performs the task of deploying and installing applications, as well as starting and stopping a context.

390

Chapter 19
Manager Servlet

Tomcat 4 and 5 come with the Manager application that you can use to manage deployed applications. Unlike other applications, Manager does not reside in the default deployment directory %CATALINA_HOME%/webapps but in %CATALINA_HOME%/server/webapps. Manager is installed when Tomcat starts because Manager has a descriptor, the manager.xml file, in the %CATALINA_HOME$/webapps directory in Tomcat 4 and the %CATALINA_HOME%/server/webapps directory in Tomcat 5.

> **Note**
> Context descriptors were discussed in Chapter 18.

This chapter describes the Manager application. It starts by outlining how to use this application to give you the feel of how Manager works. It then explains the `ContainerServlet` interface.

Using the Manager Application

The Manager application can be found in the %CATALINA_HOME%/server/webapps/manager directory for both Tomcat 4 and 5. The main servlet in this application is `ManagerServlet`. In Tomcat 4 this class belongs to the `org.apache.catalina.servlets` package, which is one of the packages in Catalina. In Tomcat 5 this class is part of the `org.apache.catalina.manager` package and is deployed as a JAR file in the WEB-INF/lib directory.

> **Note**
> Because the Manager application in Tomcat 4 is slightly simpler than that in Tomcat 5, it is a better learning tool and is therefore discussed in this chapter. You should be able to understand how the Manager application in Tomcat 5 works too, after reading this chapter.

Here are the `servlet` elements in the deployment descriptor in Tomcat 4.

```
<servlet>
  <servlet-name>Manager</servlet-name>
  <servlet-class>
    org.apache.catalina.servlets.ManagerServlet
  </servlet-class>
  <init-param>
    <param-name>debug</param-name>
    <param-value>2</param-value>
  </init-param>
</servlet>
<servlet>
  <servlet-name>HTMLManager</servlet-name>
  <servlet-class>
    org.apache.catalina.servlets.HTMLManagerServlet
  </servlet-class>
  <init-param>
    <param-name>debug</param-name>
    <param-value>2</param-value>
  </init-param>
</servlet>
```

The first servlet is `org.apache.catalina.servlets.ManagerServlet` and the second `org.apache.catalina.servlets.HTMLManagerServlet`. This chapter focuses on the `ManagerServlet` class.

The descriptor for this application, manager.xml, tells that the context path for this application is `/manager`.

```
<Context path="/manager" docBase="../server/webapps/manager"
  debug="0" privileged="true">
  <!-- Link to the user database we will get roles from -->
  <ResourceLink name="users" global="UserDatabase"
    type="org.apache.catalina.UserDatabase"/>
</Context>
```

The first `servlet-mapping` element tells you how to invoke `ManagerServlet`.

```
<servlet-mapping>
  <servlet-name>Manager</servlet-name>
  <url-pattern>/*</url-pattern>
</servlet-mapping>
```

In other words, a URL beginning with the following pattern invokes `ManagerServlet`:

```
http://localhost:8080/manager/
```

However, note that there is also this `security-constraint` element in the deployment descriptor:

```
<security-constraint>
  <web-resource-collection>
    <web-resource-name>Entire Application</web-resource-name>
    <url-pattern>/*</url-pattern>
  </web-resource-collection>
  <auth-constraint>
   <!-- NOTE:  This role is not present in the default users file -->
     <role-name>manager</role-name>
  </auth-constraint>
</security-constraint>
```

This means, the entire application is restricted to users belonging to the manager role. The `auth-login` element states that a user can be allowed access to the restricted contents if he/she can supply the correct user name and password using the BASIC authentication.

```
<login-config>
  <auth-method>BASIC</auth-method>
  <realm-name>Tomcat Manager Application</realm-name>
</login-config>
```

In Tomcat, roles and users are listed in the tomcat-users.xml file in the %CATALINA_HOME%/conf directory. Therefore, to access the Manager application, you must add a manager role with a user belonging to that role. Here is an example:

```
<?xml version='1.0' encoding='utf-8'?>
<tomcat-users>
  <role rolename="manager"/>
  <user username="tomcat" password="tomcat" roles="manager "/>
</tomcat-users>
```

With this tomcat-users.xml file, you can access the Manager application using the user name `tomcat` and password `tomcat`.

The following functions are available in the `ManagerServlet`.

- list
- start
- stop
- reload
- remove
- resources
- roles
- sessions
- undeploy

Check the servlet's `doGet` method to see how you can invoke a function.

The ContainerServlet Interface

A servlet that implements the `org.apache.catalina.ContainerServlet` interface will have access to the `StandardWrapper` object that represents it. Having access to the wrapper, it can also access the context object representing the web application, the deployer (`StandardHost` instance) in which the context resides, and other objects.

The `ContainerServlet` interface is given in Listing 19.1.

Listing 19.1: The `ContainerServlet` Interface

```
package org.apache.catalina;

public interface ContainerServlet {
  public Wrapper getWrapper();
  public void setWrapper(Wrapper wrapper);
}
```

Catalina invokes the `setWrapper` method of a servlet implementing `ContainerServlet` to pass the reference to the `StandardWrapper` representing that servlet.

Initializing ManagerServlet

As always, a servlet is represented by an `org.apache.catalina.core.StandardWrapper` instance. The first time the servlet is invoked, the `StandardWrapper` object's `loadServlet` is called, which in turns calls the servlet's `init` method. (See Chapter 11.) In the case of `ManagerServlet`, you should look at a fragment in the `loadServlet` method:

```
...
// Special handling for ContainerServlet instances
if ((servlet instanceof ContainerServlet) &&
  isContainerProvidedServlet(actualClass)) {
  ((ContainerServlet) servlet).setWrapper(this);
}

// Call the initialization method of this servlet
try {
  instanceSupport.fireInstanceEvent(InstanceEvent.BEFORE_INIT_EVENT,
    servlet);
  servlet.init(facade);
...
```

where `servlet` represents the servlet to be loaded (in this case, `ManagerServlet`).

The `if` statement in the code fragment above says that if `servlet` is an instance of `org.apache.catalina.ContainerServlet` and the `isContainerProvidedServlet` method returns `true`, call the `ContainerServlet` interface's `setWrapper` method.

The `ManagerServlet` class implements `ContainerServlet`, therefore `servlet` is an instance of `ContainerServlet`. The `isContainerProvidedServlet` method in `StandardWrapper` is given in Listing 19.2.

Listing 19.2: The `isContainerProvidedServlet` method in the `StandardWrapper` class

```
private boolean isContainerProvidedServlet(String classname) {
  if (classname.startsWith("org.apache.catalina.")) {
    return (true);
  }
  try {
    Class clazz =
      this.getClass().getClassLoader().loadClass(classname);
    return (ContainerServlet.class.isAssignableFrom(clazz));
  }
  catch (Throwable t) {
    return (false);
  }
}
```

The `classname` argument passed to `isContainerProvidedServlet` is the fully-qualified name of the `ManagerServlet`, which is `org.apache.catalina.servlets.ManagerServlet`. As such, the `isContainerProvidedServlet` method returns true.

This method also returns `true` if the servlet class inidicated by `classname` is a subtype of `ContainerServlet`, i.e. if `classname` is an interface that extends `ContainerServlet` or a class that implements `ContainerServlet`.

Note

The `java.lang.Class` class's `isAssignableFrom(Class clazz)` method returns `true` if the class or interface represented by the current `Class` object is either the same as, or is a superclass or superinterface of, the class or interface represented by the specified `clazz` parameter.

Therefore, the `loadServlet` method of the `StandardWrapper` instance representing `ManagerServlet` will call the `ManagerServlet`'s setWrapper method. Here is the implementation of the setWrapper method in ManagerServlet.

```
public void setWrapper(Wrapper wrapper) {
  this.wrapper = wrapper;
  if (wrapper == null) {
    context = null;
    deployer = null;
  }
  else {
    context = (Context) wrapper.getParent();
    deployer = (Deployer) context.getParent();
  }
}
```

Since the parameter wrapper is not null, the else block will be executed, which means context is assigned the context object representing the Manager application and deployer the StandardHost instance hosting the context. The deployer is especially important because it is used in several methods in ManagerServlet to perform various functions.

After the setWrapper method of ManagerServlet is called by the StandardWrapper class's loadServlet method, the loadServlet method calls the init method of ManagerServlet.

Listing Deployed Web Applications

You list all deployed web applications by using the following URL:

```
http://localhost:8080/manager/list
```

Here is an example of the output:

```
OK - Listed applications for virtual host localhost
/admin:stopped:0:../server/webapps/admin
/app1:running:0:C:\123data\JavaProjects\Pyrmont\webapps\app1
/manager:running:0:../server/webapps/manager
```

The URL above invokes the list method of ManagerServlet, which is presented in Listing 19.3.

Listing 19.3: The list method of ManagerServlet

```
protected void list(PrintWriter writer) {
  if (debug >= 1)
    log("list: Listing contexts for virtual host '" +
      deployer.getName() + "'");
  writer.println(sm.getString("managerServlet.listed",
    deployer.getName()));
  String contextPaths[] = deployer.findDeployedApps();
```

```
    for (int i = 0; i < contextPaths.length; i++) {
      Context context = deployer.findDeployedApp(contextPaths[i]);
      String displayPath = contextPaths[i];
      if( displayPath.equals("") )
        displayPath = "/";
      if (context != null ) {
        if (context.getAvailable()) {
          writer.println(sm.getString("managerServlet.listitem",
            displayPath, "running", ""
              + context.getManager().findSessions().length,
              context.getDocBase()));
        }
        else {
          writer.println(sm.getString("managerServlet.listitem",
            displayPath, "stopped", "0", context.getDocBase()));
        }
      }
    }
  }
}
```

The list method calls the deployer's findDeployedApps to obtain the paths of all the deployed contexts in Catalina. It then iterates the path array to get each individual context and checks whether or not the context is available. For every context that is available, the list method prints the context path, the string running, the number of user sessions, and the document base. For contexts that are unavailable, the list method prints the context path, the string stopped, 0, and the document base.

Starting A Web Application

You use the following URL to start a web application:

```
http://localhost:8080/manager/start?path=/contextPath
```

where contextPath is the context path of the application you want to start. For example, to start the admin application, you use

```
http://localhost:8080/manager/start?path=/admin
```

If the application has been started, you'll receive an error notification.

Upon receiving this URL, ManagerServlet invokes the start method, which is presented in Listing 19.4.

Listing 19.4: The **start** method of the **ManagerServlet** class

```
protected void start(PrintWriter writer, String path) {
  if (debug >= 1)
    log("start: Starting web application at '" + path + "'");
```

```
if ((path == null) || (!path.startsWith("/") && path.equals(""))) {
  writer.println(sm.getString("managerServlet.invalidPath", path));
  return;
}
String displayPath = path;
if( path.equals("/") )
  path = "";

try {
  Context context = deployer.findDeployedApp(path);
  if (context == null) {
    writer.println(sm.getString("managerServlet.noContext",
      displayPath));
    return;
  }
  deployer.start(path);
  if (context.getAvailable())
    writer.println
      (sm.getString("managerServlet.started", displayPath));
  else
    writer.println
      (sm.getString("managerServlet.startFailed", displayPath));
}
catch (Throwable t) {
  getServletContext().log
  (sm.getString("managerServlet.startFailed", displayPath), t);
  writer.println
    (sm.getString("managerServlet.startFailed", displayPath));
  writer.println(sm.getString("managerServlet.exception",
    t.toString()));
}
}
```

After some checking, the `start` method calls the deployer's
`findDeployedApp` method in the `try` block. This method returns the context
object whose path is passed to it. If the context is not `null`, the `start` method
calls the deployer's `start` method to start the application.

Stopping A Web Application

You use the following URL to stop an application:

```
http://localhost:8080/manager/stop?path=/contextPath
```

where `contextPath` is the context path of the application you want to stop. If
the application is not running, you will get an error message.

When the `ManagerServlet` receives the request, it invokes the `stop`
method. The `stop` method is given in Listing 19.5.

Listing 19.5: The `stop` method of the `ManagerServlet` class

```
protected void stop(PrintWriter writer, String path) {
  if (debug >= 1)
    log("stop: Stopping web application at '" + path + "'");
  if ((path == null) || (!path.startsWith("/") && path.equals(""))) {
    writer.println(sm.getString("managerServlet.invalidPath", path));
    return;
  }
  String displayPath = path;
  if( path.equals("/") )
    path = "";

  try {
    Context context = deployer.findDeployedApp(path);
    if (context == null) {
      writer.println(sm.getString("managerServlet.noContext",
        displayPath));
      return;
    }
    // It isn't possible for the manager to stop itself
    if (context.getPath().equals(this.context.getPath())) {
      writer.println(sm.getString("managerServlet.noSelf"));
      return;
    }
    deployer.stop(path);
    writer.println(sm.getString("managerServlet.stopped",
      displayPath));
  }
  catch (Throwable t) {
    log("ManagerServlet.stop[" + displayPath + "]", t);
    writer.println(sm.getString("managerServlet.exception",
      t.toString()));
  }
}
```

You should be able to figure out how the `stop` method works. Other methods in the `ManagerServlet` class should be easy to digest too.

Summary

In this chapter you have seen how you can use a special interface, `ContainerServlet`, to create a servlet with access to the Catalina internal classes. The Manager application that you can use to manage deployed applications has demonstrated how to obtain other objects from the wrapper object. It is very possible to design a servlet with more sophisticated functionality for managing Tomcat.

400

Chapter 20
JMX-Based Management

Chapter 19 discussed the Manager application. It showed that the `ManagerServlet` class implemented the `ContainerServlet` interface to get access to Catalina internal objects. This chapter now shows that managing Tomcat can be achieved more sophisticatedly using the Java Management Extensions (the JMX specification). For those unfamiliar with JMX, a brief introduction is given at the beginning of the chapter. In addition, this chapter explains the Commons Modeler library that Catalina uses to ease the task of writing Managed Beans, the objects used for managing other objects. Examples are offered to make understanding the use of JMX in Tomcat easier.

Introduction to JMX

So, if the `ContainerServlet` interface is good enough for the Manager application to get access to the internal body of Catalina, why should we care about JMX? Because JMX provides much greater flexibility than `ContainerServlet`. Many server-based applications, such as Tomcat, JBoss, JONAS, Geronimo, and many others, use this cool technology to manage their resources.

The JMX specification, currently at version 1.2.1, defines an open standard for managing Java objects. For example, Tomcat 4 and 5 use JMX to enable various objects (such as server, host, context, valve, and so on) in the servlet container to be flexibly and easily managed by management applications. The developers of Tomcat even made the effort to write the Admin application that acts as a management application.

A Java object that can be managed by JMX-compliant manager application is said to be a JMX manageable resource. In fact, a JMX manageable resource can also be an application, an implementation or a service, a device, a user, and so forth. A JMX manageable resource is written in Java or provides a Java wrapper.

For a Java object to be a JMX manageable resource, you must create another object called Managed Bean or MBean. The `org.apache.catalina.mbeans` package contains a number of MBeans. `ConnectorMBean`, `StandardEngineMBean`, `StandardHostMBean`, `StandardContextMBean` are examples of the Managed Beans in this package. From their name you can guess that the `ConnectMBean` class is used to manage a connector, the `StandardContextMBean` class is for managing an `org.apache.catalina.core.StandardContext` instance, and so on. Of course, you can also write an MBean that manages more than one Java object if you want to.

An MBean exposes the properties and methods of the Java object(s) it manages the management application. The management application itself does not have access to the managed Java objects directly. Therefore, you can choose any property and or method of a Java object that should be callable by the management application.

Once you have an MBean class, you need to instantiate it and register it with another Java object referred to as the MBean server. The MBean server is a central registry for all the MBeans in an application. The management application accesses the MBeans through the MBean server. Drawing an analogy between JMX and a servlet application, the management application is equivalent to a web browser. The MBean server is like a servlet container; it provides access to the managed-resources to the client (the management application). The MBeans are servlets or JSP pages. Just like the web browser never touches a servlet/JSP page directly but only through a servlet container, a management application accesses the MBeans through the MBean server.

There are four types of MBeans: standard, dynamic, open, and model. Standard MBeans are the easiest to write among the four, but offer the least flexibility. The other three come with more flexibility and we're particularly interested in model MBeans because Catalina uses this type of MBeans. Standard MBeans are discussed next to give you the look and feel of writing an MBean. Afterwards, there is a discussion of model MBeans. We skip the dynamic and open MBeans because they are not relevant to this chapter. Interested readers are referred to the JMX 1.2.1 specification document for further details.

Architecturally, the JMX specification is divided into three levels, the instrumentation level, the agent level, and the distributed services level. The MBean server resides in the agent level and the MBeans in the instrumentation level. The distributed services level will be covered in the future version of the JMX specification.

The instrumentation level of the specification defines the standard for writing JMX manageable resources, i.e. how to write MBeans. The agent level provides a specification for creating agents. An agent encapsulates an MBean server and services for handling MBeans. Agents and MBeans they manage normally reside in the same Java Virtual Machine. Because the JMX specification comes with a reference implementation, you do not need to write an MBean server of your own. The reference implementation provides a way of creating a default MBean server.

Note
Download the specification and reference implementation from http://java.sun.com/products/JavaManagement/download.html. MX4J, an open source version of JMX whose library is included in the software accompanying this book, is available from http://mx4j.sourceforge.net

Warning
The zip file that accompanies this book contains the mx4j.jar file that packages the version 2.0 beta 1 of MX4J, replacing the mx4j-jmx.jar file included in Tomcat 4.1.12. This was done in order for you to use the more recent version of JMX (version 1.2.1).

The JMX API

The reference implementation consists of a core Java library in the `javax.management` package and other packages specific to certain areas of JMX programming. This section discusses some of the more important types in the API.

MBeanServer

The `javax.management.MBeanServer` interface represents an MBean server. To create an instance of `MBeanServer`, simply use one of the methods in the `javax.management.MBeanServerFactory` class, such as the `createMBean` method.

To register an MBean with an MBeanServer, call the `registerMBean` method on the `MBeanServer` instance. The following is the signature of the `registerMBean` method.

```
public ObjectInstance registerMBean(java.lang.Object object,
  ObjectName name) throws InstanceAlreadyExistsException,
  MBeanRegistrationException, NotCompliantMBeanException
```

To the `registerMBean` method you pass the `MBean` instance you want to register and the `ObjectName` instance. An `ObjectName` instance is like a key in a `HashMap`; it uniquely identifies an `MBean`. The `registerMBean` method returns an `ObjectInstance`. The `javax.management.ObjectInstance` class encapsulates an object name of an MBean and its class name.

To retrieve an MBean or a set of MBeans matching a pattern, the `MBeanServer` interface provides two methods: `queryNames` and `queryMBeans`. The `queryNames` method returns a `java.util.Set` containing the object names of the MBeans matching the specified pattern object name. Here is the signature of the `queryName` method:

```
public java.util.Set queryNames(ObjectName name, QueryExp query)
```

The `query` argument specifies the filtering criteria.

If the `name` argument is `null` or no domain and key properties are specified, all the `ObjectName` instances of the registered MBeans will be returned. If the query is `null`, no filtering is applied.

The `queryMBeans` method is similar to `queryNames`. However, it returns a `java.util.Set` containing `ObjectInstance` objects for the selected MBeans. The `queryMBeans` method has the following signature:

```
public java.util.Set queryMBeans(ObjectName name, QueryExp query)
```

Once you have the object name of the MBean you want, you can manipulate the property of the managed resource or invoke its method exposed in the MBean.

You can call any method of the registered MBeans by calling the `MBeanServer` interface's `invoke` method. The `MBeanServer` interface's `getAttribute` and `setAttribute` methods are used for getting and setting a property of a registered MBean.

ObjectName

An MBean server is a registry for MBeans. Each of the MBeans in an MBean server is uniquely identified by an object name, just like an entry in a HashMap is uniquely identified by a key.

An object name is represented by the `javax.management.ObjectName` class. An object name consists of two parts: a domain and a set of key/value pairs. A domain is a string, and can be a blank string. In an object name, the domain is followed by a colon and one or more key/value pairs. A key is a non-blank string that may not contain any of the following characters: equal sign, comma, colon, asterisk, and question mark. The same key may only occur once in an object name.

A key and its value are separated by an equal sign, and two key/value pairs are separated by a comma. For example, the following is a valid object name with two keys:

```
myDomain:type=Car,color=blue
```

An `ObjectName` instance can also represent a property pattern for searching MBeans in an MBean server. An `ObjectName` that is a pattern uses a wildcard in its domain part or key/value pairs. A pattern `ObjectName` may have zero or more keys.

Standard MBeans

Standard MBeans are the simplest MBeans. To manage a Java object using a standard MBean, here is what you need to do:

- Create an interface named after your Java class plus the suffix MBean. For example, if the Java class you want to manage is called `Car`, the interface is called `CarMBean`.
- Modify your Java class so that it implements the interface you've created.
- Create an agent. The agent class must contain an MBeanServer.
- Create an `ObjectName` for your MBean.
- Instantiate the MBeanServer.
- Register the MBean in the MBeanServer.

The standard MBeans are the easiest to write, but using them requires your classes be modified. While modifying the classes is okay in some projects, in others (especially when the number of classes is high) this is not acceptable. Other types of MBeans allow you to manage your objects without modifying your classes.

As an example of a standard MBean, consider the following `Car` class that you want to be JMX-manageable:

```java
package ex20.pyrmont.standardmbeantest;

public class Car {
  private String color = "red";

  public String getColor() {
    return color;
  }
  public void setColor(String color) {
```

```
    this.color = color;
  }
  public void drive() {
    System.out.println("Baby you can drive my car.");
  }
}
```

The first step you need to take is modify it so that it implements the CarMBean interface. The new Car class is given in Listing 20.1:

Listing 20.1: The modified Car class

```
package ex20.pyrmont.standardmbeantest;

public class Car implements CarMBean {
  private String color = "red";

  public String getColor() {
    return color;
  }
  public void setColor(String color) {
    this.color = color;
  }
  public void drive() {
    System.out.println("Baby you can drive my car.");
  }
}
```

Now, create the CarMBean interface in Listing 20.2

Listing 20.2: The CarMBean interface

```
package ex20.pyrmont.standardmbeantest;

public interface CarMBean {
  public String getColor();
  public void setColor(String color);
  public void drive();
}
```

Basically, in the interface you declare all the methods that you want the Car class to expose. In this example, the CarMBean interface lists all the methods in the Car class. If, say, you don't want the drive method to be available to the management application, all you need to do is remove its definition from the CarMBean interface.

Finally, Listing 20.3 offers the StandardAgent class that is used to create a standard MBean and manage the Car object.

Listing 20.3: The StandardAgent class

```
package ex20.pyrmont.standardmbeantest;

import javax.management.Attribute;
```

```java
import javax.management.ObjectName;
import javax.management.MBeanServer;
import javax.management.MBeanServerFactory;

public class StandardAgent {
  private MBeanServer mBeanServer = null;
  public StandardAgent() {
    mBeanServer = MBeanServerFactory.createMBeanServer();
  }
  public MBeanServer getMBeanServer() {
    return mBeanServer;
  }
  public ObjectName createObjectName(String name) {
    ObjectName objectName = null;
    try {
      objectName = new ObjectName(name);
    }
    catch (Exception e) {
    }
    return objectName;
  }

  private void createStandardBean(ObjectName objectName,
    String managedResourceClassName) {
    try {
      mBeanServer.createMBean(managedResourceClassName, objectName);
    }
    catch(Exception e) {
    }
  }

  public static void main(String[] args) {
    StandardAgent agent = new StandardAgent();
    MBeanServer mBeanServer = agent.getMBeanServer();
    String domain = mBeanServer.getDefaultDomain();
    String managedResourceClassName =
      "ex20.pyrmont.standardmbeantest.Car";
    ObjectName objectName = agent.createObjectName(domain + ":type=" +
      managedResourceClassName);
    agent.createStandardBean(objectName, managedResourceClassName);

    // manage MBean
    try {
      Attribute colorAttribute = new Attribute("Color","blue");
      mBeanServer.setAttribute(objectName, colorAttribute);
      System.out.println(mBeanServer.getAttribute(objectName,
        "Color"));
      mBeanServer.invoke(objectName,"drive",null,null);
    }
    catch (Exception e) {
      e.printStackTrace();
    }
  }
}
```

The `StandardAgent` class is an agent that will instantiate an MBean server and use it to register a `CarMBean`. The first thing to note is the `mBeanServer` variable, to which the `StandardAgent` class's constructor assigns an `MBeanServer`. The constructor calls the `createMBeanServer` method of the `MBeanServerFactory` class.

```
public StandardAgent() {
  mBeanServer = MBeanServerFactory.createMBeanServer();
}
```

The `createMBeanServer` method returns a default `MBeanServer` object implemented by the JMX reference implementation. An advanced JMX programmer may wish to provide his/her own `MBeanServer` implementation. For this book, however, we're not interested in doing so.

The `createObjectName` method in the `StandardAgent` class in Listing 20.3 returns an instance of `ObjectName` based on the `String` argument passed to the method. The `createStandardMBean` method in `StandardAgent` calls the `createMBean` method of `MBeanServer`. The `createMBean` method accepts the class name of the managed resource and the `ObjectName` instance that uniquely identifies the created MBean for the managed resource. The `createMBean` method also registers the created MBean in the MBeanServer. Because a standard MBean follows a certain naming convention, you don't need to supply the MBean type name to the createMBean method. If the managed resource's class name is `Car`, then its MBean will be `CarMBean`.

The `main` method of `StandardAgent` starts off by creating an instance of `StandardAgent` and calls its `getMBeanServer` method to obtain a reference to the `MBeanServer` instance inside the `StandardAgent`.

```
StandardAgent agent = new StandardAgent();
MBeanServer mBeanServer = agent.getMBeanServer();
```

It then creates an `ObjectName` for the `CarMBean`. The `MBeanServer`'s default domain is used as the domain for the `ObjectName`. A key named `type` is appended to the domain. The value for type is the fully qualified name of the managed resource.

```
String domain = mBeanServer.getDefaultDomain();
String managedResourceClassName =
  "ex20.pyrmont.standardmbeantest.Car";
ObjectName objectName = agent.createObjectName(domain + ":type=" +
  managedResourceClassName);
```

The main method then calls the createStandardBean method, passing the object name and the managed resource class name.

```
agent.createStandardBean(objectName, managedResourceClassName);
```

Next, the main method manages the Car object through the CarMBean instance. It creates an Attribute object called colorAttribute to represent the Color attribute and sets the value to blue. It then invokes the setAttribute method passing the objectName and colorAttribute. It then invokes the drive method using the invoke method on the MBeanServer object.

```
// manage MBean
try {
  Attribute colorAttribute = new Attribute("Color","blue");
  mBeanServer.setAttribute(objectName, colorAttribute);
  System.out.println(mBeanServer.getAttribute(objectName,
    "Color"));
  mBeanServer.invoke(objectName,"drive",null,null);
}
```

If you run the StandardAgent class, you will see the following on your console:

```
blue
Baby you can drive my car.
```

Now, you may be wondering, why do we need to use JMX at all to manage a Java object? Anyway, from the StandardAgent class we can access the Car object directly. This is true, but the key thing here is you can choose what functionality of your object you want to expose and hide other public methods that you don't want to make available. Also, as you can see later in the "The Application" section of this chapter, the MBeanServer acts as a layer between the managed objects and the manager application.

Model MBeans

Model MBeans provide flexibility. They are harder to program than standard MBeans, but you do not need to modify your Java classes for the objects to be manageable. Using model MBeans is highly preferable if modifying the existing classes is not an option.

Using model MBeans is different from using standard MBeans. When employing a standard MBean to manage your resource, you write an interface that must be implemented by the managed resource. When using a model MBean, you do not write any interface. Instead, the `javax.management.modelmbean.ModelMBean` interface is provided for you that represents a model MBean. You just need to have an implementation for this interface. Luckily, JMX comes with the `javax.management.modelmbean.RequiredModelMBean` class, the default implementation of `ModelMBean`. You can instantiate the `RequiredModelMBean` class or its subclass.

Note
Other implementation classes for the `ModelMBean` interface are also possible. For example, the Commons Modeler library, which we will discuss in the next section, has its own implementation class that does not extend `RequiredModelMBean`.

The greatest challenge in writing a model MBean is telling your `ModelMBean` object which attributes and operations in the managed resource should be exposed to an agent. You achieve this by creating a `javax.management.modelmbean.ModelMBeanInfo` object. A `ModelMBeanInfo` object describes the constructors, attributes, operations, and event listeners exposed to an agent. Constructing a `ModelMBeanInfo` object can be a tedious task (see the example in this section), but once you have one, you just need to associate it with your `ModelMBean` object.

Using `RequiredModelMBean` as your ModelMBean implementation, there are two ways of associating your `ModelMBean` with a `ModelMBeanInfo`:

1. By passing the `ModelMBeanInfo` object to the `RequiredModelMBean` constructor.
2. By passing the `ModelMBeanInfo` object to the `setModelMBeanInfo` method on the `RequiredModelMBean` object.

After constructing a `ModelMBean`, you must associate your managed resource with it by calling the `setManagedResource` method of the `ModelMBean` interface. This method has the following signature:

```
public void setManagedResource(java.lang.Object managedResource,
   java.lang.String managedResourceType) throws MBeanException,
   RuntimeOperationsException, InstanceNotFoundException,
   InvalidTargetObjectTypeException
```

The value of the `managedResourceType` argument can be one of the following: `ObjectReference`, `Handle`, `IOR`, `EJBHandle`, or `RMIReference`. Currently, only `ObjectReference` is supported.

Then, of course, you still have to create an `ObjectName` and register the model MBean with the MBean server.

This section provides an example of using a model MBean with the same Car object as the one used in the standard MBean example. Before we discuss the example, however, let's look at the ModelMBeanInfo interface whose instance describes the attributes and operations that your managed resource will expose.

MBeanInfo and ModelMBeanInfo

The javax.management.mbean.ModelMBeanInfo interface describes the constructors, attributes, operations, and listeners exposed by a ModelMBean. A constructor is represented by the javax.management.modelmbean.ModelMBeanConstructorInfo class, an attribute by the javax.management.modelmbean.ModelMBeanAttributeInfo class, an operation by the javax.management.modelmbean.ModelMBeanOperationInfo class, and a listener by the javax.management.modelmbean.ModelMBeanNotificationInfo class. In this chapter, we're only interested in the attributes and operations.

JMX provides a default implementation of ModelMBeanInfo: the javax.management.modelmbean.ModelMBeanInfoSupport class. Here is the signature of the ModelMBeanInfoSupport class's constructor that we will use in this example:

```
public ModelMBeanInfoSupport(java.lang.String className,
  java.lang.String description, ModelMBeanAttributeInfo[] attributes,
  ModelMBeanConstructorInfo[] constructors,
  ModelMBeanOperationInfo[] operations,
  ModelMBeanNotificationInfo[] notifications)
```

You construct a ModelMBeanAttributeInfo object by using its constructor:

```
public ModelMBeanAttributeInfo(java.lang.String name,
  java.lang.String type, java.lang.String description,
  boolean isReadable, boolean isWritable,
  boolean isIs, Descriptor descriptor)
  throws RuntimeOperationsException
```

Here is the list of parameters:

- name. The name of the attribute
- type. The type or class name of the attribute
- description. The description of the attribute.
- isReadable. true if the attribute has a getter method, false otherwise.

- isWritable. true if the attribute has a setter method, `false` otherwise.
- isIs. `true` if the attribute has an `is` getter, `false` otherwise.
- descriptor. An instance of `Descriptor` containing the appropriate metadata for this instance of the `Attribute`. If it is `null` then a default descriptor will be created.

You create a `ModelMBeanOperationInfo` object using the following constructor:

```
public ModelMBeanOperationInfo(java.lang.String name,
  java.lang.String description, MBeanParameterInfo[] signature,
  java.lang.String type, int impact, Descriptor)
  throws RuntimeOperationsException
```

Here is the list of parameters:

- name. The name of the method.
- description. The description of the operation.
- signature. an array of `MBeanParameterInfo` objects describing the parameters of the method.
- type. The type of the method's return value.
- impact. The impact of the method. The value is one of the following: `INFO`, `ACTION`, `ACTION_INFO`, `UNKNOWN`.
- descriptor. An instance of `Descriptor` containing the appropriate metadata. for this instance of the `MBeanOperationInfo`.

ModelMBean Example

This example shows how to use a model MBean to manage a `Car` object whose class is presented in Listing 20.4.

Listing 20.4: The `Car` class

```
package ex20.pyrmont.modelmbeantest1;

public class Car {
  private String color = "red";
  public String getColor() {
    return color;
  }
  public void setColor(String color) {
    this.color = color;
  }
  public void drive() {
    System.out.println("Baby you can drive my car.");
  }
```

}

For a model MBean, you don't need to write an interface as in the case of a standard MBean. You simply instantiate the RequiredMBean class. Listing 20.5 provides the ModelAgent class that is used to create the MBean and manage a Car object.

Listing 20.5: The ModelAgent class

```
package ex20.pyrmont.modelmbeantest1;

import javax.management.Attribute;
import javax.management.Descriptor;
import javax.management.MalformedObjectNameException;
import javax.management.MBeanOperationInfo;
import javax.management.MBeanParameterInfo;
import javax.management.MBeanServer;
import javax.management.MBeanServerFactory;
import javax.management.ObjectName;
import javax.management.modelmbean.DescriptorSupport;
import javax.management.modelmbean.ModelMBean;
import javax.management.modelmbean.ModelMBeanAttributeInfo;
import javax.management.modelmbean.ModelMBeanInfo;
import javax.management.modelmbean.ModelMBeanInfoSupport;
import javax.management.modelmbean.ModelMBeanOperationInfo;
import javax.management.modelmbean.RequiredModelMBean;

public class ModelAgent {

  private String MANAGED_CLASS_NAME =
    "ex20.pyrmont.modelmbeantest1.Car";
  private MBeanServer mBeanServer = null;

  public ModelAgent() {
    mBeanServer = MBeanServerFactory.createMBeanServer();
  }

  public MBeanServer getMBeanServer() {
    return mBeanServer;
  }

  private ObjectName createObjectName(String name) {
    ObjectName objectName = null;
    try {
      objectName = new ObjectName(name);
    }
    catch (MalformedObjectNameException e) {
      e.printStackTrace();
    }
    return objectName;
  }

  private ModelMBean createMBean(ObjectName objectName,
    String mbeanName) {
    ModelMBeanInfo mBeanInfo = createModelMBeanInfo(objectName,
```

```
     mbeanName);
  RequiredModelMBean modelMBean = null;
  try {
    modelMBean = new RequiredModelMBean(mBeanInfo);
  }
  catch (Exception e) {
    e.printStackTrace();
  }
  return modelMBean;
}

private ModelMBeanInfo createModelMBeanInfo(ObjectName
  inMbeanObjectName, String inMbeanName) {
  ModelMBeanInfo mBeanInfo = null;
  ModelMBeanAttributeInfo[] attributes = new
    ModelMBeanAttributeInfo[1];
  ModelMBeanOperationInfo[] operations = new
    ModelMBeanOperationInfo[3];
  try {
    attributes[0] = new ModelMBeanAttributeInfo("Color",
      "java.lang.String",
      "the color.", true, true, false, null);
    operations[0] = new ModelMBeanOperationInfo("drive",
      "the drive method",
      null, "void", MBeanOperationInfo.ACTION, null);
    operations[1] = new ModelMBeanOperationInfo("getColor",
      "get color attribute",
      null, "java.lang.String", MBeanOperationInfo.ACTION, null);

    Descriptor setColorDesc = new DescriptorSupport(new String[] {
      "name=setColor", "descriptorType=operation",
      "class=" + MANAGED_CLASS_NAME, "role=operation"});
    MBeanParameterInfo[] setColorParams = new MBeanParameterInfo[] {
      (new MBeanParameterInfo("new color", "java.lang.String",
      "new Color value") )} ;
    operations[2] = new ModelMBeanOperationInfo("setColor",
      "set Color attribute", setColorParams, "void",
      MBeanOperationInfo.ACTION, setColorDesc);

    mBeanInfo  = new ModelMBeanInfoSupport(MANAGED_CLASS_NAME,
      null, attributes, null, operations, null);
  }
  catch (Exception e) {
    e.printStackTrace();
  }
  return mBeanInfo;
}

public static void main(String[] args) {
  ModelAgent agent = new ModelAgent();
  MBeanServer mBeanServer = agent.getMBeanServer();
  Car car = new Car();
  String domain = mBeanServer.getDefaultDomain();
  ObjectName objectName = agent.createObjectName(domain +
    ":type=MyCar");
  String mBeanName = "myMBean";
```

```
ModelMBean modelMBean = agent.createMBean(objectName, mBeanName);
try {
  modelMBean.setManagedResource(car, "ObjectReference");
  mBeanServer.registerMBean(modelMBean, objectName);
}
catch (Exception e) {
}

// manage the bean
try {
  Attribute attribute = new Attribute("Color", "green");
  mBeanServer.setAttribute(objectName, attribute);

  String color = (String) mBeanServer.getAttribute(objectName,
    "Color");
  System.out.println("Color:" + color);

  attribute = new Attribute("Color", "blue");
  mBeanServer.setAttribute(objectName, attribute);
  color = (String) mBeanServer.getAttribute(objectName, "Color");
  System.out.println("Color:" + color);
  mBeanServer.invoke(objectName, "drive", null, null);
}
catch (Exception e) {
  e.printStackTrace();
  }
  }
}
```

As you can see, writing model MBeans requires a lot of work, especially in declaring all the attributes and operations exposed by a managed resource. The next section will look at the Commons Modeler library that helps you write model MBeans faster.

Commons Modeler

The Commons Modeler library is part of the Apache Software Foundation's Jakarta project. It provides easy ways of writing model MBeans. The greatest help you can get from it is the fact that you don't need to write code to create a ModelMBeanInfo object.

Recall from the previous example that to construct a RequiredModelMBean instance, you need to create a ModelMBeanInfo object that you pass to the RequiredModelMBean class's constructor:

```
ModelMBeanInfo mBeanInfo = createModelMBeanInfo(objectName,
  mbeanName);
RequiredModelMBean modelMBean = null;
try {
  modelMBean = new RequiredModelMBean(mBeanInfo);
```

```
}
...
```

The `ModelMBeanInfo` object describes the attributes and operations exposed by the MBean, and writing the `createModelMBeanInfo` method is a tedious task because you have to list all the attributes and operations and pass them to the `ModelMBeanInfo`.

With Commons Modeler, you no longer need a `ModelMBeanInfo` object. Instead, description about a model MBean is encapsulated in an `org.apache.catalina.modeler.ManagedBean` object. You don't need to write code for exposing attributes and operations of an MBean. You simply write an mbean descriptor file (an XML document) that lists the MBeans you want created. For each MBean, you write the fully qualified names for both the `MBeans` class and the managed resource class, as well as the attributes and operations exposed by the MBean. You then use an `org.apache.commons.modeler.Registry` instance to read this XML document, which in turn creates an `MBeanServer` instance plus all the `ManagedBean` instances based on the XML elements in the mbean descriptor file.

You can then call the `createMBean` method of a `ManagedBean` instance to create a model MBean. After that, it's business as usual. You need to create an `ObjectName` instance and register the MBean with the MBean server. We'll now look at the format of an mbean descriptor file. Afterwards, we discuss the three most important classes in the Modeler, `Registry`, `ManagedBean`, and `BaseModelMBean`.

Note:
Tomcat 4 still uses an older version of the Modeler, with the currently deprecated methods. We will use the version that comes with Tomcat 4 in this chapter so that you can understand the MBeans in the `org.apache.catalina.mbeans` package.

MBean Descriptor

An MBean descriptor is an XML document that describes the model MBeans managed by the MBean server. An MBean descriptor starts with the following header:

```
<?xml version="1.0"?>
<!DOCTYPE mbeans-descriptors PUBLIC
 "-//Apache Software Foundation//DTD Model MBeans Configuration File"
 "http://jakarta.apache.org/commons/dtds/mbeans-descriptors.dtd">
```

It is followed by the `mbeans-descriptors` root element:

```
<mbeans-descriptors>
...
</mbeans-descriptors>
```

Inside the opening and closing `mbeans-descriptors` tags are `mbean` elements, each of which represents a model MBean. The `mbean` element can contain elements that represent attributes, operations, constructors, and notification. The following subsections discuss three elements that you need to understand Tomcat's MBean descriptor.

mbean

An `mbean` element describes a model MBean and includes the information to construct the corresponding `ModelMBeanInfo` object. The `mbean` element has the following definition:

```
<!ELEMENT mbean (descriptor?, attribute*, constructor*, notification*, operation*)>
```

The `mbean` element definition specifies that an `mbean` element can contain an optional `descriptor` element, zero or more `attribute` elements, zero or more `constructor` elements, zero or more `notification` elements, and zero or more `operation` elements.

An `mbean` element can have the following attributes:

- `className`. Fully qualified Java class name of the ModelMBean implementation. If this attribute is not present, the `org.apache.commons.modeler.BaseModelMBean` will be used.
- `description`. A description of this model MBean.
- `domain`. The MBean server's domain in which the ModelMBean created by this managed bean should be registered, when creating its `ObjectName`.
- `group`. Optional name of a "grouping classification" that can be used to select groups of similar MBean implementation classes.
- `name`. A name that uniquely identifies this model MBean. Normally, the base class name of the corresponding server component is used.
- `type`. Fully qualified Java class name of the managed resource implementation class.

attribute

You use the attribute element to describe a JavaBeans property of an MBean. The attribute element can have an optional descriptor element and can have the following attributes.

- description. A description of this attribute.
- displayName. The display name of this attribute.
- getMethod. The getter method of the property represented by the attribute element.
- is. A boolean value indicating whether or not this attribute is a boolean with an is getter method. By default, the value of the is attribute is false.
- name. The name of this JavaBeans property.
- readable. A boolean value indicating whether or not this attribute is readable by management applications. By default, the value of readable is true.
- setMethod. The setter method of the property represented by this attribute element.
- type. The fully qualified Java class name of this attribute.
- writeable. A boolean value indicating whether or not this attribute can be written by management applications. By default, this is set to true.

operation

The operation element describes a public method of the model MBean exposed to management applications. It can have zero or more parameter subelements and the following attributes:

- description. The description of this operation.
- impact. This attribute indicates the impact of this method. The possible values are ACTION (write like), ACTION-INFO (write+read like), INFO (read like), or UNKNOWN.
- name. The name of this public method.
- returnType. The fully qualified Java class name of the return type of this method.

parameter

The parameter element describes a parameter passed to a constructor or an operation. It can have the following attributes:

- description. The description of this parameter.
- name. The name of this parameter.
- type. The fully qualified Java class name of this parameter.

Example mbean Element

Catalina comes with a number of model MBeans that are all declared in the mbean-descriptors.xml file in the org.apache.catalina.mbeans package. Listing 20.6 offers the declaration of the StandardServer MBean in Tomcat 4.

Listing 20.6: The declaration of the StandardServer MBean

```
<mbean name="StandardServer"
  className="org.apache.catalina.mbeans.StandardServerMBean"
  description="Standard Server Component"
  domain="Catalina"
  group="Server"
  type="org.apache.catalina.core.StandardServer">

  <attribute name="debug"
    description="The debugging detail level for this component"
    type="int"/>
  <attribute name="managedResource"
    description="The managed resource this MBean is associated with"
    type="java.lang.Object"/>
  <attribute name="port"
    description="TCP port for shutdown messages"
    type="int"/>
  <attribute name="shutdown"
    description="Shutdown password"
    type="java.lang.String"/>
  <operation name="store"
    description="Save current state to server.xml file"
    impact="ACTION"
    returnType="void">
  </operation>
</mbean>
```

The mbean element in Listing 20.6 declares a model MBean uniquely identified as StandardServer. This MBean is represented by the org.apache.catalina.mbeans.StandardServerMBean and manages an instance of org.apache.catalina.core.StandardServer. The domain is Catalina and the group is Server.

There are four properties exposed by the model MBean: debug, managedResource, port, and shutdown, as described by the four attribute elements nested inside the mbean element. The MBean also exposes one method, store, which is described by the operation element.

Writing Your Own Model MBean Class

When using Commons Modeler, you define the type of your model MBean in the `className` attribute of your `mbean` element. By default, Commons Modeler uses the `org.apache.commons.modeler.BaseModelMBean` class. However, there are circumstances where you want to extend `BaseModelMBean`:

1. You want to override the property or method of the managed resource.
2. You want to add an attribute or operation that is not defined in the managed resource.

Catalina provides many subclasses of `BaseModelMBean` in the `org.apache.catalina.mbeans` package, and you'll learn about them shortly.

Registry

The API centers on the `org.apache.commons.modeler.Registry` class. Here are some of the things you can do with this class:

- Obtain an instance of `javax.management.MBeanServer` (so you don't need to call the `createMBeanServer` method of `javax.management.MBeanServerFactory`).
- Read an mbean descriptor file using the `loadRegistry` method.
- Create a `ManagedBean` object that you can use to construct a model MBean.

ManagedBean

A `ManagedBean` object describes a model MBean and replaces a `javax.management.MBeanInfo` object.

BaseModelMBean

The `org.apache.commons.modeler.BaseModelMBean` class implements the `javax.management.modelmbean.ModelMBean` interface. Using this class, you don't need to use the `javax.management.modelmbean.RequiredModelMBean` class.

One particularly useful field of this class is the resource field that represents the resource managed by this model MBean. The resource field has the following definition:

```
protected java.lang.Object resource;
```

Using the Modeler API

The Car class whose object we want to manage is given in Listing 20.7.

Listing 20.7: The Car class

```
package ex20.pyrmont.modelmbeantest2;

public class Car {
  public Car() {
    System.out.println("Car constructor");
  }
  private String color = "red";

  public String getColor() {
    return color;
  }
  public void setColor(String color) {
    this.color = color;
  }

  public void drive() {
    System.out.println("Baby you can drive my car.");
  }
}
```

With Commons Modeler, you don't hard code the attributes and operations of your managed object. Instead, you list them in an XML document which acts as a descriptor for your model MBean(s). In this example, such a document takes the form of the car-mbean-descriptor.xml given in Listing 20.8.

Listing 20.8: The car-mbean-descriptor.xml file

```
<?xml version="1.0"?>
<!DOCTYPE mbeans-descriptors PUBLIC
 "-//Apache Software Foundation//DTD Model MBeans Configuration File"
 "http://jakarta.apache.org/commons/dtds/mbeans-descriptors.dtd">

<mbeans-descriptors>
  <mbean name="myMBean"
    className="javax.management.modelmbean.RequiredModelMBean"
    description="The ModelMBean that manages our Car object"
    type="ex20.pyrmont.modelmbeantest.Car">

    <attribute name="Color"
      description="The car color"
```

```
      type="java.lang.String"/>
    <operation name="drive"
      description="drive method"
      impact="ACTION"
      returnType="void">
      <parameter name="driver" description="the driver parameter"
        type="java.lang.String"/>
    </operation>
  </mbean>
</mbeans-descriptors>
```

Now, you need the agent class (ModelAgent.java) in Listing 20.9.

Listing 20.9: The **ModelAgent** Class

```java
package ex20.pyrmont.modelmbeantest2;

import java.io.InputStream;
import java.net.URL;
import javax.management.Attribute;
import javax.management.MalformedObjectNameException;
import javax.management.MBeanServer;
import javax.management.ObjectName;
import javax.management.modelmbean.ModelMBean;

import org.apache.commons.modeler.ManagedBean;
import org.apache.commons.modeler.Registry;

public class ModelAgent {
  private Registry registry;
  private MBeanServer mBeanServer;

  public ModelAgent() {
    registry = createRegistry();
    try {
      mBeanServer = Registry.getServer();
    }
    catch (Throwable t) {
      t.printStackTrace(System.out);
      System.exit(1);
    }
  }

  public MBeanServer getMBeanServer() {
    return mBeanServer;
  }

  public Registry createRegistry() {
    Registry registry = null;
    try {
      URL url = ModelAgent.class.getResource
        ("/ex20/pyrmont/modelmbeantest2/car-mbean-descriptor.xml");
      InputStream stream = url.openStream();
      Registry.loadRegistry(stream);
      stream.close();
      registry = Registry.getRegistry();
```

```
    }
    catch (Throwable t) {
      System.out.println(t.toString());
    }
    return (registry);
  }

  public ModelMBean createModelMBean(String mBeanName)
    throws Exception {
    ManagedBean managed = registry.findManagedBean(mBeanName);
    if (managed == null) {
      System.out.println("ManagedBean null");
      return null;
    }
    ModelMBean mbean = managed.createMBean();
    ObjectName objectName = createObjectName();
    return mbean;
  }

  private ObjectName createObjectName() {
    ObjectName objectName = null;
    String domain = mBeanServer.getDefaultDomain();
    try {
      objectName = new ObjectName(domain + ":type=MyCar");
    }
    catch (MalformedObjectNameException e) {
      e.printStackTrace();
    }
    return objectName;
  }

  public static void main(String[] args) {
    ModelAgent agent = new ModelAgent();
    MBeanServer mBeanServer = agent.getMBeanServer();
    Car car = new Car();
    System.out.println("Creating ObjectName");
    ObjectName objectName = agent.createObjectName();
    try {
      ModelMBean modelMBean = agent.createModelMBean("myMBean");
      modelMBean.setManagedResource(car, "ObjectReference");
      mBeanServer.registerMBean(modelMBean, objectName);
    }
    catch (Exception e) {
      System.out.println(e.toString());
    }
    // manage the bean
    try {
      Attribute attribute = new Attribute("Color", "green");
      mBeanServer.setAttribute(objectName, attribute);
      String color = (String) mBeanServer.getAttribute(objectName,
        "Color");
      System.out.println("Color:" + color);

      attribute = new Attribute("Color", "blue");
      mBeanServer.setAttribute(objectName, attribute);
      color = (String) mBeanServer.getAttribute(objectName, "Color");
```

```
      System.out.println("Color:" + color);
      mBeanServer.invoke(objectName, "drive", null, null);
    }
    catch (Exception e) {
      e.printStackTrace();
    }
  }
}
```

See how the agent class is much shorter when using Commons Modeler?

Catalina's MBeans

As mentioned at the beginning of this chapter, Catalina provides a number of MBean classes in the org.apache.catalina.mbeans package. All these MBeans extend the org.apache.commons.modeler.BaseModelMBean class either directly or indirectly. This section discusses the three most important MBean classes that Tomcat 4 provides: ClassNameMBean, StandardServerMBean, and MBeanFactory. You should find no problem understanding other model MBean classes in Catalina if you can understand these three classes. The three classes are discussed in this section. In addition, the MBeanUtil class in the org.apache.catalina.mbeans package is also explained.

ClassNameMBean

The org.apache.catalina.mbeans.ClassNameMBean class extends org.apache.commons.modeler.BaseModelMBean. It provides the write-only property className that represents the class name of the managed resource. The ClassNameMBean class is given in Listing 20.10.

Listing 20.10: The `ClassNameMBean` class

```
package org.apache.catalina.mbeans;

import javax.management.MBeanException;
import javax.management.RuntimeOperationsException;
import org.apache.commons.modeler.BaseModelMBean;

public class ClassNameMBean extends BaseModelMBean {
  public ClassNameMBean()
  throws MBeanException, RuntimeOperationsException {
    super();
  }
  public String getClassName() {
    return (this.resource.getClass().getName());
```

```
    }
}
```

The `ClassNameMBean` class is an example of a subclass of `BaseModelMBean` that was written to provide a property that is not available in the managed resource itself. Many `mbean` elements defined in the mbeans-descriptors.xml file use this class as their type of Model MBean.

StandardServerMBean

The `StandardServerMBean` class extends `org.apache.commons.modeler.BaseModelMBean` to manage an instance of `org.apache.catalina.core.StandardServer`. The `StandardServerMBean` class (given in Listing 20.11) is an example of a model MBean class that is written to override a method (i.e. the `store` method) in the managed resource. When the `store` method is invoked by a management application, the `store` method in the `StandardServerMBean` (and not that in the managed StandardServer object) that gets executed.

Listing 20.11: The **StandardServerMBean** class

```
package org.apache.catalina.mbeans;

import javax.management.InstanceNotFoundException;
import javax.management.MBeanException;
import javax.management.MBeanServer;
import javax.management.RuntimeOperationsException;
import org.apache.catalina.Server;
import org.apache.catalina.ServerFactory;
import org.apache.catalina.core.StandardServer;
import org.apache.commons.modeler.BaseModelMBean;

public class StandardServerMBean extends BaseModelMBean {
  private static MBeanServer mserver = MBeanUtils.createServer();
  public StandardServerMBean()
    throws MBeanException, RuntimeOperationsException {
    super();
  }

  public synchronized void store() throws InstanceNotFoundException,
    MBeanException, RuntimeOperationsException {

    Server server = ServerFactory.getServer();
    if (server instanceof StandardServer) {
      try {
        ((StandardServer) server).store();
      }
      catch (Exception e) {
        throw new MBeanException(e, "Error updating conf/server.xml");
      }
    }
```

```
    }
  }
}
```

The `StandardServerMBean` class is an example of a model MBean class that subclasses `BaseModelMBean` to override a method in the managed resource.

MBeanFactory

The `MBeanFactory` class represents a factory object that creates all model MBeans that manage various resources in Catalina. The `MBeanFactory` class also provides methods for deleting these MBeans.

As an example, take a look at the `createStandardContext` method in Listing 20.12.

Listing 20.12: The `createStandardContext` method

```
public String createStandardContext(String parent,
  String path, String docBase) throws Exception {
  // Create a new StandardContext instance
  StandardContext context = new StandardContext();
  path = getPathStr(path);
  context.setPath(path);
  context.setDocBase(docBase);
  ContextConfig contextConfig = new ContextConfig();
  context.addLifecycleListener(contextConfig);

  // Add the new instance to its parent component
  ObjectName pname = new ObjectName(parent);
  Server server = ServerFactory.getServer();
  Service service =
    server.findService(pname.getKeyProperty("service"));
  Engine engine = (Engine) service.getContainer();
  Host host = (Host) engine.findChild(pname.getKeyProperty("host"));

  // Add context to the host
  host.addChild(context);

  // Return the corresponding MBean name
  ManagedBean managed = registry.findManagedBean("StandardContext");

  ObjectName oname =
    MBeanUtils.createObjectName(managed.getDomain(), context);
  return (oname.toString());
}
```

MBeanUtil

The org.apache.catalina.mbeans.MBeanUtil class is a utility class that provides static methods for creating various MBeans to manage Catalina objects, static methods for deleting those MBeans, and static methods for creating object names. For example, the createMBean method in Listing 20.13 creates a model MBean for a org.apache.catalina.Server object.

Listing 20.13: The `createMBean` method that creates a model MBean that manages a `Server` object.

```
public static ModelMBean createMBean(Server server) throws Exception {
  String mname = createManagedName(server);
  ManagedBean managed = registry.findManagedBean(mname);
  if (managed == null) {
    Exception e = new Exception(
      "ManagedBean is not found with "+mname);
    throw new MBeanException(e);
  }
  String domain = managed.getDomain();
  if (domain == null)
    domain = mserver.getDefaultDomain();
  ModelMBean mbean = managed.createMBean(server);
  ObjectName oname = createObjectName(domain, server);
  mserver.registerMBean(mbean, oname);
  return (mbean);
}
```

Catalina's MBeans Creation

Now that you are familiar with some of the model MBean in Catalina, we will take a look at how these MBeans are created and made available to management applications.

The server.xml file, the configuration file of Tomcat, defines the following Listener element inside the Server element:

```
<Server port="8005" shutdown="SHUTDOWN" debug="0">
  <Listener
    className="org.apache.catalina.mbeans.ServerLifecycleListener"
    debug="0"/>
...
```

This will add a listener of type org.apache.catalina.mbeans.ServerLifecycleListener to the org.apache.catalina.core.StandardServer object that represents a Server. When the StandardServer instance is started, it fires a

START_EVENT event, as defined in the `start` method of the
StandardServer class:

```
public void start() throws LifecycleException {
  ...
  lifecycle.fireLifecycleEvent(START_EVENT, null);
  ...
}
```

When the StandardServer object is stopped, a STOP_EVENT event is
triggered, as defined in its `stop` method:

```
public void stop() throws LifecycleException {
  ...
  lifecycle.fireLifecycleEvent(STOP_EVENT, null);
  ...
}
```

These events will cause the `lifecycleEvent` method of the
ServerLifecycleListener class to be executed. Listing 20.14 presents the
`lifecycleEvent` method.

Listing 20.14: The `lifecycleEvent` method of the ServerLifecycleListener class

```
public void lifecycleEvent(LifecycleEvent event) {
  Lifecycle lifecycle = event.getLifecycle();
  if (Lifecycle.START_EVENT.equals(event.getType())) {
    if (lifecycle instanceof Server) {
      // Loading additional MBean descriptors
      loadMBeanDescriptors();
      createMBeans();
    }
  }
  else if (Lifecycle.STOP_EVENT.equals(event.getType())) {
    if (lifecycle instanceof Server) {
      destroyMBeans();
    }
  }
  else if (Context.RELOAD_EVENT.equals(event.getType())) {
    if (lifecycle instanceof StandardContext) {
      StandardContext context = (StandardContext)lifecycle;
      if (context.getPrivileged()) {
        context.getServletContext().setAttribute
          (Globals.MBEAN_REGISTRY_ATTR,
        MBeanUtils.createRegistry());
        context.getServletContext().setAttribute
          (Globals.MBEAN_SERVER_ATTR,
        MBeanUtils.createServer());
      }
    }
  }
}
```

The createMBeans method is the method that creates all the MBeans in

Catalina. This method starts off by creating an instance of
MBeanFactory, a model MBean class explained in the previous section.

Listing 20.15: The `createMBeans` method in `ServerLifecycleListener`

```
protected void createMBeans() {
  try {
    MBeanFactory factory = new MBeanFactory();
    createMBeans(factory);
    createMBeans(ServerFactory.getServer());
  }
  catch (MBeanException t) {
    Exception e = t.getTargetException();
    if (e == null)
      e = t;
    log("createMBeans: MBeanException", e);
  }
  catch (Throwable t) {
    log("createMBeans: Throwable", t);
  }
}
```

The first createMBeans method uses the MBeanUtil class to create an
ObjectName for the MBeanFactory and register it in the MBean server.

The second createMBeans method takes an
org.apache.catalina.Server object and creates a model MBean for it. It
is interesting to trace this createMBeans method (presented in Listing 20.16).

Listing 20.16: The `createMBeans` method that creates an MBean for a `Server` object

```
protected void createMBeans(Server server) throws Exception {
  // Create the MBean for the Server itself
  if (debug >= 2)
    log("Creating MBean for Server " + server);
  MBeanUtils.createMBean(server);
  if (server instanceof StandardServer) {
    ((StandardServer) server).addPropertyChangeListener(this);
  }

  // Create the MBeans for the global NamingResources (if any)
  NamingResources resources = server.getGlobalNamingResources();
  if (resources != null) {
    createMBeans(resources);
  }

  // Create the MBeans for each child Service
  Service services[] = server.findServices();
  for (int i = 0; i < services.length; i++) {
    // FIXME - Warp object hierarchy not currently supported
    if (services[i].getContainer().getClass().getName().equals
      ("org.apache.catalina.connector.warp.WarpEngine")) {
      if (debug >= 1) {
```

```
      log("Skipping MBean for Service " + services[i]);
    }
    continue;
  }
  createMBeans(services[i]);
  }
}
```

Note that the createMBeans method in Listing 20.16 calls the following line in the for loop that iterates all Service objects in the StandardServer instance:

```
createMBeans(services[i]);
```

This method creates MBean instances for the services and calls the createMBeans method for creating MBean objects for all the connectors and engines in the service The createMBeans method that creates a Service MBean is given in Listing 20.17.

Listing 20.17: The **createMBeans** method that creates a **Service** MBean

```
protected void createMBeans(Service service) throws Exception {
  // Create the MBean for the Service itself
  if (debug >= 2)
    log("Creating MBean for Service " + service);
  MBeanUtils.createMBean(service);
  if (service instanceof StandardService) {
    ((StandardService) service).addPropertyChangeListener(this);
  }

  // Create the MBeans for the corresponding Connectors
  Connector connectors[] = service.findConnectors();
  for (int j = 0; j < connectors.length; j++) {
    createMBeans(connectors[j]);
  }

  // Create the MBean for the associated Engine and friends
  Engine engine = (Engine) service.getContainer();
  if (engine != null) {
    createMBeans(engine);
  }
}
```

The createMBeans(engine) method, as you might suspect, calls the createMBeans method that creates the MBeans for hosts:

```
protected void createMBeans(Engine engine) throws Exception {
  // Create the MBean for the Engine itself
  if (debug >= 2) {
    log("Creating MBean for Engine " + engine);
  }
  MBeanUtils.createMBean(engine);
  ...
```

```
    Container hosts[] = engine.findChildren();
    for (int j = 0; j < hosts.length; j++) {
      createMBeans((Host) hosts[j]);
    }
    ...
}
```

The `createMBeans(host)` method in turns creates a `ContextMBean`, like the following:

```
protected void createMBeans(Host host) throws Exception {
  ...
  MBeanUtils.createMBean(host);
  ...
  Container contexts[] = host.findChildren();
  for (int k = 0; k < contexts.length; k++) {
    createMBeans((Context) contexts[k]);
  }
  ...
}
```

The `createMBeans(context)` method is as follows:

```
protected void createMBeans(Context context) throws Exception {
  ...
  MBeanUtils.createMBean(context);
  ...
  context.addContainerListener(this);
  if (context instanceof StandardContext) {
   ((StandardContext) context).addPropertyChangeListener(this);
   ((StandardContext) context).addLifecycleListener(this);
  }

  // If the context is privileged, give a reference to it
  // in a servlet context attribute
  if (context.getPrivileged()) {
    context.getServletContext().setAttribute
      (Globals.MBEAN_REGISTRY_ATTR, MBeanUtils.createRegistry());
    context.getServletContext().setAttribute
      (Globals.MBEAN_SERVER_ATTR, MBeanUtils.createServer());
  }
  ...
}
```

If the context's `privileged` property is `true`, two attributes will be created and stored in the `ServletContext` object for the web application. The keys for those attributes are `Globals.MBEAN_REGISTRY_ATTR` and `Globals.MBEAN_SERVER_ATTR`. Here is a fragment from the `org.apache.catalina.Globals` class:

```
/**
 * The servlet context attribute under which the managed bean Registry
 * will be stored for privileged contexts (if enabled).
 */
```

```
public static final String MBEAN_REGISTRY_ATTR =
  "org.apache.catalina.Registry";

/**
 * The servlet context attribute under which the MBeanServer will be
 * stored for privileged contexts (if enabled).
 */
public static final String MBEAN_SERVER_ATTR =
  "org.apache.catalina.MBeanServer";
```

The `MBeanUtils.createRegistry` method returns a `Registry` instance.
The `MBeanUtils.createServer` method returns an instance of
`javax.management.MBeanServer` instance with which all Catalina's
MBeans are registered.

In other words, you can obtain these `Registry` and `MBeanServer` objects
from a web application whose `privileged` property is set to `true`. The next
section discusses how you can create a JMX manager application to manage
Tomcat.

The Application

The application here is a web application for administering Tomcat. It is simple
but enough to give you a general idea of how to use the MBeans exposed by
Catalina. You can use it to list all the `ObjectName` instances in Catalina, as well
as list all the contexts currently running and remove any of them.

First of all, you need to create a descriptor for the application (Listing
20.18). You must place this file in the in %CATALINA_HOME%/webapps
directory

Listing 20.18: The myadmin.xml file

```
<Context path="/myadmin" docBase="../server/webapps/myadmin" debug="8"
privileged="true" reloadable="true">
</Context>
```

One thing you need to worry about is to make sure that the `privileged`
property of the `Context` element is set to `true`. The `docBase` attribute
specifies the location of the application.

The application consists of one servlet, presented in Listing 20.19.

Listing 20.19: The **MyAdminServlet** class

```
package myadmin;

import java.io.IOException;
```

```java
import java.io.PrintWriter;
import java.net.URLEncoder;
import java.util.Iterator;
import java.util.Set;
import javax.management.MBeanServer;
import javax.management.ObjectName;
import javax.servlet.ServletException;
import javax.servlet.http.HttpServlet;
import javax.servlet.http.HttpServletRequest;
import javax.servlet.http.HttpServletResponse;
import org.apache.commons.modeler.Registry;

public class MyAdminServlet extends HttpServlet {
  private Registry registry;
  private MBeanServer mBeanServer;

  public void init() throws ServletException {
    registry = (Registry)
      getServletContext().getAttribute("org.apache.catalina.Registry");
    if(registry == null) {
      System.out.println("Registry not available");
      return;
    }
    mBeanServer = (MBeanServer) getServletContext().getAttribute(
      "org.apache.catalina.MBeanServer");
    if (mBeanServer==null) {
      System.out.println("MBeanServer not available");
      return;
    }
  }

  public void doGet(HttpServletRequest request,
    HttpServletResponse response)
    throws ServletException, IOException {

    response.setContentType("text/html");
    PrintWriter out = response.getWriter();
    if (registry==null || mBeanServer==null) {
      out.println("Registry or MBeanServer not found");
      return;
    }

    out.println("<html><head></head><body>");
    String action = request.getParameter("action");
    if ("listAllManagedBeans".equals(action)) {
      listAllManagedBeans(out);
    }
    else if ("listAllContexts".equals(action)) {
      listAllContexts(out);
    }
    else if ("removeContext".equals(action)) {
      String contextObjectName =
        request.getParameter("contextObjectName");
      removeContext(contextObjectName, out);
    }
    else {
```

```
      out.println("Invalid command");
    }
    out.println("</body></html>");
  }

  private void listAllManagedBeans(PrintWriter out) {
    String[] managedBeanNames = registry.findManagedBeans();
    for (int i=0; i<managedBeanNames.length; i++) {
      out.print(managedBeanNames[i] + "<br/>");
    }
  }

  private void listAllContexts(PrintWriter out) {
    try {
      ObjectName objName = new ObjectName("Catalina:type=Context,*");
      Set set = mBeanServer.queryNames(objName, null);
      Iterator it = set.iterator();
      while (it.hasNext()) {
        ObjectName obj = (ObjectName) it.next();
        out.print(obj +
          " <a href=?action=removeContext&contextObjectName=" +
          URLEncoder.encode(obj.toString(), "UTF-8") +
          ">remove</a><br/>");
      }
    }
    catch (Exception e) {
      out.print(e.toString());
    }
  }

  private void removeContext(String contextObjectName,
    PrintWriter out) {
    try {
      ObjectName mBeanFactoryObjectName = new
        ObjectName("Catalina:type=MBeanFactory");
      if (mBeanFactoryObjectName!=null) {
        String operation = "removeContext";
        String[] params = new String[1];
        params[0] = contextObjectName;
        String signature[] = { "java.lang.String" };
        try {
          mBeanServer.invoke(mBeanFactoryObjectName, operation,
            params, signature);
          out.println("context removed");
        }
        catch (Exception e) {
          out.print(e.toString());
        }
      }

    }
    catch (Exception e) {
    }
  }
}
```

Finally, you need the application deployment descriptor in Listing 20.20.

Listing 20.20: The web.xml file

```
<?xml version="1.0" encoding="ISO-8859-1"?>

<!DOCTYPE web-app
    PUBLIC "-//Sun Microsystems, Inc.//DTD Web Application 2.3//EN"
    "http://java.sun.com/dtd/web-app_2_3.dtd">

<web-app>
  <servlet>
    <servlet-name>myAdmin</servlet-name>
    <servlet-class>myadmin.MyAdminServlet</servlet-class>
  </servlet>
  <servlet-mapping>
    <servlet-name>myAdmin</servlet-name>
    <url-pattern>/myAdmin</url-pattern>
  </servlet-mapping>
</web-app>
```

To list all `ObjectName` instances, use the following URL:

```
http://localhost:8080/myadmin/myAdmin?action=listAllMBeans
```

You will see a list of MBean objects. Here are the first six of them:

```
MemoryUserDatabase
DigestAuthenticator
BasicAuthenticator
UserDatabaseRealm
SystemErrLogger
Group
```

To list all the contexts, use this URL:

```
http://localhost:8080/myadmin/myAdmin?action=listAllContexts
```

You will see all the running applications. To remove any of them, click the `remove` hyperlink.

Summary

In this chapter you have learned how to manage Tomcat using JMX. You have been introduced to the two of four types of MBeans and developed a simple Admin application to use the MBeans offered by Catalina.

436

Index